Why Do You Need This New Edition?

If you're wondering why you should buy this new edition of *Across Cultures: A Reader for Writers*, here are a few good reasons!

1. Because we live in an increasingly visual world and multimedia has become the primary vehicle for learning, the text features **fourteen brand new visuals**. These engaging images provide new perspectives for viewing society and culture.

2. With **approximately 20 new readings**, the eighth edition offers a fresh and updated perspective on the mulicultural issues at the heart of the text.

3. New **"Web Topics" questions** invite you to use the Internet as a resource for thinking about the essays you've read and encourage you to consider synthesizing information in written forms that push "literacy in bold new directions."

4. Additional writing topics have been included to help you better reflect on other kinds of literacies you're engaged in, **including the visual, spatial, musical, and even mathematical.**

5. **Chapter 8, "Popular Culture," has been recast** to emphasize the impact of new, frequently employed technologies, such as the Internet and text messaging. The readings featured in this revised chapter also encourage you to take a deeper look at how gaming, music, and technology are reshaping contemporary culture.

6. **Two new sets of essays are presented as a unit** within the "Family and Community," "Traditions," and "Popular Culture" chapters to spur discussion and increase interactivity among the texts.

7. **Four new essays by students** present their "take" on gender relationships, work, and traditions and illustrate a student's perspective on the key issues you'll be asked to think and write about.

8. In **Chapter 4, "Education," a new literacy narrative** by Giovanni J. Gelardi demonstrates how a visual artist perceives his work and provides guidance for how to approach images in the text and artworks in general.

Across Cultures

A Reader for Writers

Across Cultures

A Reader for Writers

EIGHTH EDITION

Sheena Gillespie
Robert Becker

Queensborough Community College
City University of New York

Longman

Boston Columbus Indianapolis New York San Francisco Upper Saddle River
Amsterdam Cape Town Dubai London Madrid Milan Munich Paris Montreal
Toronto Delhi Mexico City Sao Paulo Sydney Hong Kong Seoul Singapore Taipei Tokyo

Executive Editor: Suzanne Phelps Chambers
Editorial Assistant: Erica Schweitzer
Senior Marketing Manager: Sandra McGuire
Senior Supplements Editor: Donna Campion
Production Manager: Ellen MacElree
Project Coordination, Text Design, and Electronic Page Makeup:
    Pre-Press PMG.
Senior Cover Design Manager: Nancy Danahy
Cover Designer: Nancy Sacks
Cover Art: Hundertwasser Archive, Vienna

In appreciation for granting Pearson Education the use of *Coral Flowers*,
a donation has been made to World Wildlife Fund in honor of the artist,
Friedensreich Hundertwasser.

Photo Researcher: Rona Tuccillo
Senior Manufacturing Buyer: Dennis J. Para
Printer and Binder: R. R. Donnelley & Sons, Harrisonburg
Cover Printer: R. R. Donnelley & Sons, Harrisonburg

For permission to use copyrighted material, grateful acknowledgment is made
to the copyright holders on pp. 445–448, which are hereby made part of this
copyright page.

Library of Congress Cataloging-in-Publication Data

Across cultures : a reader for writers / [compiled by] Sheena Gillespie, Robert
Becker.—8th ed.
    p. cm.
    Includes index.
    ISBN 978-0-205-78037-2
    1. College readers.   2. English language—Rhetoric—Problems, exercises,
etc.   3. Multiculturalism—Problems, exercises, etc.   4. Report writing—
Problems, exercises, etc.   5. Culture—Problems, exercises, etc.   6. Readers—
Multiculturalism.   7. Readers—Culture. I. Gillespie, Sheena, 1938- II. Becker,
Robert. III. Title.
    PE1417.A27 2010
    808'.0427—dc22

                                                                2010000734

Longman
is an imprint of

www.pearsonhighered.com ISBN 10:   0-205-78037-7

ISBN 13: 978-0-205-78037-2

To James Geasor, Susan G. Madera and Thomas Colicino with gratitude and affection

To Barbara and Eddie

Contents

Asterisks after titles identify student writings.

Rhetorical Contents

DESCRIPTION

COMPARISON AND CONTRAST

CAUSE AND EFFECT

Preface for the Teacher

There is no such thing as a neutral educational process. Education either functions as an instrument which is used to facilitate the integration of the younger generation into the logic of the present system and bring conformity to it, or becomes "the practice of freedom," the means by which men and women deal critically and creatively with reality and discover how to participate in the transformation of their world.

—Richard Shaull

Technology isn't killing our ability to write. It's reviving it—and pushing our literacy in bold new directions.

—Clive Thompson

ACROSS CULTURES: A READER FOR WRITERS is a reader that invites students to look beyond their own society and culture. The title embodies our guiding image of a reaching out—moving beyond the immediate and the parochial to an acknowledgment and acceptance of pluralism and diversity within and among cultures. In our usage, such reaching out does not mean blending or blurring or assimilating (or hybridizing, in the biological sense). The outreach we mean may be found, first, in the selection of readings by authors from and about many countries: by North Americans writing about other cultures and about the United States' culture and subcultures; by members of ethnic subcultures in the United States, such as immigrants or their children, African Americans, or Native Americans, writing about the United States; and by persons from other cultures writing about those cultures. Second, this reaching out is encouraged by the text's apparatus, in aids to the student. Perspectives (quotations); chapter introductions; text selection headnotes; the end-of-lesson trio Interpretations, Correspondences, Applications; The Knowing Eye (reading images); and Additional Writing Topics are found in every chapter.

We began the first edition of *Across Cultures* in 1989, and since then, the number of students coming from homes that are at least bilingual and bicultural has doubled, and although we hear daily about the many facets of globalization, there has been little progress in developing pedagogy that addresses the impact of these new linguistic realities. The eighth edition of *Across Cultures* reflects this concern and we have endeavored to address the complexities of this issue by adding texts, apparatus, and assignments that will assist us in learning more about the ramifications of tapping into the rich cultures, languages, experiences, and values of our students.

The driving force behind this new edition is our desire to bring to a new generation of writers contemporary social, cultural, and technological issues. In particular, for our students who have come to know their world primarily through the screens of television and the Internet, we want to reassert the immediacy and richness of stories and ideas available through print media. By highlighting technology we hope to build on the expertise that students bring with them thereby reinforcing our commitment to the concept of students as partners in learning.

Features that are new to the eighth edition follow:

- With **eighteen new readings**, the eighth edition offers a fresh and updated perspective on the inter-cultural issues at the heart of the text.

- Because we live in an increasingly visual world and multimedia has become the primary vehicle for learning, the text features **fourteen brand new visuals.**

- Additional **"Perspectives" questions that include "Web topics"** have been added to help students use the Internet as a resource for thinking about the essays they have read. "Web topics" invite them to think about synthesizing information in written forms that push "literacy in bold new directions."

- Additional writing topics have been included that better reflect other kinds of literacies students are engaged in, **including the visual, spatial, musical, and mathematical.**

- **Two new sets of essays are presented as a unit** within the "Family and Community," "Traditions," and "Popular Culture" chapters to spur discussion and increase interactivity among the texts.

- **Four new essays by students** present their "take" on gender relationships, work, and traditions.

- **In Chapter 4, "Education," a new literacy narrative** by Giovanni J. Gelardi demonstrates how a visual artist perceives his work and provides guidance for how to approach images in the text and artworks in general.

- **Chapter Eight, "Popular Culture," has been recast** to emphasize the impact of new, frequently employed technologies, such as the Internet and text messaging.

The world of culture is a world of values. Although the good may be immaterial—truth, beauty, honor, glory—cultural good must be realized in temporal and material form. Culture consists as much in conserving values as in realizing them.

Each chapter begins with Perspectives, brief provocative quotations that stimulate thought and discussion on the chapter topic. Next come the texts—myths, folktales, essays, and short stories. Whereas many of the essays and stories reflect the seemingly endless—often tumultuous—changes in current events, our rationale for including myths and folktales is to show culture in its conserving role. Although *Across Cultures* probably pays more attention to shifts in population and to political and economic changes around the world, these changes occur against backgrounds of centuries of history and tradition, of treasured stories of origins and beginnings that give direction to the current shifting allegiances. Such stories may actually revive and sustain some cultures.

The selections we offer in *Across Cultures* cover a much greater variety of cultural trends than the table of contents indicates. For example, work, the subject of Chapter 5, leads to such related subjects as immigration, cultural displacement, family narratives, and definitions of success. Traditions, the subject of Chapter 6, leads to questions of family life, the roles of men and women, class differences, and rituals and ceremonies of all kinds.

Each text is preceded by a biographical/cultural headnote and is followed by questions—Interpretations—that provoke thinking and discussion, probe comprehension, call attention to important rhetorical features, and help the reader relate the text to the chapter topic. Comparison or cross-examination is the purpose of the questions called Correspondences, which also follow each text. The Applications section provides writing and discussion topics and follows each group of Perspectives and each text. These activities call on the student to analyze cross-cultural similarities and differences and sometimes to place themselves at crossroads. The Knowing Eye section of each chapter features images for analysis and discussion. Additional Writing Topics at the end of the chapter provide added opportunities for students to engage the chapter's theme.

Cultural commentary in our text is direct and explicit. Each chapter includes one section on general American culture by an American writer, two or three texts by writers from diverse ethnic groups within the United States writing either on the experience of those groups or on individuals within them, and several texts by writers from cultures elsewhere in the world. A Geographical Index at the back of the book indicates the worldwide scope of these texts, the better to place American culture and its own diversity in a world context for comparison.

The *Instructor's Manual* for the eighth edition of *Across Cultures* will be available only online! In addition to the flexibility afforded by Web access, the authors have created brand new content with the "Reflections on Writing" section. This "bonus chapter" is comprised of quotations from participating writers who present their impressions of their essays that appear in the text. Authors talk about the writing process, the personal significance of their essays, and additional material that will stimulate discussion of the texts. ISBN 0205780385.

We are grateful to the following reviewers for their excellent critiques and suggestions for the eighth edition of the text: Chella Courington, Santa Barbara City College; Gina Gemmel, Malone University; Diana Gruendler, Penn State University; Frank Lawrence, College of DuPage; Lori Stoltz, Rochester Community and Technical College; and Kathren A. Whitham, South Seattle Community College.

We are proud to include student essays by Thomas M. Colicino, Ramon Mendez Jr., and John Patterson. Special thanks are due to our colleagues at Queensborough and elsewhere for the essays they contributed: Trikartikaningsih Byas, Martín Kutnowski, Katherine Larios, and Charles Neuman. Last, we welcome those essays from friends old and new: Giovanni J. Gelardi, Taneisha Grant, Ariela Rutkin-Becker, and Emma Wunsch.

Giovanni J. Gelardi, En-chi Hsu, Suzanna Konecky, Mackenzie Lawrence, Zack Rutkin, Ariela Rutkin-Becker, and Elissa R. Schlau provided the new images for this edition that highlight the cross-cultural themes of the texts.

We acknowledge our gratitude to Robert Singleton, who researched folk tales, wrote new biographical headnotes, updated and improved existing headnotes, and to Isobel Pipolo for her meticulous work on the instructor's manual.

We are especially grateful for the expertise of our former student James Geasor, now adjunct in the English department, who assisted in the selection of new texts, added perspectives to the chapter on popular culture, composed questions and writing topics for several new texts, and undertook the mammoth task of translating the entire text (hard copy) into a digital file format.

Finally, we acknowledge the encouragement and support of Suzanne Phelps Chambers and Erica Schweitzer for guiding us through this edition of *Across Cultures*.

Sheena Gillespie
Robert Becker

Preface for the Student

*I think we are in the midst of a literacy revolution the likes of which we
haven't seen since Greek civilization.*

—Andrea Lunsford

Narrative is radical, creating us at the very moment it is being created.

—Toni Morrison

As teachers of writing and rhetoric, we share Andrea Lunsford's excitement about the new literacy of college students whose ability to write is
being enhanced by their technical skills. The preliminary findings of her
ongoing study indicate that frequent online writing has produced organized and persuasive prose and a sophisticated awareness of purpose and
audience.

In the eighth edition of *Across Cultures*, we invite you to celebrate
and participate in this historically unprecedented multicultural experiment by reading the narratives of writers from other cultures, both
within the United States and in many other parts of the world. Toni
Morrison, in her 1993 Nobel Lecture, talked about the power of narrative to help us understand ourselves and others. Morrison is particularly concerned that the writer's words and stories be the windows
through which both writer and reader gain knowledge not only of the
self but also of the self in relation to other people and cultures.

Old cultures, and even some not so old, such as that of the United
States, like to think that their cultures are superior. But once cultures
cross—whether such meetings add to or subtract from the sum of their
parts—they are never again the same: they can never again claim
absoluteness, exclusivity, or monopoly. To promote and foster such
meetings, or crossings, is the purpose of *Across Cultures: A Reader for
Writers*. We hope that the readings in each chapter, several of which are
written by students, will stimulate creative conversations about cultural differences as you share ideas about family, friends, gender issues,
community, education, work, choices, traditions, and popular culture
with your classmates.

At the center of each chapter are readings on a common subject or
meeting ground, but you are introduced to the chapter through a group
of brief quotations (Perspectives) to stimulate personal responses in
journal entries and collaborative explorations in group projects. Each
text is introduced with a biographical headnote that places the author in

a particular historical-geographical context. After most texts are three sets of questions: Interpretations, to provoke thinking and discussion and to call attention to specific rhetorical features; Correspondences, to encourage comparisons of cultures; and Applications, exercises to develop critical thinking and writing skills. Accordingly, you will often be asked to compare texts within, between, and among chapters.

In each chapter there is also a paired reading. Correspondences and Applications follow the second reading.

The first chapter, "Writing, the 'Writing Process,' and You," will assist you in applying the readings to your study of writing. We ask you to think of yourselves as writers joining a community of writers who will help one another as you engage in the various stages of writing narratives. The Perspective section can be used to stimulate journal writing. Application questions provide specific opportunities for you to convey what you think on a particular issue to a wider audience than just your peers through more structured writing and discussion activities. The Additional Writing Topics at the end of each chapter require you to conduct interviews, engage in debate, take positions, or reach conclusions. We have also expanded the range of writing topics to include creative writing, topics that draw upon different kinds of intelligences, as well as topics that ask/assist/require you to use the Web.

As you are also a creatively visual generation, we have added images in each chapter to encourage more complex and varied writing topics. The new prompts invite you to sharpen your observational skills, play with different voices, and make connections between the images and the chapter's texts.

When you look around your classes and your campus, you probably see a student body diverse in its many countries, ethnicities, and ages. We hope that *Across Cultures* will stimulate and encourage you to tap into the rich cultures, languages, experiences, and values of your peers.

S. G.
R. B.

Across Cultures

A Reader for Writers

1

Writing, the "Writing Process," and You

WHO ARE YOU?
What is your name? How old are you? Where are you from? Who is in your family? What are you interested in? Why are you here? Where do you want to be in five years? Your answers to these questions will help you to define yourself, to place you in a context, to help you to realize your self-identity. You are a man or a woman. Maybe you are eighteen years old, or twenty-five, or forty, or seventy, or any number between or beyond. You're from the city, the suburbs, the country. You want to be an accountant, a physician, a musician, a teacher, a professional athlete, a movie star.

Whatever your thoughts and responses are to the above questions, one thing is for certain—you are a writer. Although you may not have included this answer among those offered to the questions above, as a member of the class you are enrolled in you are a writer. Sure, in the outside world you are a son or daughter, a mother or sister, a brother or uncle. You are an artist, a someday All-Star, entrepreneur of the year, or attorney of the month. You want to become a fashion designer, a Grammy winner, a Nobel Prize winner, the president.

However, when you walk through the door into your English class, you are a writer participating in a community of writers. Here your thoughts and ideas will be committed to the written page, and the identity you establish for yourself as a writer will prove to be as important as any you might have invented prior to this time. The sooner you commit to this perception of yourself, the sooner you will trust yourself to get your words down on paper, and the easier the process of writing will become.

Yet this transformation into and acceptance of being a writer is demanding.

First of all, writing is not the same as speaking. Writing utilizes different physical actions as well as unique cognitive processes. Rather than merely translating speech into a written form, writing allows one to select more consciously the language that will be used to communicate. When you speak, you probably don't spend much time considering each word that you will use—words usually just seem to flow. Sometimes they seem to flow much too easily and quickly! Did you ever experience having words come out of your mouth and as you were saying them you thought to yourself, "Whoops! I probably shouldn't have said that!" Too late! Sometimes it seems as if words bypass our brains and emerge into the ears of our listeners all by themselves!

Writing, on the other hand, is a more deliberate and physical act. The words we want to use are still there, but now we can take our time and luxuriate in our choice of them as we put them down on the page. In fact, we can often change a word before it is committed to paper, and even when it's down we can still modify it to suit our needs. It is our ability to control more carefully the presentation of language that makes writing a unique verbal act; however, this uniqueness is—as you will see—a double-edged sword.

In this day of e-mail and instant messaging, when students like you use their cell phones to send text messages more than they do to make voice calls, we are closer than ever to emulating speech in our writing. It is quite possible to have the same "Whoops" response after replying to an IM all too quickly! The incorporation of technology into writing is a revelation that has sprouted a revolution.

Despite the changes that technology (specifically computer-based word processing programs, e-mail, instant messaging, and texting) has brought to writing, there is still one fundamental truth concerning writers and writing—as a writer, you are unique. Although many writers may share similarities, it is most unlikely that two writers will do *exactly* the same thing. In fact, it is not unusual for any single writer to alter how she or he approaches writing depending upon the task at hand. This approach to writing—the *writing process*—is unique to each writer, and, it may be argued, unique to each project undertaken. Yet there are important lessons to be learned from an examination of the choices that all writers make when encountering a writing task.

The first choice a writer makes is how to begin. How do you actually start a writing project? Some people like to sit quietly before they write, giving themselves a chance to gather their thoughts before committing them to paper. Other people like to engage in some physical activity—taking a walk or shooting some baskets—to help them clear their minds before starting. Others like to jump in, get that first sentence down, and keep on going from there. Although one of these actions might describe the way that you get started, there are other techniques that writers use to get them past that blank piece of paper staring them in the face. Three of these are freewriting, brainstorming, and journal-writing. Since you are a unique person and a unique writer, not all of these techniques will work for you. However, by giving each a serious try (indeed, the old "college try"), you might discover a tool that will help make you a more comfortable and effective writer. When this occurs, take this technique with you and incorporate it into your own writing process.

For many writers getting started is the hardest part. A bare sheet of paper can be intimidating, and the sooner that you can put words on it, the better. *Freewriting* is a technique where you write down whatever comes into your mind without consideration of language, grammar, or content. But all you'll get is garbage, you say? The idea is not to evaluate your thoughts but merely to generate them. You will have much time to consider and reconsider the words and ideas that will become your final text, but the real trick for a writer is just to get going! Sit down in a quiet place. Set a timer for five minutes and begin to write. Don't let yourself be interrupted. Don't stop for anything. If you have an itch, don't scratch it—write about scratching it. If you are feeling hungry, don't stop to grab for that cookie—write about the intensity of your hunger pains. If you get stuck and have nothing to write about, write down the colors of the rainbow, the days of the week, or the months of the year until your mind picks up a thread and starts going along it. One thing about your mind: it moves pretty quickly, and keeping up with it might prove a challenge. Do the best you can to follow it. If it stops in midthought and moves to another, stay with it! When freewriting, try to train yourself to stop in midsentence to follow your brain as it moves through the back alleys of your consciousness.

At the end of five minutes, or whenever you have set your timer to go off, go back and read what you have written. (Note how your handwriting may have deteriorated as you have gone forward!) What is the most interesting (or important) idea that you have written? What topic seems to crop up more than any other? What intriguing idea would you like to pursue? The best piece of writing that you can create is the one about something that you are interested in. Practice freewriting regularly and use it to help you find those topics that are meaningful to you.

Another technique to help you to get started is *brainstorming*. Brainstorming is similar to freewriting in that you may use it to generate ideas, but it is different in that you simply create a list of those points you think you want to make about a topic. Often, brainstorming is done as a group activity. When used in this way, group members call out responses to a recorder who sets down on paper or a chalkboard the ideas that are generated. As with freewriting, the idea is not to make judgments about the contributions that are being brainstormed. That will come later, in preparation for creating a first draft of a writing task. Rather, the object of brainstorming is to get those juices flowing and place ideas out there!

Yet another means of generating ideas is *journal-writing*. Setting your ideas to paper three or more times a week is a way to create a record of your thoughts and feelings. Note, however, that keeping a journal is not like writing in a diary. Whereas a diary is primarily a posting of daily events, journals may be quite varied and contain many kinds of entries. Sure, you might write about what happened to you during the day, but you should also be experimenting with new forms and diverse topics. Write a letter to a friend or a famous person, create lyrics to a song or a poem, sketch a landscape or a portrait, cut out and paste in a quotation, picture, or recipe that you find interesting. Of course, as you include material in your journal, be sure to comment on it. What is it about those lyrics that you find most interesting? How do they apply to your life? That picture you cut out of the magazine—what do you find intriguing about it? Why would you want to visit that place? What do you think you would find there? And that recipe you included in your journal so as not to forget it—what was the response to it when you served it to your family and/or friends? What was the verdict? Was it worth making or did you have to order in a couple of pizzas as an emergency measure?

Whatever you decide to do with your journal, remember that it should be a representation of who you are and what you think. If you choose to write only daily diarylike entries, don't be surprised if the sameness of that form causes you to lose interest in the enterprise. By giving a journal a fair try—by making it as unique as *you* are—you will not only see more clearly who you are, but you will also discover many topics to write about, some of which you might never have thought about before.

Freewriting, brainstorming, and *journal-writing* are techniques that will help you to generate ideas and get your writing started. Now that you no longer have a blank page or screen in front of you, what will you do with all that stuff?

Once you have some raw material for an essay, there are certain questions that you—and all writers—need to answer to create an effective piece. Primarily, you must consider *what* you want to say, to *whom* you want to say it, and *why* you want to convey the information.

The first decision you have to make concerns the "what"—what is it that you want to communicate? Generating ideas about your topic might have opened up several aspects of your topic to you; now you need to think about what the main point is that you want to express. This main idea about your general topic, when stated as a clear and direct sentence, is your *thesis*. There's nothing fancy about a thesis statement. It's simply a one-sentence expression of the main idea that you want to convey to your readers.

Another matter that you need to address concerns the person or people who will read your writing. This readership is called an *audience* and you need to take them into account when you create your work. Who will your readers be? How old are they? How much formal education do they have? What are their interests? Why are they reading your work? Your answers to these questions will help you to target your audience. Depending upon your topic and whom you are writing for, you may need to adjust your vocabulary, treatment of ideas, the complexity of language, and even the form that your writing takes.

Yet another concern that writers take into account when considering audience is *tone*—how one presents himself or herself to an audience. How do you want yourself and your topic to appear to your readers? Do you want to take a forceful stance with them, letting them know who's boss and in control of the information being presented? Do you want to win their sympathies and come over to your way of seeing things? Do you want to appear impartial and sway your audience with a logical presentation of information? The relationship you form with your readers—the tone that you supply to your writing—will be created by your choice of language, how you appeal to their hearts and minds, and your approach to your topic.

One final consideration you need to address is *why* you are writing your piece. Yes, you are in a writing class and you want to get a good grade. However, this answer to the question addresses your *motives* for writing rather than your *purpose*. Basically, if you are seeking some kind of tangible, material compensation—primarily either grades or money—then you are talking about motives. Your purpose for writing concerns nonmaterial objectives: you may want to entertain your readers, inform them, vent your emotions to them, or even provide a memory for them to preserve in their own minds. Chances are, you won't be able to settle on a single purpose for writing; indeed, it seems the more complex the work, the more purposes a writer has in mind for writing it. However, by assessing your purpose, audience, and meaning before creating your first draft, you will be able to more closely approach what it is that you want to convey to your readers and how you want to say it.

So now we get to putting all of this preparatory work into action, into that work of writing that we have called a *first draft*. Just its name implies that there will be (at least!) one more, so what's unique about a first, as opposed to a second, third, or fourth draft?

First drafts are where you get to work out on paper the real answers to those questions asked earlier. Although you have generated ideas and thought about your meaning, purpose, and audience, a first draft is the place where you get to try out your ideas and intentions.

When you create this draft, try to stick to your main idea (thesis), and organize information in a way that best addresses your view of audience and that achieves your purpose for writing. However, don't be surprised if when you complete this draft and read it over, you have found a new main point or discovered additional answers to some of the questions you asked yourself earlier. Quite often a first draft is where a writer truly discovers what he or she has to say. It is not unusual for a writer to declare after completing a first draft, "*Now* I have found what I really want to talk about!" There's a simple truth to this statement. How do we know what we want to say until we have said it?

Going back to the earlier discussion of speech and writing, sometimes when we speak we discover the truth of a statement only when it is too late. However, making such a discovery when creating a first draft is like finding gold! Now that you have found what you want to say, you may create a second draft that capitalizes on this knowledge. Now an opportunity presents itself for you to refine and sharpen your topic in view of your discovery. You might also reevaluate your assessment of your audience and how you might best approach your readers. In essence, a first draft is a critical step in creating an interesting and effective final essay.

But wait! With your first draft in hand, how will you go about transforming it into a completed essay? Most students try to touch up a first draft by making surface changes to it. They may alter the structure of a sentence or two, and are likely to change a few words and fix spelling errors and minor grammatical slips. Although these changes will help to increase the clarity of the essay, they will not capitalize on the hard work you have already done creating the first draft and then reassessing your meaning, purpose, and audience. To improve a first draft significantly most often calls for a writer to revise it thoroughly. Those changes mentioned above really concern *editing* and will be discussed later. What experienced writers do to a first draft almost always involves the use of *revising strategies*. These strategies are available to all writers and are the only techniques available to transform a promising first draft into a truly effective piece of writing. Here are the revising techniques available to you:

Addition: Use this technique to offer additional information to your reader. You might add only a phrase to clarify an idea, but sometimes you might need to add a sentence or even a whole paragraph to make your point strongly and clearly.

Deletion: The exact opposite of addition, deletion is used when you have too much information in your essay. Perhaps you repeat yourself or stray from your thesis. In these instances, remove that information to create a tighter, more effective, essay.

Substitution: A combination of addition and deletion, substitution requires you to replace ineffective text with phrases, sentences, or paragraphs that convey your ideas more exactly and clearly.

Rearrangement: Whereas the previous techniques have to do with the amount and effectiveness of the information you provide, rearrangement concerns the *organization* of the information in your essay. There are three techniques involved in rearranging an essay:

Moving: Use this technique to take information from one place in the essay and position it elsewhere. Sometimes a sentence or group of sentences really belongs somewhere else—move them to where they will function more effectively.

Combining: On occasion you will notice that sentences referring to the same idea appear in varied places in your essay. If you determine that these ideas ought to be placed together, you would use combining to bring them to a new location, perhaps creating a new paragraph to accommodate them.

Redistributing: The opposite of *combining*, this technique would be used to deemphasize information by taking ideas from one location and placing them in several related areas. Sometimes a body paragraph that supports your thesis tangentially can be broken up and the relevant sentences placed in other paragraphs. This will eliminate the digression you have made and strengthen the body paragraphs that are already in place.

These techniques—*adding, deleting, substituting, rearranging*—will help you to change the substance of your essay. By doing so, they will enable you to change your meaning and better adapt it to your purpose and audience. These revision strategies will encourage you to do much more than alter a word or punctuation mark, and they will help you make the kinds of changes that first drafts require to bring them to completion.

Let the power of your computer's word-processing program help you use these revising strategies. Your text is flexible and not set in stone. Highlight and cut and paste those sentences that are giving you a problem. How do they look in their new location? Not too good you say? Hit the undo icon and your text is as it was. To be doubly sure that no harm will come to your original, save the first draft (as Draft1), open the file, and immediately save the working copy as Draft2. Now if something goes terribly wrong and you can no longer undo the changes you have made, you can always revert back to your original document, Draft1. Play with your text—add, delete, substitute, and rearrange—but be sure to save your work often! Becoming familiar with the power of revision is a prerequisite to becoming a more effective writer.

By now your revised essay is pretty much where you want it. You have said what you had intended to say and have achieved your purpose in view of your intended audience. Before handing your work to your instructor or submitting it for publication, you need to take the final two steps to maximize its effectiveness—*editing* and *proofreading.*

Both of these stages have been discussed briefly earlier. *Editing* occurs when you read over your draft and examine and modify each sentence for clarity and effectiveness. Sharpen your choice of language to make certain that every word is accurate, that every word says what you want it to say. You might add, delete, or substitute a word or phrase here and there to increase the effectiveness of your text.

Proofreading is when you go over your piece for the last time, paying attention to the accuracy of every word and punctuation mark. Check the spelling of each and every word sentence by sentence—don't trust a spellchecker to find and correct errors, since it will not recognize wrong word choices (*form* instead of *from*, for example). Check grammar and punctuation to make sure that minor slips are corrected.

One problem with proofreading is that you are probably the worst person to check your work at this time! Since you have read your essay so many times, your mind often will tell your eye what to see and slight errors will go unnoticed. It's helpful to exchange papers with a classmate and to alert each other to those minor errors that fall into the proofreading category. Should you be unable to share your work, you might read your essay backward, beginning with the last sentence and ending with the first. Doing this will decontextualize your essay so that your mind does not know what to expect and your eyes will be put to work! After completing this final stage of the "writing process," your essay should be one that you are proud of and that represents your best efforts. Indeed, you have done the work that all writers need to do to write effectively.

Even so, this process of writing and revising might not be completed. Perhaps, after reading your essay, your peer group or instructor may suggest additional revisions or things to think about. In that case, assess the comments that were made and use your writing process to accommodate a new set of changes. This exchange of ideas and perceptions between a writer and his or her audience is invaluable. Learning how readers view your work and respond to your words is an important experience and an essential part of any writer's writing process. Indeed, it is by exposing yourself to these writing situations that you earn the title and identity of "writer."

What has been summarized previously are those techniques that make up the writing process. Remember, however, that every writer formulates his or her own plan to successfully complete a writing task. *Your* writing process is the sequence of steps that you find to be most helpful in creating an essay. You do not need to apply each of these steps, and frequently, steps are not followed in order. It is the nature of writing that makes these processes recursive; that is, a writer usually goes back and forth among them as the written work is produced. Oftentimes, writers revise works in process—even in the most preliminary stages. Conversely, it is plausible to generate ideas even when a piece is nearing completion.

Most important, experiment with your writing process to find the most effective way to write for *you*! Make those techniques and strategies that work best part of your personal armory of writing techniques. For example, some writers, when composing an essay, begin with the essay's body and leave the introduction for last. Their rationale is that they need to know what they have written before creating the paragraph that introduces the work. Whatever your personal preferences, keep your mind open to new techniques. Allow yourself to enjoy the freedom and potential for self-discovery that every writer may experience when setting ideas to paper.

Literacy Narratives

In *Across Cultures*, the essays by Sherman Alexie (p. 72), Susan G. Madera (p. 77), Paule Marshall (p. 185), Vincent Cremona (p. 195), Giovanni J. Gelardi (p. 198), Gloria Naylor (p. 351), and Kenneth Woo (p. 355) are "literacy narratives." A *narrative* may be defined as a story that makes a point. What, however, is literacy? According to *The American Heritage Dictionary of the English Language*, Fourth Edition, one definition of literacy is "The condition or quality of being literate, especially the ability to read and write." Certainly, the authors named above are concerned with reading and writing; this kind of literacy—linguistic literacy—is central to their personal stories. Yet, perhaps other kinds of literacy are also being addressed in these stories.

A second definition presented in *The American Heritage Dictionary* is of literacy as "the condition or quality of being knowledgeable in a particular subject or field." In this case, our representation of literacy must expand to encompass what we know and how we know it. In these instances, who we are as individuals and as individuals within society will help to form our knowledge of ourselves and our world. The things we do and the people we do them with will help to shape our definitions.

- What kind of literacy is required when hiking a trail or negotiating a subway system?

- What does one have to know to work in an office or a factory?

- How does one begin to master the technological literacy required by today's world?

- What kinds of literacy are required to play a song or create a painting?

- If you attend a house of worship, what kinds of literacy are invoked? What would someone who practices another religion need to know in order to become literate in your faith?

- How does one know how to dance, ice skate, or perform gymnastics?

- What kind of literacy is required to participate in a team sport, to be involved in a relationship, to be a member of a family?

- What does "literacy" mean to you? What kinds of literacy have you mastered? Which are you currently in the midst of learning?

Sometime this semester, your instructor might ask you to write your own literacy narrative. Perhaps, if you are asked to share your story with a classmate, a group of your peers, or with your whole class, you might observe types of literacy that you had not thought about. As your classmates share their stories, what do you notice about their literacy narratives? How is the general idea of literacy being described? What kinds of literacy are being addressed? How do these narratives compare with those published in this book?

And, as you read the literary narratives in *Across Cultures*, think about what common themes or kinds of literacy the authors are writing about. Consider how their stories resemble yours, how their depictions of literacy relate to your story and the stories of your classmates.

Composing Your Own
Literacy Narratives

If you have been asked to write a literacy narrative, there are several approaches to the assignment that you may take. Below is a method to help you formulate your ideas about your involvement with language. By following the sequence of assignments from beginning to end, you will create the kind of essay that is represented by the authors who have published their literacy narratives in the chapters of this book.

PROMPTS

- Remember back to your first writing memory, either at home or at school.

- When was the first time you realized that a piece of your writing had an effect on someone?

- When have you seen or felt language doing "harm" or causing "hurt"?

- Describe the physical location where you do your writing in as much detail as you can.

- Characterize your writing process using the metaphor of a meal. For example: What kinds of food? Home cooked? Fast food? A holiday celebration? How many courses and of what kind? Who is present when you eat? What does the table look like where you eat? Silverware? Napkins? Drinks? Rests between parts of the meal? While watching TV? Is there dessert?

- What is your favorite book? When did you read it? Why is it your favorite?

- Describe a person who has been an influence on your writing/reading/language use.

- When did you first become aware of your private voice in a public context?

- What kind of stories did you enjoy hearing as a child? Can you remember creating a story of your own?

JOURNAL-WRITING

Select one of the prompts and, without stopping, write for five minutes on anything that comes to mind related to the prompt. When the five minutes are up, select another prompt and write again for five minutes. Repeat the process again so that you have three freewritten chunks of text. Now go back and look for connections across the three chunks and rewrite them so that they form one comprehensive journal entry.

CONNECTIONS

Based upon what you have written, look through the texts in the chapter and find at least one that you can link to. Are there issues in the text that help you make sense of your journal entry? How can you use these to expand on your literacy narrative? Remember that points of conflict may be as helpful as those in common as you think about them in relation to your own writing.

REFLECTIONS

Read over the new material you have added to your narrative. How did the process of reading literacy narratives, reseeing other texts as literacy narratives, and writing your own narrative help you to think of these issues in different contexts? What insights did you gain about yourself coming into language? Do you better understand the differences between your public and private voices? How might you develop them? As you negotiate among your various roles and cultures, how will you use language to create understanding? In what contexts might you engage in the discourse of persuasion? Write a journal entry on any of these issues that seem pertinent to your literacy narrative.

CHAPTER

2

Family and Community

A REVIEW OF THE PERSPECTIVES on family, friends, and community in this chapter reflect incredible variations in cross-cultural views of social relationships, but one theme remains constant: we are social beings. The variations that exist in family, friendship, and community have been built on the changeless desire and need to reach out to one another.

The American poet Walt Whitman described the self as a "miracle of miracles, beyond statement, most spiritual and vaguest of earth's dreams, yet hardest basic fact, and only entrance to all facts." The self, as Whitman indicates, is indeed paradoxical, and if it is to remain dynamic, it must constantly evolve. To ensure self-growth, we must evaluate all that happens to us, however seemingly insignificant.

What you will encounter as you read the texts on these issues is that regardless of their ethnic and cultural backgrounds, the writers have a common interest in knowing and understanding themselves and others. You will meet people like yourself with complex personalities composed of conflicting desires, attitudes, and expressions. Like them, you play many roles—parent, child, sibling, friend, lover, employee, student. Although each of us is unique, we are also influenced by those who share our daily and communal lives. When our own personality, individualism, and sense of identity become all-important, who helps us reconcile self and society, independence and interdependence? The cross-cultural examples in this chapter may suggest some answers.

Family members are often important catalysts for reconstructing and understanding ourselves, but as we know from the Indian folktale "How the Wicked Sons Were Duped," greed within families can be a source of grief and alienation. Immigrant family relationships also add different voices to this conversation by sharing the gains and losses of diasporic experiences. In "Two Lives," for example, Maylasian immigrant Shirley Geok-Lin Lim reflects on her lack of communal identity as a "resident alien," seeing herself through the eyes of citizens as "guest, stranger, outsider, misfit, beggar."

David Brooks, in "People Like Us," casts a wider net in presenting credible evidence to support his thesis that "we don't really care about diversity all that much in America, even though we talk about it a great deal," challenging the whole notion in Toni Morrison's words that "we are people in search of a national community." Lewis (Johnson) Sawaquat, on the other hand, despite the prejudice that he experienced as a Native American, shares his aspirations that his daughter will be more fortunate.

The significance of family and individual names is explored by Tom Rosenberg, who makes a courageous decision to reclaim his Jewish heritage after three decades by changing not only his last name but his first, and by Trikartikaningsih Byas, who recalls the wrenching choice of betraying her Indonesian heritage by changing her given first name to obtain a Social Security card in the United States.

The basic importance and influence of family members, even those about whom we are ambivalent, are apparent in this cross-cultural survey of relationships. All of the texts reinforce how much our cultural and personal identities are rooted in our need for community.

Perspectives

Civilization progresses at the expense of individual happiness.
—Sigmund Freud

No people are ever as divided as those of the same blood.
—Mavis Gallant

All parents realize, or should realize, that children are not possessions, but are only lent to us, angel boarders, as it were.
—John Gregory Dunne

"Family" is not just a buzz word for reactionaries; for women, as for men, it is the symbol of the last area where one has any hope of control over one's destiny, of meeting one's most basic human needs, of nourishing that core of personhood, threatened now by vast impersonal institutions and uncontrollable corporate and government bureaucracies.
—Betty Friedan

Relationships and communion are the most significant clues surrounding the mystery of our human nature. They tell us the most about who we are.
—Susan Cahill

Friendship is by its very nature freer of deceit than any other relationship we can know because it is the bond least affected by striving for power, physical pleasure, or material profit, most liberated from any oath of duty or constancy.
—Francine du Plessix Gray

Some people are your relatives but others are your ancestors, and you choose the ones you want to have as ancestors. You create yourself out of those.
—Ralph Ellison

Talents are best nurtured in solitude; character is best formed in the stormy billows of the world.
—Johann Wolfgang von Goethe

Friendship marks a life even more deeply than love.
—Elie Wiesel

Virtue never stands alone. It is bound to have neighbors.
—Confucius

Your children need your presence more than your presents.

—Jesse Jackson

The price of hating other human beings is loving oneself less.

—Eldridge Cleaver

In search of my mother's garden I found my own.

—Alice Walker

Every man's neighbor is his looking glass.

—English proverb

Fate makes relatives, but choice makes friends.

—DeLile

I have three chairs in my house; one for solitude, two for friendship, three for society.

—Henry David Thoreau

Each friend represents a world in us, a world possibly not born until they arrive, and it is only by this meeting that a new world is born.

—Anaïs Nin

The family, not the individual, is the real molecule of society, the key link in the social chain of being.

—Robert Nisbet

Home is the place, when you have to go there, they have to take you in.

—Robert Frost

The moment we cease to hold each other, the minute we break faith with one another, the sea engulfs us and the light goes out.

—James Baldwin

We are people in search of a national community.

—Toni Morrison

Children have more need of models than of critics.

—Joseph Joubert

The family is the basic cell of government: it is where we are trained to believe that we are human beings or that we are chattel, it is where we are trained to see the sex and race divisions and become callous to injustice even if it is done to ourselves, to accept as biological a full system of authoritarian government.

—Gloria Steinem

APPLICATIONS

1. Review the perspectives for family and community and write a journal entry on the one you most agree or disagree with. Be specific.

2. Working with your group, review Frost's perspective on home and then write your own.

3. Ellison in his perspective differentiates between relatives and ancestors. What is the difference in your opinion? In what sense is it possible to choose your ancestors?

How the Wicked Sons Were Duped

A FOLKTALE FROM INDIA

Throughout the course of human history, wherever communities are formed and community life is cultivated, folklore has existed. Folklore plays a large role in our childhood and in our family and community life. Folklore based in the oral tradition—myths, legends, proverbs, and folktales—is the precursor to modern literacy. Even in contemporary societies folklore is only a cousin or a grandparent away. And wherever people live, folklore grows. India is a country of many languages, religions, sects, and cultures, and it is a land with a rich ethnic history. Below is a folktale from India that is as meaningful today as it was when it was first told hundreds, or perhaps thousands, of years ago.

A VERY WEALTHY OLD MAN, imagining that he was on the point of death, sent for his sons and divided his property among them. However, he did not die for several years afterwards; and miserable years many of them were. Besides the weariness of old age, the old fellow had to bear with much abuse and cruelty from his sons. Wretched, selfish ingrates! Previously they vied with one another in trying to please their father, hoping thus to receive more money, but now they had received their patrimony, they cared not how soon he left them—nay, the sooner the better, because he was only a needless trouble and expense. This, as we may suppose, was a great grief to the old man.

One day he met a friend and related to him all his troubles. The friend sympathized very much with him, and promised to think over the matter, and call in a little while and tell him what to do. He did so; in a few days he visited the old man and put down four bags full of stones and gravel before him.

"Look here, friend," said he. "Your sons will get to know of my coming here today, and will inquire about it. You must pretend that I came to discharge a long-standing debt with you, and that you are several thousands of rupees richer than you thought you were. Keep these bags in your own hands, and on no account let your sons get to them as long as you are alive. You will soon find them change their conduct towards you. Salám. I will come again soon to see how you are getting on."

When the young men got to hear of this further increase of wealth they began to be more attentive and pleasing to their father than ever before. And thus they continued to the day of the old man's demise, when the bags were greedily opened, and found to contain only stones and gravel!

INTERPRETATIONS

1. Write a response relating how you feel about the fact that the father has to fool his sons with the promise of wealth in return for their affections.

2. Once children have grown to adulthood and are independent of their parents' care, what obligation do parents have to them? Do parents or grandparents have a right to live out the remainder of their lives without the burden of responsibility for the economic welfare of their adult children? Explain.

3. To what degree do you think cultural traditions play a role in the treatment and care of parents and grandparents? For example, what difference do you see between how you treat your parents and grandparents and how friends of yours from different ethnic backgrounds treat their parents and grandparents?

CORRESPONDENCE

1. Read the perspective by Jesse Jackson and apply it to "How the Wicked Sons Were Duped." What is the irony of Jackson's perspective in relation to the folktale?

APPLICATION

1. Using your own words and drawing a different conclusion, retell the story describing how you would deal with (your) ungrateful children.

People Like Us

DAVID BROOKS

David Brooks has become familiar to a large audience as a commentator on "The Newshour with Jim Lehrer" and since 2003 as a columnist for The New York Times, *as a senior editor of* The Weekly Standard *from its inception in 1995 until 2003, and for the previous nine years at various posts at* The Wall Street Journal. *He has been a contributing editor at* Newsweek *and the* Atlantic Monthly *(where "People Like Us" first appeared in 2003), and as contributor to numerous other periodicals. He is the author of* Bobos in Paradise: The New Upper Class and How They Got There *and* On Paradise Drive: How We Live Now (and Always Have) in the Future Tense. *He is a frequent analyst on National Public Radio's "All Things Considered" and "The Diane Rehm Show:" Born in Toronto in 1961, he grew up in New York City and Philadelphia and graduated from the University of Chicago in 1983. He lives with his wife and three children in Montgomery County, Maryland. Brooks says here that he has never heard of or been to a truly diverse neighborhood; have you?*

MAYBE IT'S TIME to admit the obvious. We don't really care about diversity all that much in America, even though we talk about it a great deal. Maybe somewhere in this country there is a truly diverse neighborhood in which a black Pentecostal minister lives next to a white antiglobalization activist, who lives next to an Asian short-order cook, who lives next to a professional golfer, who lives next to a postmodern-literature professor and a cardiovascular surgeon. But I have never been to or heard of that neighborhood. Instead, what I have seen all around the country is people making strenuous efforts to group themselves with people who are basically like themselves.

Human beings are capable of drawing amazingly subtle social distinctions and then shaping their lives around them. In the Washington, D.C., area Democratic lawyers tend to live in suburban Maryland, and Republican lawyers tend to live in suburban Virginia. If you asked a Democratic lawyer to move from her $750,000 house in Bethesda, Maryland, to a $750,000 house in Great Falls, Virginia, she'd look at you as if you had just asked her to buy a pickup truck with a gun rack and to shove chewing tobacco in her kid's mouth. In Manhattan the owner of a $3 million SoHo loft would feel out of place moving into a $3 million

Fifth Avenue apartment. A West Hollywood interior decorator would feel dislocated if you asked him to move to Orange County. In Georgia a barista from Athens would probably not fit in serving coffee in Americus.

It is a common complaint that every place is starting to look the same. But in the information age, the late writer James Chapin once told me, every place becomes more like itself. People are less often tied down to factories and mills, and they can search for places to live on the basis of cultural affinity. Once they find a town in which people share their values, they flock there, and reinforce whatever was distinctive about the town in the first place. Once Boulder, Colorado, became known as congenial to politically progressive mountain bikers, half the politically progressive mountain bikers in the country (it seems) moved there; they made the place so culturally pure that it has become practically a parody of itself.

But people love it. Make no mistake—we are increasing our happiness by segmenting off so rigorously. We are finding places where we are comfortable and where we feel we can flourish. But the choices we make toward that end lead to the very opposite of diversity. The United States might be a diverse nation when considered as a whole, but block by block and institution by institution it is a relatively homogeneous nation.

When we use the word "diversity" today we usually mean racial integration. But even here our good intentions seem to have run into the brick wall of human nature. Over the past generation reformers have tried heroically, and in many cases successfully, to end housing discrimination. But recent patterns aren't encouraging: according to an analysis of the 2000 census data, the 1990s saw only a slight increase in the racial integration of neighborhoods in the United States. The number of middle-class and upper-middle-class African-American families is rising, but for whatever reasons—racism, psychological comfort—these families tend to congregate in predominantly black neighborhoods.

In fact, evidence suggests that some neighborhoods become more segregated over time. New suburbs in Arizona and Nevada, for example, start out reasonably well integrated. These neighborhoods don't yet have reputations, so people choose their houses for other, mostly economic reasons. But as neighborhoods age, they develop personalities (that's where the Asians live, and that's where the Hispanics live), and segmentation occurs. It could be that in a few years the new suburbs in the Southwest will be nearly as segregated as the established ones in the Northeast and the Midwest.

Even though race and ethnicity run deep in American society, we should in theory be able to find areas that are at least culturally diverse.

But here, too, people show few signs of being truly interested in building diverse communities. If you run a retail company and you're thinking of opening new stores, you can choose among dozens of consulting firms that are quite effective at locating your potential customers. They can do this because people with similar tastes and preferences tend to congregate by ZIP code.

The most famous of these precision marketing firms is Claritas, which breaks down the U.S. population into sixty-two psycho-demographic clusters, based on such factors as how much money people make, what they like to read and watch, and what products they have bought in the past. For example, the "suburban sprawl" cluster is composed of young families making about $41,000 a year and living in fast-growing places such as Burnsville, Minnesota, and Bensalem, Pennsylvania. These people are almost twice as likely as other Americans to have three-way calling. They are two and a half times as likely to buy Light n' Lively Kid Yogurt. Members of the "towns & gowns" cluster are recent college graduates in places such as Berkeley, California, and Gainesville, Florida. They are big consumers of DoveBars and *Saturday Night Live*. They tend to drive small foreign cars and to read *Rolling Stone* and *Scientific American*.

Looking through the market research, one can sometimes be amazed by how efficiently people cluster—and by how predictable we all are. If you wanted to sell imported wine, obviously you would have to find places where rich people live. But did you know that the sixteen counties with the greatest proportion of imported-wine drinkers are all in the same three metropolitan areas (New York, San Francisco, and Washington, D.C.)? If you tried to open a motor-home dealership in Montgomery County, Pennsylvania, you'd probably go broke, because people in this ring of the Philadelphia suburbs think RVs are kind of uncool. But if you traveled just a short way north, to Monroe County, Pennsylvania, you would find yourself in the fifth motor-home-friendliest county in America.

Geography is not the only way we find ourselves divided from people unlike us. Some of us watch Fox News, while others listen to NPR. Some like David Letterman, and others—typically in less urban neighborhoods—like Jay Leno. Some go to charismatic churches; some go to mainstream churches. Americans tend more and more often to marry people with education levels similar to their own, and to befriend people with backgrounds similar to their own.

My favorite illustration of this latter pattern comes from the first, noncontroversial chapter of *The Bell Curve*. Think of your twelve closest friends, Richard J. Herrnstein and Charles Murray write. If you had chosen them randomly from the American population, the odds that half of your twelve closest friends would be college graduates would be six in a thousand. The odds that half of the twelve would have advanced degrees would be less than one in a million. Have any of your twelve closest friends graduated from Harvard, Stanford, Yale, Princeton, Caltech, MIT, Duke, Dartmouth, Cornell, Columbia, Chicago, or Brown? If you chose your friends randomly from the American population, the odds against your having four or more friends from those schools would be more than a billion to one.

Many of us live in absurdly unlikely groupings, because we have organized our lives that way.

It's striking that the institutions that talk the most about diversity often practice it the least. For example, no group of people sings the diversity anthem more frequently and fervently than administrators at just such elite universities. But elite universities are amazingly undiverse in their values, politics, and mores. Professors in particular are drawn from a rather narrow segment of the population. If faculties reflected the general population, 32 percent of professors would be registered Democrats and 31 percent would be registered Republicans. Forty percent would be evangelical Christians. But a recent study of several universities by the conservative Center for the Study of Popular Culture and the American Enterprise Institute found that roughly 90 percent of those professors in the arts and sciences who had registered with a political party had registered Democratic. Fifty-seven professors at Brown were found on the voter-registration rolls. Of those, fifty-four were Democrats. Of the forty-two professors in the English, history, sociology, and political-science departments, all were Democrats. The results at Harvard, Penn State, Maryland, and the University of California at Santa Barbara were similar to the results at Brown.

What we are looking at here is human nature. People want to be around others who are roughly like themselves. That's called community. It probably would be psychologically difficult for most Brown professors to share an office with someone who was pro-life, a member of the National Rifle Association, or an evangelical Christian. It's likely that hiring committees would subtly—even unconsciously—screen out any such people they encountered. Republicans and evangelical Christians have sensed that they are not welcome at places like Brown, so they don't even consider working there. In fact, any registered Republican who contemplates a career in academia these days is both a hero and a fool. So, in a semi–self-selective pattern, brainy people with generally liberal social mores flow to academia, and brainy people with generally conservative mores flow elsewhere.

The dream of diversity is like the dream of equality. Both are based on ideals we celebrate even as we undermine them daily. (How many times have you seen someone renounce a high-paying job or pull his child from an elite college on the grounds that these things are bad for equality?) On the one hand, the situation is appalling. It is appalling that Americans know so little about one another. It is appalling that many of us are so narrow-minded that we can't tolerate a few people with ideas significantly different from our own. It's appalling that evangelical Christians are practically absent from entire professions, such as academia, the media, and filmmaking. It's appalling that people should be content to cut themselves off from everyone unlike themselves.

The segmentation of society means that often we don't even have arguments across the political divide. Within their little validating communities, liberals and conservatives circulate half-truths about the supposed awfulness of the other side. These distortions are believed because it feels good to believe them.

On the other hand, there are limits to how diverse any community can or should be. I've come to think that it is not useful to try to hammer diversity into every neighborhood and institution in the United States. Sure, Augusta National should probably admit women, and university sociology departments should probably hire a conservative or two. It would be nice if all neighborhoods had a good mixture of ethnicities. But human nature being what it is, most places and institutions are going to remain culturally homogeneous.

It's probably better to think about diverse lives, not diverse institutions. Human beings, if they are to live well, will have to move through a series of institutions and environments, which may be individually homogeneous but, taken together, will offer diverse experiences. It might also be a good idea to make national service a rite of passage for young people in this country: it would take them out of their narrow neighborhood segment and thrust them in with people unlike themselves. Finally, it's probably important for adults to get out of their own familiar circles. If you live in a coastal, socially liberal neighborhood, maybe you should take out a subscription to *The Door*, the evangelical humor magazine; or maybe you should visit Branson, Missouri. Maybe you should stop in at a megachurch. Sure, it would be superficial familiarity, but it beats the iron curtains that now separate the nation's various cultural zones.

Look around at your daily life. Are you really in touch with the broad diversity of American life? Do you care?

INTERPRETATIONS

1. Brooks maintains that people like to group themselves with others who are similar to themselves. What factors are mentioned that might provide a center of association for individuals?

2. According to Brooks, what accounts for the segregation of neighborhoods? Describe the social mechanism that he sees at work.

3. In paragraphs 13 and 14, Brooks argues that "the institutions that talk most about diversity often practice it the least." What evidence does he use to support this statement?

4. After you finish reading the essay, what conclusion do you come to about how Brooks feels about the segmentation that exists in America? What are some concrete effects of seeking out "people like us"?

CORRESPONDENCES

1. To what extent might Brooks's essay be used to explain what happens to John Wideman in "The Night I Was Nobody"?

2. Compare Brooks's essay to Linda Stanley's "Passion and the Dream" in Chapter 7. How well are Brooks's theories about community supported by Stanley's experiences?

APPLICATIONS

1. In paragraph 14, Brooks defines community as people wanting "to be around others who are roughly like themselves." Do you agree or disagree with this definition? Write a journal entry explaining your responses.

2. Draw a limited genealogical chart that shows your family (grandparents, your immediate family, and first cousins). Using some of the criteria mentioned by Brooks, try to assess how similar or different these people are. In a few paragraphs, explain your conclusions stating directly the criteria you are applying.

   Now, add to this chart those relatives who have married into the family. How do they compare to the original grouping? How do your findings compare to those of Brooks? Present your conclusions in a few paragraphs.

3. "Do you care?" What are the implications of people surrounding themselves with similar individuals? Write an essay that argues for or against the need to pursue diversity in America.

4. "Who are 'us'?"

   At a computer that has access to the Internet, point your browser to www.google.com. Type your ZIP code into the search bar and click on "Search." One of the first results you get should be something like "XXXXX Zip Code Detailed Profile—residents and real estate info" (where XXXXX is the ZIP code you initially entered) and have a Web address that starts with www.city-data. com/zips/. Click on this link. Now you should have a Web page listing some demographics for the ZIP code you initially entered. Next, for additional information, click on the highlighted text next to "City" toward the top center of the page.

What information have you learned about people in this ZIP code? How does this data relate to what Brooks has mentioned in his essay?

Changing My Name after Sixty Years

TOM ROSENBERG

What's in a name? How does one's name affect his or her life? "Changing My Name after Sixty Years" appeared in Newsweek *in 2000, a year after the author decided to change his name to the name he was born with in Berlin about six years before his family fled Nazi persecution in 1938 and settled in New York City. As "Tom Ross" he had grown up in New York, graduated from the University of Pittsburgh, and joined the Marines during the Korean War. He had lived on the West Coast, working as a political consultant with special interest in environment and outdoor recreation initiatives. In 2000 he published his first novel,* Phantom on His Wheel, *also under the name Thomas Rosenberg. You can find other short essays by Rosenberg (as well as a version of the following essay) on his blog at http://inaword.org.*

MY PARENTS LEFT NAZI GERMANY in 1938, when I was six and my mother was pregnant with my sister. They arrived in America with a lot of baggage—guilt over deserting loved ones, anger over losing their home and business, and a lifelong fear of anti-Semitism.

Shortly thereafter, whether out of fear, a desire to assimilate, or a combination of both, they changed our family name from Rosenberg to Ross. My parents were different from the immigrants who landed on Ellis Island and had their names changed by an immigration bureaucrat. My mother and father voluntarily gave up their identity and a measure of pride for an Anglicized name.

Growing up a German-Jewish kid in the Bronx in the 1940s, a time when Americans were dying in a war fought in part to save Jews from the hated Nazis, was difficult. Even my new name failed to protect me from bigotry; the neighborhood bullies knew a "sheenie" when they saw one.

The bullying only intensified the shame I felt about my family's religious and ethnic background. I spent much of my youth denying my roots and vying for my peers' acceptance as "Tom Ross." Today I look back and wonder what kind of life I might have led if my parents had kept our family name.

In the '50s, I doubt Tom Rosenberg would have been accepted as a pledge by Theta Chi, a predominantly Christian fraternity at my college. He probably would have pledged a Jewish fraternity or had the self-confidence and conviction to ignore the Greek system altogether. Tom Rosenberg might have married a Jewish woman, stayed in the East, and maintained closer ties to his Jewish family.

As it was, I moved west to San Francisco. Only after I married and became a father did I begin to acknowledge my Jewish heritage.

My first wife, a liberal Methodist, insisted that I stop running from Judaism. For years we attended both a Unitarian church and a Jewish temple. Her open-minded attitude set the tone in our household and was passed on to our three kids. As a family, we celebrated Christmas and went to temple on the High Holidays. But even though my wife and I were careful to teach our kids tolerance, their exposure to either religion was minimal. Most weekends, we took the kids on ski trips, rationalizing that the majesty of the Sierra was enough of a spiritual experience.

So last year, when I decided to tell my children that I was legally changing my name back to Rosenberg, I wondered how they would react. We were in a restaurant celebrating the publication of my first novel. After they toasted my tenacity for staying with fiction for some thirty years, I made my announcement: "I want to be remembered by the name I was born with."

I explained that the kind of discrimination and stereotyping still evident today had made me rethink the years I'd spent denying my family's history, years that I'd been ashamed to talk about with them. The present political climate—the initiatives attacking social services for immigrants, bilingual education, Affirmative Action—made me want to shout "I'm an immigrant!" My children were silent for a moment before they smiled, leaned over, and hugged me.

The memories of my years of denial continued to dog me as I told friends and family that I planned to change my name. The rabbi at the Reform temple that I belong to with my second wife suggested I go a step further. "Have you thought of taking a Hebrew first name?" he asked.

He must have seen the shocked look on my face. I wondered, is he suggesting I become more religious, more Jewish? "What's involved?" I asked hesitatingly.

The rabbi explained that the ceremony would be simple and private, just for family and friends. I would make a few remarks about why I had selected my name, and then he would say a blessing.

It took me a moment to grasp the significance of what the rabbi was proposing. He saw my name change as a chance to do more than reclaim a piece of my family's history: it was an opportunity to renew my commitment to Jewish ideals. I realized it was also a way to give my kids the sense of pride in their heritage that they had missed out on as children.

A few months later I stood at the pulpit in front of an open, lighted ark, flanked by my wife and the rabbi. Before me stood my children, holding their children. I had scribbled a few notes for my talk, but felt too emotional to use them. I held on to the lectern for support and winged it.

"Every time I step into a temple, I'm reminded that Judaism has survived for 4,000 years. It's survived because it's a positive religion. My parents, your grandparents, changed their name out of fear. I'm changing it back out of pride. I chose the name Tikvah because it means hope."

INTERPRETATIONS

1. In the last paragraph, Rosenberg says to his children, "My parents, your grandparents, changed their name out of fear. I'm changing it back out of pride." What, specifically, were Rosenberg's parents afraid of? What is the source of Rosenberg's pride?

2. In what ways does Rosenberg's decision reflect his awareness of family and community?

3. According to Rosenberg, how might his life have been different had his parents not changed their name?

APPLICATIONS

1. If you had the opportunity to give yourself a name, what would you choose? You might consider a name that describes you, or one in another language that is meaningful to you. Now, imagine yourself at a naming ceremony similar to the one Rosenberg describes. Write out a speech that explains the significance of your new name that you will deliver to your close friends and family.

2. In paragraph 7, Rosenberg briefly mentions religion and spirituality. What relationship do you think exists between these terms? How might you explain your definition of these terms and how they relate to each other?

3. What religious beliefs or customs are followed by your parents or grandparents? Do you actively participate in these beliefs and/or practices? Why or why not? What general idea governs what you choose to believe and follow?

Where the Land Is Stepped on, the Sky above It Must Be Upheld

TRIKARTIKANINGSIH BYAS

Trikartikaningsih Byas was born in Indonesia, a democratic country with the largest Muslim population but officially recognizes six religions—Islam, Catholicism, Christianity, Hinduism, Buddhism, and Indigenous Belief. After earning her B.A. in Indonesia, she came to America to complete her graduate studies (M.A. and M.Ed. in TESOL from Teachers College, Columbia University and Ph.D. in Rhetoric and Linguistics from Indiana University of Pennsylvania). As volunteers and members of the Islamic Center of Long Island (ICLI) in Westbury she and her husband are involved in cross-cultural and interfaith activities. She is currently teaching at Queensborough Community College, where she explores the issues of immigration, cross-cultural, and interfaith communication.

The Republic of Indonesia is an archipelago southeast of the Asian mainland with the greatest population density of any country in the world: 234 million people on over 13,500 islands, one of which, Java, has over 2,000 people per square mile. The principal languages are Bahasa Indonesia, English, Dutch, and Javanese, the principal religion Islam (87 percent), making Indonesia the largest Muslim nation in the world. Originally Hindu and Buddhist, Islam has been dominant since the 16th century. The Dutch gained control by the 18th century, followed by the Japanese during World War II. Nationalists, led by Sukarno, declared a republic in 1950. In 1965 a military coup resulted in General Suharto's becoming president for the next thirty-one years. After two years under Presidents Habibie and Wahid, Indonesians in 2001 elected as their first woman president Sukarno's daughter, Megawati Sukamoputri, who served until she was defeated in an election in 2004 by General Susilo Bambang Yudhoyono. Between 2004 and 2007 Indonesia has suffered a series of earthquakes, tsunamis, and floods: the death toll from the first quake alone (26 December 2004) exceeded 125,000.

WHEN I FIRST LEFT MY PARENTS' house and home country in 1990, I landed in room 214 at Whittier Hall of Teachers College Columbia University where I shared the suite with four Americans. As an Indonesian, I live by two important proverbs: *where the land is stepped on, the sky above it must be upheld,* which expects me to always respect the host community wherever I go; and *follow the way of paddy (rice), the more content it has, the lower it bows* which advises me to be humble and not attract attention. Mature and filled paddy (rice) hull will bow due to its weight, while the empty hull will stand straight. Indonesians are advised to be humble, like *paddy;* the more knowledge they acquire the lower they should bow and not attract attention.

Respecting the host culture and not attracting attention were relatively easy since being a minority was in itself a humbling experience. Though a practicing Muslim, I did not look different from my American suitemates, except for my straighter and blacker hair, darker complexion, smaller eyes, and not-so-generous nose. I wore casual clothes like they did, plus the extra layers in winter or a parasol in the summer. I did most of what my suitemates did: we had breakfast and watched TV together; we went to plays, movies and parades; on my first birthday in NYC I even joined them at *Club Baja* where they failed to persuade me to drink something more expensive and "substantial" than soda even though they were willing to pick up the tab. As a Muslim I do not drink alcoholic beverages.

In dealing with differences, I chose the strategy of yielding and avoidance. In matters not related to principles I let people have their way and I avoided situations that would be at odds with my belief. All in all, I was able to blend into the American graduate student dorm life with the help of my suitemates in my cultural learning. Even when misunderstandings occurred among us, we quickly resolved them in our discussion over breakfasts or while watching *Twin Peaks.*

Blending and being humble, however, were never easy when it comes to my name. Like many Indonesians I only have one name. I never thought that my name would pose serious challenges in this "land of the free." Seventeen letters makes my name—Trikartikaningsih. It has three parts: *Tri-kartika-ningsih. Tri* indicates the order of birth: third. *Kartika,* which means source of light or star, is the essence of my name. Finally, *ningsih* is an indicator of my gender—female. Even without having met me, most Indonesians would know that I am the third child and a female.

Arriving at Teachers College, I went straight to the International Student Office. The advisor, Nancy Bruce, told me that I needed to apply for a Social Security number so that I can register for classes and open a bank account. She took me and other international students to the Social Security Office three days later. We arrived at the office early, yet there were many people already waiting. I took a number, filled out the application form, and anxiously awaited my turn, just as I had waited in immigration check at JFK airport a week earlier. Everything was new, so I was not sure what to expect. I checked my application and the documents I had in my folder. When my number was called, I rushed to the counter. I submitted my application and was nervous when the agent flipped my application back and forth several times.

"What is your last name?" the agent asked.

"I don't have a last name," I replied. "I only have one name," I added while frantically pulling out the documents from the folder—passport, translations of birth certificate, school diplomas and transcripts—as proofs.

"Here, only one name in all my documents," I explained.

"You cannot apply if you don't have a last name," she sternly said, pushing all my documents back to me. "You must have a last name before I can accept and process your application." She signaled me to return to the waiting area and called another number.

Feeling all eyes were on me, I quietly gathered my documents and walked to where Nancy sat. I told her the situation. She was quiet as she did not know what to say. She might have never met anyone with only one very long name like me. I slumped in the chair and was feeling dizzy.

"What is wrong with having one name? Why do I have to have a last name?"

I continued the silent questioning to no avail. Then reality sank in. The host culture required a last name. I was the exception and I should not draw people's attention. If I wanted to study here, I needed a Social Security number. And to have a social security number, I needed to have a last name.

"But where do I get a last name? What name should I use? What proof of a last name do I have?"

I was baffled and ready to break down. Then I remembered my mom's words to leave the decision to *Allah* the Creator. I invoked some *du'a* (supplications) and thought about how my parents named my siblings. An inspiration came to me: separate the birth order from the rest of the name. Tri Kartikaningsih. I consoled myself thinking that my name would still appear the same, except for the space and the capital K in the middle. Then I filled out a new application form and went back to the counter.

I was quiet on the way back to campus, and after thanking Nancy, I went straight to my dorm room. I cried the whole afternoon and wanted so much to call my parents to apologize for what I did. But it was after midnight in Jakarta and they must have gone to bed already. I woke them up three hours later and told them what happened. My father was supportive of my decision, yet I sensed his dislike of anybody forcing me to change my name. He had instilled in me pride in my name and identity; what happened in the Social Security Administration Office crushed that sense of pride.

"It is OK. We understand. Just remember that you will be in the U.S. for a short while. God willing, it will not change who you are," he comforted me.

I was relieved after speaking with my parents and prayed that my anger/frustration would pass. I was wrong.

When I received the social security card in the mail with my name cut in two, I felt mutilated. I was upset, but realized I had allowed the SSA to identify me as such because I wanted to avoid "problems." I reminded myself that the card would serve some purposes. Thus, after registering for classes and opening a bank account the next morning, I buried the card at the bottom of my suitcase, hoping not to need it again. I was relieved that I did not have to use that new name on other things. To preserve my name I adopted an initial T as my first name, and used my complete name as a last name. Problems related to completing forms were solved, but not in conversation. No one can pronounce my name; thus, not wanting to draw attention to myself and to ease communication, I resorted to my nickname.

Tika is the default nickname for most *kartikas*. I was *tika* as a child and still am to some of my relatives. Nothing was wrong with *tika*, but as a curious teenager, I wanted to be different. Reviewing the alphabet while learning English in junior high, I decided to adopt the seventeenth letter as my new identity: Q, as my initial, and its Indonesian pronunciation /*ki*/ as my nickname. Since that day, I have been *kiki* to my friends and my siblings, but at the core I am still Trikartikaningsih. Most friends I made in the U.S. would know me as "kiki with ONE very long name." In fact, I prefer it to people cutting my name in places I least expected.

Two decades have passed and I have since acquired a legal last name; yet, the struggle continues. I am holding up the sky still, hoping for the day I can claim my name and identity without attracting attention or creating problems so I can continue bowing humbly as the good, mature *paddy*.

INTERPRETATIONS

1. Explain the implications of the two proverbs Byas includes in her first paragraph.

2. What profile of herself does she create in paragraphs two and three?

3. How effective is the author's use of foreshadowing in preparing the reader for her first visit to the Social Security Office? What new aspects of Byas's personality emerge in this situation?

4. Why does Byas include her parents at this point in her narrative?

5. "When I received the social security card in the mail with my name cut in two, I felt mutilated." How does Byas cope with this initial response?

6. What techniques does she use in the conclusion to unify her essay? Be specific.

CORRESPONDENCES

1. Rosenberg and Byas focus on the complexities between names and identities. To what extent did you identify with their situations? Which did you find more compelling? Explain.

2. How do the authors' focus on family and religion add dimension to their narratives? Create a brief imagined conversation with one of them on these issues.

APPLICATIONS

1. Create an extended journal entry on a conversation between yourself and Byas on the significance of names that includes your family traditions regarding them.

2. Although the focus of Byas's essay is on the trauma involved in changing her name, what other aspects of her immigration experience does she also include? Write an extended journal entry responding to her memoir. How can you imagine acting in her situation?

We Kissed the Tomato and Then the Sky

DANA WEHLE

Dana Wehle, born in Queens, New York, in 1954, now lives in Brooklyn. She is a classically trained painter with a master of fine arts. The daughter of two Holocaust survivors, her work has been recognized for its effectiveness in communicating the impact of the Holocaust on the second generation. She has a master's degree in social work and is a certified psychoanalyst with a private psychotherapy practice in Manhattan. Wehle wishes to dedicate this essay to Susan Wehle, her beloved sister who died in a Continental airplane crash in February 2009. She notes: "Such an end to Susan's life layers our family's history with yet another horrific death, this time not due to anti-semitism and hate, but random death through corporate greed."

MY PARENTS' BIG BED was not the kind to take refuge in when I was little. The two twin beds, connected by an elegant walnut headboard, were each clearly assigned. One was his, one was hers. After my father died, my mother made the monumental decision to make his side hers after forty-three years of it being the other way. She defensively explained that her motive was not to help resolve her loss, but simply to be closer to the door. In fact, the increasing number of times she got up during the night became a matter of concern to us all.

When I visited her once she was alone, I knew she would have preferred my sleeping next to her but, always needing my space, I awkwardly told her I preferred to sleep upstairs in my old room. Our love was deep and passionate, but our differences were equally as strong. For years, I had perched on a ledge waiting patiently, and sometimes not so patiently, for an opening for her to let me love her and for her to return that love for an extended period of time without tense interruption. It might have happened that the clock ran out before that opening presented itself. But, like a seagull watching for signs of food, I didn't miss my chance.

Just a year and a half after my father died, as cancer slowed her down and her need to lead was increasingly balanced by her willingness to be led, I cherished sleeping next to her. Two grown women, mother and daughter in corny, flowery nightgowns, filled this once forbidding bed in precious unity. Night after night, our arms stretched across the crack between the beds as our hands warmly joined. With just one reading light easing the darkness, I now viewed the room from her vantage point. In this space that enveloped us both, my mother would share her disbelief at her illness, her increasing symptoms and pains and even her unanswerable questions. I would say, "Pfeh!"; and she would say, "That's right. Pfeh!" Each lying on our own side, we were fully on the same side in sharing the sadness and the anger. We talked about Karl, her first husband, and my father and how blessed she felt for having loved two such loving men. She asked me if I was happy with my husband, and I said "very." We bonded as two women who shared the thankfulness of knowing this type of love.

Once, I crawled on her side and kissed her soft cheek. She gave me her special "Safta"* kiss. I kissed her hand and retreated to my side of the enormous bed. In the middle of the night, I was awakened by her moans of pain, which she did not recall in the morning. Keeping to her routine, I made the bed in just the right way: the bedspread did not touch the floor, the quilts were not bumpy, and the throw pillows were not carelessly placed. In spite of this, she became cold when the temperature was warm; full when she ate only a spoonful; and tired when her day had barely begun.

The big bed, now perfectly made in its flowery pastel-colored spread with matching pillows, holds all these memories plus the last— her lying there no longer able to warmly hold my hand.

• • •

Who would have believed that in my lifetime I would have gotten to share meditation space with my mother? But in her last weeks, when the pain of cancer slowed her down, this fast-moving, always self-sufficient woman was too tired to run. She did not stop running all at once, however. It was gradual, more like the increasing presence of the left hand in a piano composition, where the effect of the grave bass notes emerges in time.

For my mother, shopping was once the beginning of a long day that included swimming forty laps, cooking up a storm, writing letters, doing "administrative work," and trying to sit dqwn to write the last essay in a series on her Holocaust experiences. At this time, shopping alone wore her out. As she would say, "she couldn't anymore." How trapped she must have felt. Her survivor instincts told her she had to

*"Safta" means grandmother in Hebrew. This kiss had no name when my siblings and I were young but my mother called it "the safta kiss" with the grandchildren. It can't be described, it has to be experienced.

find new doors. Though she could no longer will her body to do more, she still had command over her mind and soul. At seventy-nine, this Czech Jewish woman who was set in her ways opened herself up to a "New Age" experience.

We meditated in two green-and-white lawn chairs, inhaling and exhaling as we felt the earth's energy travel through our bodies. We visualized ourselves as eagles flying above Floral Park and landing at Jones Beach. We watched the ocean come forward and recede as we observed our breathing doing the same. We felt the rhythm of nature and the universe and experienced ourselves being part of the whole. Guided by ancient wisdom, we tried to find balance within the extremes and centeredness in the moment. After we embraced memories of the past at Jones Beach and absorbed the ocean's lessons, we slowly traveled back to Queens. We landed and gently opened our eyes. My mother and I were sitting in the driveway in the sun, hearing the birds sing, the neighbors rattle their garbage cans, and the dogs bark as we listened to the silence.

One week later, two weeks before her death, we sat in a sculpture park with two dear friends. My mother enthusiastically suggested that she lead us through a meditation. I got to share this sacred space with her; this space she could create only because even at this desperate time, she was open to expansion. I still hear her saying "I feel the wind caressing my face."

• • •

She sat there with a weak smile on her face as her fading eyes suddenly filled with the recognition of a world once known. Around the large dining room table, my mother, my sisters, and I were assembled. My brother went between this room and another, changing CDs as we all tried to decide which music to play at her funeral. The surrealism of the moment was not lost.

I sat directly across from her and caught the flash of light in her sunken eyes as the Beethoven piece we played at my father's funeral filled the air. I think the others missed this flash as they continued to discuss the options. I requested that we be silent and share the experience.

If music can be worn out, this Beethoven concerto would have been destroyed by how often my mother listened to it after my father's death. After a year or so, however, this same CD became lethal for her as she could no longer bear the pain that it evoked. On this day before her own death and one and a half years after my father's, with fresh ears, she received this music as an offering from heaven.

My mother described our relationship as love/hate. But at that time, when only I seemed to know what filled her heart, I knew what she meant by her last direct words to me: "It always amazed me how you would sometimes know what I was feeling without my saying the words."

Dear Ma, I had a dream a few days after you died and all I remember is you sitting at the end of the table smiling at me as you knew I knew the profound joy you were feeling at the moment Daddy's music filled your soul.

• • •

Oddly, my mother's death has given me a sense of completion in a way similar to my finishing a painting. Drawn studies, painted studies, notes, and art materials fill my studio as the residue of final works. Audio tapes and journals crammed with ponderings about my parents' future deaths fill my drawers, which, with my memories, are the stuff of my latest final work. I prepared for the day when I could no longer hear their voices by taping their sweetest answering machine messages. One year after my father's death Ma left these:

Are you home? Daninko? OK. I just came from the city. I wanted to report to you, OK? Thank you, Bye-bye. (October 1996)

Hi Dana. Are you there? Are you home? Oh. What a pity. Channel 13. Danny Kaye. So, I thought you would laugh. Anyhow, Bye-bye. (December 1996)

My mother's urgency defined her life-affirming existence, yet it was also a constant reminder to me of her emotional scars. She beat death so many times, from the gas chambers to critical illnesses. She was just beginning to beat her paralyzing grief after my father's death. Now, her obsessive race, which she so ably finessed over her lifetime, was over.

This seventy-nine-year-old woman was a juggler extraordinaire, but a juggler's art is both exhilarating and unsettling to watch. Warding off the sound of shattering plates, my mother looked straight ahead till the very end. One quiet night, however, she did confess that she was not sure whether she or the cancer was in control. When the terror of death found its way through her thick defenses, my mother found solace in knowing she would be with my father when she died.

The last of her messages was left thirty-four days before her end, and it went like this:

Hi Dana. I am just reporting. I am chewing my breakfast very slowly. I came from swimming . . . and I will rest . . . and then I will go to get the drug. And I had a very good, peaceful night.

And also Dr. Li called me, how I am feeling after that tea. So, that was very nice. I hope you are fine. I am just reporting. Bye-bye. (May 1997)

I suppose it's because she had no regrets, and because I now have many answers to questions that occupied me since I was young, that I feel some sense of completion. Both finishing a painting and saying goodbye to someone you love require time to reflect upon moments that are just right as well as unanswered questions.

Hello? Dani? Are you home? That's Ma. Are you there? Dana? OK, so I just wanted to know what is going on. I didn't hear from you, so I wanted to make sure that you are OK. So call me if you feel up to it. OK? Bye-bye. (March 1997)

Ma. I'm here. Where are you?

• • •

The house is still intact; the pillows on the couch are still scrunched from someone's weight; the flowers in the vases are still more alive than dead; the mail is still coming to a woman who was alive less than a month ago and to a man long gone. My home. My house where I grew up. My parents' house. My mother's house.

Soon my mother's beloved tomato plants, still green, will bear the red harvest that she knew she would not live to see. The piano, which once eloquently spoke for my father through his strong fingers and passionate heart, will be among the things removed. The smell of cardboard boxes mingling with the sight of frenzied dust particles will signal that the pain of saying goodbye is near.

I comfort myself by knowing that my mother's refined artistic sensibility will filter into my home when some of her artwork and belongings will become my own. I look forward to honoring my promise to my father to organize "the stuff downstairs" into an archive. This stuff (rare, Browning photographs and documents from before the war; my parents' published writings as witnesses to the Holocaust; materials from my father's years as administrative head of the Jewish Community in Prague, hospital administrator, and Czech Jewish historian; as well as newer family memorabilia) has always been, and will always be, a defiant symbol of their survival. I feel calmed by the honor of this task.

Though the breakdown has not yet started, I have already felt compelled to rescue a remnant of my mother's favorite shirt from being used simply as a rag. The familiar battle between a need to hold on and a voice that says let go has begun. I guess that saying good-bye to her, to him again, and to the house will mean separating from the rags. I guess that the struggle itself will bestow honor upon them and the home they created.

• • •

Today is September 4, 1997, and always counting the time since my father died, I just realized that today is exactly one year and ten months since his death. Ma died on June 11 and I now count both their days, though hers is still counted only in months. The house has been totally dismantled, and its stark emptiness is especially pronounced when strangers come to check out whether they want to make it their home. Like the sound of a wailing Greek chorus, the lamenting of old neighbors, family, and dear friends counters the silent indifference of those who pass through with no feeling. A sweet, subtle reminder of the way Ma sounded when she answered the phone by one of those who loved her the most brings it all back.

Last week, my husband and I picked a juicy red tomato off the stem. Holding each other tightly, we kissed this symbol of life, each other, and then the sky. Our hands could not part. This was our goodbye. Later on, my sister and I held each other. We cried. We prayed. We laughed in our childhood bedroom, as we got one last touch of the textured linoleum tiles that used to bruise our hands while we endlessly practiced to be in the "Jacks Olympics." Filled with the joy of sharing, we said our goodbye.

• • •

Today is September 4, 2000, and I still have not stopped saying goodbye. Tonight, about five years since my father died and about three years since my mother died, the beautiful bright moon suddenly appeared outside my window. Memories of my parents, like the moon, often emergé unexpectedly as sources of light surrounded by darkness. Some nights, when sleep is eluding me, I am struck by the power of memory. Once, while thinking about someone's wedding plans, my eyes got overwhelmed with tears because all I could think about was how gleaming my father's eyes were when he shared in the joy of my wedding just two weeks before he died. Another time, while watching a poignant late night "Roseanne" rerun, I suddenly cried reckless tears because all I could think about was how loving my mother was when she brought me homemade soup while I was recovering from surgery one year before she died.

Each time my tears of loss turn into tears of gratitude, I say goodbye again. Each time my tears of loss turn into tears of gratitude, I feel the wind caressing my face.

INTERPRETATIONS

1. The author refers several times to her mother's urgency. Does this word also describe the author? What examples can you cite? What is the underlying reason for her urgency?

2. Time is an important theme in this essay. What direct and indirect techniques does the author use to suggest the passing of time?

3. Characterize the author's relationship with her mother. What different aspects of this relationship does she portray in the essay?

4. Analyze her father's role in the essay. What symbols does the author associate with him? How do these add unity to the memoir?

CORRESPONDENCES

1. Walker's perspective reflects upon the links between her mother and herself. To what extent is this also true of Wehle's text?

2. Cahill's perspective addresses relationships and communion. Find examples of each in Wehle's text and analyze their effect.

APPLICATIONS

1. Wehle uses many literary techniques to enhance theme. With your group members, cite examples of foreshadowing, similes, and metaphors. To what senses do they appeal? Are there examples that indicate Wehle's interest in the visual arts? Why does she end her essay with a line that occurs earlier? How has its meaning changed?

2. Wehle discusses part of her mother's history and the values she communicated. Write an essay analyzing the impact that your family's history and values have had on you. Be specific.

3. Review the answering machine tapes in Wehle's essay. What do they reveal about her mother? What do they add to knowledge of the author? Is this an effective method for writing memoirs? Why or why not?

Focusing on Friends

STEVE TESICH

Steve Tesich (1943–1996) was born in Yugoslavia and immigrated to the United States when he was fourteen. He is best known for the original screenplay Breaking Away *(1979), for which he won an Academy Award. He also wrote the screenplays* Eyewitness *(1981) and* Four Friends *(1981); many plays for the theater, including* Passing Game *(1977),* The Road *(1978), and* Division Street *(1980); and a novel,* Summer Crossing *(1982). A recurring theme in Tesich's work is the plight of the outsider. Before reading Tesich's essay, brainstorm on the word "friend."*

WHEN I THINK OF PEOPLE who were my good friends, I see them all, as I do everything else from my life, in cinematic terms. The camera work is entirely different for men and women.

I remember all the women in almost extreme close-ups. The settings are different—apartments, restaurants—but they're all interiors, as if I had never spent a single minute with a single woman outside. They're looking right at me, these women in these extreme close-ups; the lighting is exquisite, worthy of a Fellini or Fosse film, and their lips are moving. They're telling me something important or reacting to something even more important that I've told them. It's the kind of movie where you tell people to keep quiet when they chew their popcorn too loudly.

The boys and men who were my friends are in an entirely different movie. No close-ups here. No exquisite lighting. The camera work is rather shaky but the background is moving. We're going somewhere, on foot, on bicycles, in cars. The ritual of motion, of action, makes up for the inconsequential nature of the dialogue. It's a much sloppier film, this film that is not really a film but a memory of real friends: Slobo, Louie, Sam. Male friends. I've loved all three of them. I assumed they knew this, but I never told them.

Quite the contrary is true in my female films. In close-up after close-up, I am telling every woman who I ever loved that I love her, and then lingering on yet another close-up of her face for a reaction. There is a perfectly appropriate musical score playing while I wait. And if I wait long enough, I get an answer. I am loved. I am not loved. Language clears up the suspense. The emotion is nailed down.

Therein lies the difference, I think, between my friendships with men and with women. I can tell women I love them. Not only can I tell them, I am compulsive about it. I can hardly wait to tell them. But I can't tell the men. I just can't. And they can't tell me. Emotions are never nailed down. They run wild, and I and my male friends chase after them, on foot, on bicycles, in cars, keeping the quarry in sight but never catching up.

My first friend was Slobo. I was still living in Yugoslavia at the time, and not far from my house there was an old German truck left abandoned after the war. It had no wheels. No windshield. No doors. But the steering wheel was intact. Slobo and I flew to America in that truck. It was our airplane. Even now, I remember the background moving as we took off down the street, across Europe, across the Atlantic. We were inseparable. The best of friends. Naturally, not one word concerning the nature of our feelings for one another was ever exchanged. It was all done in actions.

The inevitable would happen at least once a day. As we were flying over the Atlantic, there came, out of nowhere, that wonderful moment: engine failure! "We'll have to bail out," I shouted. "A-a-a-a-a!" Slobo made the sound of the failing engine. Then he would turn and look me in the eye: "I can't swim," he'd say. "Fear not." I put my hand on his shoulder. "I'll drag you to shore." And, with that, both of us would tumble out of the truck onto the dusty street. I swam through the dust. Slobo drowned in the dust, coughing, gagging. "Sharks!" he cried. But I always saved him. The next day the ritual would be repeated, only then it would be my turn to say "I can't swim," and Slobo would save me. We saved each other from certain death over a hundred times, until finally a day came when I really left for America with my mother and sister. Slobo and I stood at the train station. We were there to say good-bye, but, since we weren't that good at saying things and since he couldn't save me, he just cried until the train started to move.

The best friend I had in high school was Louie. It now seems to me that I was totally monogamous when it came to male friends. I would have several girl friends but only one real male friend. Louie was it at that time. We were both athletes, and one day we decided to "run till we drop." We just wanted to know what it was like. Skinny Louie set the pace as we ran around our high-school track. Lap after lap. Four laps to a mile. Mile after mile we ran. I had the reputation as being a big-time jock. Louie didn't. But this was Louie's day. There was a bounce in his step and, when he turned back to look at me, his eyes were gleaming with the thrill of it all. I finally dropped. Louie still looked fresh; he seemed capable, on that day, of running forever. But we were the best of friends, and so he stopped. "That's it," he lied,

"I couldn't go another step farther." It was an act of love. Naturally, I said nothing.

Louie got killed in Vietnam. Several weeks after his funeral, I went to his mother's house, and, because she was a woman, I tried to tell her how much I had loved her son. It was not a good scene. Although I was telling the truth, my words sounded like lies. It was all very painful and embarrassing. I kept thinking how sorry I was that I had never told Louie himself.

Sam is my best friend now, and has been for many years. A few years ago, we were swimming at a beach in East Hampton. The Atlantic! The very Atlantic I had flown over in my German truck with Slobo. We had swum out pretty far from the shore when both of us simultaneously thought we spotted a shark. Water is not only a good conductor of electricity but of panic as well. We began splashing like madmen toward shore. Suddenly, at the height of my panic, I realized how much I loved my friend, what an irreplaceable friend he was, and, although I was the faster swimmer, I fell back to protect him. Naturally, the shark in the end proved to be imaginary. But not my feelings for my friend. For several days after that I wanted to share my discovery with him, to tell him how much I love him. Fortunately, I didn't.

I say fortunately because on reflection, there seems to be sufficient evidence to indicate that, if anybody was cheated and shortchanged by me, it was the women, the girls, the very recipients of my uncensored emotions. Yes, I could hardly wait to tell them I loved them. I did love them. But once I told them, something stopped. The emotion was nailed down, but, with it, the enthusiasm and the energy to prove it was nailed down, too. I can remember my voice saying to almost all of them, at one time or another: "I told you I love you. What else do you want?" I can now recoil at the impatient hostility of that voice but I can't deny it was mine.

The tyranny of self-censorship forced me, in my relations with male friends, to seek alternatives to language. And just because I could never be sure they understood exactly how I felt about them, I was forced to look for ways to prove it. That is, I now think how it should be. It is time to make adjustments. It is time to pull back the camera, free the women I know, and myself, from those merciless close-ups and have the background move.

INTERPRETATIONS

1. Contrast Tesich's treatment of male and female friends in his cinematic imagination and in his real life.

2. To what extent do you agree with Tesich that telling a person you love him or her "nails down" the emotion?

3. By moving from the general to the specific, Tesich is able to present Slobo, Louie, and Sam in some detail. How do his portrayals of them clarify his purpose? How do they affect you as his audience?

CORRESPONDENCES

1. Review the Nin perspective on friendship. How does it apply to Tesich's relationships with his male friends?

2. Apply the du Plessix Gray perspective on friendship to Tesich's portrayal of his friendships with women. To what extent do you treat male and female friends differently?

APPLICATIONS

1. In addition to contrasting friendships between men and women and women and men, Tesich also defines friendship in general. Discuss his ideas about friendship with your group. To what extent do you agree with his gender distinctions? Do your friendships fit into the categories he discusses? Write a summary of your conclusions.

2. From the title to the last sentence, much of the language is from the world of filmmaking. How does this language help Tesich clarify his meaning and purpose? Support your point of view with specific examples.

3. How do you differentiate between an acquaintance and a friend? Do you consider someone you "hang out" with frequently your friend? Write a journal entry on these questions.

Treasures

MAHWASH SHOAIB

Mahwash Shoaib (b. 1973), a native of Pakistan, is a graduate of the University of Punjab and currently a graduate student at the Graduate School and University Center of CUNY in New York City. She is a poet, a writer, and a translator of poetry from her native Urdu language into English. Keenly interested in philosophy as a way of life, she devotes her time between the study of language and literature, writing, and bibliophilia. Her aim is to realize her creative potential in both fiction and poetry. Before reading Shoaib's essay, freewrite on one of your "treasures."

Pakistan, formerly a part of India, became a dominion in 1947. In 1956, an Islamic Republic was proclaimed. For the next thirty-five years, government consisted of a series of elected prime ministers alternating with military coup d'etats. In 1988, Benazir Bhutto became the first female leader of a Muslim nation when she was elected prime minister. In the years that followed, dissolved governments and a military coup compromised the nation's parliamentary process. The 2007 assassination of Bhutto, who had returned from exile to seek re-election, and tensions between the current government and Taliban militants signal continued political uncertainty.

THEY ARE ALL WAITING FOR ME. *I slowly lift the dress out of the wrappings of tissue. It is indeed beautiful. The velvet is a majestic russet color; the embroidery is of real silver thread and fills the neck of the* kameez[1] *in the shape of a bow. The slightly dull sequins still blink on the velvet. There are solid creases where the cloth was folded; here the velvet shines with a fiercer intensity than below the folds which reveal lighter mysteries. When I pass my hand over it, the velvet smooths down. As I wear the dress for the first time, I am amazed at how snugly it fits me, as if it were made just for me. The dress is not mine; it was a part of my grandmother's trousseau. In fact, this is what my grandfather brought for her to wear on their* nikkah.[2] *She wore it only once and then put it away; then my youngest* khala,[3] *her last daughter to be married, wore it; and now, the dress is being worn for the third time by me. I feel it on my body and try to imagine how my grandmother must have felt on the nuptial day, adorned*

---

[1] A long shirt worn with pants called shalwar.
[2] Traditional Muslim marriage ceremony.
[3] Aunt, mother's sister.

48

in this dress. My young cousins ask me impatiently from outside the door if I need any help. I open the door and come out feeling a little shy. Everyone stops talking and tells me how nice I look in her dress, the women admiring how immaculately preserved it is and how much it would cost today to have something like that made.

Everyone, young and old, his children and grandchildren, called him Abbaji, with love. Last year, January 1 was a very joyous occasion for us because we celebrated Abbaji's ninety-fifth birthday. Eleven of his fifteen children managed to gather in the same house that day. I promised him that five years from now we would celebrate his century-marking birthday and everyone would be there.

Today there is an unusual number of people in my grandfather's house because it is Eid, the day at the end of Ramazan, when we celebrate the end of fasting and offer prayers of gratitude to Allah. Not only are two of my khalas here with their families, but just a few moments ago my grandmother's brother, my mother's mamoon,[4] *came in with his wife and daughters. Their bright, jocund voices shimmering through the walls, now everyone is sitting together in the living room talking and drinking tea while the children are playing all over the house. Spicy aromas emanating from the family kitchen are mingling with delicate perfumes on crisply-ironed clothes to form one warm embrace.*

Although every time the phone rang at night we would be filled with dread, no one was prepared for the news. This year on the midnight of January 1, we were awakened by a phone call telling us that Abbaji had died. Later on I found out that Abbaji had died calling out for every one of his children, few of whom were with him at that time. That is why I cannot reconcile the fact that I wasn't there at the time when he wanted to gather all his seeds. The distance does nothing to dissipate the agony and anger; only it makes the grief more unbearable. How can you triumph distance and time to tell someone that you love him, something you thought you would always have time for?

After a few minutes I excuse myself and go to my grandfather's room to show him the dress. My eldest mamoon *is sitting beside my grandfather and when he sees me entering with my cousins behind me, he leaves the room grumbling that these children do not leave any corner of the house in peace. The girls, somewhat bored now, run off to play. As I sit down on his bed, my* khala *also comes in the room after having served the latest guests. Abbaji is*

---

[4]Uncle, mother's brother.

lying in his bed, supported by pillows, and smiles at me kindly. Through the
open door I see the tree casting a long shadow in the coral evening.

My earliest memories are associated with Abbaji because I spent my
early childhood under the eyes of my grandparents in their *haveli*, the
huge fort-like house that Abbaji had before he moved to the smaller
house, after my grandmother's death. His voracious appetite for reading
instilled in me a respect for books. Once when I was ten or eleven years
old, we went to spend our winter vacations with him. I brought along my
arsenal of books to while away time and one of the books was Robert
Louis Stevenson's *Treasure Island*. One afternoon when I was tired of
playing with my cousins, I went to look for the novel. After a long search
I came out on the veranda and found Abbaji basking in the hazy sunlight
and reading the book. I remember feeling a concoction of mild surprise
and delectation even then that my own grandfather was reading and
enjoying the same book that had made me so happy. Then at times he
would tell me a tale within a tale. One evening very long ago when he
was young, Abbaji was sitting on a rock by a frothy river reading a book.
In the book an incident was described in great detail in which a snake
slithers off a rock and falls into the river; at that very moment, a snake,
out of nowhere, sprang on the rock right in front of him and landed into
the gushing waters. At the end of the tale, Abbaji would chuckle with
merry perplexity; I would try to picture a young boy with a book in his
hands at the edge of a river, his shadow extending before him, frightened
by the sudden appearance of a lithe snake, and my blood would race
with adventure. This is what a child's trove of bright and diffused memories is made up of—shared words and shared silences.

I ask him, Abbaji, how does the dress look? He puts on his glasses and looks
at me from head to toe, tells me that it is very beautiful and asks when did I have
it made. I do not realize but my khala *guesses immediately and laughingly asks*
him if he does not recognize it. My grandfather, with a short embarrassed laugh,
says no. I then tell him that it is the dress that my grandmother wore for her
wedding. He asks incredulously if it is true, and we talk about how many people
came to visit us today and how much I'll miss this day when I go back. After
some time I come out of his room a little hurt and disappointed.

When I look at the pictures I took of Abbaji last year, I still wonder
at the kind smile touching the tired liquid eyes of a man who had seen
life and still found it amusing. His presence was a spiritual focus to
which his scattered progeny drifted back time and again. Family legend has it that when he was sixteen or seventeen, Abbaji ran away from
his home in Afghanistan because of an escalating bloody dispute about

his father's estate, to which he was the sole heir. And I ask myself, what do I truly know of my grandfather? I do remember so many times when he came to visit us at our house in Lahore, the weddings, births and birthdays we celebrated. But I also remember the times when he used to pick up the loosened skin from his hands remorsefully. So, in sad nostalgia, what matters most . . . the freedom from pain of a loved one or the lost inert moments of happiness induced by him?

There are still a lot of guests in the living room and I mingle with them. One of my cousins and I pose for a special picture of me in the dress. Just when the camera flashes, I remember that I forgot to take off the thick woolen socks peeking from under it.

I have lost my bearings. It seems that right when I was beginning to convince myself that the tunnel was not so dimly lit, life slapped me full in the face of my meager certitude. A catharsis is unwelcome and the fear for the mortality of my loved ones is fresh. I have found that treasures that bind you by the spirit are hard to keep. The dress, the pictures are still tangible; the person whose presence was hope is no more. I keep returning to times and events and places and images in a tiding circuit until I am unsure of where I started from. Suddenly I am frightened of the new year.

INTERPRETATIONS

1. Why do you think Shoaib begins her essay with a detailed description of her grandmother's wedding dress?

2. Shoaib's memoir juxtaposes past and present in alternating paragraphs. Analyze the effects of this technique on her purpose and meaning. How does she use this technique to reflect on her relationship with Abbaji?

3. Characterize Abbaji. Which of his traits have most influenced the author? How would you describe their relationship? Do you have a similar relationship with any member of your family?

CORRESPONDENCES

1. Review Friedan's perspective on families and discuss its relevance to the texts by Shoaib and Lim (page 17).

2. Shoaib and Wehle write about the death of a close family member. Compare and contrast their responses to loss.

APPLICATIONS

1. Shoaib's essay focuses on her portrayal of her grandfather, but in the italicized passages she also reveals herself. Write a portrait of the author using these paragraphs.

2. Freewrite about an older family member who intrigues you and about whom you would like to know more. Interview family members or friends for information about him or her, and write a description based on your interviews.

3. Shoaib and Wehle recall an experience that represents a turning point in their lives. If you have had such an experience (it need not be about death), write an essay comparing its effects when it first occurred and now as you view it in retrospect.

4. Note how Shoaib uses visual cues in the text to signal different voices and tones. If you examine the italicized and the non-italicized sections of the essay, what kinds of music are evoked by each of these font types? How would you describe these kinds of music to a reader?

5. It is possible to look at Shoaib's first paragraph as a journal entry. Try to write a journal entry about something that is happening in this essay from the perspective of one of the other participants.

Two Lives

SHIRLEY GEOK-LIN LIM

*Shirley Geok-Lin Lim (b. 1944 in Malaysia) once told Contemporary Authors:
"I was born in a tropical colony of the British Empire. The English language
was only one of three (Malay and Hokkien being the other two) languages that
surrounded me but it is my language of choice. . . . Much of my writing life is
composed of negotiating multiple identities, multiple societies, multiple
desires, and multiple genres. I have published poetry, short fiction, criticism,
and autobiographical essays, and I worked on my novel* (Joss and Gold, published in 2001; in 2006 she published Sister Swing) *for a long time. I am an
Asian, a Westerner, and a woman, and I have known desperate hunger, in the
presence of which one must be committed to speak. . . ." She has also published
a memoir* Among the White Moon Faces: An Asian-American Memoir
of Homelands *(1997). Lim received her B.A. at the University of Malaysia,
Kuala Lumpur. She immigrated to the United States in 1969 and became a
U.S. citizen. In 1971 she obtained an M.A. and in 1973 a Ph.D. from Brandeis
University. She has taught at the University of Malaysia, in Australia, at the
University of Hong Kong, at several units of the City University of New York,
and at the University of California, Santa Barbara. She has received numerous
awards. As you read, watch for signs that Lim learned valuable lessons from
her unpleasant experience of being a daughter far from her family.*

NO ONE WHO HAS NOT LEFT EVERYTHING behind her—every acquaintance,
tree, corner lamp post, brother, lover—understands the peculiar
remorse of the resident alien. Unlike the happy immigrant who sees the
United States as a vast real-estate advertisement selling a neighborly
future, the person who enters the country as a resident alien is neither
here nor there. Without family, house, or society, she views herself
through the eyes of citizens: guest, stranger, outsider, misfit, beggar.
Transient like the drunks asleep by the steps down to the subway, her
bodily presence is a wraith, less than smoke among the 250 million in
the nation. Were she to fall in front of the screeching wheels of the
Number Four Lexington line, her death would be noted by no one,
mourned by none, except if the news should arrive weeks later, twelve
thousand miles away.

A resident alien has walked out of a community's living memory,
out of social structures in which her identity is folded, like a bud in a

tree, to take on the raw stinks of public bathrooms and the shapes of shadows in parks. She holds her breath as she walks through the American city counting the afternoon hours. Memory for her is a great mourning, a death of the living. The alien resident mourns even as she chooses to abandon. Her memory, like her guilt and early love, is involuntary but her choice of the United States is willful.

For what? She asks the question over and over again. At first, she asks it every day. Then as she begins to feel comfortable in the body of a stranger, she asks it occasionally, when the weekend stretches over the Sunday papers and the television news does not seem enough, or when the racks of dresses in the department stores fail to amuse. Finally, she forgets what it feels like not to be a stranger. She has found work that keeps her busy, or better still, tired. She has found a lover, a child, a telephone friend, the American equivalents for the opacity of her childhood. The dense solidity of Asian society becomes a thin story. At some point, she no longer considers exchanging the remote relationships that pass as American social life for those crowded rooms in Asia, the unhappy family circles. And were those rooms really that crowded, the family so intensely unhappy? . . .

It was the waste of time I minded most, a sludgy feeling that took over October and November. In September, almost a year after my arrival at Brandeis, Father had written to say he had been diagnosed with throat cancer. He was seeking medical care in Malacca. "Don't come home," his letter ended, "I don't want you to interrupt your studies."

I told no one. Food stuck in my throat whenever I thought of Father. The thought was like a fishbone, sharp and nagging. I couldn't speak of him.

Another short letter arrived from China without a return address. I read it over and over in the safety of my room. "I am doing well," it said. "My white blood cells have gone up, and I am feeling stronger." The small black-and-white photograph that fell out of the envelope showed that he was lying. The shirt draped over his body like a sheet over a child, although his face was old and sad.

For a few months, the letters came from China without a forwarding address: he was staying near the clinic in Canton, noted for its cancer cures. He wrote irregularly. Like a careful student, perhaps because he was lonely, he sent the laboratory reports on his white blood count. His letters were optimistic to begin with. The white blood-cell numbers had improved; he was enjoying this Chinese city he had never seen before, visiting parks, zoos, and museums, with a new friend also undergoing treatment at the clinic. Then a letter arrived complaining of homesickness. He wanted to be home with the family; he missed Malaysian food.

When Thanksgiving came, the Castle emptied out. Julie and Carol returned to Brooklyn and Missouri. On Friday I picked up a letter from my mailbox. The rice-paper-fine aerogramme rustled as I spread it out to read the ball-point print that smeared across the crumpled blue surface. It was a letter from Second Brother, and I was immediately afraid, for Second Brother had never written to me before. "We buried Father two weeks ago," he wrote.

I stared at the words and calculated the time. Two weeks ago, and a week for the aerogramme to cross the world to reach me in Massachusetts. It was unimaginable that Father, the source of whatever drove me, that total enveloping wretchedness of involuntary love, my eternal bond, my body's and heart's DNA, had been dead for almost a month. The world had a hole in it, it was rent, and I would never heal.

Maggie came knocking at my door just as I finished reading Second Brother's letter. An orphan left with a trust fund, she was slowly completing her graduate studies, while spending most of her time volunteering to help with the animals in the zoo. She wanted to know if I had had any pumpkin pie yet for Thanksgiving. Would I go with her to the cafeteria for a piece of pie? I was still holding Second Brother's blue aerogramme in my hand.

"My father's dead," I said to her. Why was I telling her this? Would I have said the same thing if the janitor had knocked on the door to fix the radiator? "He died three weeks ago."

"Oh," she said. "I'm sorry." I could see that she was. Tall and big-boned, Maggie was deep water, quiet-spoken, all reserve.

I paid for my pie and coffee at the cafeteria and watched her eat. She left the crust and scraped the brown gooey filling carefully with her fork till it was all gone. My throat hurt. Then I returned alone to my room. I knew Maggie would never visit me again. I had been too painful for her.

At first I didn't cry. It wasn't Father's death that drove hardest at me, it was that he had been dead for more than two weeks already, and I hadn't known all that time that he had gone. "We didn't think you should come home," Second Brother wrote. The grief and the guilt lay beyond tears. Months later, in Brooklyn where I was sharing a studio apartment with Charles, the Brandeis graduate student whom I would later marry, I woke up in the middle of the night, my face drenched with tears. I had wept in my sleep for Father.

A month after the news of Father's death, Second Brother sent me a package of papers from Father's belongings. Father had kept all my old school record books, annual school certificates of achievement, examination diplomas, yellowed letters of recommendation from high school teachers, and Malaysian citizenship documents. On an unmailed aero-gramme sheet, Father had scrawled in a shaky hand, "I want you to come home now."

My brother also sent me a diary Father had kept in the last weeks of his life. Only a few pages were filled, and all the entries were addressed to me. In the early entries, he wrote he was hopeful he would recover, and he did not want me to return home because it was so important for me to continue my studies. In the second to last entry, he asked that I hurry home; he didn't believe he had much time left and he wanted to see me. In the very last entry, addressing me as his dear daughter, he wrote that although he knew I would do so, still he asked that I promise to take care of my brothers and sister, Peng's children. The entry was very short and the handwriting erratic. My father had willed his chil-dren to me.

The day I received the package, I emptied my bank account and sent the few hundred dollars in it to Peng. With it, my letter promised that I would send her as much as I could each month. For a long time, every U.S. dollar rang as precious Malaysian currency for me to remit. A ten-dollar shirt? I paid for it and guiltily counted the groceries the money could have bought for Father's family. I disapproved of my growing consumerism. The pastries that gleamed, sugar-encrusted, at Dunkin' Donuts, which I eyed longingly, would buy copy books for my half-brothers. For the next few years, I carried my father's ghostly pres-ence through department stores and restaurants. His sad smile was a mirage of poverty. I saw my half-siblings ragged and hungry whenever I glanced at a sales tag, and every month, I made out a bank draft to Peng and mailed it out as an exorcism.

An exorcism I could not explain to Charles, my American husband. How could one eat well if one's family was starving? For Chinese, eat-ing is both material and cultural. We feed our hungry ghosts before we may feed ourselves. Ancestors are ravenous, and can die of neglect. Our fathers' children are also ourselves. The self is paltry, phantas-magoric; it leaks and slips away. It is the family, parents, siblings, cousins, that signify the meaning of the self, and beyond the family, the extended community.

In writing the bank drafts I remained my father's daughter, return-ing to Father the bargain we had made. This is the meaning of blood— to give, because you cannot eat unless the family is also eating. For years, I woke up nights, heart beating wildly. Oh Asia, that nets its chil-dren in ties of blood so binding that they cut the spirit.

INTERPRETATIONS

1. How does Lim characterize the "resident alien" in paragraphs 1 and 2? What is the connection between the "resident alien" and the "alien resident"?

2. What is the effect of Lim's recording the process of her father's illness and death?

3. Why does she include the entries from her father's diaries? How would you describe the relationship she and her father shared?

4. How do you interpret the last line of her essay? What examples of her spirit's being "cut" can you cite?

CORRESPONDENCES

1. Wehle and Lim record their responses to the death of a parent. Compare and contrast their reactions to that experience.

2. How do Shoaib and Lim use mood and tone to enhance theme?

APPLICATIONS

1. Write a journal entry on the title of Lim's essay.

2. Lim writes that she disapproves of her "growing consumerism." What examples does she cite? Do you and your group members think of yourselves as consumers? Is it easy to resist being a consumer in today's society? Summarize your group's discussion.

3. Lim writes about her sorrow and guilt as she distances herself from her native culture. If you have had a similar experience, write a short essay describing how you resolved the paradox of being a "resident alien" and "an alien resident."

4. Who is Lim describing in paragraphs 1 and 2 of this essay? What do you imagine this person to look like? Draw a sketch of this individual. Then, using your sketch to guide you, write a detailed description of this person.

For My Indian Daughter

LEWIS (JOHNSON) SAWAQUAT

Lewis (Johnson) Sawaquat (b. 1935), is a member of the Ottawa tribe, whose last official chief was his great-grandfather. He was raised in Harbor Springs, in northern Michigan near Mackinac Island. He learned to be a surveyor while in the U.S. Army in Korea and after he left the Army continued for thirty years to practice the profession for the Soil Conservation Service of the U.S. Department of Agriculture. He also attended the Art Institute and the University of Chicago. In writing for and about his daughter, Gaia, who later graduated from Yale University, Sawaquat describes his personal journey toward greater ethnic pride. After he retired in 1990, Sawaquat became for a while the "cultural traditionalist," a sort of spiritual/cultural advisor for the Grand Traverse Band of his tribe. He adopted his Indian name after "For My Indian Daughter" was published in Newsweek *in 1983. It was named National Essay of the Year in 1986.*

MY LITTLE GIRL IS SINGING HERSELF to sleep upstairs, her voice mingling with the sounds of the birds outside in the old maple trees. She is two and I am nearly 50, and I am very taken with her. She came along late in my life, unexpected and unbidden, a startling gift.

Today at the beach my chubby-legged, brown-skinned daughter ran laughing into the water as fast as she could. My wife and I laughed watching her, until we heard behind us a low guttural curse and then an unpleasant voice raised in an imitation war whoop.

I turned to see a fat man in a bathing suit, white and soft as a grub, as he covered his mouth and prepared to make the Indian war cry again. He was middle-aged, younger than I, and had three little children lined up next to him, grinning foolishly. My wife suggested we leave the beach, and I agreed.

I knew the man was not unusual in his feelings against Indians. His beach behavior might have been socially unacceptable to more civilized whites, but his basic view of Indians is expressed daily in our small town, frequently on the editorial pages of the county newspaper, as white people speak out against Indian fishing rights and land rights, saying in essence, "Those Indians are taking our fish, our land." It doesn't matter to them that we were here first, that the U.S. Supreme Court has ruled in our favor. It matters to them that we have something they want, and they hate us for it. Backlash is the common explanation of the attacks on Indians, the bumper stickers that say, "Spear an Indian, Save a Fish," but I know better. The hatred of Indians goes back to the beginning when white people came to this country. For me it goes back to my childhood in Harbor Springs, Michigan.

Harbor Springs is now a summer resort for the very affluent, but a hundred years ago it was the Indian village of my Ottawa ancestors. My grandmother, Anna Showanessy, and other Indians like her, had their land there taken by treaty, by fraud, by violence, by theft. They remembered how whites had burned down the village at Burt Lake in 1900 and pushed the Indians out. These were the stories in my family.

When I was a boy my mother told me to walk down the alleys in Harbor Springs and not to wear my orange football sweater out of the house. This way I would not stand out, not be noticed, and not be a target.

I wore my orange sweater anyway and deliberately avoided the alleys. I was the biggest person I knew and wasn't really afraid. But I met my comeuppance when I enlisted in the U.S. Army. One night all the men in my barracks gathered together and, gang-fashion, pulled me into the shower and scrubbed me down with rough brushes used for floors, saying, "We won't have any dirty Indians in our outfit." It is a point of irony that I was cleaner than any of them. Later in Korea I learned how to kill, how to bully, how to hate Koreans. I came out of the war tougher than ever and, strangely, white.

I went to college, got married, lived in La Porte, Indiana, worked as a surveyor and raised three boys. I headed Boy Scout groups, never thinking it odd when the Scouts did imitation Indian dances, imitation Indian lore.

One day when I was 35 or thereabouts I heard about an Indian powwow. My father used to attend them and so with great curiosity and a strange joy at discovering a part of my heritage, I decided the thing to do to get ready for this big event was to have my friend make me a spear in his forge. The steel was fine and blue and iridescent. The feathers on the shaft were bright and proud.

In a dusty state fairground in southern Indiana, I found white people dressed as Indians. I learned they were "hobbyists," that is, it was their hobby and leisure pastime to masquerade as Indians on weekends. I felt ridiculous with my spear, and I left.

It was years before I could tell anyone of the embarrassment of this weekend and see any humor in it. But in a way it was that weekend, for all its silliness, that was my awakening. I realized I didn't know who I was. I didn't have an Indian name. I didn't speak the Indian language. I didn't know the Indian customs. Dimly I remembered the Ottawa word for dog, but it was a baby word, *kahgee*, not the full word, *muhkahgee*, which I was later to learn. Even more hazily I remembered a naming ceremony (my own). I remembered legs dancing around me, dust. Where had that been? Who had I been? "Suwaukquat," my mother told me when I asked, "where the tree begins to grow."

That was 1968, and I was not the only Indian in the country who was feeling the need to remember who he or she was. There were others. They had powwows, real ones, and eventually I found them. Together we researched our past, a search that for me culminated in the Longest Walk, a march on Washington in 1978. Maybe because I now know what it means to be Indian, it surprises me that others don't. Of course there aren't very many of us left. The chances of an average person knowing an average Indian in an average lifetime are pretty slim.

Still, I was amused one day when my small, four-year-old neighbor looked at me as I was hoeing in my garden and said, "You aren't a real Indian, are you?" Scotty is little, talkative, likable. Finally I said, "I'm a real Indian." He looked at me for a moment and then said, squinting into the sun, "Then where's your horse and feathers?" The child was simply a smaller, whiter version of my own ignorant self years before. We'd both seen too much TV, that's all. He was not to be blamed. And so, in a way, the moronic man on the beach today is blameless. We come full circle to realize other people are like ourselves, as discomfiting as that may be sometimes.

As I sit in my old chair on my porch, in a light that is fading so the leaves are barely distinguishable against the sky, I can picture my girl asleep upstairs. I would like to prepare her for what's to come, take her each step of the way saying, there's a place to avoid, here's what I know about this, but much of what's before her she must go through alone. She must pass through pain and joy and solitude and community to discover her own inner self that is unlike any other and come through that passage to the place where she sees all people are one, and in so seeing may live her life in a brighter future.

INTERPRETATIONS

1. What audience besides his daughter is Sawaquat writing for? Cite evidence. Why do you suppose he waited until he was nearly fifty and had a daughter—he has three other children, boys—to express these thoughts?

2. "I didn't know who I was." What do we have to know about ourselves before we know who we are? How important is ancestry

to a sense of identity? What should be our attitude toward our ancestry—or ancestries?

3. Until he asked his mother, Sawaquat did not know his Indian name. Why do you suppose she withheld it? How do you think you would feel to discover that you had another name? Why?

4. What was involved in Sawaquat "finding himself"? Why must such a search be conducted with others? How did white society delay the search and make it difficult?

CORRESPONDENCES

1. Feelings of alienation and displacement are expressed by both Lim and Sawaquat. Explain their causes and effects. How are they reconciled in each text?

2. Review Morrison's perspective and discuss its relevance to Sawaquat's essay. Does pursuing ethnic identity preclude searching for a national community? Explain.

APPLICATIONS

1. "We come full circle to realize other people are like ourselves, as discomfiting as that may be sometimes." To what extent do you agree with Sawaquat? Write a summary of your group's discussions.

2. Write an essay on a part of your cultural heritage you might someday want to share with your children.

3. In paragraph 14 Sawaquat says of his daughter: "She must pass through pain and joy and solitude and community to discover her own inner self that is unlike any other . . ." To what extent do you agree? Write a journal entry of an experience that corresponds to Sawaquat's comment.

4. In this essay Lewis Sawaquat writes: "The chances of an average person knowing an average Indian in an average lifetime are pretty slim." Hopefully, the following Web sites will help a reader begin to bridge this knowledge gap.

   http://www.indiancountry.com

   http://www.turtletrack.org

   http://www.navajohopiobserver.com

The Night I Was Nobody

JOHN EDGAR WIDEMAN

John Edgar Wideman (b. 1941 in Washington, D.C.) has written nine novels since A Glance Away, *in 1967, the year after graduating from Oxford University on a Rhodes scholarship. He has written in a variety of forms, such as short story and autobiography, but his usual technique is to combine biography with fiction, as in his latest novel,* Fanon *(2008), based on Frantz Fanon, the Afro-Caribbean psychiatrist and anti-colonial writer who influenced the Algerian revolution. Many relationships and difficulties in this novel reflect Wideman's own life, such as having a brother serving a life term in prison. Wideman grew up in a Pittsburgh ghetto, and was recruited by the University of Pennsylvania on a basketball scholarship. He told one interviewer, "I always wanted to play pro basketball—ever since I saw a ball and learned you could make money at it." Wideman has been a professor of English at the University of Massachusetts–Amherst and is now a professor of Africana Studies at Brown University. Watch how in this selection from* Esquire *the frequently mentioned subject of weather becomes "racial weather" and try to decide what racism and weather have in common.*

ON JULY 4TH, THE FIREWORKS DAY, the day for picnics and patriotic speeches, I was in Clovis, New Mexico, to watch my daughter, Jamila, and her team, the Central Massachusetts Cougars, compete in the Junior Olympics Basketball national tourney. During our ten-day visit to Clovis the weather had been bizarre. Hailstones as large as golf balls. Torrents of rain flooding streets hubcap deep. Running through the pelting rain from their van to a gym, Jamila and several teammates cramming through a doorway had looked back just in time to see a funnel cloud touch down a few blocks away. Continuous sheet lightning had shattered the horizon, crackling for hours night and day. Spectacular, off-the-charts weather flexing its muscles, reminding people what little control they had over their lives.

Hail rat-tat-tatting against our windshield our first day in town wasn't exactly a warm welcome, but things got better fast. Clovis people were glad to see us and the mini-spike we triggered in the local economy. Hospitable, generous, our hosts lavished upon us the same hands-on affection and attention to detail that had transformed an unpromising place in the middle of nowhere into a very livable community.

On top of all that, the Cougars were kicking butt, so the night of July 3rd I wanted to celebrate with a frozen margarita. I couldn't pry anybody else away from "Bubba's," the movable feast of beer, chips, and chatter the adults traveling with the Cougars improvised nightly in the King's Inn Motel parking lot, so I drove off alone to find one perfect margarita.

Inside the door of Kelley's Bar and Lounge I was flagged by a guy collecting a cover charge and told I couldn't enter wearing my Malcolm X hat. I asked why; the guy hesitated, conferred for a moment with his partner, then declared that Malcolm X hats were against the dress code. For a split second I thought it might be that *no* caps were allowed in Kelley's. But the door crew and two or three others hanging around the entrance-way all wore the billed caps ubiquitous in New Mexico, duplicates of mine, except theirs sported the logos of feed stores and truck stops instead of a silver X.

What careened through my mind in the next couple of minutes is essentially unsayable but included scenes from my own half-century of life as a black man, clips from five hundred years of black/white meetings on slave ships, auction blocks, plantations, basketball courts, in the Supreme Court's marble halls, in beds, back alleys and back rooms, kisses and lynch ropes and contracts for millions of dollars so a black face will grace a cereal box. To tease away my anger I tried joking with folks in other places. Hey, Spike Lee. That hat you gave me on the set of the Malcolm movie in Cairo ain't legal in Clovis.

But nothing about these white guys barring my way was really funny. Part of me wanted to get down and dirty. Curse the suckers. Were they prepared to do battle to keep me and my cap out? Another voice said, Be cool. Don't sully your hands. Walk away and call the cops or a lawyer. Forget these chumps. Sue the owner. Or should I win hearts and minds? Look, fellas, I understand why the X on my cap might offend or scare you. You probably don't know much about Malcolm. The incredible metamorphoses of his thinking, his soul. By the time he was assassinated he wasn't a racist, didn't advocate violence. He was trying to make sense of America's impossible history, free himself, free us from the crippling legacy of race hate and oppression.

While all the above occupied my mind, my body, on its own, had assumed a gunfighter's vigilance, hands ready at sides, head cocked, weight poised, eyes tight and hard on the doorkeeper yet alert to anything stirring on the periphery. Many other eyes, all in white faces, were checking out the entranceway, recognizing the ingredients of a racial incident. Hadn't they witnessed Los Angeles going berserk on their TV screens just a couple months ago? That truck driver beaten nearly to death in the street, those packs of black hoodlums burning and looting? Invisible lines were being drawn in the air, in the sand, invisible chips bristled on shoulders.

The weather again. Our American racial weather, turbulent, unchanging in its changeability, its power to rock us and stun us and smack us from our routines and tear us apart as if none of our cities, our pieties, our promises, our dreams, ever stood a chance of holding on. The racial weather. Outside us, then suddenly, unforgettably, unforgivingly inside, reminding us of what we've only pretended to have forgotten. Our limits, our flaws. The lies and compromises we practice to avoid dealing honestly with the contradictions of race. How dependent we are on luck to survive—*when* we survive—the racial weather.

One minute you're a person, the next moment somebody starts treating you as if you're not. Often it happens just that way, just that suddenly. Particularly if you are a black man in America. Race and racism are a force larger than individuals, more powerful than law or education or government or the church, a force able to wipe these institutions away in the charged moments, minuscule or mountainous, when black and white come face to face. In Watts in 1965,[1] or a few less-than-glorious minutes in Clovis, New Mexico, on the eve of the day that commemorates our country's freedom, our inalienable right as a nation, as citizens, to life, liberty, equality, the pursuit of happiness, those precepts and principles that still look good on paper but are often as worthless as a sheet of newspaper to protect you in a storm if you're a black man at the wrong time in the wrong place.

None of this is news, is it? Not July 3rd in Clovis, when a tiny misfire occurred, or yesterday in your town or tomorrow in mine? But haven't we made progress? Aren't things much better than they used to be? Hasn't enough been done?

We ask the wrong questions when we look around and see a handful of fabulously wealthy black people, a few others entering the middle classes. Far more striking than the positive changes are the abiding patterns and assumptions that have not changed. Not all black people are mired in social pathology, but the bottom rung of the ladder of opportunity (and the space *beneath* the bottom rung) is still defined by the color of the people trapped there—and many *are* still trapped there, no doubt about it, because their status was inherited, determined generation after generation by blood, by color. Once, all black people

[1]*Watts in 1965:* In August of 1965, a police traffic stop provoked six days of rioting in which thirty-four people died in the Watts neighborhood of Los Angeles—Eds.

were legally excluded from full participation in the mainstream. Then fewer. Now only some. But the mechanisms of disenfranchisement that originally separated African Americans from other Americans persist, if not legally, then in the apartheid mind-set, convictions and practices of the majority. The seeds sleep but don't die. Ten who suffer from exclusion today can become ten thousand tomorrow. Racial weather can change that quickly.

How would the bouncer have responded if I'd calmly declared, "This is a free country, I can wear any hat I choose"? Would he thank me for standing up for our shared birthright? Or would he have to admit, if pushed, that American rights belong only to *some* Americans, white Americans?

We didn't get that far in our conversation. We usually don't. The girls' faces pulled me from the edge—girls of all colors, sizes, shapes, gritty kids bonding through hard clean competition. Weren't these guys who didn't like my X cap kids too? Who did they think I was? What did they think they were protecting? I backed out, backed down, climbed in my car and drove away from Kelley's. After all, I didn't want Kelley's. I wanted a frozen margarita and a mellow celebration. So I bought plenty of ice and the ingredients for a margarita and rejoined the festivities at Bubba's. Everybody volunteered to go back with me to Kelley's, but I didn't want to spoil the victory party, taint our daughters' accomplishments, erase the high marks Clovis had earned hosting us.

But I haven't forgotten what happened in Kelley's. I write about it now because this is my country, the country where my sons and daughter are growing up, and your daughters and sons, and the crisis, the affliction, the same ole, same ole waste of life continues across the land, the nightmarish weather of racism, starbursts of misery in the dark.

The statistics of inequality don't demonstrate a "black crisis"—that perspective confuses cause and victim, solutions and responsibility. When the rain falls, it falls on us all. The bad news about black men— that they die sooner and more violently than white men, are more ravaged by unemployment and lack of opportunity, are more exposed to drugs, disease, broken families, and police brutality, more likely to go to jail than college, more cheated by the inertia and callousness of a government that represents and protects the most needy the least—this is not a "black problem," but a *national* shame affecting us all. Wrenching ourselves free from the long nightmare of racism will require collective determination, countless individual acts of will, gutsy, informed, unselfish. To imagine the terrible cost of not healing ourselves, we must first imagine how good it would feel to be healed.

INTERPRETATIONS

1. Comment on the first sentence of Wideman's essay. Why does he choose to mention these particular events? What do they have in common?

2. Wideman uses the metaphor of weather throughout the essay, beginning in the first paragraph with a literal description of the weather they encountered. To what extent does the last sentence foreshadow his encounter at Kelley's bar in paragraph 4?

3. What mood does he create in the second paragraph? What is the main reason that the people of Clovis are happy to entertain the fans attending the Junior Olympics?

4. Wideman is denied admission to Kelley's bar because of his Malcolm X hat. What associations do you have with Malcolm X? Why does Wideman mention that the hat was a present from Spike Lee?

5. Trace the course of the weather metaphor in paragraphs 8, 10, 11, and 15. What are the symbolic implications of the connections he makes between weather and racism?

6. Review Wideman's penultimate paragraph in which he states his reasons for writing about this incident. To what extent do you agree or disagree with his concluding sentence?

CORRESPONDENCES

1. Review Baldwin's perspective and discuss its relevance to Wideman's essay. What does each imply about the importance of community?

2. Wideman and Sawaquat record their experiences with racism initially because of their children but also because of their hope that it will be eradicated. To what extent do you share their hopes? What actions, if any, do you imagine taking to help eradicate racism?

APPLICATIONS

1. Write a journal entry responding to the title of Wideman's essay. Under what circumstances can you imagine feeling like a nobody?

2. Check the Internet for more information on Malcolm X and/or Spike Lee and write an essay on your impressions of one or both of them.

3. Discuss with your group Wideman's response to the situation at Kelley's bar. Should he have confronted the bouncer and taken a stand or withdrawn because of the young girls, including his daughter, who were participating in the Junior Olympics? What can you imagine doing in his situation? Record your group's responses.

Solidarity

CHARLES NEUMAN

Charles Neuman has two dogs who love to swim. He enjoys outdoor activities with his three sons, playing jazz and classical piano, and building wooden boats. A self-described "friendly introvert," Neuman finds family life, even with all of its challenges, to be surprisingly invigorating. He gives credit to his wife, who is a special education teacher on Long Island, where Neuman and his family live. Neuman teaches physics and astronomy at Queensborough Community College (CUNY).

A FEW WEEKS AGO I went on my first walk for a cause, the Walk for Autism, at Jones Beach. I wasn't sure why I was going exactly, but I thought it might be a nice thing to do with my son.

When we arrived, I was emotionally moved by the large congregation of people there. I didn't know what to make of it. It was overwhelming. My mind took many pictures of the scenes I saw, as we worked our way through the crowds to sign in. I saw a kid having a characteristic "meltdown." I was exposed to various messages, some about finding a cure for autism, others about a particular child for whom a group was walking. One message was controversial, and I turned away from it quickly so as not to get distracted by the issue. Besides, this did not seem like the place to have divisive thoughts. I saw a group of adults with autism. My eye lingered a bit as I walked past them, trying to picture my son among them as an adult. Thoughts of the future always raise the questions "Where will he be?" and "Who will take care of him when I'm gone?"

Mostly I just saw people. Purposeful people. People who were going about their business. Not mourning. Not angry. Not jubilant. Just busy people. I could relate. The events of that day were part of our busy everyday life. Our life might not be typical—my other children know their brother is different—but it feels routine to us. Thousands of us brought our atypical but routine daily lives to this event.

I was walking individually, but most people were organized into groups, or "teams," each with its own T-shirt. There was the "Team for Patrick," the "Team for Sean." Some teams held up enlarged pictures of the autistic child they represented. It seemed as if the entire Smithtown school district showed up—they were everywhere. What brought out all these people? Why were the teams so large? How could one child with a disorder motivate so many people? I didn't understand. It was apparently more than just about raising money for a cause. I heard one mother tell her child, "You see all these people? They all came out just for you." Somehow, that hit home. Everyone came out for every individual who was represented.

The walk itself was nice. It was a sunny day, and there was a pleasant ocean breeze. We were all walking together. Thousands of people. We didn't know each other, there was no "theme song," and there was really nothing uniting us except for a connection to autism, usually through a child or a relative.

Why was I walking? Halfway through the walk, I still didn't know. I didn't know much about the organization for which we were raising money, so I wasn't primarily walking for the organization. I didn't feel like I was walking for a cure either. Although it would certainly be nice if more children could develop typically, thoughts of a cure are generally not on my mind. I don't go around thinking there is something "wrong" with my son, such that he needs to be "fixed." He's just different and has different needs than most children. I also wasn't at the walk to seek comfort. There's no reason for anyone to feel sorry for me for having a healthy, wonderful son who loves swimming, music, and other activities. So why was I there?

I think the main reason I walked was to experience a connection with all of these people who were touched by autism in some way. I didn't need to shake hands with anyone, or even exchange a knowing nod. We all knew. We knew what it means to have someone different in our lives. And we were all walking. I took in the experience of simply walking alongside these people.

I felt safe. I knew I wouldn't need to explain anything to anyone. Nobody would look over involuntarily if my son made a verbal outburst with no linguistic meaning, nobody would appear uncomfortable if my son jumped around with movement that would seem erratic to an outsider, nobody would ask my son what his name was or how old he was and assume that he would answer, and nobody would have to be polite and accepting. I could let my guard down and be myself.

We could all just be. And we had a common purpose. To be together.

INTERPRETATIONS

1. In which paragraph do you think Neuman provides his definition of "community"? What evidence are you able to provide to support your answer?

2. In paragraph 3, Neuman uses the phrase "atypical but routine" to describe daily life. What do you think he means? What in your life is "atypical but routine"?

CORRESPONDENCES

1. In "People Like Us" David Brooks explores the living patterns of modern Americans. How do you think his ideas relate to the group of people depicted in "Solidarity"?

2. Several of the writers in this chapter address the issue of misconceptions about people and/or discrimination against them. Select one essay where you notice this theme and relate it to "Solidarity."

   For your consideration: One way of examining pertinent issues is to explore the "us" and "them" within the essay. What groups are being defined? What conflicts arise? How do you feel about these issues in the context of larger definitions of both community and solidarity?

APPLICATIONS

1. Write a narrative about an experience you had when you joined a group of people that had a common goal (sports team, hobbyist club, religious retreat, political campaign). In your story, explain why you joined this group, how you felt the first time that you participated in the group, and how you felt about the group experience after taking part in it for a period of time. Be sure to express your thinking about "community" as you tell your story.

2. Imagine that you were interviewing one of the people holding a sign that read "Team for Patrick" or "Team for Sean." What questions would you ask that person? What answers do you think that person might provide? To help you formulate both your questions and answers, explore the websites listed below. Next, write out your interview in the form of a dialogue.

   http://www.autismspeaks.org/

   http://www.ninds.nih.gov/disorders/autism/detail_autism.htm

   http://www.autism-society.org/

Literacy Narratives

Sherman Alexie and Susan Madera both write stories about how their engagement with language affects their view of themselves, other people, and society in general. Alexie, building upon his father's love of books, forges his own self-identify from his mastery of texts. Madera recreates herself after a tenuous start with college. Both writers share a belief in the power of words to shape lives. How does your use of language influence your relationships with the people closest to you? To what extent are you an invention of the language that you use?

The Joy of Reading and Writing: Superman and Me

SHERMAN ALEXIE

Sherman Alexie (b. 1966) tells us in this article much of what we need to know about him. But we also need to know that he attended the Spokane Indian Reservation school until the eighth grade, when he chose to travel thirty-two miles to the high school in Reardan, Washington, a village of 608, where he was the only Indian until his twin sisters joined him a year later. From there he went to Gonzaga University in Spokane, and received his B.A. from Washington State University. His first book was a poetry collection, The Business of Fancydancing, *published in 1992, which Alexie turned into a film in 1993. Between Alexie's first novel,* Reservation Blues, *published in 1995, and his latest,* Flight: A Novel, *published in 2007, he has published many volumes of poems and short stories, as well as the novel* Indian Killer *(1996). (One of his short-story collections is called* The Toughest Indian in the World *[2000], a title you might remember when you read in the article: "I refused to fail. I was smart. I was arrogant. I was lucky. I read books late into the night. . . .) In 2007 he published* The Absolutely True Diary of a Part-Time Indian, *Alexie's first juvenile fiction, with a protagonist who lives on Spokane Reservation and goes to a school where he is the only Indian. The Diary is fiction, and the title should alert you that Alexie is "a man who often speaks of his childhood in the third-person . . . ." He still lives on the reservation.*

Approximately 1,100 Spokane Tribal members live on the reservation where Alexie grew up. Alexie's father is a Coeur d'Alene Indian, and his mother is a Spokane Indian. The Spokane Indians are of the Interior Salish group, which has inhabited northeastern Washington, northern Idaho, and western Montana for centuries. "Spokane" is generally accepted as meaning "Sun People" or "Children of the Sun." The living cycle of the Spokane was integral to their economic and social life. In the spring, the winter camps dispersed to gather food, hunt, and fish. By early summer, salmon fishing, hunting, and rootdigging were the main activities. Summer was the time of year when intertribal activities were at the highest, since neighboring tribes joined the Spokanes for root and berry gathering. This tradition of socializing is carried on today with the Indian powwows, which begin in June and end in September. Visiting, games, and ceremonial dancing are important parts in the social life of today's Indians.

I LEARNED TO READ WITH A *SUPERMAN* COMIC BOOK. Simple enough, I suppose. I cannot recall which particular Superman comic book I read, nor can I remember which villain he fought in that issue. I cannot remember the plot, nor the means by which I obtained the comic book. What I can remember is this: I was three years old, a Spokane Indian boy living with his family on the Spokane Indian Reservation in eastern Washington state. We were poor by most standards, but one of my parents usually managed to find some minimum-wage job or another, which made us middle-class by reservation standards. I had a brother and three sisters. We lived on a combination of irregular paychecks, hope, fear, and government surplus food.

My father, who is one of the few Indians who went to Catholic school on purpose, was an avid reader of westerns, spy thrillers, murder mysteries, gangster epics, basketball player biographies, and anything else he could find. He bought his books by the pound at Dutch's Pawn Shop, Goodwill, Salvation Army, and Value Village. When he had extra money, he bought new novels at supermarkets, convenience stores and hospital gift shops. Our house was filled with books. They were stacked in crazy piles in the bathroom, bedrooms, and living room. In a fit of unemployment-inspired creative energy, my father built a set of bookshelves and soon filled them with a random assortment of books about the Kennedy assassination, Watergate, the Vietnam War, and the entire twenty-three book series of the Apache westerns. My father loved books, and since I loved my father with an aching devotion, I decided to love books as well.

I can remember picking up my father's books before I could read. The words themselves were mostly foreign, but I still remember the exact moment when I first understood, with a sudden clarity, the purpose of a paragraph. I didn't have the vocabulary to say "paragraph," but I realized that a paragraph was a fence that held words. The words inside a paragraph worked together for a common purpose. They had some specific reason for being inside the same fence. This knowledge delighted me. I began to think of everything in terms of paragraphs. Our reservation was a small paragraph within the United States. My family's house was a paragraph, distinct from the other paragraphs of the LeBrets to the north, the Fords to our south, and the Tribal School to the west. Inside our house, each family member existed as a separate paragraph but still had genetics and common experiences to link us. Now, using this logic, I can see my changed family as an essay of seven paragraphs: mother, father, older brother, the deceased sister, my younger twin sisters, and our adopted little brother.

At the same time I was seeing the world in paragraphs, I also picked up the *Superman* comic book. Each panel, complete with picture, dialogue, and narrative, was a three-dimensional paragraph. In one panel, Superman breaks through a door. His suit is red, blue, and yellow. The brown door shatters into many pieces. I look at the narrative above the picture. I cannot read the words, but I assume it tells me that "Superman is breaking down the door." Aloud, I pretend to read the words and say, "Superman is breaking down the door." Words, dialogue, also float out of Superman's mouth. Because he is breaking down the door, I assume he says, "I am breaking down the door." Once again, I pretend to read the words and say aloud, "I am breaking down the door." In this way, I learned to read.

This might be an interesting story all by itself. A little Indian boy teaches himself to read at an early age and advances quickly. He reads *Grapes of Wrath* in kindergarten when other children are struggling through Dick and Jane. If he'd been anything but an Indian boy living on the reservation, he might have been called a prodigy. But he is an Indian boy living on the reservation and is simply an oddity. He grows into a man who often speaks of his childhood in the third-person, as if it will somehow dull the pain and make him sound more modest about his talents.

A smart Indian is a dangerous person, widely feared and ridiculed by Indians and non-Indians alike. I fought with my classmates on a daily basis. They wanted me to stay quiet when the non-Indian teacher asked for answers, for volunteers, for help. We were Indian children who were expected to be stupid. Most lived up to those expectations inside the classroom but subverted them on the outside. They struggled with basic reading in school but could remember how to sing a few dozen powwow songs. They were monosyllabic in front of their non-Indian teachers but could tell complicated stories and jokes at the dinner table. They submissively ducked their heads when confronted by a non-Indian adult but would slug it out with the Indian bully who was ten years older. As Indian children, we were expected to fail in the non-Indian world. Those who failed were ceremonially accepted by other Indians and appropriately pitied by non-Indians.

I refused to fail. I was smart. I was arrogant. I was lucky. I read books late into the night, until I could barely keep my eyes open. I read books at recess, then during lunch, and in the few minutes left after I had finished my classroom assignments. I read books in the car when my family traveled to powwows or basketball games. In shopping malls, I ran to the bookstores and read bits and pieces of as many books as I could. I read the books my father brought home from the pawnshops and secondhand. I read the books I borrowed from the library.

I read the backs of cereal boxes. I read the newspaper. I read the bulletins posted on the walls of the school, the clinic, the tribal offices, the post office. I read junk mail. I read auto-repair manuals. I read magazines. I read anything that had words and paragraphs. I read with equal parts joy and desperation. I loved those books, but I also knew that love had only one purpose. I was trying to save my life.

Despite all the books I read, I am still surprised I became a writer. I was going to be a pediatrician. These days, I write novels, short stories, and poems. I visit schools and teach creative writing to Indian kids. In all my years in the reservation school system, I was never taught how to write poetry, short stories, or novels. I was certainly never taught that Indians wrote poetry, short stories, and novels. Writing was something beyond Indians. I cannot recall a single time that a guest teacher visited the reservation. There must have been visiting teachers. Who were they? Where are they now? Do they exist? I visit the schools as often as possible. The Indian kids crowd the classroom. Many are writing their own poems, short stories, and novels. They have read my books. They have read many other books. They look at me with bright eyes and arrogant wonder. They are trying to save their lives. Then there are the sullen and already defeated Indian kids who sit in the back rows and ignore me with theatrical precision. The pages of their notebooks are empty. They carry neither pencil nor pen. They stare out the window. They refuse and resist. "Books," I say to them. "Books," I say. I throw my weight against their locked doors. The door holds. I am smart. I am arrogant. I am lucky. I am trying to save our lives.

INTERPRETATIONS

1. The purpose of an introduction is to engage the reader. How well does Alexie's first paragraph accomplish this? Cite effective examples.

2. What role does his father play in his literacy acquisition? Is there someone who played a similar role in your learning to read?

3. How effectively does Alexie use the metaphor of a fence as a framing device for his essay? Trace its development in each paragraph.

4. In paragraph 4, Alexie returns to the theme of literacy as empowerment. Why does he reintroduce Superman? To what effect?

5. Alexie devotes subsequent paragraphs to personal history and cultural stereotypes. Explain the effects of the latter with respect to teachers, non-Indian, and Indian students.

6. Review Alexie's conclusion. Why does he devote so much time to visiting Indian schools? What is the effect of his ending his essay with the symbol of the door?

APPLICATIONS

1. "I read anything that had words and paragraphs. I read with equal parts of joy and desperation. I loved those books, but I also knew that love had only one purpose. I was trying to save my life." Write a journal response to each of Alexie's statements. What is the effect of juxtaposing joy and desperation? How do you react to his linking reading with saving his life?

2. Alexie writes ". . . I realized that a paragraph was a fence that held words." To what extent is this metaphor dependent upon an understanding of another kind of literacy? What literacy is being invoked?

3. In his second paragraph, Alexie writes: "My father, who is one of the few Indians who went to Catholic school on purpose . . ." What do the last two words of this quoted phrase tell you about the literacies present on the reservation?

One Voice

SUSAN G. MADERA

Susan G. Madera was born and raised in Little Italy in New York City. She received her A.A. degree from Queensborough Community College in 2003 and continued her education at Queens College, where she earned a B.A. in English and Secondary Education in 2005. She is currently pursuing an M.A. in Liberal Studies at Queens College. She resides in Queens, New York, with her husband and two sons.

GROWING UP, I KNEW TWO LANGUAGES: English, and neighborhood. The former was taught at school, and the latter was learned at home, from family and friends. I could read and write in English, but I spoke neighborhood. "What is neighborhood?" you may ask. That is the language spoken in the neighborhood of my youth, Little Italy. It is a language full of slang words, and colloquialisms. Where I grew up, almost everyone spoke neighborhood.

As a child, I attended Transfiguration, a small Catholic grammar school in Chinatown. This school was several blocks away from our cramped, fifth floor apartment in a walk-up building on Broome Street. It was a financial hardship for all five children in our family to attend this school. My father worked two strenuous jobs so that we could enjoy the benefits of a good education. I wore my plaid jumper, crisp white blouse, and red uniform tie with pride each day. I was getting the best education that money could buy. My father said that if I studied hard, I was going to be "someone" when I grew up.

In grammar school, the most difficult subject I studied was English. There were so many complicated rules to memorize! To me, it was a foreign language—mysterious, and intriguing, but not a language that I spoke fluently. I was not alone in my feelings of dismay. Many of the students in my class were having difficulty learning this new language.

I remember Dominick Mazzocchi asking, "How can you say *ain't* ain't a word?"

The teacher responded, "Not only is it not a word, but that was a double negative!"

Dominick responded, "Double what? I wish you would talk English! None of us is understanding you."

"You mean, none of us *are* understanding you," remarked the teacher.

Dominick screamed, "We don't talk like you do!" He was sent to the principal's office.

The truth is, we did not speak alike. Although we were getting a great education in school, it was the language we learned outside of school that determined our speech. The effect on my language skills was a tremendous one, albeit negative. I could not speak English properly.

Once outside the neighborhood, this language hindered me. I was not always understood clearly, or was mocked. "What do you mean, you want to 'take' a haircut?," asked the hairdresser. "Where do you want to take it?" He began to laugh at me. I was so embarrassed. How could he not understand me? The language I picked up on the streets was a part of me, but as I grew up I wanted to get as far away from it as possible. It embarrassed me. In this case, being bilingual was not a blessing, it was a curse.

In high school, I began to use the rules taught to me in my English classes in grammar school. More than anything, I wanted to speak like everyone else. I tried my best, but was unsuccessful. The only way I could stop speaking neighborhood was to take a knife and cut the tongue from my mouth! In my junior year, I was approached by my English teacher who asked if I would like to write for the school paper. "I can't do that!," I exclaimed, "I don't talk right!" She then told me that although I did not speak correctly, I wrote correctly. My written work showed no trace of my flawed speech. She had so much confidence in me that she wanted me to edit the paper as well. I was flabbergasted, and quickly accepted the position. When my first story was published, I was amazed at the response I received from my peers. No one believed that I had written it! I could, indeed, write in proper English. This gave me hope. Perhaps, one day, I might also be able to speak correctly. I felt very much like M. Bella Mirabella, who described how she felt when she accomplished her goals. She wrote, "I was no longer the proverbial small child looking in the shop window."[1] I too was no longer on the outside looking in.

Success at last!

After high school, I attended Brooklyn College. Walking on campus for the first time was like browsing through a travel brochure. I was transformed into a tourist. There were trees everywhere. Although I was only in Brooklyn, I felt far from the city streets of Manhattan. I was

---

[1]M. Bella Mirabella. "The Education of an Italian-American Girl Child." *Liberating Memory*. Ed. Janet Zandy (Rutgers University Press, 1995), pp. 162–172.

in a different world. This was not like the small Catholic schools I had attended. I was alone, and afraid, but determined.

On the first day of classes, I was overwhelmed with feelings of anxiety. I was so excited, I could hardly breathe. That feeling of excitement was soon transformed into a feeling of terror. One of my professors had decided to make my life miserable. He taught Speech 101. On the first day of class, he had each student read aloud from our text book to determine the quality of their speech. He then proceeded to demean me, my heritage and my education. That day was only the first of many. He proceeded to make a fool of me each and every day our class met. That first, and last, semester at Brooklyn College was a dream that turned into a nightmare. José Torres (page 160) writes that you should not let someone else's opinion of you affect your self-worth. Unfortunately, this professor's opinion of me was so low, and his personal attacks were so painful, that I had lost all confidence in myself. It took years for me to gain that confidence back. I decided that college was not for me, and I went into the working world.

I was lucky enough to get a position as a typist in a very prestigious company, Morgan Guaranty. I began my career in the typing pool, typing on an IBM typewriter. Within a year, word processors came into the office, and I was thrilled to be picked as one of the people trained to use one. During this time, I met a wonderful man who would change my life forever—Michael. We dated for two years, and were married at Most Precious Blood Church, in Little Italy.

My personal life was wonderful, so too was my professional life. Over the next few years, I got small promotions within my department. Each promotion brought much more responsibility, with a little more money. One day, at review time, I was called into a meeting. When I walked into the dimly lit conference room, I was surprised to see several assistant vice presidents and a vice president with my supervisor. I immediately broke into a cold sweat. What had I done wrong? My years of "dedication, hard work, and knowledge of the English language" had brought me to their attention. Knowledge of the English language! They were joking, they had to be. They proceeded to make me an offer I could not refuse—my own department. I was dumbfounded when offered this position, but accepted quickly, before they changed their minds. I headed a department of word processors in the investment research department. This success was much larger than the one achieved in high school. I was now being accepted in the business world.

I eventually left Morgan on maternity leave with my first child. Upon my return, I was to be trained on the new IBM computers, and become supervisor of an even larger group of people. Once our son was born and I looked into his sparkling eyes, I knew I could not leave him to the care of a baby-sitter. When I returned three months later, it was to resign my position.

I am still a supervisor, but of our home. Michael is now twelve years old, and Matthew is six. Unfortunately, our children have a bit of neighborhood in them. I take the blame for this. As Dr. Benjamin Spock says about childhood development, "Between 3 and 5 years they were, generally, cozy, affectionate family children who proudly patterned their activities, table manners, and speech after their parents."[2] Our children's speech patterns were picked up from the main caregiver in our home, me. When I hear one of our boys say something incorrectly, I explain why it is wrong, and tell him the correct way to say it. My husband often tells me that I should be an English teacher because I am always correcting their grammar. I want our children to have the benefit of a strong background in English. I know the downfalls of not speaking properly, and I do not want them to experience them, as I have.

To say that I have conquered all my fears of the English language would be untrue. Twenty-one years after walking away from Brooklyn College, I am back in school at Queensborough Community College. What was the first class I decided to take? Why English, of course. I am as determined as ever to speak English as well as possible. I am doing well in my class, and I am proud of myself. I am also quite glad that QCC has decided to give me the three credits I earned in Speech at Brooklyn College, although I barely passed, with a grade of D. I could not have taken that class again.

Over the years, I have gained confidence in myself as a writer. The way I speak does not exemplify who I am; however, my writing is a true expression of the person I am inside. When I write, words come from deep inside of me, and spill out onto the page. I never stop to correct myself, as I would if I were speaking. I may speak two languages, but I write with one voice.

INTERPRETATIONS

1. What distinctions does Madera make between the language of school and the language of the neighborhood?

2. Why does she regard being bilingual as a "curse" rather than a "blessing"?

---

[2] Dr. Benjamin Spock and Michael B. Rothenberg, M.D., *Dr. Spock's Baby and Child Care* (New York: Pocket Books, 1985).

3. What roles do her teachers play in her acquisition of written language?

4. What point does she make about her "two languages" in her conclusion?

APPLICATIONS

1. Do you, like Madera, have a "writing self" and a "speaking self"? How do they differ? What does each express about your identity?

2. The opening sentence to Susan G. Madera's essay is: "Growing up, I knew two languages: English, and neighborhood." What literacies are implied in this statement? What is involved in the literacy of "neighborhood"? What knowledge do you bring to your understanding of your neighborhood?

3. What literacy is presented in Madera's anecdote about Dominick Mazzocchi? What assumptions about literacy are made?

4. How does Madera ultimately resolve the conflict between the literacies of English and neighborhood? To what extent have you negotiated these same literacies and the demands they make upon you?

The Knowing Eye

Alan S. Maltz

Zack Rutkin

En-chi Hsu

READING IMAGES

1. Which of these photographs depict "family"? Which show "community"? Explain your answers.
2. Crucial to many definitions of family or community is the idea of sharing or giving. As you examine these photographs, what do you think is being shared or given?

MAKING CONNECTIONS

1. Which essay (or essays) in this chapter seem(s) to match these photographs? What similarities do you notice?

2. Select one "Perspective" (see pages 17–18) to summarize each photograph. After making your choices, are the quotations and photographs interchangeable? What have you learned about the interplay of words and images?

WORDS AND IMAGES

1. Which image do you like the most? Why? Present your findings in an argumentation and persuasion essay.

2. As you examine the photograph of the two children walking together, what do you think they would be talking about? First, write a dialogue of ten lines that illustrates the conversation they might have as sisters. Next, write another dialogue of ten lines with the assumption that they are not related. What do you observe about the dialogues that you have created? How does the presence or absence of family relations influence the dialogues that you have written?

Additional Writing Topics

1. In "Solidarity," Neuman talks about finding a sense of community through his participating with his son in the march for autism. If you had a similar experience in marching for a cause to which you are committed, write an essay describing your thoughts and feelings as concisely as Newnan.

2. Several writers in this unit focus on the complex roles that memory plays in constructing the self. Write an essay in which you recount at least two memories and explain their significance in shaping your identity.

3. Several selections focus on family members and their influence. Why are families so important? Write an essay answering this question. Use examples from this chapter and your own experience.

4. Does the observance of customs, rituals, or traditions promote unity and continuity within the family? What rituals have your family shared over the years? How have these contributed to family relationships? Write an essay explaining how the observance of rituals helps preserve the family.

5. Review Nin's perspective on friendship (page 18). What does it suggest about possibilities in relationships? Are old friends necessarily one's best friends? Write an essay comparing two friendships of varying durations. How has each contributed to your knowledge of yourself? How do the relationships differ?

6. You have been introduced to several families in this chapter. Imagine being invited to spend a weekend with one of them. Which family would you choose and why? What would you expect from such a visit? Cite evidence from the text to support your expectations.

7. Several writers in this chapter discuss the transition from family to community. Write an essay focusing on a particular experience that enabled you to have such a transition. To what extent were you able to make a connection between your private and public worlds?

8. Interview three members of your group or three friends about their family structure and parental roles. Focus on at least three specific areas that might include information regarding economic issues, discipline, decisions, and other factors you consider relevant. Write an essay analyzing your findings.

9. According to the contemporary writer and critic Susan Sontag, "a family's photograph album is generally about the extended family—and, often, is all that remains of it." What role do photographs play in your immediate and extended family? Write an essay describing selected family photographs that support Sontag's thesis.

CHAPTER

3

Gender Issues

F EW ASPECTS OF CONTEMPORARY LIFE in North America and other parts of the world have changed more radically in the last two decades than those focusing on women in the workplace, gender roles in marriage, women's sexuality, divorce, communication between men and women, child custody, and sexual preference.

The texts on gender issues present a number of points of view on the relationship between men and women and their perceptions of each other. The writers explore, among other things, why various cultures have constructed different images of men and women at different points in their history.

They invite you to examine these changing cross-cultural concepts of masculinity and femininity and to evaluate the degree to which they have affected both men and women in their individual quests for identity, as well as the radical changes in the structure of the family. Some of the writers ask you to decide whether gender conflicts should be confronted or avoided, whereas others pose possibilities for freeing both sexes from the confines of traditional roles.

The most recurrent and controversial aspects of gender relations found in these texts is the debate between patriarchs and feminists. In some, the traditional idea of male supremacy has left its mark, and in others it is vigorously rejected, shattering intrapersonal and intracultural harmony.

Sexual orientation and sexual preference are current controversies particularly in the realm of "Queer Theory," in which scholars propose that human sexuality is a social construct based on culture rather than nature. They argue that in many cultures outside of the United States bisexuality and homosexuality are accepted, releasing both males and females from the confines of traditional sexual roles. Obviously, such reconsiderations are complex, involving not only individual and social values but moral and religious beliefs.

The texts in this chapter reflect the complexity of gender issues. Natalia Ginzburg in "He and I" explores the nuances of love and friendship from a female perspective, whereas Kate Chopin in "The Storm" presents the duality of the storm as a physical event that prevents the characters from carrying out their routines, and on the symbolic level as a passionate moment of sexual intimacy that will be remembered, not regretted or repeated. Gillianne Duncan explains why so many women feel ambivalent about their physical appearance, and Thomas Colicino presents gender relationships from a male's perspective. In "Shrouded in Contradiction," Gelareh Asayesh reveals her ambivalence to hijab—Islamic covering—"Sometimes I hate it. Sometimes I value it." The controversial issue of sexual preference is the focus of the texts by Dennis Altman and Anna Quindlen.

As you join the debate concerning feminists, patriarchs, homosexuals, and lesbians in these texts from various cultures and traditions, you are invited to speculate on questions such as the following: Are men rightly in charge of the family and tribe? Should women be accorded the same personal, political, and economic rights as men? Can the family survive the challenge to traditionalism created by changing personal and economic gender roles? Are women who return to the workplace surrendering their matriarchal role of nurturing the family and tribe? How have cultural attitudes toward homosexuals and lesbians resulted in political and sexual exclusion? What new definitions are needed for the concept of love?

Perspectives

Masculinity and Femininity may stand on either side of a mile-high wall, yet women and men share beds and homes, histories and children. So while racial and ethnographic stereotypes are fueled by segregation and prohibit familiarity . . . sexual stereotypes are formed in intimacy. This is what makes them unique, and uniquely troubling.

—*Judith Levine*

Marriage is a lottery in which men stake their liberty and women their happiness.

—*Virginia des Rieux*

We need to draw on images of collaborative caring by both men and women as a model of responsibility.

—*Mary Catherine Bateson*

Marriage must be a relation either of sympathy or of conquest.

—*George Eliot*

In sum, "homophobia" is a form of acute conventionality. We should do our best to help humankind over this illness, since heterosexuals who are free of it tend to have much better lives than heterosexuals who are not.

—*George Weinberg*

Indeed, it is my experience that both men and women are fundamentally human, and that there is very little mystery about either sex, except for the exasperating mysteriousness of human beings in general.

—*Dorothy Sayers*

Marriage comes with more myths attached to it than a six-volume set of ancient Greek history.

—*Steven Tesich*

A good marriage is that in which each appoints the other the guardian of his solitude.

—*Rainer Maria Rilke*

Love will redeem a man and change his entire character and existence; lack of love will literally drive a woman crazy.

—*Jean Anouilh*

Japan is the land where dawn doesn't break without a woman. Distant mountains move when wives speak.

—Japanese Proverbs

Not people die but worlds die in them.

—Yevgeny Yevtushenko

A child becomes an adult when he realizes that he has a right not only to be right but also to be wrong.

—Thomas Szasz

The word love has by no means the same sense for both sexes, and this is one of the serious misunderstandings that divide them.

—Simone de Beauvoir

Growing up homosexual was to grow up normally but displaced; to experience romantic love, but with the wrong person; to entertain grand ambitions, but of the unacceptable sort; to seek a gradual self-awakening, but in secret, not in public.

—Andrew Sullivan

Women have served all these centuries as looking-glasses possessing the magic and delicious power of reflecting the figure of man at twice its natural size.

—Virginia Woolf

The legal subordination of one sex to another is wrong in itself and now one of the chief hindrances to human improvement.

—John Stuart Mill

Males become so accustomed to masking their true emotions that it seems like second nature.

—Mark Zmarzly

After marriage, a woman's sight becomes so keen that she can see right through her husband without looking at him, and a man's so dull that he can look right through his wife without seeing her.

—Helen Rowland

APPLICATIONS

1. Review the various perspectives on marriage. What do they suggest about this intimate relationship? Select the one with which you are most in agreement and compare your choice with those of your group. What consensus, if any, did you reach?

2. Working with members of your group, devise a questionnaire that asks respondents about positive traits associated with masculinity and femininity. Distribute the questionnaire to ten or twelve class-mates or co-workers. Write an analysis of their responses.

3. Discuss Zmarzly's perspective with your group. To what extent do you agree with him? What cultural and social factors account for males suppressing their emotions? What solutions are there?

The Wise Daughter

SWAHILI FOLKTALE

Swahili is spoken widely in East Africa and is an official language of Kenya and Tanzania. What are your associations with the word "wise"?

THERE WAS ONCE A YOUNG MAN whose parents died and left him a hundred cattle. He was lonely after the death of his parents, so he decided to get married. He went to his neighbors and asked them to help him find a wife.

Soon one of the neighbors came to tell him that he had found the most beautiful girl in the country for him to marry. "The girl is very good and wise and beautiful, and her father is very wealthy," he said. "Her father owns six thousand cattle."

The young man became very excited when he heard about this girl. But then he asked, "How much is the bride price?"

"The father wants a hundred cattle," was the reply.

"A hundred cattle! That is all I have. How will we be able to live?" replied the young man.

"Well, make up your mind. I have to take an answer to the father soon," said the neighbor.

The young man thought, "I cannot live without this girl." So he said, "Go and tell the father that I want to marry his daughter."

So the two were married. But after they returned home, they quickly ran out of food, and the young man had to herd cattle for a neighbor to get anything to eat. What he got was not very much for a young lady who was used to eating well and living in style.

One day as the young wife was sitting outside the house, a strange man came by and was struck by her beauty. He decided to try to seduce her and sent a message to her. The young wife told him that she could not make up her mind and he would have to come back later.

Several months later, the girl's father came to visit. She was very upset because she did not have anything to feed him. But on that same day, the seducer came back. So the young wife told the seducer that she would give in to his requests if he would bring her some meat to cook for her father.

Soon the seducer returned with the meat and the girl went inside to cook it. Her husband returned, and he and her father sat down to eat and have a good time. The seducer was standing outside listening.

Soon he became angry and went inside to see what was happening. The young husband, who was hospitable, invited him in.

The young wife then brought in the meat and said, "Eat, you three fools."

"Why do you call us fools?" the three men said all together.

"Well, Father," the girl replied. "You are a fool because you sold something precious for something worthless. You had only one daughter and traded her for a hundred cattle when you already had six thousand."

"You are right," said her father. "I was a fool."

"As for you, husband," she went on. "You inherited only a hundred cattle and you went and spent them all on me, leaving us nothing to eat. You could have married another woman for ten or twenty cows. That is why you were a fool."

"And why am I a fool?" asked the seducer.

"You are the biggest fool of all. You thought you could get for one piece of meat what had been bought for a hundred cattle."

At that, the seducer ran away as fast as he could. Then the father said, "You are a wise daughter. When I get home, I will send your husband three hundred cattle so that you shall live in comfort."

INTERPRETATIONS

1. Is this tale about how *not* to make choices? Explain your answer.

2. Evaluate the daughter's role in the story. Was she wise or just practical? What is the difference?

CORRESPONDENCES

1. Review the Eliot perspective and discuss its relevance to "The Wise Daughter." Is there a conqueror in this tale? Explain.

2. Apply Anouilh's perspective to "The Wise Daughter." To what extent does it apply to the husband and the seducer? Explain.

APPLICATIONS

1. Consult a dictionary or thesaurus entry for "wisdom." Which connotations best express your associations with wisdom? Can wisdom be taught? Do you think of yourself as wise? Explain.

2. Create a portrait of someone you know or admire that you consider wise.

Apollo and Daphne

GREEK LEGEND

*Greece reached the height of its achievements and power in the fifth century
B.C. Its accomplishments in art, architecture, science, mathematics, philosophy, drama, literature, and democracy became legacies for future generations
in countries all over the world. In later centuries, Greece fell under the rule of
Rome, Turkey, and other nations. In 1829, it won independence from Turkey
and became a kingdom. A republic was formed in 1924. During World War
II, occupation by Germans, Italians, and Bulgarians was met by guerrilla
warfare against the occupying armies. Subsequent struggles led to the reestab-
lishment of the monarchy, juntas, and finally socialist government.*

DAPHNE [GREEK FOR "LAUREL"] was a wood nymph, the daughter of the
river god Peneus. She was one of those free-spirited women in mythol-
ogy who was more interested in hunting and fishing than in men. Her
father despaired that she would ever marry; he was more interested in
grandchildren than in having still more game to eat.

The god Apollo saw Daphne one day and fell instantly in love
with her. He was unable to think of anything but her and he pursued
her to no avail. Daphne was absolutely indifferent to his attentions; it
mattered not whether he was god or mortal. She also knew that relationships with gods were often complicated and even dangerous. She
was, after all, half divine, yet mortal. Finally Apollo chased her
through the forests until she was stricken with fear. There was no way
that she could outrun him, so she cried for her father to save her with
a miracle.

Suddenly, she felt her feet become rooted in the earth. She could not
move. Leaves began to sprout from her arms—she had become a living
laurel tree. The gods have a way of sorting things out of the most desperate situations, so they made the laurel tree the sacred tree of Apollo.

To this day, whether at poetry contests or athletic events, both
within the purview of Apollo, the winner is crowned with laurels.

INTERPRETATIONS

1. What is your definition of a free spirit? Do you think of yourself as
    being one? Explain.

2. Is Apollo's love for Daphne obsessive? To what extent is he responsible for his fate?

3. Consult a source on laurel trees and explain their significance with respect to Daphne.

CORRESPONDENCES

1. Review the Rilke perspective. What could Apollo have learned from it? To what extent do you agree with his point of view about solitude in relationships?

2. Review the Japanese proverbs and discuss their relevance to Apollo and Daphne.

APPLICATIONS

1. Discuss with your group the degree to which Daphne's being a free spirit conflicts with parental expectations. To what extent is this still the case? Write a summary of your conclusions.

2. What role does possessiveness often play in intimate relationships? Focus on dating perspectives from male and female members of your group and discuss the degree to which they affect attitudes toward freedom in close gender relationships.

Shrouded in Contradiction

GELAREH ASAYESH

Gelareh Asayesh was born in 1962 in Tehran, Iran. She earned a B.A. in journalism from the University of North Carolina in 1983, and from that year until 1988 she was a reporter for The Miami Herald. *She worked for* The Baltimore Sun *from 1989 to 1992, when she became a freelance writer. Her memoir* Saffron Sky: A Life Between Iran and America, *published in 1999, tells the story of her life in Iran, her immigration, and the beginning of her life in the United States. She wanted to "map the emotional landscape of the immigrant," to "retain her essential core" while becoming "something new." "Shrouded in Contradiction" was first published in* The New York Times Magazine *in 2001.*

The Islamic Republic of Iran (formerly Persia), with a population of about 67 million people, lies between the Middle East and Southeast Asia, bordered on the west by Turkey and Iraq and on the east by Pakistan. Since the Islamic Revolution of 1979 (led by Shiite Ayatollah Ruholla Khomeini) established a theocracy, the country has been ruled by a religious head, an ayatollah, although a secular president and representatives are also elected. When militants seized sixty-two Americans at the U.S. Embassy in that same year, the United States severed diplomatic relations. A more moderate president, Mohammad Khatami, elected in 1997, gave promise of improved U.S.-Iranian relations, but the current president, Mahmoud Ahmadinejad, and a crisis over nuclear power, have set back relations between the two countries.

I GREW UP WEARING THE MINISKIRT to school, the veil to the mosque. In the Tehran of my childhood, women in bright sundresses shared the sidewalk with women swathed in black. The tension between the two ways of life was palpable. As a schoolgirl, I often cringed when my bare legs got leering or contemptuous glances. Yet, at times, I long for the days when I could walk the streets of my country with the wind in my hair. When clothes were clothes. In today's Iran, whatever I wear sends a message. If it's a chador, it embarrasses my Westernized relatives. If it's a skimpy scarf, I risk being accused of stepping on the blood of the martyrs who died in the war with Iraq. Each time I return to Tehran, I wait until the last possible moment, when my plane lands on the tarmac, to don the scarf and long jacket that many Iranian women wear in lieu of a veil. To wear *hijab*—Islamic covering—is to invite contradiction. Sometimes I hate it. Sometimes I value it.

Most of the time, I don't even notice it. It's annoying, but so is wearing pantyhose to work. It ruins my hair, but so does the humidity in Florida, where I live. For many women, the veil is neither a symbol nor a statement. It's simply what they wear, as their mothers did before them. Something to dry your face with after your ablutions before prayer. A place for a toddler to hide when he's feeling shy. Even for a woman like me, who wears it with a hint of rebellion, *hijab* is just not that big a deal.

Except when it is.

"Sister, what kind of get-up is this?" a woman in black, one of a pair, asks me one summer day on the Caspian shore. I am standing in line to ride a gondola up a mountain, where I'll savor some ice cream along with vistas of sea and forest. Women in chadors stand wilting in the heat, faces gleaming with sweat. Women in makeup and clunky heels wear knee-length jackets with pants, their hair daringly exposed beneath sheer scarves.

None have been more daring than I. I've wound my scarf into a turban, leaving my neck bare to the breeze. The woman in black is a government employee paid to police public morals. "Fix your scarf at once!" she snaps.

"But I'm hot," I say.

"You're hot?" she exclaims. "Don't you think we all are?"

I start unwinding my makeshift turban. "The men aren't hot," I mutter.

Her companion looks at me in shocked reproach. "Sister, this isn't about men and women," she says, shaking her head. "This is about Islam."

I want to argue. I feel like a child. Defiant, but powerless. Burning with injustice, but also with a hint of shame. I do as I am told, feeling acutely conscious of the bare skin I am covering. In policing my sexuality, these women have made me more aware of it.

The veil masks erotic freedom, but its advocates believe *hijab* transcends the erotic—or expands it. In the West, we think of passion as a fever of the body, not the soul. In the East, Sufi poets used earthly passion as a metaphor; the beloved they celebrated was God. Where I come from, people are more likely to find delicious passion in the mosque than in the bedroom.

There are times when I feel a hint of this passion. A few years after my encounter on the Caspian, I go to the wake of a family friend. Sitting in a mosque in Mashhad, I grip a slippery black veil with one hand and a prayer book with the other. In the center of the hall, there's a stack of Koranic texts decorated with green-and-black calligraphy, a vase of white gladioluses and a large photograph of the dearly departed. Along the walls, women wait quietly.

From the men's side of the mosque, the mullah's voice rises in lament. His voice is deep and plaintive, oddly compelling. I bow my head, sequestered in my veil while at my side a community of women pray and weep with increasing abandon. I remember from girlhood this sense of being exquisitely alone in the company of others. Sometimes I have cried as well, free to weep without having to offer an explanation. Perhaps they are right, those mystics who believe that physical love is an obstacle to spiritual love; those architects of mosques who abstained from images of earthly life, decorating their work with geometric shapes that they believed freed the soul to slip from its worldly moorings. I do not aspire to such lofty sentiments. All I know is that such moments of passionate abandon, within the circle of invisibility created by the veil, offer an emotional catharsis every bit as potent as any sexual release.

Outside, the rain pours from a sullen sky. I make my farewells and walk toward the car, where my driver waits. My veil is wicking muddy water from the sidewalk. I gather up the wet and grimy folds with distaste, longing to be home, where I can cast off this curtain of cloth that gives with one hand, takes away with the other.

INTERPRETATIONS

1. In the first paragraph, Asayesh longs for the days "when clothes were clothes." What do you think she means by this statement?

2. "For many women, the veil is neither a symbol nor a statement. It's simply what they wear, as their mothers did before them." Do you think that this statement applies to Asayesh? What specific examples can you find to support your answer?

3. In the incident that occurs on the Caspian shore, a woman who is employed to "police public morals" says to Asayesh, "Sister, this isn't about men and women. This is about Islam." Asayesh then writes, "I want to argue. I feel like a child. Defiant, but powerless." What arguments do you think Asayesh would present to the woman? What do you think is the primary issue—gender or religious belief?

CORRESPONDENCES

1. Asayesh and Gary Soto ("To Be a Man") both struggle against society. To what extent are their struggles dependent upon their gender?

2. Create a conversation between Asayesh and Duncan in your journal and compare your responses with others in your group. What consensus, if any, did you reach?

APPLICATIONS

1. Was there a time in your life when your choice of clothing was in conflict with the expectations of others? Write a narrative about this event where you explain the incident and your feelings about it as it occurred. Also, include your thoughts and reflections about society and personal choice.

2. How does the clothing that men and women wear reflect society's views and expectations of them? Look through a couple of fashion magazines or watch a few music videos. In your journal, jot down what you notice about the clothing that the men and women are wearing. Now, in a formal essay, discuss similarities and differences in the ways that men and women are portrayed. What messages are presented about the roles of men and women in these visual media? What conclusions might you come to about the relationship between gender, clothing, and society? Try to include specific examples to support your views.

3. Enter a place of worship. What do you observe about the clothing that people are wearing? Is the clothing appropriate to the setting? Does the setting dictate behaviors to be followed?

   After returning from this place, try to recall specific details in your journal. Then, in class, discuss your findings with your group. What general conclusions has the group come to?

To Be a Man

GARY SOTO

Gary Soto was born April 12, 1952, in Fresno, California, to Manuel and Angie Soto, whose Mexican heritage was important in his upbringing. He graduated in 1974 from California State–Fresno, and in 1976 he received an M.A. in creative writing from the University of California at Irvine. Between 1979 and 1993 he taught English at the University of California at Berkeley, where he now lives, but he has been a full-time writer since 1992. He is the author of numerous volumes of poetry, among them The Elements of San Joaquin *(1977), a grim picture of Mexican-American life, and* Black Hair *(1985), which focuses on his friends and family. One of Soto's memoirs,* Living Up the Street: Narrative Recollections, *received a Before Columbus Foundation American Book Award in 1985. More recent publications have included a novel,* Amnesia in a Republican County *(2003), four young-adult novels (three of them in 2006 and 2007), a collection of stories,* Help Wanted *(2005), and two more collections of poems. Soto has produced a film and a libretto for the Los Angeles Opera. He also serves as Young People's Ambassador for the California Rural Legal Assistance and the United Farm Workers of America. "To Be a Man" will, if you let it, take you back to the days when you were first learning how to look for a job. What memories do you have of those days?*

HOW STRANGE IT IS to consider the dishevelled man sprawled out against a store front with the rustling noise of newspaper in his lap. Although we see him from our cars and say "poor guy," we keep speeding toward jobs, careers, and people who will open our wallets, however wide, to stuff them with money.

I wanted to be that man when I was a kid of ten or so, and told Mother how I wanted my life. She stood at the stove staring down at me, eyes narrowed, and said I didn't know what I was talking about. She buttered a tortilla, rolled it fat as a telescope, and told me to eat it outside. While I tore into my before-dinner-snack, I shook my head at my mother because I knew what it was all about. Earlier in the week (and the week before), I had pulled a lawn mower, block after block, in search of work. I earned a few quarters, but more often screen doors slapped shut with an "I'm sorry," or milky stares scared me to the next house.

I pulled my lawn mower into the housing projects that were a block from where we lived. A heavy woman with veined legs and jowls like a fat purse, said, "Boy, you in the wrong place. We poor here."

It struck me like a ball. They were poor, but I didn't even recognize them. I left the projects and tried houses with little luck, and began to wonder if they too housed the poor. If they did, I thought, then where were the rich? I walked for blocks, asking at messy houses until I was so far from home I was lost.

That day I decided to become a hobo. If it was that difficult pulling quarters from a closed hand, it would be even more difficult plucking dollars from greedy pockets. I wanted to give up, to be a nobody in thrown-away clothes, because it was too much work to be a man. I looked at my stepfather who was beaten from work, from the seventeen years that he hunched over a conveyor belt, stuffing boxes with paperback books that ran down the belt quick as rats. Home from work, he sat in his oily chair with his eyes unmoved by television, by the kids, by his wife in the kitchen beating a round steak with a mallet. He sat dazed by hard labor and bitterness yellowed his face. If his hands could have spoken to him, they would have asked to die. They were tired, bleeding like hearts from the inside.

I couldn't do the same: work like a man. I knew I had the strength to wake from an alley, walk, and eat little. I knew I could give away the life that the television asked me to believe in, and live on fruit trees and the watery soup of the Mission.

But my ambition—that little screen in the mind with good movies— projected me as a priest, then a baseball coach, then a priest again, until here I am now raking a cracker across a cheesy dip at a faculty cocktail party. I'm looking the part and living well—the car, the house, and the suits in the closet. Some days this is where I want to be. On other days I want out, such as the day I was in a committee meeting among PhDs. In an odd moment I saw them as pieces of talking meat and, like meat we pick up to examine closely at supermarkets, they were soulless, dead, and fixed with marked prices. I watched their mouths move up and down with busy words that did not connect. As they finished mouthing one sentence to start on another, they just made up words removed from their feelings.

It's been twenty years since I went door to door. Now I am living this other life that seems a dream. How did I get here? What line on my palm arched into a small fortune? I sit before students, before grade books, before other professors talking about books they've yet to write, so surprised that I'm far from that man on the sidewalk, but not so far that he couldn't wake up one day, walk a few pissy steps saying, "It's time," and embrace me for life.

INTERPRETATIONS

1. Why do you think Soto's mother responds the way she does when he announced to her that he wanted to be like the man depicted in paragraph 1?

2. Why did Soto, as a child, decide to be a hobo? What do you think of his reasoning?

3. How do you think Soto feels about how he has chosen to live his life? How do his decisions represent his vision of what it means to be a man?

CORRESPONDENCES

1. Compare the societal pressures that Soto feels as a man with those felt by Asayesh as a woman (see "Shrouded in Contradiction," page 96).

2. Fathers and sons are the subject of several texts in this chapter. After reading a couple of the following essays, what did you learn about male gender roles? What qualities are grown men supposed to have? Possible readings include Quindlen, Barone, and Chopin.

APPLICATIONS

1. What does it mean to be a "man" or a "woman"? Write a definition essay that explores just one of these terms. Be sure to provide clear examples and to use details. (Note how Soto uses descriptive language to help you to see the people he presents in his essay.)

2. What is "the life that the television asked me to believe in" (paragraph 6)?

    Watch a commercial television station for one hour. As you watch, keep a list of those assumptions and expectations (regarding social status, consumerism, ethnicity, gender roles) that are being presented to you. Remember to log commercials as well as show content.

    After you have finished viewing the show or shows, consult your list. How has life been represented on the TV screen? More specifically, what "needs" or "wants" have been presented to you?

    Give careful consideration to your observations and your thoughts about them. Then, from your list, write an essay that explains your definition of both "needs" and "wants." Use examples from your TV viewing log to support your ideas.

3. Write a dialogue of ten lines that is derived from the exchange between the ten-year-old Soto and his mother that is described in paragraph 2. Now add a third person—Soto as the grown man described in paragraphs 7 and 8—who comments upon the ongoing exchange. What impact do Soto's life experiences have upon what he says to his mother and his younger self?

4. Three primary men are presented in Soto's essay: the man described in paragraph 1, the father described in paragraph 5, and the man (Soto) described in paragraph 7. From Soto's descriptions, draw a picture of each man, showing how each one illustrates what it is "to be a man." (Alternatively, you might cut out photos from a magazine or take the photographs yourself.) Share your drawings with your classmates, letting them explain the definitions that they interpret from your works.

Man-Made Misery

THOMAS M. COLICINO

Thomas M. Colicino would like to thank all the educators, families, friends, and others that inspire and encourage his writing. Mr. Colicino is currently enrolled in Queensborough Community College, where he was majoring in science and mathematics but is now proud to be discovering where his true talents and interests lie. Mr. Colicino is reassured in learning that there is a Nobel Prize in Literature.

WE MET ONE AFTERNOON on a lush green hill in our sophomore year of high school and talked about our classes, teachers and mutual friends. I was immediately fond of her laugh and cute inflections in her voice. She made me happy and inspired confidence; I mean she was laughing, not running away and I was charmed when she remembered me in the halls.

Come senior year, both of us had enrolled in the same elective science course. Katherine sat right behind me. I am not one to be in a rush to do anything and as I packed my things after every class, she would be there. In several weeks time our conversation would carry on until we were leaving the building. The next evolution found us spending our free time together in the neighborhood diner. And just as I lit the candle on her birthday muffin, wishing that our friendship would soon wither and die, she flinched amidst the fireworks. She asked me bluntly, "You do know I have a boyfriend?" "Yeah," I lied, "We're just friends. Happy birthday, Katherine." Becoming embarrassed at my own emotions for her on her birthday made me feel foolish for wanting so badly something I couldn't have. Why she never mentioned him puzzled me, and it didn't take long for me to completely forget about him.

I met her boyfriend at one of the city's fundraising walks. It seemed Katherine and I would be "just friends" forever. Yet, we walked most of the walk together, without him. A month later Katherine and I were dancing together in Lincoln Center. I got tired, found my head in her lap as we rested beside the fountain—and before anyone throws up—I'll just say I kissed her. Now I was the boyfriend, a guardian, a confidant, a romantic rocker with an all access pass.

We became a couple blessed by bountiful brunches. Rummaging through thrift shops. Holding hands. Taking walks. Having those casual talks that turn into flirtatious flights. A summer of movies, museums, pancakes, parks, picnics, and a ride on the Circle Line proved to me the wonders of romance. Until the school bells rang, I to my CUNY and she to her SUNY.[1] Though we made no pact, no binding commitment to each other.

I liked Katherine, but she was my first and only. My logic holds that there are many women in the world. I am curious. Sometimes a girl on the train was a little sexier. Once a girl I knew and liked before showed an interest after Katherine and I were involved. Sometimes I just couldn't deal with the idea of commitment. A flurry of "what ifs?" descended and I grew insecure. "What if we couldn't afford to visit each other?" "What if talking on the phone was languishing?" "What if either of us had a change in heart?" So in the spirit of being loving and considerate I "let her go" and suggested we see other people. She agreed to an open relationship.

I visited Katherine once upstate and as fulfilling as that visit was we proceeded to fall out of touch for nearly a month. She eventually came to visit me only to act in a strange and distant manner. Apparently she had found another man to fill my space and hers. I was crushed and angry though she hadn't cheated in any way. The elation I initially felt of having someone I really wanted was marred by the implication that I wasn't fit to keep her. I feared I was irrevocably inadequate.

Does having a girlfriend get any less complicated? Had I asked for too much? Had I not done enough? Would it have ended anyway? I have tried to let it roll off my back. I am young and now I'm single, but I miss having a girlfriend. I knew as I first met her that Katherine could keep me happy, yet we didn't have the devotion it takes to stick together. I cut short our sizzling summer romance. And though I have met other girls, contentment has never graced my mind and I truly miss being happy.

INTERPRETATIONS

1. Where in the essay do you think the narrator first reveals his romantic feelings for Katherine? What makes you think so?

2. If this essay had a moral, what would it be? Create a moral to this story and then explain it fully in a few paragraphs.

3. Colicino writes in the final paragraph, "I knew as I first met her that Katherine could keep me happy, yet we didn't have the devotion it takes to stick together." This sentence provides one explanation as to why the relationship did not last. What others can you find in the essay?

[1]CUNY, the City University of New York, contains twenty-three institutions within New York City. SUNY, the State University of New York, is comprised of sixty-four campuses mostly outside NYC.

CORRESPONDENCES

1. Read the final paragraph of Ginzburg's essay (page 131) where she reminisces about "that one evening he walked me back to the *pensione* where I was living; we walked together along the *Via Nazionale*." How might this paragraph relate to Colicino's narrator's relationship with Katherine? If he and Katherine *had* stayed together, how well does Ginzburg's relationship with her husband predict what might have happened to them? Explain your reasons for your beliefs.

2. How do you feel about what happens between Calixta and Alcée on that stormy day (see page 134)? How do these responses relate to what you think about what happens between Katherine and Colicino's narrator? To what extent do you think gender motivates the actions of the people in both readings? Explain your answers fully.

APPLICATIONS

1. People end relationships for a variety of reasons. Conduct ten interviews with friends, classmates, family members, or other people you know to find out why they have ended a relationship (or had one ended). Along with each person's response to your questions, record the gender of your interviewee. With the data you have collected, create a pie chart to illustrate your findings. (Remember to record gender as part of the description for each part of your pie. To learn more about pie charts—what they do and how you can make them, check the website below.) Next, write an essay explaining your findings. You might devote each body paragraph to explaining fully each of the primary reasons for ending relationships that you have discovered (the largest slices of your pie). What generalizations might you make about how gender influences the reasons for a breakup?

   http://nces.ed.gov/nceskids/graphing/Classic/pie.asp

   (Yes, it's for kids, but it's a good site all the same! Remember to check the JPEG option at the bottom of the graph creator tool to print your completed chart. Also, be sure to select a "Large" or "Xtra-Large" chart.)

2. Dear _____ .

   As the writer of an advice column, what would you say to both the young man and young woman depicted in Colicino's essay? When writing your columns (one for each person), remember to be honest, tactful, and brief. Now examine the two advice columns you have written. To what extent do you think your gender has influenced your responses? Write a brief journal entry that presents and explains your answer to this question.

Why Are Gay Men So Feared?

DENNIS ALTMAN

Born in 1943 in Sydney, Australia, Dennis Altman is a Reader in Politics at La Trobe University in Melbourne, Australia. Among his works are AIDS in the Mind *(1986) and* Paper Ambassadors *(1991). The excerpt from the article below appeared in the* New Internationalist *in November 1989.*

GAY MEN ARE THE VICTIMS of insults, prejudice, abuse, violence, sometimes murder. Why are gay men hated by so many other men? Some maintain that homosexuality is unnatural or a threat to the family. But celibacy is also unnatural, yet nuns and priests are not regularly attacked. And there is also a good case to be made that homosexuality actually *strengthens* the family by liberating some adults from child-bearing duties and so increasing the pool of adults available to look after children.

But the real objection to homosexuality (and lesbianism) is undoubtedly more deep-seated: It is threatening because it seems to challenge the conventional roles governing a person's sex, and the female and male roles in society. The assertion of homosexual identity clearly challenges the apparent naturalness of gender roles.

Men are particularly prone to use anger and violence against those they think are undermining their masculinity. And it is here that we can find at least some of the roots of homophobia and gay-bashing.

As Freud understood, most societies are built upon a set of relationships between men: Most powerful institutions like parliaments and business corporations are male-dominated. And this "male bonding" demands a certain degree of sexual sublimation.

In many societies, the links between men are much stronger than the relations that link them to women. But these bonds are social rather than individual, and for this reason need to be strictly governed. Armies, for example, depend upon a very strong sense of male solidarity, though this does not allow for too close an emotional tie between any *specific* pair of men.

Thus the most extreme homophobia is often found among tightly knit groups of men, who need to deny any sexual component to their bonding as well as boost their group solidarity by turning violently on "fags" or "queers," who are defined as completely alien. This is a phenomenon found among teenage gangs, policemen, and soldiers.

A particularly prominent example of this was Germany's Nazi Party, which shortly after coming to power purged those of its members who were tempted to turn the hypermasculinity of Nazism into an excuse for overt homosexual behavior.

Many observers of sexual violence have argued that the most virulent queer-basher is attacking the homosexual potential in himself—a potential that he has learned to suppress. Because homosexuality is "un-masculine," those who struggle with feelings of homosexuality (often unacknowledged) will be particularly tempted to resolve them through "masculine" expressions of violence. In court cases involving violence against gay men, the idea of preserving one's male honor is often pleaded as a defense.

Homophobia has effects that go far beyond those individuals against whom it is directed. Like racism and sexism, it is an expression of hatred that harms the perpetrator as well as the victim; the insecurities, fears, and sexual hang-ups that lead young men to go out looking for "fags" to beat up are dangerous to the entire society.

Those societies that are best able to accept homosexuals are also societies that are able to accept assertive women and gentle men, and they tend to be less prone to the violence produced by hypermasculinity.

INTERPRETATIONS

1. To what extent do you agree with Altman that homosexuality and lesbianism are feared because they challenge "the apparent naturalness of gender roles"?

2. What, according to Altman, is the connection between homosexuality and violence?

CORRESPONDENCES

1. Review Sullivan's perspective and discuss its application to Altman's essay.

2. Review Weinberg's perspective on homophobia and discuss its application to Altman's essay. How does it support or contradict Altman's point of view?

APPLICATIONS

1. Discuss with your group the question posed in Altman's title. To what extent do you agree that both homosexuals and lesbians are feared?

2. Review paragraph 8 of Altman's essay and write a persuasive essay agreeing or disagreeing with his point of view. You may include your emotional as well as your intellectual responses to his thesis.

3. Films such as *Angels in America, My Own Private Idaho,* and *Suddenly Last Summer* explore sexual difference. Select one and write a journal entry on your responses.

Gay

ANNA QUINDLEN

Anna Quindlen (b. 1953 in Philadelphia) graduated from Barnard College in New York City in 1974. She was a reporter for The New York Post *from 1974 to 1977, and between 1977 and 1995 she held a variety of positions at* The New York Times. *She has received many awards, among them the Pulitzer Prize in 1992. For ten years after 1999 she wrote a biweekly column for* Newsweek. *She has written five novels:* Object Lessons *(1991);* One True Thing *(1994), made into a movie in 1998 starring Meryl Streep and William Hurt;* Black and Blue *(1998), a selection of Oprah Winfrey's book club and made into a movie starring Anthony La Paglia and Mary Stuart Masterson, which aired on CBS;* Blessings *(2002), and* Rise and Shine *(2006). Quindlen is the author of the nonfiction* Living Out Loud *(1988), from which the following essay comes,* How Reading Changed My Life *(1998), A* Short Guide to a Happy Life *(2000), and* Being Perfect *(2005). She holds honorary doctorates from Dartmouth College, Denison University, Moravian College, Mount Holyoke College, Smith College, and Stevens Institute of Technology. Married and the mother of three children, she lives in New York City. Quindlen told an interviewer that she is most "at home in the rocky emotional terrain of marriage, parenthood, secret desires and self-doubts." What evidence of these interests and qualities do you find in "Gay"?*

WHEN HE WENT HOME LAST YEAR, he realized for the first time that he would be buried there, in the small, gritty industrial town he had loathed for as long as he could remember. He looked out the window of his bedroom and saw the siding on the house next door and knew that he was trapped, as surely as if he had never left for the city. Late one night, before he was to go back to his own apartment, his father tried to have a conversation with him, halting and slow, about drug use and the damage it could do to your body. At that moment he understood that it would be more soothing to his parents to think that he was a heroin addict than that he was a homosexual.

This is part of the story of a friend of a friend of mine. She went to his funeral not too long ago. The funeral home forced the family to pay extra to embalm him. Luckily, the local paper did not need to print the cause of death. His parents' friends did not ask what killed him, and his parents didn't talk about it. He had AIDS. His parents had figured out at the same time that he was dying and that he slept with men. He tried to talk to them about his illness; he didn't want to discuss his homosexuality. That would have been too hard for them all.

Never have the lines between sex and death been so close, the chasm between parent and child so wide. His parents hoped almost until the end that some nice girl would "cure" him. They even hinted broadly that my friend might be that nice girl. After the funeral, as she helped with the dishes in their small kitchen with the window onto the backyard, she lost her temper at the subterfuge and said to his mother: "He was gay. Why is that more terrible than that he is dead?" The mother did not speak, but raised her hands from the soapy water and held them up as though to ward off the words.

I suppose this is true of many parents. For some it is simply that they think homosexuality is against God, against nature, condemns their sons to hell. For others it is something else, more difficult to put into words. It makes their children too different from them. We do not want our children to be too different—so different that they face social disapprobation and ostracism, so different that they die before we do. His parents did not know any homosexuals, or at least they did not believe they did. His parents did not know what homosexuals were like.

They are like us. They are us. Isn't that true? And yet, there is a difference. Perhaps mothers sometimes have an easier time accepting this. After all, they must accept early on that there are profound sexual differences between them and their sons. Fathers think their boys will be basically like them. Sometimes they are. And sometimes, in a way that comes to mean so much, they are not.

I have thought of this a fair amount because I am the mother of sons. I have managed to convince myself that I love my children so much that nothing they could do would turn me against them, or away from them, that nothing would make me take their pictures off the bureau and hide them in a drawer. A friend says I am fooling myself, that I would at least be disappointed and perhaps distressed if, like his, my sons' sexual orientation was not hetero. Maybe he's right. There are some obvious reasons to feel that way. If the incidence of AIDS remains higher among homosexuals than among heterosexuals, it would be one less thing they could die of. If societal prejudices remain constant, it would be one less thing they could be ostracized for.

But this I think I know: I think I could live with having a son who was homosexual. But it would break my heart if he was homosexual and felt that he could not tell me so, felt that I was not the kind of mother who could hear that particular truth. That is a kind of death, too, and it kills both your life with your child and all you have left after the funeral: the relationship that can live on inside you, if you have nurtured it.

In the days following his death, the mother of my friend's friend mourned the fact that she had known little of his life, had not wanted to know. "I spent too much time worrying about what he was," she said. Not who. What. And it turned out that there was not enough time, not with almost daily obituaries of people barely three decades old, dead of a disease she had never heard of when she first wondered about the kind of friends her boy had and why he didn't date more.

It reminded me that often we take our sweet time dealing with the things that we do not like about our children: the marriage we could not accept, the profession we disapproved of, the sexual orientation we may hate and fear. Sometimes we vow that we will never, never accept those things. The stories my friend told me about the illness, the death, the funeral and, especially, about the parents reminded me that sometimes we do not have all the time we think to make our peace with who our children are. It reminded me that "never" can last a long, long time, perhaps much longer than we intended, deep in our hearts, when we first invoked its terrible endless power.

INTERPRETATIONS

1. Why do you think the gay man's parents would prefer "to think that he was a heroin addict rather than that he was a homosexual"?
2. To what extent do you agree with Quindlen that parents are reluctant to accept children who are too different from them?
3. What is Quindlen's supposition about being the mother of a homosexual? Do you agree with her? Why or why not?

CORRESPONDENCES

1. Compare and contrast societal attitudes toward sexual preference in the texts by Quindlen and Altman.
2. Is Quindlen seeking only to inform her audience or does she wish also to persuade? Compare her purpose and tone with that of Altman.

APPLICATIONS

1. Imagine yourself as the young gay man and write a letter to your parents explaining your sexual preference.

2. Discuss with your group the implications of AIDS for your generation and its effects on gender relationships and on individual and family lives.

3. The film *Longtime Companion* portrays the responses of a group of friends confronting the reality of AIDS. Rent the videotape and write a review of the film, including the characters' reactions to their situation.

Why Do We Hate Our Bodies?

GILLIANNE N. DUNCAN

Gillianne Duncan enrolled in Queensborough Community College in 2000 but because of family and financial issues had to drop out. She grew up in a single mother household and her mother remarried when she was ten years old. She has four sisters and four nieces of varying ages and is disgusted by the images her nieces are surrounded by. Her co-workers and oldest niece were the inspirations for her essay as she listened to the way they talked about their bodies.

Gillianne is currently completing her A.A. and intends to pursue her B.A. and possibly a teaching career.

ALL WEEK LONG I HAVE BEEN hearing women complain about their bodies when I asked them how much *they* liked themselves. One of my co-workers I believe had noticed a flaw in every part of her body just about, and then got mad when my co-workers and I told her she was beautiful but she just did not notice it. It was scary and sad to see a beautiful young woman say and act the way she did, but we all understood, to some degree, because we were all her. Everybody had a flaw that he or she wanted changed but when asked why they wanted the change they said so that they could look better. When I asked better than who or what nobody had an answer they just wanted to look better. So I asked if they hated their bodies and all said no, but after sitting and listening I heard all my co-workers talking about going to the gym, dieting, surgeries they would have if they had money, and even starvation. But they all claim not to hate their bodies. How can you love something you treat so badly? If your body and you were married, you would go to jail for domestic violence.

In the article "Why Don't We Like the Human Body" by Barbara Ehrenreich, she tries to explain or bring to light the love-hate relationship with the horror movies and the human body. She compares our addiction to exercise and dieting to some crazy serial killer that hacks people up and eats them or plays with their rotting bodies. Ehrenreich also points out our fascination or need to see this kind of violence toward the human body. But I wonder what her thoughts would be if she ever saw the show *Nip/Tuck*; to me that is worse than any horror flick. Then there is the makeover show *Extreme Makeover*, where every week they pick two friends that feel that they are homely; they then take them away from their families for months and give them all the plastic surgeries they want and then when it is over a big party to show off their new look. They give them complete makeovers, changing their hair, teeth, bodies and of course attitude. Everything is done with surgery. They give the people liposuction, tummy tucks, breast implants, collagen injection, Botox, porcelain veneers, face lifts, and whatever else they feel they need, or that the show feels that the person needs to have done.

For the people at home the producers have decided that it would be more interesting if we saw every step of the transformation from hating the old body to loving the new and improved one that was built. We get to see every procedure, all implants and injections and removals, all dental work and every chemical peel, we at home get to see what the friends cannot see because there are no mirrors allowed until the very end of the show.

It is a horror show. They pull two victims in, then they beat them with images of how they could look, then they cut them up and add foreign objects to them. Then they abuse them some more, because now that they are healing from the many surgeries, they are starved, made to "work out" (a torture technique very popular nowadays), and then dressed up and put on parade like a circus monkey. It is horrible. And no body is free from ridicule. Last week (October 20, 2006), they had on the show a deaf man and his best friend, who was a burn victim with scars all over her body, and both of them got what some would call "the works." (Yes, the handicapped are not safe from the power of mass media.) Between the two of them they had everything nipped and/or tucked. At the end of the show not only do they recap the surgeries but, they also tell you the price, just to say you can look like this for only fifteen thousand dollars or monthly installments of two hundred and fifty dollars (and yes we do take Discover).

Extreme Makeover is like the show *This Old House* with Bob Vila. The same concept, take out some walls and add some paint, a few nails, drywall, a little plaster and perfect old into new. It might not be completely fair to compare a plastic surgery show to a fix it yourself show, mainly because they did not do it themselves, but it is a horror show, and I blame the media for its creation. Without the media's constant need to make people feel bad about themselves shows like *Nip/Tuck*, *Extreme Makeover*, and *Dr. 90210* would not exist. But they do, as a reminder that we are not perfect, these shows reinforce the ideas and beliefs of hatred towards the body. Mostly and without concern for the female body. Why must the media attack women so much? My answer, the world is run by men and a small amount of over achieving women with low self-esteem. Okay, so women are supposed to be weak and helpless making them easy prey, but what about men? Would not a man make a good victim? They are stronger, faster and considered to be more rational, making for a better hunt. So if guys make better prey would they also not make better subjects for shows about makeovers? The producers of the show *The Swan* should make a male version where they take fifteen average looking guys and give them implants and liposuction, torture them mentally, starve them, place them on a crazy exercise plan and then place them on parade to be judged to see which of the men are the most handsome. But that will never happen, there will be episodes where men will get surgery and there will be episodes where men will be subjected to horrible treatments in order to obtain better ratings or to show that some shows are equal in their selection of victims, but there will never be an entire show or season where men are treated the same way as women.

I am not a big fan of horror movies nor am I a fan of makeover shows. I believe both to be sick and demeaning towards human life, but the only difference is that a horror movie is not real. They are only there to scare and shake you; they are a form of entertainment for those who like to be scared. Makeover shows are based around real people that think very little of themselves, generally people that are not very beautiful but are far from being absolutely horrible looking. These shows like many other forms of media never address the real issues or point people into a positive direction that will lead them away from self-hate. If we thought of our bodies as a loved one, we would take care of them better. Like any great relationship it takes work and compromise. If we stopped trying to look like Barbie and Ken dolls and stopped listening and allowing the media to tell us that we are fat, ugly and our bodies are our enemies, maybe we will make a new friend or find a lover in the body we were given. If we cannot we will always just be prey for the crazy sicko murderer that wants to see us hacked up or that greasy plastic surgeon that only wants to dissect our bodies and transform us into something not human.

INTERPRETATIONS

1. At the end of her first paragraph, Duncan writes, "If your body and you were married, you would go to jail for domestic violence." What do you think she means by this statement? Why do you agree or disagree with it?

2. According to Duncan, why do people hate their bodies? To what extent do you agree with her perceptions?

3. In paragraph 5, Duncan addresses gender in the selection of subjects for the television shows that she has described. Why do you think that females, rather than males, are most often chosen for these shows? What does Duncan believe?

CORRESPONDENCES

1. How are the television shows that Duncan discusses similar to horror movies? How does what Duncan describes relate to what Stephen King presents in his essay "Why We Crave Horror Movies"? (Chapter 8)

2. Duncan writes about how gender is the primary consideration in the selection of subjects for television shows like *Nip/Tuck* and *Extreme Makeover* and that these shows contribute to the problems women face. Soto informs us that his concepts of masculinity were also shaped by television shows. Given what society expects of them, which gender has a tougher time?

APPLICATIONS

1. What qualities would your dream partner possess?

    Create an equation that takes into account such aspects as personality, emotional makeup, and physical characteristics. Try to compute a mathematical formula such as $a + b + c + \ldots = x$ where a, b, and c stand for personal qualities and characteristics (e.g., *patience, understanding, generosity, intellect, curiosity, musical ability, physical strength, adventurousness* . . .) and x equals "*the perfect partner.*" Where is physical beauty in your equation? What does its location tell you about the value you place upon it?

2. Scan the covers of several popular magazines. What general conclusions can you make about the physical traits of those people who appear in the photographs? Write an analysis essay that examines the meaning of beauty in America.

3. Most likely, you have heard someone say, "Beauty is only skin deep." In view of Duncan's essay, do you think that we have gone too far as a society in what we will do to acquire beauty? Write an essay that articulates your response to this question. Like Duncan, provide plenty of specific examples to back up your views. In addition, in a second draft of your work, pay careful attention to the exact words you use to maximize your impact. Apply images and connotative (charged) language to increase the appeal your essay will have for a reader.

The Gravity of Mark Buehrle

JASON BARONE

Jason Barone (b. 1982) was born in Queens, New York, and at age four moved to Canada. He lived in Oakville, Ontario, for fifteen years before returning to New York. He is currently pursuing his B.A. in Media Studies at Hunter College and hopes to become a sportswriter for a major publication or for the Anaheim Angels. As you read about Barone's expectations of his father, compare them with your idea about what a father should be.

I LIVE IN PARADISE as well as Pandemonium. I grew up in the beautiful town of Oakville, which lies only a 30-minute car ride west of Toronto. During my elementary years my life was a much younger version of *Everybody Loves Raymond*. In fact, when you look closely, you will find a great deal of similarities between the fictional Barones on that show and the real life Barones in my family. During high school I attended Appleby College, which was a private high school that backs onto Lake Ontario. The old red brick school buildings that spread throughout the campus and our quaint little chapel complete with stained glass windows could make you believe that life just could not get any better. My house was part of a collection of houses in the "Fairway Hills" community that slowly crept onto the Glen Abby golf course. For those of you who watch the PGA, you have probably seen my house in the background when the Canadian Open is played.

Over the years my friends have more or less stayed the same. The only real change with them has been the setting for where we hung out: from the portable steps to the dining hall to now at the downtown pub, The King's Arm's. It would all sound like paradise if not for the fact that five years ago my parents got divorced.

This heart-crushing news was delivered to family and friends in January 1998. I found out in December 1997, just as Christmas Eve passed into Christmas. To no surprise, Christmas has turned from an exciting time into nothing. I overcompensate for this by always wanting to have the tree, the lights, and our *Alvin and the Chipmunks Christmas* CD all roaring at full force a few weeks before Christmas. My guess is that I do this so that my mother, younger brother, and sister are too distracted to see how empty my eyes are.

We had come down from Canada to visit my Mom's side of the family and were staying with an uncle in New Jersey. It was on the ride back to Jersey when my brother, sister, and I had all fallen asleep in the back of my Dad's Jeep. I had awakened, but my eyes for some reason had not opened; it had never happened before, and it's never happened since. To be truthful, I don't know how long I was up, I just remember the fighting. Everything was "discussed." Have you ever cried while frantically trying to keep motionless and expressionless? It's like a shiver that doesn't end. My parents still think I was asleep the whole time.

After that, I found myself praying every day, sometimes even multiple times. A sense of doom had overcome me and I was reaching out to the one person who might be able to help save my family. This went on for about a month until one Saturday afternoon while I was talking on the phone with my friend Patrick. I've heard how when bad news is delivered, the recipient seems to know what is going to be said before a word is spoken. Personally, I never bought into that. However, when my mother—in a calm and monotonous tone—said "Tell your friend you'll call him back, I need to tell you something," I immediately knew.

I have never received the Eucharist since.

• • •

"Did you talk to your mother?"
"Yes."
"OK, well."
"Did you cheat on her?"
"Yes."
I still wish that I had slammed the phone down at that moment; something to put him in his place. After my mom had told me, we sat there in silence for what felt like ten minutes (in truth it was closer to ten seconds). It was during that time that I was screaming at myself to keep composed, for Mommy. Eventually, I broke down. I had not even been on the job for two minutes and already I broke down; how was I going to do this for years after?

After a divorce most children and their fathers are not able to maintain a close relationship as the years pass. By the time most of these children are young adults, they often have little or no emotional intimacy left with their father. When they do talk, write, or get together—which is not often—too many of these fathers and their young adult children feel uncomfortable and emotionally distant. Their relationship has often dwindled into a fairly superficial one—more like a distant uncle who knows as little about the children's present lives as they know about his. Usually there is not animosity or resentment as much as indifference, awkwardness, and an underlying anxiety about what to say or do around each other. But for other young adults and their fathers, the lingering animosity and pain related to the parents' divorce continues to drive a wedge between them (Nielsen).

It was then that I decided I needed a new role model because I could no longer look at my dad in awe. I now shake my head while I let out a big sigh. Before the divorce, my dad and I used to really have something special. He came to all my baseball games and the majority of my practices. He himself had been all state in baseball and he was able to teach me things about the game that many kids didn't know. When we went to Blue Jays games, he always pointed out things like positioning, stance, and vision. Whenever I had a question about anything, he always had the answer. Now to most this may seem boring, but I couldn't get enough of it. I gorged myself on baseball, and he was my chef. In the years since, it became a big deal if we had a conversation that was longer than a few syllables. Some days I could go through a whole conversation with little more than a few low hums of acknowledgment to whatever he said. It became apparent that unless we were talking about sports, we would end up fighting. Yet whenever he called, there was a private joy inside of me. Knives were flying at my mother's back from all directions.

My father has since moved to Cleveland, and while we are now able to get along it's more of a friendly relationship than that of a father and son. His words no longer carry any weight.

There are times when I miss my dad. I remember once I was at my best friend's house, and he, his dad, and I were standing around the kitchen talking and joking around. My friend told his dad "You're not so tough now that I'm as tall as you." So as one could imagine, this had to be proved, and a friendly wrestling match ensued. As I watched my friend embarrass himself, I found myself envious because it was things like this that I realized I was unable to experience. Every once in a while, one of my friends would tell a funny story that they remember about my dad. I would nod and give a half-hearted smile, but it didn't matter any more. It had all been tarnished.

Last summer I visited him in Cleveland, and we had decided to take a little road trip to Detroit to see the Tigers play the White Sox. In the bottom of the first, we saw the White Sox pitcher take the mound. A few of his season's statistics flashed on the scoreboard under his name, Mark Buehrle. "Is he any good?" The question took me by surprise, more so when I looked over to see my dad looking up at me the way I used to do to him when I was younger. I rattled out an answer, but I could not get over the question. Wasn't *I* supposed to be asking *him* that? For five years before that, we rarely spoke. Silence had reversed our roles.

• • •

WORKS CITED

Nielsen, Linda. "College Aged Students With Divorced Parents: Facts and Fiction." *College Student Journal* 33.4 (1999): 543–73.

INTERPRETATIONS

1. What associations do you have with the words "paradise" and "pandemonium"? What effect does Barone achieve by juxtaposing them in the first sentence?
2. Why does Barone focus on his responses to at least six Christmases after the divorce of his parents?
3. Throughout the essay Barone inserts short, objective, declarative statements such as "I have never received the Eucharist since" to reflect his subjective states. Find at least two others and discuss what they reveal about his emotional responses to the divorce.
4. What is the effect of including Nielsen's citation in his essay? Which of the possible responses that Nielsen cites best parallels Barone's?
5. Characterize Barone's relationship with his father before the divorce. How does it change? Does he judge his father too harshly? Why or why not?

CORRESPONDENCES

1. According to Yevtushenko's perspective, "not people die but worlds die in them." Although Barone's father did not literally die, how did his unfaithfulness alter his son's world? To what extent do you empathize with his reaction? Explain.
2. Analyze with your group the thematic and symbolic implications of the titles of Barone's and Soto's texts.

APPLICATIONS

1. Assume the role of Barone's father and write an essay imagining how he would explain his unfaithfulness, his emotional reactions to the changes in their relationship, and the reversal of roles that occurs at the end of the essay.
2. If you *really* wanted to get to know someone, what questions would you ask of that person to learn about him or her?

    Think carefully about questions that would provide little information and those that would yield essential facts and insights.

Now, make up a list of the five questions you think are most important to ask. Next, pair up with a classmate who you do not know very well and ask that person your five questions. Be sure to take notes as your questions are answered! After you have asked your questions, reverse the process. After all five questions have been asked and answered by both you and your classmate, separate from each other and use your notes to create a "character sketch." (Perhaps the first thing you might do is change the name of the person you interviewed to preserve his or her privacy.) When creating your sketch, what information will you include and what will you leave out? What information might you manipulate to make your "character" more interesting?

He and I

NATALIA GINZBURG

Natalia Ginzburg (née Levi) was born in Palermo, Sicily, in 1916 and died in Rome in 1991. A prolific novelist, essayist, and playwright, her literary works are renowned for their honesty and integrity. During World War II her family was placed under house arrest by the anti-Semitic fascist regime in Italy (Ginzburg's father was Jewish), and her husband, the Jewish publisher and political activist Leone Ginzburg, was tortured and murdered by the Nazis for running an underground newspaper. She married again in 1950 to Gabriele Baldini, a musicologist and professor of English Literature. Her relationship with Baldini is one of the central themes of the essay below. "He and I" is part of a collection of personal essays published by Ginzburg under the title, The Little Virtues *(1962). Many of Ginzburg's personal essays reveal to us that much of what we learn about life is found in the familiar surroundings of home and neighborhood, in our relationships with others, in the everyday world we all experience. Ginzburg's writing teaches us that within life's little virtues sometimes we find the grand ones. All we need to do is take them to heart when we find them.*

HE ALWAYS FEELS HOT. I always feel cold. In the summer when it is really hot he does nothing but complain about how hot he feels. He is irritated if he sees me put a jumper on in the evening.

He speaks several languages well; I do not speak any well. He manages—in his own way—to speak even the languages that he doesn't know.

He has an excellent sense of direction. I have none at all. After one day in a foreign city he can move about in it as thoughtlessly as a butterfly. I get lost in my own city; I have to ask directions so that I can get back home again. He hates asking directions; when we go by car to a town we don't know he doesn't want to ask directions and tells me to look at the map. I don't know how to read maps and I get confused by all the little red circles and he loses his temper.

He loves the theatre, painting, music, especially music. I do not understand music at all, painting doesn't mean much to me and I get bored at the theatre. I love and understand one thing in the world and that is poetry.

He loves museums, and I will go if I am forced to but with an unpleasant sense of effort and duty. He loves libraries and I hate them.

123

He loves travelling, unfamiliar foreign cities, restaurants. I would like to stay at home all the time and never move.

All the same I follow him on all his journeys. I follow him to museums, to churches, to the opera. I even follow him to concerts, where I fall asleep.

Because he knows the conductors and the singers, after the performance is over he likes to go and congratulate them. I follow him down long corridors lined with the singers' dressing-rooms and listen to him talking to people dressed as cardinals and kings.

He is not shy; I am shy. Occasionally however I have seen him be shy. With the police when they come over to the car armed with a notebook and pencil. Then he is shy, thinking he is in the wrong.

And even when he doesn't think he is in the wrong. I think he has a respect for established authority. I am afraid of established authority, but he isn't. He respects it. There is a difference. When I see a policeman coming to fine me I immediately think he is going to haul me off to prison. He doesn't think about prison; but out of respect, he becomes shy and polite.

During the Montesi trial,[1] because of his respect for established authority, we had very violent arguments.

He likes tagliatelle, lamb, cherries, red wine. I like minestrone, bread soup, omelletes, green vegetables.

He often says I don't understand anything about food, that I am like a great strong fat friar—one of those friars who devour soup made from greens in the darkness of their monasteries; but he, oh he is refined and has a sensitive palate. In restaurants he makes long inquiries about the wines; he has them bring two or three bottles then looks at them and considers the matter, and slowly stokes his beard.

There are certain restaurants in England where the waiter goes through a little ritual; he pours some wine into a glass so that the customer can test whether he likes it or not. He used to hate this ritual and always prevented the waiter from carrying it out by taking the bottle from him. I used to argue with him about this and say that you should let people carry out their prescribed tasks.

And in the same way he never lets the usherette at the cinema direct him to his seat. He immediately gives her a tip but dashes off to a completely different place from the one she shows him with her torch.

---

[1]A notorious homicide case that took place in Italy during the early 1950s, and the prime suspect in the murder was the son of then Italian premier Mario Scelba. The case was postwar Italy's biggest political scandal and nearly brought down Scelba's clerico-capitalist government.

At the cinema he likes to sit very close to the screen. If we go with friends and they look for seats a long way from the screen, as most people do, he sits by himself in the front row. I can see well whether I am close to the screen or far away from it, but when we are with friends I stay with them out of politeness; all the same it upsets me because I could be next to him two inches from the screen, and when I don't sit next to him he gets annoyed with me.

We both love the cinema, and we are ready to see almost any kind of film at almost any time of day. But he knows the history of the cinema in great detail; he remembers old directors and actors who have disappeared and been forgotten long ago, and he is ready to travel miles into the most distant suburbs in search of some ancient silent film in which an actor appears—perhaps just for a few seconds—whom he affectionately associates with memories of his early childhood. I remember one Sunday afternoon in London; somewhere in the distant suburbs on the edge of the countryside they were showing a film from the 1930s, about the French Revolution, which he had seen as a child, and in which a famous actress of that time appeared for a moment or two. We set off by car in search of the street, which was a very long way off; it was raining, there was a fog, and we drove for hour after hour through identical suburbs, between rows of little grey houses, gutters and railings; I had the map on my knees and I couldn't read it and he lost his temper; at last, we found the cinema and sat in the completely deserted auditorium. But after a quarter of an hour, immediately after the brief appearance of the actress who was so important to him, he already wanted to go.

I on the other hand, after seeing so many streets, wanted to see how the film ended. I don't remember whether we did what he wanted or what I wanted; probably what he wanted, so that we left after a quarter of an hour, also because it was late—though we had to set off early in the afternoon it was already time for dinner. But when I begged him to tell me how the film ended I didn't get a very satisfactory answer; because, he said, the story wasn't all that important, the only thing that mattered was those few moments, that actress's curls, gestures, profile.

I never remember actors' names, and as I am not good at remembering faces it is often difficult for me to recognize even the most famous of them. This infuriates him; his scorn increases as I ask him whether it was this one or that one; "You don't mean to tell me," he says, "you don't mean to tell me that you didn't recognize William Holden!"[2]

---

[2]World-famous movie actor who starred in many films from the 1940s through the 1960s such as *Our Town, The Bridge on the River Kwai,* and *Stalag 17,* for which he won the Academy Award for Best Actor.

And in fact I didn't recognize William Holden. All the same, I love the cinema too; but although I have been seeing films for years I haven't been able to provide myself with any sort of cinematic education. But he has made an education of it for himself and he does this with whatever attracts his curiosity; I don't know how to make myself an education out of anything, even those things that I love best in my life; they stay with me as scattered images, nourishing my life with memories and emotions but without filling the void, the desert of my education.

He tells me I have no curiosity, but this is not true. I am curious about a few, a very few things. And when I have got to know them I retain scattered impressions of them, or the cadence of a phrase, or a word. But my world, in which these completely unrelated (unless in some secret fashion unbeknown to me) impressions and cadences rise to the surface, is a sad, barren place. His world, on the other hand, is green and populous and richly cultivated; it is a fertile, well-watered countryside in which woods, meadows, orchards and villages flourish.

Everything I do is done laboriously, with great difficulty and uncertainty. I am very lazy, and if I want to finish anything it is absolutely essential that I spend hours stretched out on the sofa. He is never idle, and is always doing something; when he goes to lie down in the afternoons he takes proofs to correct or a book full of notes; he wants us to go to the cinema, then to a reception, then to the theatre—all on the same day. In one day he succeeds in doing, and in making me do, a mass of different things, and in meeting extremely diverse kinds of people. If I am alone and try to act as he does I get nothing at all done, because I get stuck all afternoon somewhere I had meant to stay for half an hour, or because I get lost and cannot find the right street, or because the most boring person and the one I least wanted to meet drags me off to the place I least wanted to go.

If I tell him how my afternoon has turned out he says that it is a completely wasted afternoon and is amused and makes fun of me and loses his temper; and he says that without him I am good for nothing.

I don't know how to manage my time; he does.

He likes receptions. He dresses casually, when everyone else is dressed formally; the idea of changing his clothes in order to go to a reception never enters his head. He even goes in his old raincoat and crumpled hat; a woolen hat which he bought in London and which he wears pulled down over his eyes. He only stays for half an hour; he enjoys chatting with a glass in his hand for half an hour; he eats lots of *hors d'oeuvres*, and I eat almost none because when I see him eating so many I feel that I at least must be well-mannered and show some self-control and not eat too much; after half an hour, just as I am beginning to feel at ease and to enjoy myself, he gets impatient and drags me away.

I don't know how to dance and he does.

I don't know how to type and he does.

I don't know how to drive. If I suggest that I should get a licence too he disagrees. He says I would never manage it. I think he likes me to be dependent on him for some things.

I don't know how to sing and he does. He is a baritone. Perhaps he would have been a famous singer if he had studied singing.

Perhaps he would have been a conductor if he had studied music. When he listens to records he conducts the orchestra with a pencil. And he types and answers the telephone at the same time. He is a man who is able to do many things at once.

He is a professor and I think he is a good one.

He could have been many things. But he has no regrets about those professions he did not take up. I could only ever have followed one profession—the one I chose and which I have followed almost since childhood. And I don't have any regrets either about the professions I did not take up, but then I couldn't have succeeded at any of them.

I write stories, and for many years I have worked for a publishing house.

I don't work badly, or particularly well. All the same I am well aware of the fact that I would have been unable to work anywhere else. I get on well with my colleagues and my boss. I think that if I did not have the support of their friendship I would soon have become worn out and unable to work any longer.

For a long time I thought that one day I would be able to write screenplays for the cinema. But I never had the opportunity, or I did not know how to find it. Now I have lost all hope of writing screenplays. He wrote screenplays for a while, when he was younger. And he has worked in a publishing house. He has written stories. He has done all the things that I have done and many others too.

He is a good mimic, and he does an old countess especially well. Perhaps he could also have been an actor.

Once, in London, he sang in a theatre. He was Job. He had to hire evening clothes; and there he was, in his evening clothes, in front of a kind of lectern; and he sang. He sang the words of Job; the piece called for something between speaking and singing.[3] And I, in my box, was dying of fright. I was afraid he would get flustered, or that the trousers of his evening clothes would fall down.

[3]The concert in which her husband played a prominent role could have been a performance of the oratorio *Job* by Sir Hubert Parry. The classical oratorio utilizes both spoken word and singing, and it was, and still is, not uncommon for amateur provincial groups to stage elaborate classical works.

He was surrounded by men in evening clothes and women in long dresses, who were the angels and devils and other characters in Job.

It was a great success, and they said that he was very good.

If I loved music I would love it passionately. But I don't understand it, and when he persuades me to go to concerts with him my mind wanders off and I think of my own affairs. Or I fall sound asleep.

I like to sing. I don't know how to sing and I sing completely out of tune; but I sing all the same—occasionally, very quietly, when I am alone. I know that I sing out of tune because others have told me so; my voice must be like the yowling of a cat. But I am not—in myself—aware of this, and singing gives me real pleasure. If he hears me he mimics me; he says that my singing is something quite separate from music, something invented by me. When I was a child I used to yowl tunes I had made up. It was a long wailing kind of melody that brought tears to my eyes.

It doesn't matter to me that I don't understand painting or the figurative arts, but it does hurt me that I don't love music; and I feel that my mind suffers from the absence of this love. But there is nothing I can do about it, I will never understand or love music. If I occasionally hear a piece of music that I like I don't know how to remember it; and how can I love something that I can't remember?

It is the words of a song that I remember. I can repeat words that I love over and over again. I repeat the tune that accompanies them too, in my own yowling fashion, and I experience a kind of happiness as I yowl.

When I am writing it seems to me that I follow a musical cadence or rhythm. Perhaps music was very close to my world, and my world could not, for whatever reason, make contact with it.

In my house there is music all day long. He keeps the radio on all day. Or plays records. Every now and again I protest a little and ask for a little silence in which to work; but he says that such beautiful music is certainly conducive to any kind of work.

He has bought an incredible number of records. He says that he owns one of the finest collections in the world.

In the morning when he is still in his dressing gown and dripping water from his bath, he turns the radio on, sits down at the typewriter and begins his strenuous, noisy, stormy day. He is superabundant in everything; he fills the bath to overflowing, and the same with the teapot and his cup of tea. He has an enormous number of shirts and ties. On the other hand he rarely buys shoes.

His mother says that as a child he was a model of order and precision; apparently once, on a rainy day, he was wearing white boots and white clothes and had to cross some muddy streams in the country—at the end of his walk he was immaculate and his clothes and boots had not one spot of mud on them. There is no trace in him of that former immaculate little boy. His clothes are always covered in stains. He has become extremely untidy.

But he scrupulously keeps all the gas bills. In drawers I find old gas bills, which he refuses to throw away, from houses we left long ago.

I also find old, shrivelled Tuscan cigars, and cigarette holders made from cherry wood.

I smoke a brand of king-size, filterless cigarettes called *Stop*, and he smokes Tuscan cigars.

I am very untidy. But as I have got older I have come to miss tidiness, and I sometimes furiously tidy up all the cupboards. I think this is because I remember my mother's tidiness. I rearrange the linen and blanket cupboards and in the summer I reline every drawer with strips of white cloth. I rarely rearrange my papers because my mother didn't write and had no papers. My tidiness and untidiness are full of complicated feelings of regret and sadness. His untidiness is triumphant. He has decided that it is proper and legitimate for a studious person like himself to have an untidy desk.

He does not help me get over my indecisiveness, or the way I hesitate before doing anything, or my sense of guilt. He tends to make fun of every tiny thing I do. If I go shopping in the market he follows me and spies on me. He makes fun of the way I shop, of the way I weigh the oranges in my hand unerringly choosing, he says, the worst in the whole market; he ridicules me for spending an hour over the shopping, buying onions at one stall, celery at another and fruit at another. Sometimes he does the shopping to show me how quickly he can do it; he unhesitatingly buys everything from one stall and then manages to get the basket delivered to the house. He doesn't buy celery because he cannot abide it.

And so—more than ever—I feel I do everything inadequately or mistakenly. But if I once find out that he has made a mistake I tell him so over and over again until he is exasperated. I can be very annoying at times.

His rages are unpredictable, and bubble over like the head on beer. My rages are unpredictable too, but his quickly disappear whereas mine leave a noisy nagging tail behind them which must be very annoying—like the complaining yowl of a cat.

Sometimes in the midst of his rage I start to cry, and instead of quietening him down and making him feel sorry for me this infuriates him all the more. He says my tears are just play-acting, and perhaps he is right. Because in the middle of my tears and his rage I am completely calm.

I never cry when I am really unhappy.

There was a time when I used to hurl plates and crockery on the floor during my rages. But not any more. Perhaps because I am older and my rages are less violent, and also because I dare not lay a finger on our plates now; we bought them one day in London, in the Portobello Road, and I am very fond of them.

The price of those plates, and of many other things we have bought, immediately underwent a substantial reduction in his memory. He likes to think he did not spend very much and that he got a bargain. I know the price of that dinnerware service—it was £16, but he says £12. And it is the same with the picture of King Lear that is in our dining room, and which he also bought in the Portobello Road (and then cleaned with onions and potatoes); now he says he paid a certain sum for it, but I remember that it was much more than that.

Some years ago he bought twelve bedside mats in a department store. He bought them because they were cheap, and he thought he ought to buy them; and he bought them as an argument against me because he considered me to be incapable of buying things for the house. They were made of mud-colored matting and they quickly became very unattractive; they took on a corpse-like rigidity and were hung from a wire line on the kitchen balcony, and I hated them. I used to remind him of them, as an example of bad shopping; but he would say that they had cost very little indeed, almost nothing. It was a long time before I could bring myself to throw them out—because there were so many of them, and because just as I was about to get rid of them it occurred to me that I could use them for rags. He and I both find throwing things away difficult; it must be a kind of Jewish caution in me, and the result of my extreme indecisiveness; in him it must be a defence against his impulsiveness and open-handedness.

He buys enormous quantities of bicarbonate of soda and aspirins.

Now and again he is ill with some mysterious ailment of his own; he can't explain what he feels and stays in bed for a day completely wrapped up in the sheets; nothing is visible except his beard and the tip of his red nose. Then he takes bicarbonate of soda and aspirins in doses suitable for a horse, and says that I cannot understand because I am always well, I am like those great fat strong friars who go out in the wind and in all weathers and come to no harm; he on the other hand is sensitive and delicate and suffers from mysterious ailments. Then in the evening he is better and goes into the kitchen and cooks himself some tagliatelle.

When he was a young man he was slim, handsome and finely built; he did not have a beard but long, soft moustaches instead, and he looked like the actor Robert Donat. He was like that about twenty years ago when I first knew him, and I remember that he used to wear an elegant kind of Scottish flannel shirt. I remember that one evening he walked me back to the *pensione* where I was living; we walked together along the *Via Nazionale*. I already felt that I was very old and had been through a great deal and had made many mistakes, and he seemed a boy to me, light years away from me. I don't remember what we talked about on that evening walking along the *Via Nazionale*; nothing important, I suppose, and the idea that we would become husband and wife was light years away from me. Then we lost sight of each other, and when we met again he no longer looked like Robert Donat, but more like Balzac.[4] When we met again he still wore his Scottish shirts but on him now they looked like garments for a polar expedition; now he had his beard and on his head he wore his ridiculous crumpled woolen hat; everything about him put you in mind of an imminent departure for the North Pole. Because, although he always feels hot, he has the habit of dressing as if he were surrounded by snow, ice and polar bears; or he dresses like a Brazilian coffee-planter, but he always dresses differently from everyone else.

If I remind him of that walk along the *Via Nazionale* he says he remembers it, but I know he is lying and that he remembers nothing; and I sometimes ask myself if it was us, these two people, almost twenty years ago on the *Via Nazionale*, two people who conversed so politely, so urbanely, as the sun was setting; who chatted a little about everything perhaps and about nothing; two friends talking, two young intellectuals out for a walk; so young, so educated, so uninvolved, so ready to judge one another with kind impartiality; so ready to say goodbye to one another for ever, as the sun set, at the corner of the street.

—*Translated by Dick Davis*

INTERPRETATIONS

1. How would you describe Ginzburg's style of writing? What separates her style from other authors you have read and what makes her approach to telling her story so effective?

---

[4]British-born Robert Donat was a stage and screen actor whose superior acting ability, sophisticated demeanor, and handsome appearance endeared him to many fans, especially in Europe. Nineteenth-century novelist and playwright Honoré de Balzac is considered by many critics the greatest French novelist of all time. Balzac had health problems, which led to weight problems and a rather ungainly appearance, and his dedication to his writing craft left most of his contemporary critics believing he was a misanthrope.

2. Ginzburg begins "He and I" with a statement of absolute polarity: "He always feels hot, I always feel cold." Although they appear to have little in common, as the story unfolds Ginzburg uses shifts in tone and point of view to give a more subtle account of what makes their relationship a meaningful one. For example, even though her husband, a self-taught musician, loves music and she admits that she doesn't understand music, she admires his courage to sing and perform in public. What other examples in the essay indicate that Ginzburg moves beyond simple opposition in order to create a more mutual compatibility?

3. Ginzburg gives many small but significant details about herself and her husband that bring to light the peculiarities of personality that can only be observed in a close, lasting relationship. What do these details reveal to you about the nature of their relationship?

4. The author states that her husband has the tendency to lose his temper and go into rages. She also states that at times his rages bring her to tears, yet, "He says my tears are just play-acting, and perhaps he is right. Because in the middle of my tears and his rage I am completely calm. I never cry when I am really unhappy." What do you think Ginzburg means by this statement? Is this observation by Ginzburg influenced by her relationship with her husband or is it something that lies on a deeper, more personal, level? Use examples from the text to justify your answer.

5. In the last two paragraphs of the essay, Ginzburg reminisces about their first meeting to make the reader aware of the consequence of memory. How do you interpret this last paragraph in relation to the rest of the essay? Why do you think Ginzburg ends the essay by summoning the past?

CORRESPONDENCES

1. Review Rowland's perspective at the beginning of this chapter. What evidence is there in Ginzburg's essay that either qualifies or dismisses Rowland's assertion? Give details from the text to explain your answer.

2. Pretend you are Natalia Ginzburg and write a response to any one of the perspectives on marriage found at the beginning of this chapter. What evidence from the text will help you determine your response to your chosen perspective?

APPLICATIONS

1. Early in the essay we learn that both Ginzburg and her husband share a love for the cinema yet they are drawn to the cinema for different reasons. With your group, analyze the paragraphs where she talks of their love for the cinema and discuss how the cinema affects each of them. In what way does their love for the cinema help you gain insight into their characters?

2. The theme of love has been fertile ground for poets and songwriters for centuries. Countless songs and poems have been written about love and companionship. Choose a song or poem about love or an intimate relationship between two people you are familiar with that resonates with you. Write an essay where you interpret the message of the song or poem and explain why it has the impact it does on your thoughts and feelings about love and companionship.

3. Compare and contrast Ginzburg's relationship with her husband to a relationship that you have either experienced or observed in others. What are the similarities and differences between Ginzburg's relationship with her partner and the relationship you have had with your partner or noticed in other relationships?

The Storm

KATE, CHOPIN (1851–1904)

Chopin was born in St. Louis, and moved to New Orleans when she married a Louisiana Creole. Her short stories and novels usually take place in that locale. Her last novel, The Awakening *(1899), found a new audience during the women's movement of the 1960s, not only because it examined a woman's search for personal identity but also for its interest in financial and sexual autonomy.*

I

The leaves were so still that even Bibi thought it was going to rain. Bobinôt, who was accustomed to converse on terms of perfect equality with his little son, called the child's attention to certain sombre clouds that were rolling with sinister intention from the west, accompanied by a sullen, threatening roar. They were at Friedheimer's store and decided to remain there till the storm had passed. They sat within the door on two empty kegs. Bibi was four years old and looked very wise.

"Mama'll be 'fraid, yes," he suggested with blinking eyes.

"She'll shut the house. Maybe she got Sylvie helpin' her this evenin'," Bobinôt responded reassuringly.

"No; she ent got Sylvie. Syhrie was helpin' her yistiday," piped Bibi.

Bobinôt arose and going across to the counter purchased a can of shrimps, of which Calixta was very fond. Then he returned to his perch on the keg and sat stolidly holding the can of shrimps while the storm burst. It shook the wooden store and seemed to be ripping great furrows in the distant field. Bibi laid his little hand on his father's knee and was not afraid.

II

Calixta, at home, felt no uneasiness for their safety. She sat at a side window sewing furiously on a sewing machine. She was greatly occupied and did not notice the approaching storm. But she felt very warm and often stopped to mop her face on which the perspiration gathered in beads. She unfastened her white sacque at the throat. It began to grow dark, and suddenly realizing the situation she got up hurriedly and went about closing windows and doors.

Out on the small front gallery she hung Bobinôt's Sunday clothes to air and she hastened out to gather them before the rain fell. As she stepped outside, Alcée Laballière rode in at the gate. She had not seen him very often since her marriage, and never alone. She stood there with Bobinôt's coat in her hands, and the big rain drops began to fall. Alcée rode his horse under the shelter of a side projection where the chickens had huddled and there were plows and a harrow piled up in the corner.

"May I come and wait on your gallery till the storm is over, Calixta?" he asked. "Come 'long in, M'sieur Alcée."

His voice and her own startled her as if from a trance, and she seized Bobinôt's—vest. Alcée, mounting to the porch, grabbed the trousers and snatched Bibi's braided jacket that was about to be carried away by a sudden gust of wind. He expressed an intention to remain outside, but it was soon apparent that he might as well have been out in the open: the water beat in upon the boards in driving sheets, and he went inside, closing the door after him. It was even necessary to put something beneath the door to keep the water out.

"My! what a rain! It's good two years sense it rain' like that," exclaimed Calixta as she rolled up a piece of bagging and Alcée helped her to thrust it beneath the crack.

She was a little fuller of figure than five years before when she married; but she had lost nothing of her vivacity. Her blue eyes still retained their melting quality; and her yellow hair, dishevelled by the wind and rain, kinked more stubbornly than ever about her ears and temples.

The rain beat upon the low, shingled roof with a force and clatter that threatened to break an entrance and deluge them there. They were in the dining room—the sitting room—the general utility room. Adjoining was her bed room, with Bibi's couch along side her own. The door stood open, and the room with its white, monumental bed, its closed shutters, looked dim and mysterious.

Alcée flung himself into a rocker and Calixta nervously began to gather up from the floor the lengths of a cotton sheet which she had been sewing.

"If this keeps up, *Dieu said*[1] if the levees goin' to stan' it!" she exclaimed.

"What have you got to do with the levees?"

"I got enough to do! An' there's Bobinôt with Bibi out in that storm—if he only didn't left Friedheimer's!"

---

[1] God knows.

"Let us hope, Calixta, that Bobinôt's got sense enough to come in out of a cyclone."

She went and stood at the window with a greatly disturbed look on her face. She wiped the frame that was clouded with moisture. It was stiflingly hot. Alcée got up and joined her at the window, looking over her shoulder. The rain was coming down in sheets obscuring the view of far-off cabins and enveloping the distant wood in a gray mist. The playing of the lightning was incessant. A bolt struck a tall chinaberry tree at the edge of the field. It filled all visible space with a blinding glare and the crash seemed to invade the very boards they stood upon.

Calixta put her hands to her eyes, and with a cry, staggered backward. Alcée's arm encircled her, and for an instant he drew her close and spasmodically to him.

"*Bonté!*"[2] she cried, releasing herself from his encircling arm and retreating from the window, "the house'll go next! If I only knew w'ere Bibi was!" She would not compose herself; she would not be seated. Alcée clasped her shoulders and looked into her face. The contact of her warm palpitating body when he had unthinkingly drawn her into his arms, had aroused all the old-time infatuation and desire for her flesh.

"Calixta," he said, "don't be frightened. Nothing can happen. The house is too low to be struck, with so many tall trees standing about. There! aren't you going to be quiet? say, aren't you," He pushed her hair back from her face that was warm and steaming. Her lips were as red and moist as pomegranate seed. Her white neck and a glimpse of her full, firm bosom disturbed him powerfully. As she glanced up at him the fear in her liquid blue eyes had given place to a drowsy gleam that unconsciously betrayed a sensuous desire. He looked down into her eyes and there was nothing for biro to do but to gather her lips in a kiss. It reminded him of Assumption.

"Do you remember—in Assumption, Calixta?" he asked in a low voice broken by passion. Oh! she remembered; for in Assumption he had kissed her and kissed and kissed her; until his senses would well nigh fail, and to save her he would resort to a desperate flight. If she was not an immaculate dove in those days, she was still inviolate; a passionate creature whose very defenselessness had made her defense, against which his honor forbade him to prevail. Now—well, now—her lips seemed in a manner free to be tasted, as well as her round, white throat and her whiter breasts.

---

[2]"Goodness!"

They did not heed the crashing torrents, and the roar of the elements made her laugh as she lay in his arms. She was a revelation in that dim, mysterious chamber; as white as the couch she lay upon. Her firm, elastic flesh that was knowing for the first time its birthright, was like a creamy lily that the sun invites to contribute its breath and perfume to the undying life of the world.

The generous abundance of her passion, without guile or trickery, was like a white flame which penetrated and found response in depths of his own sensuous nature that had never yet been reached.

When he touched her breasts they gave themselves up in quivering ecstasy, inviting his lips. Her mouth was a fountain of delight. And when he possessed her, they seemed to swoon together at the very borderland of life's mystery.

He stayed cushioned upon her, breathless, dazed, enervated, with his heart beating like a hammer upon her. With one hand she clasped his head, her lips lightly touching his forehead. The other hand stroked with a soothing rhythm his muscular shoulders.

The growl of the thunder was distant and passing away. The rain beat softly upon the shingles, inviting them to drowsiness and sleep. But they dared not yield.

The rain was over; and the sun was turning the glistening green world into a palace of gems. Calixta, on the gallery, watched Alcée ride away. He turned and smiled at her with a beaming face; and she lifted her pretty chin in the air and laughed aloud.

III

Bobinôt and Bibi, trudging home, stopped without at the cistern to make themselves presentable.

"My! Bibi, w'at will yo' mama say! You ought to be ashame'. You oughtn' put on those good pants. Look at 'em! An' that mud on yo' collar! How you got that mud on yo' collar, Bibi? I never saw such a boy!" Bibi was the picture of pathetic resignation. Bobinôt was the embodiment of serious solicitude as he strove to remove from his own person and his son's the signs of their tramp over heavy roads and through wet fields. He scraped the mud off Bibi's bare legs and feet with a stick and carefully removed all traces from his heavy brogans. Then, prepared for the worst—the meeting with an over-scrupulous housewife, they entered cautiously at the back door.

Calixta was preparing supper. She had set the table and was dripping coffee at the hearth. She sprang up as they came in.

"Oh, Bobinôt! You back! My! but I was uneasy. W'ere you been during the rain? An' Bibi? he ain't wet? he ain't hurt?" She had clasped Bibi and was kissing him effusively. Bobinôt's explanations and apologies which he had been composing all along the way, died on his lips as Calixta felt him to see if he were dry, and seemed to express nothing but satisfaction at their safe return.

"I brought you some shrimps, Calixta," offered Bobinôt, hauling the can from his ample side pocket and laying it on the table.

"Shrimps! Oh, Bobinôt! you too good fo' anything!" and she gave him a smacking kiss on the cheek that resounded. "*J'vous réponds,*[3] we'll have a feas' tonight! umph-umph!"

Bobinôt and Bibi began to relax and enjoy themselves, and when the three seated themselves at table they laughed much and so loud that anyone might have heard them as far away as Laballière's.

IV

Alcée Laballière wrote to his wife, Clarisse, that night. It was a loving letter, full of tender solicitude. He told her not to hurry back, but if she and the babies liked it at Biloxi, to stay a month longer. He was getting on nicely; and though he missed them, he was willing to bear the separation a while longer—realizing that their health and pleasure were the first things to be considered.

V

As for Clarisse, she was charmed upon receiving her husband's letter. She and the babies were doing well. The society was agreeable; many of her old friends and acquaintances were at the bay. And the first free breath since her marriage seemed to restore the pleasant liberty of her maiden days. Devoted as she was to her husband, their intimate conjugal life was something which she was more than willing to forego for a while.

So the storm passed and everyone was happy.

INTERPRETATIONS

1. What evidence does Chopin present about the past relationship of Calixta and Alcée? Is it important for the reader to know about this relationship? Explain your answer.

2. How does Chopin use point of view to develop characterization in the first two sections of the story?

3. What is the symbolic significance of the storm? What chain of events does it set in motion?

4. Pay particular attention to Chopin's use of language in the story. How do her images reflect her attitude toward her characters? Does

---

[3]I tell you.

her choice of words imply judgment or empathy? Select evidence from the text to justify your point of view.

CORRESPONDENCES

1. Create a conversation on gender roles between Chopin and Duncan and compare your responses to those of your group members.
2. Review Sayer's Perspective in Correspondences and discuss its relevance to the gender relationships in "The Storm."

APPLICATIONS

1. Discuss with your group your responses to the last sentence of the story. Do you agree with Chopin's conclusion? Why or why not? Summarize your group's responses. Did you reach a consensus?
2. Chopin chose not to publish this story during her lifetime. How might readers in the 1890s have responded to her lack of condemnation of adultery or to the fact that both Calixta and Alcée enjoy their sexual encounter as equals? Working with your group, debate whether you accept or reject Calixta's and Alcée's attitudes toward marriage and infidelity.

The Knowing Eye

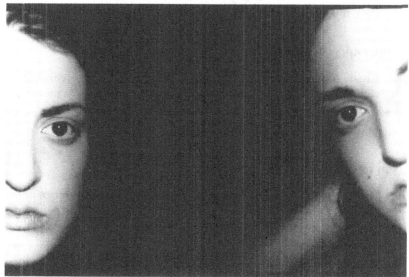

Emma Wunsch

The New Woman — Wash Day.
Copyright 1901 by Underwood & Underwood.

Library of Congress; Underwood and Underwood

140

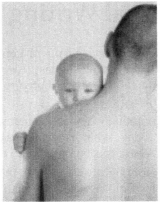

Mara Denardo

READING IMAGES

1. How does each photograph address "gender issues"? What message about gender and identity is being given by each photographer?

2. When do you think each of these photographs was taken? How might the extent to which each one represents a political/social climate help you to arrange them chronologically.

MAKING CONNECTIONS

1. How does the photograph of the man and woman ("The New Woman—Wash Day") relate to the one of the man carrying the baby?

2. What is the tone or mood presented in the photograph of the faces? Which essays do you think best correspond to this feeling?

WORDS AND IMAGES

1. The photograph showing the laundering of clothing confronts the issue of gender roles. Are there certain jobs that you think are gender specific? If so, what are they? Why do you think they should be available only to men or to women? After thinking and writing about these questions, compare your responses with those from the members of your peer group. How are your ideas similar to and different from those of your classmates? What consensus opinion has been formed?

2. What would the people from the second photograph say about the situation presented in the third photograph? Create a dialogue that captures this conversation.

Additional Writing Topics

1. To what extent have your concepts of gender roles and gender relationships changed during the last five years? Write an essay that analyzes the factors that contributed to your modifying your point of view on these issues.

2. Write an essay discussing whether it is realistic to expect marriage to last a lifetime today. What expectations do most people have about marriage? What expectations should they have?

3. Are gender roles more rigidly assigned in the United States than in other countries? In some cultures, for example, it is not unusual for men to express affection for one another or even to cry in public. Write an essay discussing how cultural expectations affect gender sterereotypes.

4. Societal and cultural attitudes toward masculinity and femininity are the focus of the texts by Soto, Duncan, and Asayesh. How does your attitude toward this emotionally charged subject compare to theirs? Write an essay defining your concepts and analyzing your emotional reactions to them.

5. Create an extended conversation between Ginsburg and Chopin on marriage and gender roles. On what aspects might they agree? Disagree? Do you consider Ginzburg a feminist? What is your response to Chopin's concept of fidelity in "The Storm"?

6. Bring to class four advertisements from current magazines featuring dress styles for men and women. Analyze with your group the images they intend to communicate. To what extent are they based on gender stereotypes? What do they "promise" the consumer?

7. From the perspective of a parent, write a letter explaining to your daughter what it means to be a woman or to your son explaining what it means to be a man.

8. Brainstorm with your group on your concepts of fatherhood. What images and emotions does the word evoke? What responsibilities are fathers expected to assume in the family? How has the role of father changed in the last decade?

9. Societal and familial attitudes toward homosexuality are explored by Altman and Quindlen. Write an essay analyzing your emotional associations with this topic.

CHAPTER

4

Education

HUMAN BEINGS SHOW A WONDERFUL capacity to learn and unlearn—if it were not so you would not see such diversity in this and in all the other chapters of this book. "The greatest happiness of man as a thinking being," said Goethe, "is to know what is knowable and quietly to revere what is unknowable." Several cross-cultural texts clearly support Goethe's notion of the joy of learning, including the old folktale "The Bar of Gold," "A View from the Bridge," "Always Living in Spanish," and "Poets in the Kitchen."

In "A View from the Bridge," Cherokee Paul McDonald recounts a chance encounter with a remarkable young boy with whom he established a relationship, however brief. Through this experience he is able to revive a sense of wonder about what we can learn if we maintain curiosity and are open to possibilities. Taneisha Grant in "When the Simulated Patient Is for Real" contrasts what she learned theoretically about treating a complex patient as opposed to treating one in actuality. Like McDonald, she also learned something about herself through this encounter.

Education is also an important issue to politicians, educators, and parents, and the pendulum swings back and forth constantly as to what aspects of the educational system should be reevaluated. Currently, the national spotlight is on assessment and measuring students' performance through a series of standardized tests beginning in third grade and continuing through college.

Another "hot" issue is bilingual education, a matter of controversy in several states despite the large numbers of students in public schools for whom English is not a first language. Critics of bilingual education claim that this approach delays the acquisition of English and a student's ability to achieve proficiency in the language of public discourse.

143

The more extreme groups view bilingualism as a threat to national unity, and that has prompted the formation of English-only movements.

Defenders of bilingualism argue that forcing students to abandon their private language is pedagogically unsound, and often psychologically debilitating. For example, Eva Hoffman, forced to leave her native Poland in 1959 at age thirteen, describes in her memoir, *Lost in Translation*, the trauma of linguistic dispossession as she struggled to learn English in school in Vancouver, Canada. "Blind rage, helpless rage is rage that has no words—rage that overwhelms one with darkness."

Several texts in this chapter focus on the crucial and controversial implications of the connections between language and culture. Is it desirable and possible for public schools to perform this mission without robbing students of their natal language and culture? Is it possible to achieve biculturalism, as well as bilingualism? Is it possible to tolerate— even respect—other religions, systems of law, forms of art, and languages without losing respect for one's own? Is our idea of culture clear and distinct enough to speak of absolute boundaries between cultures? If we accept the concept of cultural differences, even cultural boundaries, is cultural exclusiveness the goal we want to pursue?

In "Always Living in Spanish," Marjorie Agosín talks about the "solitude of exile" that she has experienced since leaving her native Chile (then under the dictatorship of the Pinochet regime), and her years at a high school in Georgia where her "poor English and accent were the cause of ridicule and insult." José Torres emphasizes the importance of education and the link between language and power, and Chang-Rae Lee recalls his mother's powerlessness expressed by her silence as a Korean immigrant in the United States.

Is a person educated who knows only his or her own culture as it is at that moment? Carlos Fuentes, the eminent contemporary Mexican writer would respond negatively, as he is convinced that "cultures only flourish in contact with others; they perish in isolation." Anyone who knows the history of his or her own culture expects change. But at what price? By what vehicle? Preparation for the global culture of the twenty-first century surely requires your generation to forge new definitions of an educated person.

Perspectives

Only the curious have, if they live, a tale worth telling at all.
—Alastair Reid

Not to transmit an experience is to betray it.
—Etie Wiesel

I hear and I forget. I see and I remember, I do and I understand.
—Chinese proverb

Education is what survives when what has been learnt has been forgotten.
— B. F. Skinner

Sexist language, racist language, theistic language—all are typical of the policing languages of mastery, and cannot, do not, permit new knowledge or encourage the mutual exchange of ideas.
— Toni Morrison

Learning to read books—or pictures, or films—is not just a matter of acquiring information from texts, it is a matter of learning to read and write the texts of our lives.
—Robert Scholes

What I wish for all students is some release from the clammy grip of the future. I wish them a chance to savor each segment of their education as an experience in itself and not as a grim preparation for the next step. I wish them the right to experiment, to trip and fall, to learn that defeat is as instructive as victory and is not the end of the world.
—William Zinsser

Education is not a product: mark, diploma, job, money—in that order: it is a process, a never-ending one.
—Bel Kaufman

Education is hanging around until you've caught on.
—Robert Frost

Put yourself in a different room, that's what the mind is for.
—Margaret Atwood

Teachers are the door. You enter yourself.
—Chinese proverb

145

Education is not the filling of a pail, but the lighting of a fire.

—*William Butler Yeats*

I am still learning.

—*Michelangelo*

Shall I teach you what knowledge is? When you know a thing, to recognize that you know it, and when you do not know a thing, to recognize that you do not know it. That is knowledge.

—*Confucius*

Education! Which of the various me's do you propose to educate, and which do you propose to suppress?

—*D. H. Lawrence*

By doubting we are led to enquire: By enquiry we perceive the truth.

—*Abelard*

The greatest difficulty in education is to get experience from ideas.

—*George Santayana*

It is above all by the imagination that we achieve perception, and compassion, and hope.

—*Ursula K. Le Guin*

I have always come to life after coming to books.

—*Jorge Luis Borges*

Power is the ability to take one's place in whatever discourse is essential to action and the right to have one's part matter.

—*Carolyn Heilbrun*

. . . That is what learning is. You suddenly understand something you've understood all your life, but in a new way.

—*Doris Lessing*

Knowledge is power.

—*Francis Bacon*

The mind is an enchanting thing.

—*Marianne Moore*

But it is not hard work which is dreary; it is superficial work. That is always boring in the long run, and it has always seemed strange to me that in our endless discussions about education so little stress is ever laid on the pleasure of becoming an educated person, the enormous interest it adds to life. To be able to be caught up into the world of thought—that is to be educated.

—Edith Hamilton

It ought to be embarrassing, in this age of celebration of America's diversity, that the schools have been so slow to move toward teaching about our nation's diverse religious traditions. . . . After all, if the material is well taught, many children will be intrigued by what will be for many their first exposure to religious traditions different from their own—or, in some instances, to any religious tradition at all.

—Stephen L. Carter

APPLICATIONS

1. Discuss Hamilton's description of an educated person. To what extent has your education been pleasurable? How has it made your life more interesting? What does it mean to you "to be caught up in the world of thought"?

2. Abelard and Reid focus on the importance of curiosity in acquiring knowledge and becoming an interesting person. Have you been encouraged by your teachers to ask questions? Do you consider yourself curious? Has curiosity played a positive role in your education? Cite one or two examples.

3. Discuss Zinsser's perspective on education. To what extent do you agree that it is important "to trip and fall" and that defeat or failure may be used constructively? How can these views be reconciled with the pressures facing today's college students? Write a summary of your group's discussion.

The Bar of Gold

A FOLKTALE

The Bar of Gold is a folktale of unknown origin. This folk story was first published in 1910 by T. Y. Crowell & Company and is part of an anthology of folktales compiled by Lilian Gask titled Folk Tales from Many Lands. *The stories in this anthology are interesting to read and the book includes a series of illustrations drawn by noted stylist Willy Pogany.* Folk Tales from Many Lands *is available to read online at* http://digital.library.upenn.edu/women/gask/tales/tales.html.

LONG YEARS AGO there lived a poor labouring man who never knew what it was to sleep in peace. Whether the times were good or bad, he was haunted by fears for the morrow, and this constant worrying caused him to look so thin and worn that the neighbouring farmers hesitated to give him work. He was steady and frugal, and had never been known to waste his time in the village inn, or indulge in foolish pleasures—in fact, a worthier man could not be found, and his friends agreed in saying that he certainly deserved success, though this never came his way.

One day, as he sat by the roadside with his head on his hands, a kindly and charitable doctor from the town close by stopped his carriage to ask him what was the matter.

"You seem in trouble, my good man," he said. "Tell me what I can do to help you."

Encouraged by the sympathy in his voice, "Weeping John," as he was called, poured out his woes, to which the doctor listened with much attention.

"If I should fall sick," the poor man finished by saying, "what would happen to my little children, and the wife whom I love more dearly than life itself? They would surely starve, for even as it is they often go hungry to bed. Surely a more unfortunate man has never been born—I toil early and late, and this is my reward." And once more he buried his face in his hands, while bitter sobs shook his ill-clad shoulders.

"Come, come!" said the doctor briskly. "Get up at once, man, and I will do my best for you. I can see that if you do not kill worry, worry will kill you."

Helping the poor fellow into his carriage, he told the coachman to drive straight home, and when they arrived at his comfortable mansion, he led him into his surgery.

"See here," he cried, pointing to a shining bar in a glass case, "that bar of gold was bequeathed to me by my father, who was once as poor as you are now. By means of the strictest economy, and hard work, he managed to save sufficient money to purchase this safeguard against want. When it came to me, I too was poor, but by following his example, and keeping a brave heart, in cloud and storm as well as sunshine, I have now amassed a fortune that is more than sufficient for my needs. Therefore, I will now hand over to you the bar of gold, since I no longer require it. Its possession will give you confidence for the future. Do not break into it if you can avoid it, and remember that sighing and weeping should be left to weak women and girls."

The labourer thanked him with much fervour, and, hiding the bar of gold beneath his coat, sped joyfully homeward.

As he and his wife sat over the fire, which they were now no longer afraid to replenish, he told her all that the good doctor had said, and they agreed that unless the worst came to the worst, they would never touch that bar of gold.

"The knowledge that we have it safely hidden in the cellar," said his wife, "will keep from us all anxiety. And now, John, you must do your best to make a fortune, so that we may be able to hand it on to our dear children."

From that day John was a changed man. He sang and whistled merrily as he went about his work, and bore himself like a prosperous citizen. His cheeks filled out, and his eye grew bright; no longer did he waste his leisure in lamentations, but dug and planted his little garden until it yielded him richly of the fruits of the earth, and the proceeds helped to swell the silver coins in his good wife's stocking.

The farmer who had before employed him when short of hands was so impressed with his altered looks that he took him permanently into his service, and with regular food and sufficient clothing John's delicate children grew strong and hardy.

"That bar of gold has brought us luck," he would sometimes say blithely to his wife, who held her tongue like a wise woman, although she was tempted to remind him that the "luck" had come since he had given up weeping and lamentations concerning the future.

One summer's evening, long afterwards, as they sat in the wide porch, while their grandchildren played in the meadow beyond, and the lowing of the cows on their peaceful farm mingled with the little people's merry shouts, a stranger came up the pathway and begged for alms. Though torn and tattered, and gaunt with hunger, he had an air of gentleness and refinement, and, full of compassion, the worthy couple invited him in to rest. They set before him the best they had, and, when he tried to express his gratitude, John laid his hand on his shoulder.

"My friend," he said, "Providence has been good to us, and blessed the labour of our hands. In times gone by, however, I was as wretched as you appeared to be when you crossed the road, and it is owing to a stranger's kindness that I am in my present position."

He went on to tell him of the bar of gold, and, after a long look at his wife, who nodded her head as if well pleased, he went and fetched it from the cellar, where it had lain hidden all these years.

"There!" he exclaimed. "I am going to give it to you. I shall not want it now, and my children are all well settled. It is fitting that you should have it, since your need is very great."

Now the stranger understood the science of metals, for he was a learned man who had fallen on evil times. As he took the gleaming bar in his hands, while murmuring his astonished thanks, he knew by its weight that it was not gold.

"You have made a mistake, my friends," he cried. "This bar is not what you think it, though I own that most men would be deceived."

Greatly surprised, the old woman took it from him, and polished it with her apron in order to show him how brightly it gleamed. As she did so, an inscription appeared, which neither she nor her husband had noticed before. Both listened with great interest as the stranger read it out for them.

"It is less a matter of actual want," it ran, "than the fear of what the morrow will bring, which causes the unhappiness of the poor. Then tread the path of life with courage, for it is clear that at last you will reach the end of your journey."

When the stranger paused there was a dead silence, for the old man and woman were thinking many things, and words do not come quickly when one is deeply moved. At last John offered the stranger a tremulous apology for the disappointment he must be suffering through their innocent mistake.

"On the contrary," he replied warmly, "the lesson that bar has taught me is worth far more than any money that you could give me. I shall make a new start in life, and, remembering that we fail through fear, will henceforth bear myself as a brave man should."

So saying, he bade them adieu, and passed out into the fragrant twilight.

INTERPRETATIONS

1. What is the source of "Weeping John's" anxiety at the outset of the folktale? What does the doctor say about John's anxiety?

2. How does John's wife view the effect of the bar of gold on her husband? Explain.

3. In what way does the bar of gold act as the catalyst in changing the lives of the characters that come in possession of the bar of gold? Be specific.

4. What is the significance behind the bar of gold having no material value? How does its lack of material value influence the outcome of the story?

5. Reread the inscription on the bar of gold. Although the inscription states that fear of the morrow causes the unhappiness of the poor, fear and anxiety do not discriminate. How would you reword the inscription to have its message applicable to people from all walks of life?

CORRESPONDENCE

1. "All that glitters is not gold" is an age-old phrase made famous by William Shakespeare in his play *The Merchant of Venice*. What is your interpretation of this phrase and what connection can you make between the phrase and "The Bar of Gold"?

APPLICATIONS

1. Make a list of principles you aspire to in life. Leave a space between each entry for your thoughts, and be honest. From the list you create and in the space you provide, write down what you believe to be the core value of each principle on your list. When you are finished, answer the following question: How does the list you created reveal the type of person you are?

2. "Worry often gives a small thing a big shadow." This Swedish proverb tells us that sometimes we allow the small worries in life to consume us to the point that they appear much greater than they are. Write a letter offering advice and guidance to a friend or loved one who you know is overwhelmed with worry.

A View from the Bridge

CHEROKEE PAUL MCDONALD

Cherokee Paul McDonald (b. 1949) is a fiction writer and journalist. In his most recent book, Into the Green *(2001), he records his tour of duty as an Army lieutenant during the Vietnam War. He later joined the police department in Fort Lauderdale, where he served for ten years, and in 1991 published* Blue Truth, *a memoir of his years in the police force that includes graphic descriptions of crimes he had to deal with. "A View from the Bridge" was published in* Sunshine *(1990), a Florida sporting magazine.*

I WAS COMING UP ON THE LITTLE BRIDGE in the Rio Vista neighborhood of Fort Lauderdale, deepening my stride and my breathing to negotiate the slight incline without altering my pace. And then, as I neared the crest, I saw the kid.

He was a lumpy little guy with baggy shorts, a faded T-shirt and heavy sweat socks falling down over old sneakers.

Partially covering his shaggy blond hair was one of those blue baseball caps with gold braid on the bill and a sailfish patch sewn onto the peak. Covering his eyes and part of his face was a pair of those stupid-looking '50s-style wrap-around sunglasses.

He was fumbling with a beat-up rod and reel, and he had a little bait bucket by his feet. I puffed on by, glancing down into the empty bucket as I passed.

"Hey, mister! Would you help me, please?"

The shrill voice penetrated my jogger's concentration, and I was determined to ignore it. But for some reason, I stopped.

With my hands on my hips and the sweat dripping from my nose I asked, "What do you want, kid?"

"Would you please help me find my shrimp? It's my last one and I've been getting bites and I know I can catch a fish if I can just find that shrimp. He jumped outta my hand as I was getting him from the bucket."

Exasperated, I walked slowly back to the kid, and pointed.

"There's the damn shrimp by your left foot. You stopped me for *that?*"

As I said it, the kid reached down and trapped the shrimp.

"Thanks a lot, mister," he said.

I watched as the kid dropped the baited hook down into the canal. Then I turned to start back down the bridge.

That's when the kid let out a "Hey! Hey!" and the prettiest tarpon I'd ever seen came almost six feet out of the water, twisting and turning as he fell through the air.

"I got one!" the kid yelled as the fish hit the water with a loud splash and took off down the canal.

I watched the line being burned off the reel at an alarming rate. The kid's left hand held the crank while the extended fingers felt for the drag setting.

"No, kid!" I shouted, "Leave the drag alone . . . just keep that damn rod tip up!"

Then I glanced at the reel and saw there were just a few loops of line left on the spool.

"Why don't you get yourself some decent equipment?" I said, but before the kid could answer I saw the line go slack.

"Ohhh, I lost him," the kid said. I saw the flash of silver as the fish turned.

"Crank, kid, crank! You didn't lose him. He's coming back toward you. Bring in the slack!"

The kid cranked like mad, and a beautiful grin spread across his face.

"He's heading in for the pilings," I said. "Keep him out of those pilings!"

The kid played it perfectly. When the fish made its play for the pilings, he kept just enough pressure on to force the fish out. When the water exploded and the silver missile hurled into the air, the kid kept the rod tip up and the line tight.

As the fish came to the surface and began a slow circle in the middle of the canal, I said, "Whooee, is that a nice fish or what?"

The kid didn't say anything, so I said, "Okay, move to the edge of the bridge and I'll climb down to the seawall and pull him out."

When I reached the seawall I pulled in the leader, leaving the fish lying on its side in the water.

"How's that?" I said.

"Hey, mister, tell me what it looks like."

"Look down here and check him out," I said. "He's beautiful."

But then I looked up into those stupid-looking sunglasses and it hit me. The kid was blind.

"Could you tell me what he looks like, mister?" he said again.

"Well, he's just under three, uh, he's about as long as one of your arms," I said. "I'd guess he goes about 15, 20 pounds. He's mostly silver, but the silver is somehow made up of *all* the colors, if you know what I mean." I stopped. "Do you know what I mean by colors?"

The kid nodded.

"Okay. He has all these big scales, like armor all over his body. They're silver too, and when he moves they sparkle. He has a strong body and a large powerful tail. He has big round eyes, bigger than a quarter, and a lower jaw that sticks out past the upper one and is very tough. His belly is almost white and his back is a gunmetal gray. When he jumped he came out of the water about six feet, and his scales caught the sun and flashed it all over the place."

By now the fish had righted itself, and I could see the bright-red gills as the gill plates opened and closed. I explained this to the kid, and then said, more to myself, "He's a beauty."

"Can you get him off the hook?" the kid asked. "I don't want to kill him."

I watched as the tarpon began to slowly swim away, tired but still alive.

By the time I got back up to the top of the bridge the kid had his line secured and his bait bucket in one hand.

He grinned and said, "Just in time. My mom drops me off here, and she'll be back to pick me up any minute."

He used the back of one hand to wipe his nose.

"Thanks for helping me catch that tarpon," he said, "and for helping me to see it."

I looked at him, shook my head, and said, "No, my friend, thank you for letting *me* see that fish."

I took off, but before I got far the kid yelled again.

"Hey, mister!"

I stopped.

"Someday I'm gonna catch a sailfish and a blue marlin and a giant tuna and *all* those big sportfish!"

As I looked into those sunglasses I knew he probably would. I wished I could be there when it happened.

INTERPRETATIONS

1. McDonald uses foreshadowing to convey to the reader that the boy is blind. What clues did he provide and at what point did you realize that he could not see? Why does it take the narrator so long to realize this? How does his attitude change toward the boy after he gains this knowledge?

2. Identify the sensory language that the author uses to describe the tarpon to the boy. What changes does he make in his language in the process? What does the boy know about fishing?

3. McDonald uses dialogue throughout the essay. Why is this effective for this situation? Be specific.

4. What did you find most interesting about the boy by the end of his encounter with the narrator? Do you believe that he will achieve his goal of catching "all those big sportfish"? Why or why not?

5. Why does the narrator thank the boy for allowing him to see the fish? How has the narrator changed as a result of their meeting?

CORRESPONDENCES

1. Review Le Guin's perspective and write a journal entry on its relevance to "A View from the Bridge."

2. Review Kaufman's perspective and discuss its relevance to "A View from the Bridge."

APPLICATIONS

1. Consult your thesaurus on "view" and "bridge" and write an essay on the multiple meanings of the title. Is irony implicit in the title? Explain.

2. Experiment with your group in describing an object or a bird, flower, butterfly, or goldfish to someone who cannot see. Use sensory language—smell, touch, texture, and color—to create a vivid verbal picture. What did you learn about language through this exercise?

3. The jogger and the young boy are strangers to each other but share a passion for fishing. Write an essay on the various roles that the tarpon plays in their encounter.

Mute in an English-Only World

CHANG-RAE LEE

Chang-Rae Lee (b. 1965, in Seoul, Korea) has taught creative writing at Princeton University since 2002. For the preceding four years he taught writing at Hunter College of the City University of New York. His father was a psychiatrist practicing in Westchester County, New York, and Lee attended Phillips Exeter Academy and Yale (B.A., 1987). He earned an M.A. from the University of Oregon in 1993. He is the author of the novels Native Speaker *(1994), for which he earned the Hemingway Foundation/ PEN Award in 1995;* A Gesture Life *(1999); and* Aloft *(2004). In 1999* The New Yorker *named Lee one of the twenty best American writers under the age of forty. The following essay, originally published in* The New York Times *in 1996, shows his typical interest in language and identity. What accommodations do you think should be made for immigrants who don't speak English?*

WHEN I READ OF THE TROUBLES in Palisades Park, New Jersey, over the proliferation of Korean language signs along its main commercial strip, I unexpectedly sympathized with the frustrations, resentments and fears of the longtime residents. They clearly felt alienated and even unwelcome in a vital part of their community. The town, like seven others in New Jersey, has passed laws requiring that half of any commercial sign in a foreign language be in English.

Now I certainly would never tolerate any exclusionary ideas about who could rightfully settle and belong in the town. But having been raised in a Korean immigrant family, I saw every day the exacting price and power of language, especially with my mother, who was an outsider in an English-only world.

In the first years we lived in America, my mother could speak only the most basic English, and she often encountered great difficulty whenever she went out.

We lived in New Rochelle, New York in the early 70s, and most of the local businesses were run by the descendants of immigrants who, generations ago, had come to the suburbs from New York City. Proudly dotting Main Street and North Avenue were Italian pastry and cheese shops, Jewish tailors and cleaners and Polish and German butchers and bakers. If my mother's marketing couldn't wait until the weekend, when my father had free time, she would often hold off until I came home from school to buy the groceries.

Though I was only six or seven years old, she insisted that I go out shopping with her and my younger sister. I mostly loathed the task, partly because it meant I couldn't spend the afternoon playing catch with my friends but also because I knew our errands would inevitably lead to an awkward scene, and that I would have to speak up to help my mother.

I was just learning the language myself, but I was a quick study, as children are with new tongues. I had spent kindergarten in almost complete silence, hearing only the high nasality of my teacher and comprehending little but the cranky wails and cries of my classmates. But soon, seemingly mere months later, I had already become a terrible ham and mimic, and I would crack up my father with impressions of teachers, his friends and even himself. My mother scolded me for aping his speech, and the one time I attempted to make light of hers I rated a roundhouse smack on my bottom.

For her, the English language was not very funny. It usually meant trouble and a good dose of shame, and sometimes real hurt. Although she had a good reading knowledge of the language from university classes in South Korea, she had never practiced actual conversation. So in America, she used English flashcards and phrase books and watched television with us kids. And she faithfully carried a pocket workbook illustrated with stick-figure people and compound sentences to be filled in.

But none of it seemed to do her much good. Staying mostly at home to care for us, she didn't have many chances to try out sundry words and phrases. When she did, say, at the window of the post office, her readied speech would stall, freeze, sometimes altogether collapse.

One day was unusually harrowing. We ventured downtown in the new Ford Country Squire my father had bought her, an enormous station wagon that seemed as long—and deft—as an ocean liner. We were shopping for a special meal for guests visiting that weekend, and my mother had heard that a particular butcher carried fresh oxtails, which she needed for a traditional soup.

We'd never been inside the shop, but my mother would pause before its window, which was always lined with whole hams, crown roasts and ropes of plump handmade sausages. She greatly esteemed the bounty with her eyes, and my sister and I did also, but despite our desirous cries she'd turn us away and instead buy the packaged links at the Finast supermarket, where she felt comfortable looking them over and could easily spot the price. And, of course, not have to talk.

But that day she was resolved. The butcher store was crowded, and as we stepped inside the door jingled a welcome. No one seemed to notice. We waited for some time, and people who entered after us were now being served. Finally, an old woman nudged my mother and waved a little ticket, which we hadn't taken. We patiently waited again, until one of the beefy men behind the glass display hollered our number.

My mother pulled us forward and began searching the cases, but the oxtails were nowhere to be found. The man, his big arms crossed, sharply said, "Come on, lady, whaddya want?" This unnerved her, and she somehow blurted the Korean word for oxtail, soggori.

The butcher looked as if my mother had put something sour in his mouth, and he glanced back at the lighted board and called the next number.

Before I knew it, she had rushed us outside and back in the wagon, which she had double-parked because of the crowd. She was furious, almost vibrating with fear and grief, and I could see she was about to cry.

She wanted to go back inside, but now the driver of the car we were blocking wanted to pull out. She was shooing us away. My mother, who had just earned her driver's license, started furiously working the pedals. But in her haste she must have flooded the engine, for it wouldn't turn over. The driver started honking and then another car began honking as well, and soon the entire street was shrieking at us.

In the following years, my mother grew steadily more comfortable with English. In Korean, she could be fiery, stern, deeply funny and ironic; in English, just slightly less so. If she was never quite fluent, she gained enough confidence to make herself clearly known to anyone, and particularly to me.

Five years ago, she died of cancer, and some months after we buried her I found myself in the driveway of my father's house, washing her sedan. I liked taking care of her things; it made me feel close to her. While I was cleaning out the glove compartment, I found her pocket English workbook, the one with the silly illustrations. I hadn't seen it in nearly twenty years. The yellowed pages were brittle and dog-eared. She had fashioned a plain-paper wrapping for it, and I wondered whether she meant to protect the book or hide it.

I don't doubt that she would have appreciated doing the family shopping on the new Broad Avenue of Palisades Park. But I like to think, too, that she would have understood those who now complain about the Korean-only signs.

I wonder what these same people would have done if they had seen my mother studying her English workbook—or lost in a store. Would they have nodded gently at her? Would they have lent a kind word?

INTERPRETATIONS

1. What issues does Lee raise in the first paragraph?

2. What is his purpose in this essay? Is he seeking to inform or persuade his readers on the English-only debate? Cite evidence for your point of view.

3. How effectively does Lee's mother's workbook function literally and symbolically in the text?

A Letter to a Child Like Me

JOSÉ TORRES

José Torres (1936–2009) was raised in poverty in Puerto Rico. After winning a silver medal in the 1956 Olympic Games, he became a professional boxer and had a successful career that culminated in his winning the light-heavyweight boxing championship in 1965. A long interview with Torres on his life and career appears in In This Corner: 42 World Champions Tell Their Stories *(1994) by Peter Heller. Torres himself was the author of* Fire and Fear: The Inside Story of Mike Tyson *(1989). The following essay offers advice to young people of his ethnic background.*

DEAR PEDRITO:

You're thirteen now, and you must certainly be aware that there are some people in this country who refer to you as "Hispanic." That is, you're a member of a minority group. You read newspapers and magazines, you watch television, so you know that the world is moving into the twenty-first century faced with big problems, enormous possibilities, huge mysteries. I worry that you might not be fully prepared for the journey.

The statistics are scary. They show us Hispanics facing a sea of trouble. The United States has 250 million people, a little more than 20 million of whom are of Hispanic descent. That's only 8 percent of this nation's total population. We're also the youngest ethnic group in the nation. We earn the lowest salaries, and, in cities where we have a large concentration of Hispanics, we have the highest school dropout rate. In New York City, example, we comprise 25.7 percent of the high school dropouts, 42.7 percent of pregnant teenagers and 8.9 percent of the unemployed.

It should not be too hard for you to understand, my friend, that these statistics hurt us a lot. That means that many of our young people end up badly, as both victims and perpetrators. Some blame us for these conditions, despite our minuscule stock in this country and the fact the overwhelming majority of us are hardworking, decent, law-abiding citizens.

Still, you should realize that the world is not made up of statistics but of individuals. By the year 2030, you'll be my age, and what you do now is going to determine what you'll be doing then.

I've had my defeats; I've made my share of mistakes. But I've also learned something along the way. Let me tell you about a few of them. You didn't ask for this advice, but I'm going to give it to you anyway.

Let's start with a fundamental human problem, and I don't mean race or religion or origin. I mean fear. Fright, my young friend, may be the first serious enemy you have to face in our society. It's the most destructive emotional bogeyman there is. Cold feet, panic, depression, and violence are all symptoms of fear—when it's out of control. But this feeling, ironically, can also trigger courage, alertness, objectivity. You must learn not to try to rid yourself of this basic human emotion but to manipulate it for your own advantage. You cannot surrender to fear, but you *can* use it as a kind of fuel. Once you learn to control fear—to make it work for you—it will become one of your best friends.

I learned this the hard way. I was a boxer. I became a world champion, but on my way up the ladder I found Frankie Kid Anslem, a tough young Philadelphian made of steel. The match proceeded, to my increasing dismay, with me hitting and Anslem smiling. At one point, I remember, I let go a particularly left hook-right cross combination. The punches landed flush on his jaw, but he simply riposted with a smile—and some hard leather of his own.

Suddenly, I found myself struggling for my life. I was afraid. For two rounds—the eighth and ninth—Anslem and I seemed contestants in an evil struggle. My punches seemed to give him energy and pleasure! Unexpectedly, my chest began to burn, my legs weakened, my lungs gasped for air. I felt exhausted. I was dying! Thoughts of defeat and humiliation assailed me. I was grappling with these facts when I saw Anslem's jaw exposed and, reaching from somewhere beyond my terror, I threw a straight right with all my might. And Anslem lost his smile and dropped like an old shoe.

My fatigue disappeared. I felt good, happy, invigorated. Fear had overtaken me, been recognized, then resolved and manipulated for a positive result.

I was obliged to learn about handling fear through the brutal trade of boxing. I didn't have the option now open to you, my young friend. I was one of seven poor kids who lived under many layers of an underdeveloped subculture. I chose a tough profession because two black boxers—a heavyweight champion named Joe Louis, and a middleweight marvel called Sugar Ray Robinson—showed me the way. They lived far away from my hometown in Puerto Rico. But I knew them. I wanted to be like them.

Looking back, I wonder what my choice would have been if real alternatives had been available when I was your age. Don't get me wrong. I'm very proud of my first profession. To be recognized as the best in the world at what you do, even if only for a moment, is a wonderful experience. Still, I was very much aware that boxing was a temporary activity intended only for the young. And so I had a pretty good idea of what your choice should not be if you're given a chance to become an artist, a corporate executive, a doctor, a lawyer, an engineer, a writer, or a prizefighter—though it should be *my* choice.

Whatever your ambition, you must educate yourself. School is a great gift our society offers you. It provides the key for your future. You must accept this gift, not disdain it. School is where you'll learn about your country and your world and your life in both. You also discover the conflicts and contradictions of history. You'll unlock the treasure chest of the world's literature and begin to sense the beauty of music and art. You'll acquire the tools of abstract thinking, of science and mathematics—and the computer, perhaps the primary instrument of the world you'll inherit.

At home, you should learn about compassion and dignity and care. You should realize that the workings of an individual's heart and soul can be as important as the histories of the great battles, military generals, dictators and kings. Most of all, you should learn that it's *you* who are responsible for your future.

There is a basic principle you should never forget: Don't be ruled by other people's low expectation of you! It almost happened to me. I grew up in Playa de Ponce, a small *barrio* in the southern part of Puerto Rico, an island 100 miles long and 35 miles wide, with a dense population today of more than 3.3 million—1,000 human beings per square mile. I was only five when I first noticed the American military men—many of them tall, blond, and blue-eyed—wearing a variety of uniforms, roaming the streets of my neighborhood and picking up the prettiest girls. They seemed to own Playa de Ponce. Their attitude in the streets and their country's constant military victories, which we witnessed at the movie houses, became symbols of these young men's "obvious superiority." By comparison, we Puerto Ricans felt limited, inadequate.

To catch up, I volunteered to serve in the U.S. Army as soon as I became of age. And, for some mysterious reason, I joined its boxing team. My first four opponents were two compatriots and two black men from the Virgin Islands, all of whom I had no trouble disposing of. But just before my fifth fight—against one of those tall, blond, blue-eyed "superior" American soldiers, doubt started to creep into my mind. Yet, despite my worries, after three rounds of tough boxing, I overcame. I won! I had discovered the equality of the human race.

Your best defense against the ignorance of bigots and haters is pride in your own heritage. That's why you must learn your own history. Do it now. Don't wait until you are in college. You don't need teachers. Go to the library. Ask your parents and relatives and friends.

Be proud of your ethnicity and language. Don't be afraid to use it. Don't give up to the stupidity of those know-nothings who insist one language is better than two or three. You should know, and be proud, that in the Western Hemisphere more people speak Spanish than English; that Español was the language of the Hemisphere's first university—the Santo Tomás de Aquino University in the Dominican Republic, founded in 1538—and of the books in its first library. When you discover the long and honorable tradition to which you belong, your pride will soar.

So do not lose the language of your parents, which is also yours. Instead, refine your skill in it. If you're having trouble with grammar or writing, take courses in Spanish. Go to the library and read Cervantes' *Don Quixote*, the first full-fledged novel, or the works of the hundreds of great modern Hispanic authors, such as Gabriel García Márquez, Lola Rodriguez de Tió, Carlos Fuentes, Mario Vargas Llosa, Octavio Paz, Jorge Luis Borges, and Oscar Hijuelos, the 1990 Pulitzer Prize winner in fiction (who writes in English). Read them in both languages; know the strength of both. This is the treasure that no one can ever beat.

Puerto Rico is a nearly imperceptible dot on the map, my friend. Still, this small island recently had five boxing champions at the same time. And consider this: Baseball star Reggie Jackson; the great entertainer Sammy Davis, Jr.; Dr. Joaquín Balaguer, poet, writer and six-time president of the Dominican Republic; the renowned cellist Pablo Casals all had one thing in common—one of their parents was Puerto Rican. The film and stage star Rita Moreno, a Puerto Rican, is one of the few performers ever to win an Oscar, a Tony, a Grammy, and an Emmy award. José Ferrer, a proud Puerto Rican, was once selected as the American citizen with the finest English diction in the United States. Ferrer also won an Oscar for his brilliant performance in the classic film *Cyrano de Bergerac*. Dr. Raul García Rinaidi, a physician of world prominence and a native Puerto Rican, helped invent six instruments now used in cardiovascular surgery. Arturo Alfonso Schomburg, a native Puerto Rican, made extensive investigation into Black history. In his honor, the New York Public Library system erected the Schomburg Center for Research in Black Culture.

The contribution of Hispanics to the development of the United States of America has been vast and unquestionable. But much more remains to be done, my friend. Every member of society must work together in order to survive together.

We live in a country where more than 27 million people can't read or write well enough to take a driving test, and many can't recognize "danger," or "poison." Every eight seconds of the school day a student drops out; every sixty seconds a teenager has a baby; every six minutes a child is arrested for drugs; every year, the schools graduate 700,000 who cannot read their diplomas.

Most of them are *not* Hispanics. Yet, many of these victims are the same people who, day after day, throw themselves in front of a TV set and become passive, docile ghosts, allowing their lives to be easily controlled by others. Television, with its emphasis on package images and quick bites, discourages thought and imagination. Studies indicate that chronic televiewers develop problems with their thinking processes and articulation. Excessive viewing dulls the most indispensable muscle—the brain.

Instead of watching TV, read and write. Words are the symbols of reality, and a well-read person, skilled at decoding those symbols, is better able to comprehend and think about the real world.

Many years ago, the great Japanese artist, Katsushika Hokusai lay on his deathbed at age 89. Experts say no one could paint better than Hokusai during his prime, and many are convinced that his work is as good as—or better than—today's top artists. But Hokusai was never satisfied with his triumphs and successes. "If I could live one more year," he said, "I could learn how to draw."

You, my young friend, would do well to become like Hokusai—a person who can lead a humble but useful and productive life, free of harm and, most important, free of the influences that generate hate, murder, suicide, and death. If you choose to spend your time not reading, thinking, and creating, but watching TV and learning how to deceive, cheat, and lie, then you become another person out there perpetuating the cycle of ignorance that leads to poverty, suffering, and despair. But if you commit yourself to a lifetime of honest work—if you assure yourself that a day in which you are unable to produce anything positive is a tragically misspent day—then, my friend, the twenty-first century is yours.

Go and get it!

INTERPRETATIONS

1. Why does Torres begin his letter by citing mainly negative statistics about Hispanics and then go on to say that "the world is not made up of statistics but of individuals"?

2. Torres tells his young friend that fear may be his greatest enemy. How did Torres overcome his own fear? To what extent do you agree or disagree about the negative power of fear?

3. "School is a great gift our society offers you." What evidence does he cite to support his thesis? How do your experiences with school correspond to Torres's expectation?

4. "Be proud of your ethnicity and language." What evidence did you find most convincing regarding this advice?

5. Respond to Torres's views on watching television, particularly to his comment about television's dulling the brain.

CORRESPONDENCES

1. Lee focuses on the connection between language and powerlessness, whereas Torres emphasizes the relation between language and power. What factors account for differences in their points of view?

2. What conversation can you imagine Lee and Torres sharing on the issue of bilingualism? What would you add to the debate?

APPLICATIONS

1. Write a journal entry responding to Lee's title. Can you imagine being mute in a culture whose native language is not English? How might you respond in a situation similar to the one in the butcher's shop?

2. Listen to the sounds of a language that you do not understand. Listen for rhythms and melodies. How would you describe this language as a song?

3. According to Torres, "Television, with its emphasis on packaged images and quick bites, discourages thought and imagination." Debate this issue with your group, citing examples from your own experience that support or refute Torres. What consensus did you reach?

4. Create a concept map of the types of learning or education that Torres presents in his essay. To learn more about concept mapping, check the following Web sites:

   http://www.cotf.edu/ete/pb12.html

   http://users.edte.utwente.nl/lanzing/cm_home.htm

Always Living in Spanish

MARJORIE AGOSÍN

Marjorie Agosín was born in 1955 in Bethesda, Maryland, but spent her child-hood in Chile. She immigrated with her family to the United States just before Salvador Allende's government was overthrown by the dictatorship of Augusto Pinochet. The holder of a B.A. from the University of Georgia and a Ph.D. from Indiana University–Bloomington, she teaches in the Department of Spanish at Wellesley College. Author of more than forty books, Agosín writes in many forms: poetry, short fiction, autobiography, essays, longer works of nonfiction, as well as editing collections of other writers' work, such as her recent Writing Toward Hope: The Literature of Human Rights in Latin America *(2007).* A Cross and a Star: Memoirs of a Jewish Girl in Chile *(1995) illustrates her cross-cultural and human rights interests: it is about her family's life in a small town in southern Chile (Osorno) from the perspective of her mother, who was excluded from all schools except the one for orphans and Indians. Two other books, both published in 1996, also explore human rights issues:* Tapestries of Hope, Threads of Love: The Arpillera Movement in Chile 1974–1994 *and* Ashes of Revolt: Essays on Human Rights. *Between 1980 and 2004 she published eight books of poetry. Agosín is the winner of the 1995 Letros de Oro Award, and in 1998 the Chilean government bestowed on Agosín the Gabriela Mistral Medal of Honor for Lifetime Achievement. See if Agosín whets your appetite to know more about the details of her life.*

Agosín comes by her interest in human rights naturally. Chile's popu-lation, largely urban, is 95 percent European and Mestizo and 3 percent Indian. Salvador Allende, a Marxist, was elected president in 1970, but three years later General Augusto Pinochet seized power and ruled until 1990. Under his military dictatorship nearly three thousand people were executed, "disappeared," or died as a result of torture and other kinds of political violence.

IN THE EVENINGS in the northern hemisphere, I repeat the ancient ritual that I observed as a child in the southern hemisphere: going out while the night is still warm and trying to recognize the stars as it begins to grow dark silently. In the sky of my country, Chile, that long and wide stretch of land that the poets blessed and dictators abused, I could eas-ily name the stars: the three Marias, the Southern Cross, and the three Lilies, names of beloved and courageous women.

But here in the United States, where I have lived since I was a young girl, the solitude of exile makes me feel that so little is mine, that not even the sky has the same constellations, the trees and the fauna the same names or sounds, or the rubbish the same smell. How does one recover the familiar? How does one name the unfamiliar? How can one be another or live in a foreign language? These are the dilemmas of one who writes in Spanish and lives in translation.

Since my earliest childhood in Chile I lived with the tempos and the melodies of a multiplicity of tongues: German, Yiddish, Russian, Turkish, and many Latin songs. Because everyone was from somewhere else, my relatives laughed, sang, and fought in a Babylon of languages. Spanish was reserved for matters of extreme seriousness, for commercial transactions, or for illnesses, but everyone's mother tongue was always associated with the memory of spaces inhabited in the past: the shtetl, the flowering and vast Vienna avenues, the minarets of Turkey, and the Ladino whispers of Toledo. When my paternal grandmother sang old songs in Turkish, her voice and body assumed the passion of one who was there in the city of Istanbul, gazing by turns toward the west and the east.

Destiny and the always ambiguous nature of history continued my family's enforced migration, and because of it I, too, became one who had to live and speak in translation. The disappearances, torture, and clandestine deaths in my country in the early seventies drove us to the United States, that other America that looked with suspicion at those who did not speak English and especially those who came from the supposedly uncivilized regions of Latin America. I had left a dangerous place that was my home, only to arrive in a dangerous place that was not: a high school in the small town of Athens, Georgia, where my poor English and my accent were the cause of ridicule and insult. The only way I could recover my usurped country and my Chilean childhood was by continuing to write in Spanish, the same way my grandparents had sung in their own tongues in diasporic sites.

The new and learned English language did not fit with the visceral emotions and themes that my poetry contained, but by writing in Spanish I could recover fragrances, spoken rhythms, and the passion of my own identity. Daily I felt the need to translate myself for the strangers living all around me, to tell them why we were in Georgia, why we are different, why we had fled, why my accent was so thick, and why I did not look Hispanic. Only at night, writing poems in Spanish, could I return to my senses, and soothe my own sorrow over what I had left behind.

This is how I became a Chilean poet who wrote in Spanish and lived in the southern United States. And then, one day, a poem of mine was translated and published in the English language. Finally, for the first time since I had left Chile, I felt I didn't have to explain myself. My poem, expressed in another language, spoke for itself . . . and for me.

Sometimes the austere sounds of English help me bear the solitude of knowing that I am foreign and so far away from those about whom I write. I must admit I would like more opportunities to read in Spanish to people whose language and culture is also mine, to join in our common heritage and in the feast of our sounds. I would also like readers of English to understand the beauty of the spoken word in Spanish, that constant flow of oxytonic and paraoxytonic syllables (*Verde que te quiero verdo*), the joy of writing—of dancing—in another language. I believe that many exiles share the unresolvable torment of not being able to live in the language of their childhood.

I miss that undulating and sensuous language of mine, those baroque descriptions, the sense of being and feeling that Spanish gives me. It is perhaps for this reason that I have chosen and will always choose to write in Spanish. Nothing else from my childhood world remains. My country seems to be frozen in gestures of silence and oblivion. My relatives have died, and I have grown up not knowing a young generation of cousins and nieces and nephews. Many of my friends disappeared, others were tortured, and the most fortunate, like me, became guardians of memory. For us, to write in Spanish is to always be in active pursuit of memory. I seek to recapture a world lost to me on that sorrowful afternoon when the blue electric sky and the Andean cordillera bade me farewell. On that, my last Chilean day, I carried under my arm my innocence recorded in a little blue notebook I kept even then. Gradually that diary filled with memoranda, poems written in free verse, descriptions of dreams and of the thresholds of my house surrounded by cherry trees and gardenias. To write in Spanish is for me a gesture of survival. And because of translation, my memory has now become a part of the memory of many others.

Translators are not traitors, as the proverb says, but rather splendid friends in this great human community of language.

INTERPRETATIONS

1. Brainstorm on the multiple meanings in Agosín's title.
2. What evidence does she provide to support her statement that she "left a place that was my home, only to arrive in a dangerous place that was not."
3. Agosín offers several reasons as to why she will always write in Spanish. Which do you find most convincing?
4. Explain the conclusion of her essay.

CORRESPONDENCES

1. What conversation can you imagine Torres and Agosín sharing on the issue of biculturalism? What would you add to the debate?

2. Compare and contrast the tone of Agosín's and Lee's texts. How is purpose related to tone in each essay?

APPLICATIONS

1. Discuss with your group Agosín's statement that she believes that "many exiles share the unresolvable torment of not being able to live in the language of their childhood." If this is also your experience, what would you add to the examples Agosín offers?

2. Agosín discloses much about herself as a result of her family's "forced migration" from Chile to the United States. If you have had a similar experience, write an essay about what you learned about yourself.

3. Write a journal entry on the relationship between language and identity according to Agosín.

The Mistress of Make Believe

DORIS VILORIA

Doris Viloria (b. 1972) was brought up and educated in Queens, New York, and is a graduate of Queens College–City University of New York (CUNY). As you read Viloria's essay, find evidence to support her introductory paragraph.

SHE WAS HUGE, but in a majestic awe-inspiring way like a mountain that only added to her enigma. The word fat never came to mind.

"Good morning class," she'd briskly salute each day, as she marched in on stiletto heels. Her hair would be piled high on her head, in a fountain of honey blond and gray tendrils that was most undoubtedly dyed. The heady scent of lilacs drenched the room as she entered; a tornado of fragrances, heavy makeup, and shopping bags, her gaudy jewelry sending out smart metallic clinks. She always squeezed herself into tight "form fitting" cashmere turtlenecks, which emphasized her rather copious stomach and voluptuous bosom and created the illusion of a kind of fanciful, woman-caterpillar hybrid. Then shifting her bulk considerably, she would sit atop her tall, rickety wooden swivel chair, crossing her legs jauntily, and bringing one polished long red fingernail to her lips. As her meaty arms settled on her lectern, one perfectly tweezed eyebrow languidly drifted up like a cobra, contemplating the class.

"Aaah," she'd purr in her thick coppery, baritone New England accent, as she towered over us, her mouth curling up in a sly grin. "How many of you are ready to let your imagination take you off to distant mystical lands?"

Together we explored the unbridled savagery of William Golding's *The Lord of the Flies* , the silent yearnings and personal betrayals of John Knowles' *A Separate Peace* , and the coming of age in the heart of injustice of a young girl in Harper Lee's *To Kill a Mockingbird*. Golding's desolate, desperate island sprang to life as she needled us with questions.

"Is man simply a beast temporarily tamed by years of affecting proper etiquette, whose mask might drop if taken out of his 'civilized' environment?" she'd fire at us. "How would any of you react if placed in a jungle where your actions were accountable to no one? Would you aspire to rule as a belligerent dictator, or would you struggle to maintain your moralistic humanity and preserve democracy?"

Having thus spat out these challenges she would take a long draught of steaming black coffee from her styrofoam cup, leaving a sharp stain of fuschia lipstick on the rim. Then in a smokey, hypnotic tone she would read a passage from the book. The mood became trance-like as we followed her into the story. Afterwards, those characters would linger about the room like inspirational phantoms as I slaved over my writing assignment.

Creating solely on pure instinct and guided by the illuminations of those benevolent daimons, I wrote a short story based on a gripping, terrifying nightmare I'd had. It was as though I had exorcised all the horrors of my dream from myself, and they had metamorphosized into a story that had a life of its own. With a feeling of deep-seated pride and accomplishment, I turned it in.

Walking out of class one day, I heard that unmistakable voice ask for a moment of my time. I was brimming with curiosity as I approached her desk. Those penetrating blue eyes gazed at me with a mixture of respect and mischief. Tapping my story gently on her desk, she inclined that lion's mane of a head to the side and whispered in a close and confidential way, "Where did it come from?"

My eyes darted about the room as I searched for some response. Finally, I turned to her levelly and said honestly, "It just sort of wove itself."

Nodding her head in understanding after what seemed like an hour, she handed me the paper. "It really is very special," she said with a sigh. "You have a way with words that is a talent, a gift. I expect you to be a woman of great individual distinction."

Those words have bolstered me like iron saviors through countless fits of self-doubt and introspection over the past few years. I walked out of the room that day with charmed visions of exquisitely soaring dragonflies before me. The spell has never waned.

INTERPRETATIONS

1. What scene and what group of people do you assume the author to be describing? How effective is that description? What purpose does the description seem intended to serve?

2. How do you interpret the question "Where did it [the story] come from?" How important to the meaning of the essay is this question?

3. How would this essay be affected if the story itself were included or appended here?

4. The last paragraph is perhaps the most important in terms of the meaning of the essay. Comment on the effectiveness of saving this information until the end.

CORRESPONDENCES

1. Review Moore's perspective. How does it apply to Viloria's educational experience? How many "enchanting" minds are there in her essay?

2. Review Borges's perspective on books. To what extent does it apply to Viloria's essay? To your own experiences with reading?

APPLICATIONS

1. Viloria is excited by using language effectively. You may be creative in another medium, such as photography, music, art, or dance. Write an essay describing your creative process and the emotions it evokes.

2. Write a journal entry describing the teacher from whom you learned most. Re-create the classroom environment. How was it conducive to learning? Describe a learning activity that excited you.

3. Write a journal entry comparing and contrasting an experience with reading or writing that took place outside of the classroom. How was it different from reading or writing in school?

4. Notice Viloria's use of details in this essay. From her description, create a drawing of "The Mistress of Make Believe." Which details in the text have you focused upon in your artwork?

From Dropout to Graduate

LAURA KUEHN

Laura Kuehn (b. 1976) was raised in Ellisville, Illinois, and graduated from high school in 1994. She moved to New York City in 2000 and two years later enrolled in Queensborough Community College (CUNY). After a two-year break in her studies, she graduated with an A.A. degree with honors from Queensborough and will continue her studies for the B.A. degree at Queens College (CUNY). She hopes that her essay will encourage students returning to college after a break in their studies.

WHEN I WAS FOURTEEN AND A FRESHMAN in high school, I, like many of my classmates, began thinking of college. Of course, back then my expectations weren't so much on academics as they were on other things. College was all about experiencing the first taste of parental freedom, meeting new and interesting people, late night cram sessions, and most importantly . . . partying! Or so that's how my girlfriends and I imagined it to be. However, many years would pass, long after graduating high school, before I would get my chance at college. And when I finally got there, the last thing on my mind was partying.

Soon after high school, even before I was eighteen, I moved out of my family's home to live with my boyfriend. A couple of years later he and I would be married with a mortgage. I suppose I could have gone to college then, but between taking care of a husband, a home, and maintaining my two part-time jobs I was exhausted. But that's what happens. Looking back, it seems to me that the longer I waited to attend college the bigger the obstacles were to get there. Before I knew it I was in my mid-twenties, divorced, bankrupt, and uneducated. I had been through a slew of dead-end jobs and was all out frustrated. That's when I packed up and moved to New York City. Luck was on my side though, and within several months I was managing a successful yet small club in Manhattan, so I decided to consider college again.

After years of being out of high school I was terrified of the thought of college. It no longer was about the social aspect, but rather the academics. I can still recall vividly the day a good friend went with me to check out a college campus. I became so consumed with self-doubt that I had a full blown anxiety attack. My friend sat with me in the parking lot as my tears flowed and listened to me profess my ineptitude. But I mustered up the courage and a month later took the entrance exam to my local community college. To my own amazement I scored quite well on portions of the exam.

In the spring of 2001, almost seven years after high school, I began attending my first college courses at Queensborough Community College. I was exempted from English 101 and allowed to immediately take English 102 Honors. I also took a simple math course. I was thrilled! And I was overwhelmed! My first semester of college only seemed to prove what I had feared all along. My full-time job that paid the bills was a priority and it left virtually no time for my studies. I endured that first semester and barely scraped by one more. Consequently, I finished out my second semester and begrudgingly left my newfound college life behind.

So, for a while, I accepted things as they were. And at first things were good. I had a good paying job and could afford a better life. But as the years went by I realized that I had peaked. I saw no advancement. No ladder of success to climb higher and higher. I managed that club for over three and a half years and never once requested vacation time. I was never late and sometimes worked twelve-hour shifts. Why? Because I was scared. Without an education to back me up I was afraid to lose the job. I was trapped. And miserable. Once again I found myself thinking of college, but this time things would be different. Nothing was going to get in my way. I prepared myself for a rough road ahead.

I registered for two courses in the spring of 2004. I studied hard and did well. Yet I knew I needed to make some drastic changes if I was going to make my second attempt at college work. So that fall I quit my job and focused all my energy on school. By the end of the fall 2004 semester I was on the dean's list and accepted back into the Honor's program. To pay the bills I did whatever odd job would fit into my school schedule. One day I'd be tending bar or waiting tables and the next I'd be doing makeup or hair for a photo shoot. It didn't matter as long as I could study.

The further I got into my school career the more excited I became. Sure I was poorer, lonelier, and more frustrated than ever! But I was happier than ever. In the spring of 2006 I graduated with honors from Queensborough Community College with an associate's degree in liberal arts and sciences. To some it may seem minuscule, but to me it was empowering.

Soon I will be starting classes at Queens College and I plan on continuing my academic success. Things are much different than when I first began QCC. Now I know my own strength and determination, and I have confidence in myself. I agreed to write this essay about my journey because I know that I'm not alone. There are countless others like myself who deprive themselves of an education because they think it's too late. As adults, we have jobs, spouses, children, bills, and many other responsibilities that we can't simply overlook. However, we also have a responsibility to ourselves. I can't say where I'll be in five years (who can?), but I do know that my chances of having a better life are greater with an education. My college experience thus far has had a positive effect. I know, without any doubt, that every sacrifice I've made or will make has been worth it. My education is priceless to me. It is something that no one can take away.

INTERPRETATIONS

1. Why did Kuehn drop out of college? Why did she return?
2. How did Kuehn approach college the first time she enrolled? How about the second time? What similarities and/or differences do you notice?
3. How does Kuehn feel after completing her associate's degree?

CORRESPONDENCES

1. What might Kuehn have learned from reading Torres's "A Letter to a Child Like Me"?
2. Kuehn's essay is in certain ways a literacy narrative. How does her story compare with those of Marshall (page 173) and Cremona (page 195)?

APPLICATIONS

1. How did you decide to enroll in college? Write your story!

   Try to clarify in your narrative your motives and motivations for attending college, your expectations of it, and the realities you encountered in your first semester. How does your story compare with Kuehn's?
2. What must a student have to succeed in college?

   Make a list of five characteristics that you think are most important. Compare these items with those on the lists of the members of your peer group. What three characteristics can you all agree on? Be prepared to explain to your whole class why these three qualities are essential.
3. Some people think it best that all students take a year off before attending college. What do you think of this idea? As you present your reasons in an essay, explain what you might have done in that year between high school and college.

The Fender-Bender

RAMÓN "TIANGUIS" PÉREZ

Ramón "Tianguis" Pérez is an undocumented alien. Of necessity he does not disclose information about his life or his whereabouts. "The Fender-Bender" is an excerpt from his book Diary of an Undocumented Immigrant *(1991) and gives a glimpse of his life in this country.*

ONE NIGHT AFTER WORK, I drive Rolando's old car to visit some friends, and then head towards home. At a light, I come to a stop too late, leaving the front end of the car poking into the crosswalk. I shift into reverse, but as I am backing up, I strike the van behind me. Its driver immediately gets out to inspect the damage to his vehicle. He's a tall Anglo-Saxon, dressed in a deep blue work uniform. After looking at his car, he walks up to the window of the car I'm driving.

"Your driver's license," he says, a little enraged.

"I didn't bring it," I tell him.

He scratches his head. He is breathing heavily with fury.

"Okay," he says. "You park up ahead while I call a patrolman."

The idea of calling the police doesn't sound good to me, but the accident is my fault. So I drive around the corner and park at the curb. I turn off the motor and hit the steering wheel with one fist. I don't have a driver's license. I've never applied for one. Nor do I have with me the identification card that I bought in San Antonio. Without immigration papers, without a driving permit, and having hit another car, I feel as if I'm just one step away from Mexico.

I get out of the car. The white man comes over and stands right in front of me. He's almost two feet taller.

"If you're going to drive, why don't you carry your license?" he asks in an accusatory tone.

"I didn't bring it," I say, for lack of any other defense.

I look at the damage to his car. It's minor, only a scratch on the paint and a pimple-sized dent.

"I'm sorry," I say. "Tell me how much it will cost to fix, and I'll pay for it; that's no problem." I'm talking to him in English, and he seems to understand.

"This car isn't mine," he says. "It belongs to the company I work for. I'm sorry, but I've got to report this to the police, so that I don't have to pay for the damage." "That's no problem," I tell him again. "I can pay for it."

After we've exchanged these words, he seems less irritated. But he says he'd prefer for the police to come, so that they can report that the dent wasn't his fault.

While we wait, he walks from one side to the other, looking down the avenue this way and that, hoping that the police will appear.

Then he goes over to the van to look at the dent.

"It's not much," he says. "If it was my car, there wouldn't be any problems, and you could go on."

After a few minutes, the long-awaited police car arrives. Only one officer is inside. He's a Chicano, short and of medium complexion, with short, curly hair. On getting out of the car, he walks straight towards the Anglo.

The two exchange a few words.

"Is that him?" he asks, pointing at me.

The Anglo nods his head.

Speaking in English, the policeman orders me to stand in front of the car and to put my hands on the hood. He searches me and finds only the car keys and my billfold with a few dollars in it. He asks for my driver's license.

"I don't have it," I answer in Spanish.

He wrinkles his face into a frown, and casting a glance at the Anglo, shakes his head in disapproval of me.

"That's the way these Mexicans are," he says.

He turns back towards me, asking for identification. I tell him I don't have that, either.

"You're an illegal, eh?" he says.

I won't answer.

"An illegal," he says to himself.

"Where do you live?" he continues. He's still speaking in English.

I tell him my address.

"Do you have anything with you to prove that you live at that address?" he asks.

I think for a minute, then realize that in the glove compartment is a letter that my parents sent to me several weeks earlier.

I show him the envelope and he immediately begins to write something in a little book that he carries in his back pocket. He walks to the back of my car and copies the license plate number. Then he goes over to his car and talks into his radio. After he talks, someone answers.

Then he asks me for the name of the car's owner.

He goes over to where the Anglo is standing. I can't quite hear what they're saying. But when the two of them go over to look at the dent in the van, I hear the cop tell the Anglo that if he wants, he can file charges against me. The Anglo shakes his head and explains what he had earlier explained to me, about only needing for the police to certify that he wasn't responsible for the accident. The Anglo says that he doesn't want to accuse me of anything because the damage is light.

"If you want, I can take him to jail," the cop insists.

The Anglo turns him down again.

"If you'd rather, we can report him to Immigration," the cop continues.

Just as at the first, I am now almost sure that I'll be making a forced trip to Tijuana. I find myself searching my memory for my uncle's telephone number, and to my relief, I remember it. I am waiting for the Anglo to say yes, confirming my expectations of the trip. But instead, he says no, and though I remain silent, I feel appreciation for him. I ask myself why the Chicano is determined to harm me. I didn't really expect him to favor me, just because we're of the same ancestry, but on the other hand, once I had admitted my guilt, I expected him to treat me at least fairly. But even against the white man's wishes, he's trying to make matters worse for me. I've known several Chicanos with whom, joking around, I've reminded them that their roots are in Mexico. But very few of them see it that way. Several have told me how when they were children, their parents would take them to vacation in different states of Mexico, but their own feeling, they've said, is, "I am an American citizen!" Finally, the Anglo, with the justifying paper in his hands, says goodbye to the cop, thanks him for his services, gets into his van and drives away.

The cop stands in the street in a pensive mood. I imagine that he's trying to think of a way to punish me.

"Put the key in the ignition," he orders me.

I do as he says.

Then he orders me to roll up the windows and lock the doors.

"Now, go on, walking," he says.

I go off taking slow steps. The cop gets in his patrol car and stays there, waiting. I turn the corner after two blocks and look out for my car, but the cop is still parked beside it. I begin looking for a coat hanger, and after a good while, find one by a curb of the street. I keep walking, keeping about two blocks away from the car. While I walk, I bend the coat hanger into the form I'll need. As if I'd called for it, a speeding car goes past. When it comes to the avenue where my car is parked, it makes a turn. It is going so fast that its wheels screech as it rounds the corner. The cop turns on the blinking lights of his patrol car and leaving black marks on the pavement beneath it, shoots out to chase the speeder. I go up to my car and with my palms force a window open a crack. Then I insert the clothes hanger in the crack and raise the lock lever. It's a simple task, one that I'd already performed. This wasn't the first time that I'd been locked out of a car, though always before, it was because I'd forgotten to remove my keys.

INTERPRETATIONS

1. Compare and contrast the attitudes of the Anglo driver and the Chicano cop at the scene of the fender-bender.
2. Why do you think the Anglo chooses not to report the illegal alien to Immigration? Does it surprise you that the cop is intent on punishing the Mexican? Why or why not?
3. Characterize the tone of the narrative. Is it objective? Subjective? Ironic?

CORRESPONDENCES

1. Create a conversation between Torres and Pérez on the topic of illegal immigrants.
2. Assume the persona of the Chicano cop and write a journal entry defending his point of view. What did you learn from this experience?

APPLICATIONS

1. Discuss with your group stereotyping in "The Fender-Bender."
2. Review the last paragraph of the essay. What does it reveal about the attitude of the "illegal" toward his situation? Write an essay discussing the thematic implications of the author's use of irony in "The Fender-Bender."
3. The rights and status of illegal aliens became the subject of national debate in recent decades, resulting in severe penalties and legal restrictions. What is your point of view? Do you think, for example, that "illegals" pose a threat to the job market, given the fact that most of them are involved in menial tasks and paid below minimum wage? Summarize your discussion.

When the Simulated Patient Is for Real

TANEISHA GRANT

Taneisha Grant was born in Portland, Jamaica, and migrated to the United States at age 14. She received a B.S. in Biology from the City College of the City University of NY and then completed medical school at Albert Einstein College of Medicine in the Bronx, New York. She later completed postgraduate, medical residency training in the Yale Primary Care Internal Medicine Program.

I WALKED INTO THE EMERGENCY ROOM early one morning and was welcomed by the sounds of a man yelling profanities while struggling against his restraints. He was screaming to be released as he was being held against his will. He was going to file claims of police brutality because he was just an innocent pedestrian who had been approached and beaten by police officers in the early morning hours. He was irate because their attack was unwarranted.

He had not been engaging in any suspicious activity. To make matters worse, he was hungry and demanded to be brought a breakfast tray. If he did not get a tray instantly, ". . . things were going to really start getting ugly."

He was handcuffed to the stretcher and a police officer kept watch close by. Since it was still quite early there was little else competing for my attention. That would likely change quickly, though, which is in keeping with the high-paced energy of the oftentimes chaotic emergency room. This man was making quite a scene and he definitely had everyone's attention, but we watched silently from a distance.

He was a twenty-four-year-old black man under arrest for disorderly conduct. The police had made a detour to the emergency room en route to the police station, where he would be booked for the noted offense. During the attempt at arrest, the police officers used a baton and the man sustained a 2 centimeter laceration to the area just above his right eye. He needed to have sutures placed and he was to be my patient.

The doctor whose shift I was assuming had not had a chance to examine this patient yet and apologized to me for what she guessed would be a difficult encounter. I will refer to this patient as Mr. G.

180

Mr. G is the personification of the irate, belligerent patient that you always dread dealing with because he is usually implacable. This is the patient that everyone avoids just so that he does not become even more riled up. This had been the case here, too. There is very little that anyone can say or do to satisfy him short of removing his handcuffs and discharging him from the ER. This is not an option.

Usually, so many "offenses" have transpired by the time the examining physician approaches him, that all the patient's grievances are taken out on that doctor. Medical students and residents receive training for situations like these and I sifted through my "mental Rolodex" of "patient types."

The aggressive patient, the sexual patient, the highly educated patient and the angry patient were a few simulated patient scenarios from my training that came to mind. I remembered working with actors who pantomimed these potential encounters with my classmates and me. Unfortunately, I couldn't think of one where the patient was ever this angry or so seemingly physically threatening. I did not remember a case where there were police involved and a patient was in custody.

I have visited patients in prisons and patients who have needed to be involuntarily committed to psychiatric institutions. This was a different situation. I took a deep breath and approached Mr. G, who was about twice my size.

I tried to appear as brave and calm as possible as I approached him. I was more concerned about being physically harmed than about receiving some verbal onslaught. I knew that the latter was inevitable if past behavior was any predictor. I tried to take comfort in the fact that he was handcuffed, that there was a police officer at the bedside and that I was surrounded by people in the emergency room.

I introduced myself as Dr. Grant and told him that I was there to suture his laceration. He confirmed my status by inspecting my badge but still seemed very annoyed and turned away from me.

His posture softened after I said that I was sorry to see him so upset and wanted to know how he sustained his injury. I already knew the story but I was trying to create some rapport. I was doubtful that he would have the patience to go down the rapport-building path with me but I kept talking anyway. It helped to keep my mind off my own nervousness.

To my surprise he answered my questions and eventually turned to face me. He repeated the same story that he had been yelling out for the thirty minutes before I saw him while I cleaned and examined the extent of his wound. He felt as if his rights had been violated, that he was being treated like a criminal and that he wanted me to call his mother.

Mr. G did not allow me to use a syringe that the medical student working with me had pre-filled with lidocaine intended to numb the skin. He insisted that we get all new supplies; break all seals, open all needles and fill all syringes in front of him. He also wanted step-by-step instructions about what I was doing. I complied.

I placed four sutures and then went to telephone his mother.

I went back and told Mr. G that his mother was on her way to the hospital. He thanked me quietly and I walked away realizing that my heart was racing.

The profile of an angry, handcuffed man in police custody possibly intoxicated by drugs is enough to make someone reproachable. I was proud of myself for having accomplished my task. There are some technicalities involved in placing sutures, but beyond that I was proud of myself because I had decided not to prejudge Mr. G.

The contradictions in Mr. G's character were so striking. He was a tough guy (or so he made us believe) who wanted his mommy, a hungry man dependent on us for food. I suspect that a lot of his outbursts and "machismo" stemmed from a place of fear, vulnerability, perceived personal insignificance and suspicion of the medical system and doctors.

I wonder if I was able to have a successful interaction with him because I used the patient-centered interviewing skills that I learnt in medical school or if it was because our skins were of the same color. It was probably a bit of both.

I also remembered my multi-cultural seminars from medical school and how my teachers strived to teach cultural awareness and sensitivity. . . . These are important lessons but there are times when classroom didactics are not enough.

In practicing medicine and treating sick, vulnerable people, I've found it best to rely not only on the lessons from my medical school training. I often draw from experiences that I have had outside of my workplace—I think of times when I go to the doctor and feel overwhelmed and frustrated. I remember that patients may have low health literacy or may project emotions that are not related to the situation at hand.

I try to empathize with my patients because I realize that the medical encounter can be intimidating. It must be even more so when you feel as if your basic human rights are being violated.

I realize that each of my patients is unique. Each may be a victim of circumstance, a product of an environment and community that is subject to hate, malice and prejudice of every kind. My encounter with Mr. G strengthened my belief that every patient should remain just that—my patient, unshrouded by race, criminal implications, gender and socioeconomic status in my perceptions.

I also embrace education in all its forms, from the formal to the informal. This is where "the art" of medicine comes into play. Keeping that human inter-connectedness in mind is sometimes what makes a potentially volatile situation much more pleasant.

This encounter was a reminder to me that even after twenty-eight years of schooling, my education continues, both inside and outside the classroom. I look forward to many more lessons.

INTERPRETATIONS

1. What do you think Grant ultimately learns from her encounter with Mr. G.? How does she acquire this knowledge?

2. Why does Mr. G. insist upon receiving new supplies and witnessing their unpacking? What does Grant's willingness to comply with his demands say about her?

3. At the end of the essay, Grant states: "I also embrace education in all its forms, from the formal to the informal." Where does she present evidence of each type of learning? Provide specific examples.

CORRESPONDENCES

1. When you examine the narrators of McDonald's "A View from the Bridge" and Grant's "When the Simulated Patient Is for Real," what do you observe about how they act and how they are affected by their experiences? What changes in their behavior do you notice as the events of the story unfold?

2. Although Grant's patient and the young writer portrayed in Doris Viloria's essay "The Mistress of Make Believe" are worlds apart in many ways, what similarities might you find? What general message might the experiences of both of these people convey?

APPLICATIONS

1. One primary theme of Grant's essay is the contrast between what she has learned in school and what she has learned on the job. What do you think is most important: book learning or experience? In an argumentation and persuasion essay, support only one of these as being most important to you. State a clear thesis and use each body paragraph to develop fully one supporting argument. Also remember to create an introduction that grabs a reader's attention and a conclusion that summarizes what you have said but that also makes your essay memorable!

2. *All I Really Need to Know I Learned in Kindergarten* is the title of a
    popular book published several years ago. As you reflect back on
    your education, in what grade do you think you learned all that
    you needed to know? (Think in terms of academics, social experi-
    ences, self-knowledge, creative expression.) Write a literacy narra-
    tive (see pages 10–13) that tells about this year, why it is important
    to you, and what you learned.

Literacy Narratives

The literacy narratives of Paule Marshall and Vincent Cremona involve metaphors—a figure of speech that makes an implicit comparison between two dissimilar things. A metaphor is complex, inventive, subtle, and powerful. It can transform people, places, objects, and ideas into whatever the writer imagines them to be. Successful metaphors make it possible for us as readers to "see" things in new ways. What is your response, for example, to the metaphor that "the heart is a lonely hunter"? In Paule Marshall's narrative, her poets inform us that "the sea ain' got no back door," whereas Vincent Cremona transforms a familiar metaphor from the workplace into one that describes his writing style. As you read their narratives, think of a metaphor that you might use to describe your writing.

Giovanni Gelardi utilizes another literary term, symbolism, when describing how he has created a work of art. Discussing his desire to "bring to viewers a point of view or a complex of feelings or thoughts" when they "read" his assemblage, Gelardi explores how visual literacy informs his work. What is your reaction as you view the artwork through the artist's eyes?

---

from Poets in the Kitchen

PAULE MARSHALL

Paule Marshall (b. 1929 in Brooklyn, New York) learned storytelling from her mother, a native of Barbados, whose West Indian friends used to gather in Marshall's home after a hard day of "scrubbing floor." She graduated from Brooklyn College in 1953 and received a Guggenheim fellowship in 1960. She was a librarian in New York City public libraries before working for Our World, *a popular 1950s African-American magazine. In 1959, Marshall's first novel,* Brown Girl, Brownstones, *was published. The novel is set in what Marshall calls "Bajan [Barbadian] Brooklyn" and according to one reader, expresses "in a lyrical, powerful language a culturally distinct and expansive world." Marshall's other novels include* Soul Clap Hands and Sing *(1961),* The Chosen Place, The Timeless People *(1969),* Praisesong *for the Widow (1983), and* Daughters

(1991). Her most recent novel, The Fisher King, for which she received the Dos Passos Prize for Literature, was published in 2000. In 1992 she became a MacArthur Fellow. She has been a lecturer on black literature and a teacher of creative writing at numerous universities, and is currently a professor of English at New York University.

The history of Barbados, the most easterly of the West Indies, begins with the arrival of an English ship in 1605 and with British settlers at the uninhabited island in 1627. Slavery was abolished in 1834. The island, 80 percent of whose population of 256,000 is of African descent, declared its independence from Britain in 1966 but remains within the Commonwealth.

SOME YEARS AGO, when I was teaching a graduate seminar in fiction at Columbia University, a well-known male novelist visited my class to speak on his development as a writer. In discussing his formative years, he didn't realize it but he seriously endangered his life by remarking that women writers are luckier than those of his sex because they usually spend so much time as children around their mothers and their mothers' friends in the kitchen.

What did he say that for? The women students immediately forgot about being in awe of him and began readying their attack for the question and answer period later on. Even I bristled. There again was that awful image of women locked away from the world in the kitchen with only each other to talk to, and their daughters locked in with them.

But my guest wasn't really being sexist or trying to be provocative or even spoiling for a fight. What he meant—when he got around to examining himself more fully—was that, given the way children are (or were) raised in our society, with little girls kept closer to home and their mothers, the women writer stands a better chance of being exposed, while growing up, to the kind of talk that goes on among women, more often than not in the kitchen; and that this experience gives her an edge over her male counterpart by instilling in her an appreciation for ordinary speech.

It was clear that my guest lecturer attached great importance to this, which is understandable. Common speech and the plain, workaday words that make it up are, after all, the stock in trade of some of the best fiction writers. They are the principal means by which a character in a novel or story reveals himself and gives voice sometimes to profound feelings and complex ideas about himself and the world. Perhaps the proper measure of a writer's talent is his skill in rendering everyday speech—when it is appropriate to his story—as well as his ability to tap, to exploit, the beauty, poetry and wisdom it often contains.

"If you say what's on your mind in the language that comes to you from your parents and your street and friends you'll probably say something beautiful." Grace Paley[1] tells this, she says, to her students at the beginning of every writing course.

It's all a matter of exposure and a training of the ear for the would-be writer in those early years of his or her apprenticeship. And, according to my guest lecturer, this training, the best of it, often takes place in as unglamorous a setting as the kitchen.

He didn't know it, but he was essentially describing my experience as a little girl. I grew up among poets. Now they didn't look like poets—whatever that breed is supposed to look like. Nothing about them suggested that poetry was their calling. They were just a group of ordinary housewives and mothers, my mother included, who dressed in a way (shapeless housedresses, dowdy felt hats and long, dark, solemn coats) that made it impossible for me to imagine they had ever been young.

Nor did they do what poets were supposed to do—spend their days in an attic room writing verses. They never put pen to paper except to write occasionally to their relatives in Barbados. "I take my pen in hand hoping these few lines will find you in health as they leave me fair for the time being," was the way their letters invariably began. Rather, their day was spent "scrubbing floor," as they described the work they did.

Several mornings a week these unknown bards would put an apron and a pair of old house shoes in a shopping bag and take the train or streetcar from our section of Brooklyn out to Flatbush. There, those who didn't have steady jobs would wait on certain designated corners for the white housewives in the neighborhood to come along and bargain with them over pay for a day's work cleaning their houses. This was the ritual even in the winter.

Later, armed with the few dollars they had earned, which in their vocabulary became "a few raw-mouth pennies," they made their way back to our neighborhood, where they would sometimes stop off to have a cup of tea or cocoa together before going home to cook dinner for their husbands and children.

The basement kitchen of the brownstone house where my family lived was the usual gathering place. Once inside the warm safety of its walls the women threw off the drab coats and hats, seated themselves at the large center table, drank their cups of tea or cocoa, and talked. While my sister and I sat at a smaller table over in a corner doing our homework, they talked—endlessly, passionately, poetically, and with impressive range. No subject was beyond them. True, they would indulge in the usual gossip: whose husband was running with whom, whose daughter looked slightly "in the way" (pregnant) under her bridal gown

[1]Contemporary American fiction writer.

as she walked down the aisle. That sort of thing. But they also tackled the great issues of the time. They were always, for example, discussing the state of the economy. It was the mid- and late 30s then, and the aftershock of the Depression, with its soup lines and suicides on Wall Street, was still being felt.

Some people, they declared, didn't know how to deal with adversity. They didn't know that you had to "tie up your belly" (hold in the pain, that is) when things got rough and go on with life. They took their image from the bellyband that is tied around the stomach of a newborn baby to keep the navel pressed in.

They talked politics. Roosevelt was their hero. He had come along and rescued the country with relief and jobs, and in gratitude they christened their sons Franklin and Delano and hoped they would live up to the names.

If F.D.R. was their hero, Marcus Garvey was their God. The name of the fiery, Jamaican-born black nationalist of the '20s was constantly invoked around the table. For he had been their leader when they first came to the United States from the West Indies shortly after World War I. They had contributed to his organization, the United Negro Improvement Association (UNIA), out of their meager salaries, bought shares in his ill-fated Black Star Shipping Line, and at the height of the movement they had marched as members of his "nurses' brigade" in their white uniforms on Seventh Avenue in Harlem during the great Garvey Day parades. Garvey: He lived on through the power of their memories.

And their talk was of war and rumors of wars. They raged against World War II when it broke out in Europe, blaming it on the politicians. "It's these politicians. They're the ones always starting up all this lot of war. But what they care? It's the poor people got to suffer and mothers with their sons." If it was *their* sons, they swore they would keep them out of the Army by giving them soap to eat each day to make their hearts sound defective. Hitler? He was for them "the devil incarnate."

Then there was home. They reminisced often and at length about home. The old country, Barbados—or Bimshire, as they affectionately called it. The little Caribbean island in the sun they loved but had to leave. "Poor—poor but sweet" was the way they remembered it.

And naturally they discussed their adopted home. America came in for both good and bad marks. They lashed out at it for the racism they encountered. They took to task some of the people they worked for, especially those who gave them only a hard-boiled egg and a few spoonfuls of cottage cheese for lunch. "As if anybody can scrub floor on an egg and some cheese that don't have no taste to it!"

Yet although they caught H in "this man country," as they called America, it was nonetheless a place where "you could at least see your way to make a dollar." That much they acknowledged. They might even one day accumulate enough dollars, with both them and their husbands working, to buy the brownstone houses which, like my family, they were only leasing at that period. This was their consuming ambition: to "buy house" and to see the children through.

There was no way for me to understand it at the time, but the talk that filled the kitchen those afternoons was highly functional. It served as therapy, the cheapest kind available to my mother and her friends. Not only did it help them recover from the long wait on the corner that morning and the bargaining over their labor, it restored them to a sense of themselves and reaffirmed their self-worth. Through language they were able to overcome the humiliations of the workday.

But more than therapy, that freewheeling, wide-ranging, exuberant talk functioned as an outlet for the tremendous creative energy they possessed. They were women in whom the need for self-expression was strong, and since language was the only vehicle readily available to them they made of it an art form that—in keeping with the African tradition in which art and life are one—was an integral part of their lives.

And their talk was a refuge. They never really ceased being baffled and overwhelmed by America—its vastness, complexity and power. Its strange customs and laws. At a level beyond words they remained fearful and in awe. Their uneasiness and fear were even reflected in their attitude toward the children they had given birth to in this country. They referred to those like myself, the little Brooklyn-born Bajans (Barbadians), as "these New York children" and complained that they couldn't discipline us properly because of the laws here. "You can't beat these children as you would like, you know, because the authorities in this place will dash you in jail for them. After all, these is New York children." Not only were we different, American, we had, as they saw it, escaped their ultimate authority.

Confronted therefore by a world they could not encompass, which even limited their rights as parents, and at the same time finding themselves permanently separated from the world they had known, they took refuge in language. "Language is the only homeland," Czeslaw Milosz, the emigré Polish writer and Nobel Laureate, has said. This is what it became for the women at the kitchen table.

It served another purpose also, I suspect. My mother and her friends were after all the female counterpart of Ralph Ellison's invisible man.[2] Indeed, you might say they suffered a triple invisibility, being

---

[2]Title of novel published in 1947 that has become the seminal metaphor for African-Americans.

black, female and foreigners. They really didn't count in American society except as a source of cheap labor. But given the kind of women they were, they couldn't tolerate the fact of their invisibility, their powerlessness. And they fought back, using the only weapon at their command: the spoken word.

Those late afternoon conversations on a wide range of topics were a way for them to feel they exercised some measure of control over their lives and the events that shaped them. "Soully-gal, talk yuh talk!" they were always exhorting each other. "In this man world you got to take yuh mouth and make a gun!" They were in control, if only verbally and if only for the two hours or so that they remained in our house.

For me, sitting over in the corner, being seen but not heard, which was the rule for children in those days, it wasn't only what the women talked about—the content—but the way they put things—their style. The insight, irony, wit, and humor they brought to their stories and discussions and their poet's inventiveness and daring with language— which of course I could only sense but not define back then.

They had taken the standard English taught them in the primary schools of Barbados and transformed it into an idiom, an instrument that more adequately described them—changing around the syntax and imposing their own rhythm and accent so that the sentences were more pleasing to their ears. They added the few African sounds and words that had survived, such as the derisive suck-teeth sound and the word "yam," meaning to eat. And to make it more vivid, more in keeping with their expressive quality, they brought to bear a raft of metaphors, parables, Biblical quotations, sayings and the like:

"The sea ain' got no back door," they would say, meaning that it wasn't like a house where if there was a fire you could run out the back. Meaning that it was not to be trifled with. And meaning perhaps in a larger sense that man should treat all of nature with caution and respect.

"I has read hell by heart and called every generation blessed!" They sometimes went in for hyperbole.

A woman expecting a baby was never said to be pregnant. They never used that word. Rather, she was "in the way" or, better yet, "tumbling big." "Guess who I butt up on in the market the other day tumbling big again!"

And a woman with a reputation of being too free with her sexual favors was known in their book as a "thoroughfare"—the sense of men like a steady stream of cars moving up and down the road of her life. Or she might be dubbed "a free-bee," which was my favorite of the two. I liked the image it conjured up of a woman scandalous perhaps but independent, who flitted from one flower to another in a garden of male beauties, sampling their nectar, taking her pleasure at will, the roles reversed.

And nothing, no matter how beautiful, was ever described as simply beautiful. It was always "beautiful-ugly": the beautiful-ugly dress, the beautiful-ugly house, the beautiful-ugly car. Why the word "ugly," I used to wonder, when the thing they were referring to was beautiful, and they knew it. Why the antonym, the contradiction, the linking of opposites? It used to puzzle me greatly as a child.

There is the theory in linguistics which states that the idiom of a people, the way they use language, reflects not only the most fundamental views they hold of themselves and the world but their very conception of reality. Perhaps in using the term "beautiful-ugly" to describe nearly everything, my mother and her friends were expressing what they believed to be a fundamental dualism in life: the idea that a thing is at the same time its opposite, and that these opposites, these contradictions make up the whole. But theirs was not a Manichaean brand of dualism[3] that sees matter, flesh, the body, as inherently evil, because they constantly addressed each other as "soully-gal"—soul: spirit; gal: the body, flesh, the visible self. And it was clear from their tone that they gave one as much weight and importance as the other. They had never heard of the mind/body split.

As for God, they summed up His essential attitude in a phrase, "God," they would say, "don' love ugly and He ain' stuck on pretty."

Using everyday speech, the simple commonplace words—but always with imagination and skill—they gave voice to the most complex ideas. Flannery O'Connor[4] would have approved of how they made ordinary language work, as she put it, "double-time," stretching, shading, deepening its meaning. Like Joseph Conrad[5] they were always trying to infuse new life in the "old old words worn thin . . . by . . . careless usage." And the goals of their oral art were the same as his: "to make you hear, to make you feel . . . to make you *see*." This was their guiding esthetic.

By the time I was eight or nine, I graduated from the corner of the kitchen to the neighborhood library, and thus from the spoken to the written word. The Macon Street Branch of the Brooklyn Public Library was an imposing half block long edifice of heavy gray masonry, with glass-paneled doors at the front and two tall metal torches symbolizing the light that comes of learning flanking the wide steps outside.

[3]Religious sect founded in 276 A.D. in Persia, which teaches the release of the spirit from matter through asceticism.
[4]American writer (1925–1964).
[5]British fiction writer (1857–1924).

The inside was just as impressive. More steps—of pale marble with gleaming brass railings at the center and sides—led up to the circulation desk, and a great pendulum clock gazed down from the balcony stacks that faced the entrance. Usually stationed at the top of the steps like the guards outside Buckingham Palace was the custodian, a stern-faced West Indian type who for years, until I was old enough to obtain an adult card, would immediately shoo me with one hand into the Children's Room and with the other threaten me into silence, a finger to his lips. You would have thought he was the chief librarian and not just someone whose job it was to keep the brass polished and the clock wound. I put him in a story called "Barbados" years later and had terrible things happen to him at the end.

I was sheltered from the storm of adolescence in the Macon Street library, reading voraciously, indiscriminately, everything from Jane Austen to Zane Grey, but with a special passion for the long, full-blown, richly detailed eighteenth- and nineteenth-century picaresque tales: *Tom Jones*, *Great Expectations*, *Vanity Fair*.

But although I loved nearly everything I read and would enter fully into the lives of the characters—indeed, would cease being myself and become them—I sensed a lack after a time. Something I couldn't quite define was missing. And then one day, browsing in the poetry section, I came across a book by someone called Paul Laurence Dunbar, and opening it I found the photograph of a wistful, sad-eyed poet who to my surprise was black. I turned to a poem at random. "Little brown-baby wif spa'klin'/eyes/Come to yo' pappy an' set on his knee." Although I had a little difficulty at first with the words in dialect, the poem spoke to me as nothing I had read before of the closeness, the special relationship I had had with my father, who by then had become an ardent believer in Father Divine and gone to live in Father's "kingdom" in Harlem. Reading it helped to ease somewhat the tight knot of sorrow and longing I carried around in my chest that refused to go away. I read another poem, "Lias! Lias! Bless de Lawd!/Don' you know de day's/erbroad?/Ef you don' get up, you scamp/Dey'll be trouble in dis camp." I laughed. It reminded me of the way my mother sometimes yelled at my sister and me to get out of bed in the mornings.

And another: "Seen my lady home las' night/Jump back, honey, jump back./Hel'/huh han'/an'/sque'z it tight . . ." About love between a black man and a black woman. I had never seen that written about before and it roused in me all kinds of delicious feelings and hopes.

And I began to search then for books and stories and poems about "The Race" (as it was put back then), about my people. While not abandoning Thackeray, Fielding, Dickens and the others, I started asking the reference librarian, who was white, for books by Negro writers, although I must admit I did so at first with a feeling of shame—the shame I and many others used to experience in those days whenever the word "Negro" or "colored" came up.

No grade school literature teacher of mine had ever mentioned Dunbar or James Weldon Johnson or Langston Hughes.[6] I didn't know that Zora Neale Hurston[7] existed and was busy writing and being published during those years. Nor was I made aware of people like Frederick Douglass and Harriet Tubman[8]—their spirit and example—or the great 19th-century abolitionist and feminist Sojourner Truth. There wasn't even Negro History Week when I attended P.S. 35 on Decatur Street!

What I needed, what all the kids—West Indian and native black American alike—with whom I grew up needed, was an equivalent of the Jewish shul, someplace where we could go after school—the schools that were shortchanging us—and read works by those like ourselves and learn about our history.

It was around that time also that I began harboring the dangerous thought of someday trying to write myself. Perhaps a poem about an apple tree, although I had never seen one. Or the story of a girl who could magically transplant herself to wherever she wanted to be in the world—such as Father Divine's kingdom in Harlem. Dunbar—his dark, eloquent face, his large volume of poems—permitted me to dream that I might someday write, and with something of the power with words my mother and her friends possessed.

When people at readings and writers' conferences ask me who my major influences were, they are sometimes a little disappointed when I don't immediately name the usual literary giants. True, I am indebted to those writers, white and black, whom I read during my formative years and still read for instruction and pleasure. But they were preceded in my life by another set of giants whom I always acknowledge before all others: the group of women around the table long ago. They taught me my first lesson in the narrative art. They trained my ear. They set a standard of excellence. This is why the best of my work must be attributed to them; it stands as testimony to the rich legacy of language and culture they so freely passed on to me in the wordshop of the kitchen.

---

[6]Paul Laurence Dunbar (1870–1906), James Weldon Johnson (1871–1938), Langston Hughes (1902–1967)—African-American poets of the Harlem Renaissance.
[7]African-American novelist (1901–1961).
[8]Frederick Douglass (1817–1895), Harriet Turban (1820–1193)—African-American abolitionists.

INTERPRETATIONS

1. Were the "poets in the kitchen" as interesting on paper as in their conversations? What does Marshall think their orality revealed about them? Cite two or three examples.

2. Marshall's "unknown bards" use language to combat their powerlessness in a culture in which they experienced the "triple invisibility of being black, female and foreigners." Which expressions best reflect this?

APPLICATIONS

1. In what contexts do Marshall's poets view language as a refuge? How do you respond to this concept?

2. What kind of literacy is Marshall writing about when she speaks of her early upbringing? What must a participant in kitchen conversation be aware of? What other kinds of literacy might be invoked by "these unknown bards"?

3. Later on in her life, Marshall comes to understand and value another kind of literacy that she has discovered in the "Macon Street Branch of the Brooklyn Public Library." What kind of literacy is this? How is it related to the kinds of literacies that she has described earlier?

4. "It was around that time also that I began harboring the dangerous thought of someday trying to write myself." Why does Marshall use the word "dangerous"? How does her consideration of becoming a writer affect her perceptions of literacy? What happens to your sense of literacy when you engage in a writing task?

My Pen Writes in Blue and White

VINCENT CREMONA

Vincent Cremona grew up in a middle-class neighborhood on Long Island, New York. He is currently working full-time while pursuing his education in the evening at Queensborough Community College, CUNY.

SOME PEOPLE SAY THAT THEY SEE THINGS in black and white. I tend to view things a little bit differently. I like to say that I see things in blue and white. Certain things that I will see, or hear, or read, and I will say, "This is blue." Other times I will come to the conclusion, "That is white." Sometimes I can even view things as blue and white at the same time. I have been taught, though unintentionally, to view things in this manner since I first learned to read and write.

The manner in which I now write, and communicate for that matter, has been directly affected by the two major influences in my life, my parents. Even though my parents communicate in two completely different ways, I have borrowed from both of them. I am reminded of the words of Richard Rodriguez when he lamented, "I now speak in the chromium accents of my grammar school classmates . . ." I, myself, have taken the plain, frank, honest words of my father and joined them with the proper and formal words of my mother to form the dialect that I now speak. This combination has given me the ability to communicate in many different ways.

When I say that I see things as blue, I mean that I view them as basic, bold, and workman-like. I see things from a blue-collar point of view. I have learned to view things in this manner from my father. A truck driver by trade, my father was a card-carrying member of the International Brotherhood of Teamsters, Local 851. My father was cut in the Jimmy Hoffa mold, in that Jimmy Hoffa believed that most Americans are basically hard-working individuals, who have respect for one another, as they face the trials and tribulations of providing a good home life for their families. As a union man, there is a lot of pride and patriotism in his words. He would say things like, "A day's work for a day's pay." It was said by Barbara Brandt that, "For many Americans today, paid work is not just a way to make money but is a crucial source of their self-worth." These words could easily be used to describe my father's attitude towards work. Work was a way of life for my father.

The most interesting thing to me was not his work, but rather my father's relationship with his co-workers. I would go to union meetings with my father and listen to the men talk about politics, finances, and all aspects of life. I was amazed that at such a young age, I could understand everything that they were saying. They spoke in a plain, although loud and brash, English. When I read their union-oriented propaganda, I noticed that it too was easy to understand. These were not complicated men. No one was out to impress or upstage anyone else. These men were union brothers, unmistakably blue-collared, and proud of it.

While I was listening to my father with one ear, my other was always pointed towards my mother. Although my mother also spoke English, like my father, they hardly sounded similar. My mother speaks what I like to call white-collar English. My mother is an office manager at a law firm. She goes to work all cleaned and pressed, briefcase in hand. When I listen to her talk about work, all I would hear was legalese. My mother uses words with many syllables and plenty of letters. She speaks in a very proper and clear voice. When she writes, she does so in a manner that makes the most ordinary things seem complicated. I remember she once wrote me a note for school that read, "Vincent will be unable to attend the upcoming academic function due to a prior commitment." I think she was trying to tell my teacher that I couldn't go on a class trip because we were going on vacation, but I am not really sure.

My mother aligned herself more with Emily Post because she believed the manner in which you talk, or write, or act in a certain situation would determine whether you have acted with class and dignity. My mother is all about being proper, no matter what the situation. Her I's are always dotted and her T's are always crossed. In my mother's white-collared world, the manner in which you conduct yourself has a direct influence on your career.

Learning to see things from these two different points of view has had a dramatic effect on the way I communicate. It is also very evident in my writing. I recently had to write a letter to an airline that had canceled my flight home from vacation, causing me to miss work on Monday. Needless to say, this cancellation was a tremendous inconvenience to me. I conveyed those feelings to the airline, in the bold, brash words of my father, in the beginning of the letter. Then, I used the poignant and legal sounding terms of my mother to convince them that they had better make restitution to me. I received a check from the airline only a few weeks later.

Since most of my writing is now done at work, I can see examples of my dual dialects all over my desk. I am a foreman at a construction company. The people who work directly under me are union construction workers. When I write their work orders, I do it in plain, ordinary, laymen's terms. I do this not because I think they will not understand, but because I know this is the way they choose to communicate.

When I write the same work orders for my supervisors, I write them completely differently. My supervisors are made up of accountants, architects, and other assorted managers and executives. When I communicate with them, whether it is via e-mail, fax, memo, or report, I do it in a very professional manner. The terms I use are very technical and official sounding. I know this is the way it has to be in the corporate world.

Even the writings that I do for school have the traces of these two viewpoints. When I am asked to do a serious business paper, for instance, I tend to write very professionally. I use the long-winded terms used by my professors and textbooks. On the other hand, when I am asked to write about more common ideas, like my experiences, or about myself, I write differently. I prefer to write in a more basic, everyday English. I like to write to the point and from the heart. When it is appropriate, I can even write from both perspectives at the same time. Some people may have to work at this, but to me it comes naturally.

All of my writing, now, I can see as either blue, or white, or some shade thereof. I used to think this made me write like two different people, with different personalities. Now I feel that I have the voice of one author, with a broadened horizon.

INTERPRETATIONS

1. How effective is Cremona's metaphor for describing his writing process? Try to create one to describe yours.
2. How do his parents' prose styles differ? Which do you prefer? How has he used both to his advantage?

APPLICATIONS

1. Review Cremona's last paragraph. What point does he make about language and identity?
2. What view of literacy does each of Cremona's parents represent? What evidence do you find to support your analysis?
3. In the fourth paragraph of the essay, Cremona recounts going to his father's union meetings. What kind of literacy did he observe at those times?
4. Who is Emily Post (mentioned in paragraph 6)? What kind of literacy does she represent? Who is an "Emily Post" in your life?
5. How does Cremona ultimately integrate the literacies that he presents in the essay? How well do you relate to what the author has written about? In what situations do you find yourself navigating among seemingly conflicting definitions of literacy?

"Multiple Dimensions of Love": From the Artist's Eyes

GIOVANNI J. GELARDI

Giovanni Gelardi was born in Trapani, Sicily in 1965. At the age of seven, his family immigrated to the United States. He grew up in Brooklyn, New York, where he acquired a street-smart education. Growing up surrounded by an ethnically diverse population gave him a greater understanding and respect for different cultures and religions. Upon graduating high school, he joined the United States Army. After serving six years of duty and being released with two honorable discharges, he next enrolled in Queens College for a few semesters. Always fascinated as a child by his mentor, the genius Leonardo da Vinci, he decided to become a self-taught artist, creating and constructing assemblages that address a variety of subjects.

I'M A SELF-TAUGHT ARTIST. My surroundings are my canvas and platform. I am not limited to any particular medium or subject matter. My works have an inter-connection of all things. My passion for art and a better world allows me to create artworks that have a story to tell. As an artist I want to bring to viewers a point of view or a complex of feelings or thoughts when they see my works. At the very least, I want to convey a sense of beauty, mystery and fantasy.

My process for creating art consists of combining and assembling multiple disciplines and media into my works. For "Multiple Dimensions of Love" I used cut-outs from books, found objects, pine wood and materials that I purchased. The case for the assemblage is a wine crate that held three bottles, and I built the window myself. "Multiple Dimensions of Love" is 13 inches high by 10.5 inches wide and took me fifteen months—from January, 2004 to March, 2005—start to finish. Each piece I create is a work in progress and is totally magical from the beginning until completion.

The biggest challenge that I faced was how to put these pieces together to make them feel like they belong together with nature and look very natural like the wood which I left untouched. I really didn't have any problem in building the piece except gluing a few hundred leaves together. I started by first putting a border with leaves around the crate and then the tree. From there it took a life of its own. I couldn't believe how many times I was left speechless when I would add a piece in the box. It was all magical to me! I just can't explain how each piece came to my mind and how they all tell the story. Everything fell into place. The box looks so natural and beautiful—just like love and the different couples that engage in this natural act.

The titles that I give my works have a purpose and meaning. "Multiple Dimensions of Love" deals with a social myth and a moral problem. The subject is Love. Who has the right and authority to say what it is and with whom it should be? The social myth that my work is addressing is homosexuality. Is it right? Is it wrong? It's a very sensitive subject with lots of misleading information and misguidance by people who have certain false beliefs and/or hatred and do not understand the power of love. In my opinion, no one should determine the lives and actions of two individuals who partake in the ultimate feeling between two human beings.

A painting or assemblage can represent and/or express the truth in many ways. As a visual artist, truth to me means facts, scientific evidence, physical proof and common sense. One can write a factual statement with paint on a canvas or glue a newspaper clipping with facts on a wooden box. You can use a photograph with a particular scene or a copy of a book cover that you know expresses the truth.

I use history, science, politics, religion and many other subjects to express my thoughts and feelings in my works. Whether past or present, I feel a strong connection to and interest in the subject matter I choose. Like a true journalist who gathers facts to write his or her story, I tell my story through my assemblage art. My thirst for knowledge and the truth allows me to study and gather information to better understand my subjects and be able to give a more accurate account of the story. I read articles about the subject matter. I watch documentaries about it. I listen to stories on television. And, for "Multiple Dimensions of Love," I gathered statistics about how states, countries and military forces treat the subject and the laws that they have for such a matter. For example, some states, like Massachusetts and Connecticut, allow same sex marriage. Some countries, such as the United States and Turkey, are against homosexuals in the military, while twenty-six other countries like Israel, Canada and the United Kingdom allow gays in the military.

My narratives are literal and symbolic. By literal I mean that the object represents what it physically is. A pair of shoes is a pair of shoes. A car is a car. The doves in my assemblage are just that, two doves flying free. The birds on top of the bench are also literally just two birds. By symbolic I mean that an object is not used for what it appears as to the naked eye, but for how the artist transforms it and uses it to represent something else. For example, a blue marble can symbolically represent planet earth. I use the two red cardinals literally and symbolically. Literally the red cardinals are two birds on top of a tree and look natural in their environment. But symbolically I use male birds which are colored bright red in nature to represent a love between two male partners in a home that is represented by a nest. In addition, the couple kissing on the upper branches of the tree signifies a heterosexual relationship.

"Multiple Dimensions of Love" deals with cycles of life that are represented by the four seasons and three different types of love, which I show literally and symbolically. The first thing that I want to bring into focus for the viewers is the autumn tree and a bombardment of leaves placed everywhere. I initially want viewers to feel that they are outside and experiencing the autumn season with the red, orange, yellow, and green leaves falling from the tree and carpeting the ground. I left all the wood raw, so when viewers are looking at the assemblage, they will see and feel something natural, like the birds flying free, and the squirrels cavorting on the footstool of the loveseat. I represent the season of spring using the lady with flowers on her dress. In the painting by Sandro Botticelli (1444–1510) titled "The Birth of Venus," the lady with flowers on her dress is Flora, Goddess of Flowers and Spring. Summer, on the other hand, is represented by a couple wearing summer clothes. The girl is wearing shorts and a half- cut shirt. The boy is wearing a short-sleeve shirt.

Through the transparent tree I want viewers to focus their attention next on the window, located in the center of the box. I want them to contemplate the scenery. By looking out of the window, I want them to get a sense that they are no longer outside but inside, watching the snow falling and experiencing the winter season. Keeping their eyes on the window and then scanning from left to right, they see a mirror and a doorframe. These two objects elaborate further that viewers are inside a home, and both pieces give the feeling of being in two different places or dimensions.

Taking a closer look at the bottom of the box, viewers see a furniture set, a plaque hanging on the tree with an inscription, and a lady with flowers on her dress who is trying to cover something or someone with her cloth. Both furniture pieces look like they could be for outside use in a park or a person's backyard.

The three kinds of love that I describe and represent in my assemblage are a love between a man and a woman, a love between a man and a man, and a love between a woman and a woman. The couple on the tree represents a heterosexual couple. The two red male cardinals on the tree symbolically represent two male humans together. The way that I represent the two female humans in my assemblage is as follows: first the goddess of spring is literally used to represent a woman whom I pair up with the plaque. In the painting by Botticelli, Flora is about to cover the naked body of Venus, the Goddess of Love. In my assemblage she is about to cover the plaque, which I use literally to describe what love is from the Bible. 1 Corinthians 13; 4-7 says: "Love is patient, love is kind. It does not envy, it does not boast, it is not proud. It is not rude, it is not self-seeking, it is not easily angered, it keeps no record of wrongs. Love does not delight in evil but rejoices with the truth. It always protects, always trusts, always hopes, always perseveres." Symbolically, the plaque represents the female partner of the metaphorical goddess of love, Venus, who is being covered by the cloth. The lady is literally and symbolically used to represent both a woman and Venus, allowing me to complete the third kind of love. Since the plaque talks about love and Venus represents love, the two together re-enact the scene from the Botticelli painting.

After reading the plaque, I would like viewers to zoom out and continue to scatter their eyes around the assemblage looking for other clues to meaning and the final pieces of the story. A viewer should be seeing a big red heart appearing to be growing from the tree or possibly a red helium balloon just released floating into the sky. The pulsating heart, a symbol of love, looks like a pomegranate aril, ready to burst its precious cargo all around the world. Going on an incline from right to left, the viewer sees a couple in love on top of the tree. This couple represents two ideas: the love between two heterosexual people and the summer season. I use the silvery moon, top left, literally to represent the night sky and to enhance the feeling of being outside. Symbolically the moon is used to represent love and romance.

The last piece of the assemblage is a disc sitting on the tree just above the plaque. It is made of a spectrum of colors which represents the rainbow and the cycles of colors that the four seasons bring to us each year. These colors are also used to represent the gay flag, which is used in parades and protests and has six horizontal stripes. Starting from the top of the flag and working our way down are red, orange, yellow, green, blue and purple.

Whether an art work is to be seen from a realistic point of view or as an abstract form, seeing a piece of art work for the first time can have a dramatic affect on the observer. It can even cause someone to have a life-time changing experience. An artist puts his or her body, mind and soul on the line when showing his or her art works. If someone sees a piece of art that says something to his or her inner consciousness, the viewer should learn more about the artist. Doing this can open up a Pandora's box full of treasures and mystery. Another hint that I would give a viewer is to look at art from different distances and angles. A person can get a better perspective and find hidden clues to meaning that are not seen just by looking straight forward.

Looking at a picture of an art work, whether the work is two or three-dimensional, is not the same as seeing it in real life. The eye can uncover the layers of depth up to a certain point and the viewer can get an idea where the objects stand from one another, but the true texture and depth of a work of art can only, I believe, be felt by having it in front of you, especially if the work is a three-dimensional piece like "Multiple Dimensions of Love." By looking at an art work live, the viewer is able to see the flow of the objects in relation to themselves and get a better sense of what the artist is trying to convey through movement and space.

INTERPRETATIONS

1. Gelardi states that his "narratives are literal and symbolic." Where in the essay does he explain these terms? Where do these ideas manifest themselves in the artwork (see pp. 203–204)?

2. According to Gelardi, how does he select the materials he uses to create the assemblage? What meaning does he say he wants to convey through these choices?

3. Throughout the essay, and directly in its final two paragraphs, Gelardi offers advice to viewers regarding how to think about and approach a work of art. How might you apply some of his ideas to one of the images in this chapter and to other photographs appearing in this book?

Giovanni J. Gelardi

"Multiple Dimensions of Love"

Detail of the couple on the tree.

Detail of the window.

The Knowing Eye

U.S. State Department/USAID

READING IMAGES

1. When you hear the word "education," what *image* comes to mind? How do these photographs illustrate your visual definition of the word?

2. Which part of each photograph captures your attention? Why do you think the photographer has chosen to make this person/object the focus of the image?

MAKING CONNECTIONS

1. There are many ways to learn, and people generally favor a few methods. How do these photographs and the kinds of learning they convey relate to the essays you have read in this chapter? Which essays seem to address the kind of learning implied by the first, second, and third photograph respectively?

Arnold Asrelsky

2. Which photograph do you think best illustrates a reading from this chapter? Which reading does it recall? What connections do you make between the written text and the visual one?

WORDS AND IMAGES

1. These photographs depict different ways that people learn. Which photograph is closer to depicting the way that you learn? If you have not already written a "Literacy Narrative" (see pages 10–13), write an essay that describes how you learn things best.

2. How do you relate to the classroom experience depicted in the first photograph? Write a comparison and contrast essay that examines your early education and that takes into account some of the following criteria: the number of students in the class,

Leon Brooks

classroom architecture and decoration, student posture, student attentiveness, teaching methods, and class composition (in terms of gender, clothing worn). Remember to state a clear thesis!

3. Review the last two paragraphs of Gelardi's essay (pp. 201–202), where he makes specific recommendations concerning how to view a work of art. Then examine the photograph of the museum goers. What does the body posture of the people in the photograph tell you about the physical aspects of learning in this environment? Now visit an art museum or gallery and concentrate on one work of your choice. Look at this work from one position for a few minutes. Then, take five steps back and reexamine the work. Repeat this procedure from another physical location. Write an essay about what you have learned about viewing art (and about learning in general) from this experience. Where possible, include direct quotations from Gelardi's essay.

Additional Writing Topics

1. Write an essay discussing Agosín's concept that one's first language is the most vivid and crucial key to identity as it links memories, emotions, and a sense of place. Include in your essay specific examples from your own experience.

2. "Words themselves are innocuous; it is the consensus that gives them true power." Using a word that has powerful emotional connotations for you, write an essay defining that word as common usage has defined it and analyzing your emotional reactions to it.

3. Review the Kaufman perspective. What are the ramifications of viewing education as a process rather than a product? To what extent do the selections in this chapter support or refute Kaufman? Write an essay responding to these questions, concluding with your views on this issue.

4. Discuss with your group an educational experience that occurred outside of school. What did you learn from it? From the experience of group members?

5. Should a teacher serve as a role model for students? How important is it that he or she be a member of the students' ethnic group? Do teachers have too much or too little influence on their students? Write an essay that answers these questions.

6. Review Reid's perspective on curiosity and write an essay on the role of curiosity in the learning process described by Viloria and Torres. Is it possible to learn without being curious? Why or why not?

7. Grant concludes her essay with the reflection that "even after twenty-eight years of formal schooling, my education continues, both inside and outside the classroom. I look forward to many more lessons." Write an extended journal entry on your philosophy of education, using as does Grant a specific experience that influenced it.

8. Some educational theorists argue that because students have grown up with television they prefer the visual to the linear—the image to the word. For such learners, "a picture is worth a thousand words." To what extent do you agree? How has the visual affected information processing? Should more visual techniques of communication be incorporated into the classroom? Write an essay responding to these questions.

CHAPTER

5

Work

A TTITUDES TOWARD WORK and the workplace are constantly changing. Traditionally, work was viewed as something to endure to support one's family, an effort rewarded by a pension and Social Security. Younger people have different expectations. Some desire economic success and job satisfaction; others prefer to shun the pressures of the corporate world and work for themselves.

We spend a great deal of our lives choosing, preparing for, and doing our work. "What do you do?" is perhaps the first question we want to ask of a new acquaintance. "Talking shop" is supposed to be taboo everywhere except at the office, factory, or construction site, yet no taboo is more frequently, and more gladly broken. For many people, the workplace is life. Talk about it ranges from the personal to the particular to the abstract, whatever one's culture.

The workplace is also changing rapidly. Technological expertise is in demand and will be rewarded by economic gains for those with innovative ideas and appropriate education. The increasing presence of women poses a challenge to traditional career choices and criteria for promotion, and attitudes toward work itself vary widely. For some, the workplace is a vital community, whereas others regard it as a location in which to perform a service. The notion of staying with one company for a lifetime or even making only one career choice is alien to many, and the concept of loyalty between employer and employee and vice versa is no longer assumed.

As you will discover, attitudes toward work and its value differ among cultures and exist in a matrix of customs, traditions, education, and class. Few people seem to think of work as a vocation or a passion despite the fact that they will spend a great part of their lives making a living. Two texts from Native American writers place work in the context of the former. Chief Smohalla thinks of work as interfering with dreams while Michael Dorris in "Life Stories" informs us that in his culture, a young man leaving his village for the first time was expected to benefit from his solitary journey, and "through this unique prism, abstractly preserved in a vivid memory or song, a boy caught foresight of his adult persona and of his vocation, the two inextricably linked."

In "Essential Work" John Patterson's focus is on his grandfather, who spent four decades as a steel worker beginning at 18 and ending at 62 working for the same company. "Instead of resting or playing bingo my grandfather employed his time and his energies in strengthening our family." On the other hand, Andrew Curry, in "Why We Work," concedes that although some people work because they enjoy it, or want to make money, most people work because they "have no other choice."

The most negative treatment of work in the United States is Gary Soto's "Black Hair," a grueling account of a summer job at Valley Tire Factory that made him keenly aware of the effects of the destructive power of hopelessness that caused his co-workers to no longer value themselves, whereas R. K. Narayan examines the personal and professional commitment expected by employers in his native India. Lalita Gandbhir discusses the issue of affirmative action in the workplace from a multicultural perspective, while Thomas Colicino focuses on the right time to quit.

As you explore the complexities, even controversies, and changes in the workplace and attitudes toward work, you may decide that now is a good time to join the conversation on these issues.

Perspectives

Work spares us from three great evils: boredom, vice and need.
—Voltaire

The ability to take pride in your own work is one of the hallmarks of sanity. Take away the ability to both work and be proud of it and you can drive anyone insane.
—Nikki Giovanni

If people are highly successful in their professions they lose their senses. Sound goes. They have no time to listen to music. Speech goes. They have no time for conversation. They lose their sense of proportion—the relations between one thing and another. Humanity goes.
—Virginia Woolf

Work is a necessity for man. Man invented the alarm clock.
—Pablo Picasso

Life is a continual distraction which does not allow us to reflect on that from which we are distracted.
—Franz Kafka

Each of you has a call, a vocation, which beckons you from the deepest places of your soul.
—David Hilfiker

He that maketh haste to be rich shall not be innocent.
—Proverbs 28:20

A job as a human right is a principle that applies to men as well as women. But women have more cause to fight for it.
—Gloria Steinem

The workplace performs the function of community.
—Robert Schrank

This book, being about work, is, by its very nature, about violence—to the spirit as well as the body.
—Studs Terkel

In fact, there is perhaps only one human being in a thousand who is passionately interested in his job for the job's sake.
—Dorothy Sayers

More and more, we take for granted that work must be destitute of pleasure. More and more, we assume that if we want to be pleased we must wait until evening, or the weekend, or vacation, or retirement. More and more, our farms and forests resemble our factories and offices, which in turn more and more resemble prisons—why else should we be so eager to escape them? We recognize defeated landscapes by the absence of pleasure from them. We are defeated at work because our work gives us no pleasure.

—*Wendell Berry*

Increased means and increased leisure are the two civilizers of man.
—*Benjamin Disraeli*

We are not far from the time when a man after a hard weekend of leisure will thankfully go back to work.
—*Russell Baker*

APPLICATIONS

1. According to Schrank, "the workplace performs the function of community." To what extent do you agree or disagree? Is it possible to establish community in competitive environments? What factors contribute to your feeling at home in the workplace?

2. Discuss Picasso's perspective with your group. Do you think there is a connection between work and time? What is your attitude toward time? Are you punctual for school, work, and leisure activities? Does lateness in others bother you? Summarize your discussion.

3. According to Berry, "we are defeated at work because work gives us no pleasure." To what kind of work is Berry referring? What factors account for boredom in the workplace? What is the difference between a job and a vocation? How would you diminish drudgery in the workplace?

My Young Men Shall Never Work

CHIEF SMOHALLA
AS TOLD BY HERBERT J. SPINDEN

The Nez Percé are a tribe of American Indians, formerly occupying much of the Pacific Northwest, whose reservation is in Idaho.

Because Native Americans resisted giving up their homes and nomadic way of life to become farmers, white people have often called them lazy, stubborn, and impractical. But to Indians, whose homes, land, and hunting were sacred, anything that threatened any one of these threatened their whole system of beliefs and values, in short, their very lives.

MY YOUNG MEN SHALL NEVER WORK. Men who work cannot dream and wisdom comes in dreams.

You ask me to plow the ground. Shall I take a knife and tear my mother's breast? Then when I die she will not take me to her bosom to rest.

You ask me to dig for stone. Shall I dig under her skin for bones? Then when I die I cannot enter her body to be born again.

You ask me to cut grass and make hay and sell it and be rich like white men. But how dare I cut off my mother's hair?

It is a bad law and my people cannot obey it. I want my people to stay with me here. All the dead men will come to life again. We must wait here in the house of our fathers and be ready to meet them in the body of our mother.

INTERPRETATIONS

1. Are the Nez Percé objecting to all work? Would you define work to include hunting?

2. What is the Nez Percé's reason for rejecting what they call "work"? What do they value more than work? How common is it for a culture to place the highest value on something other than work? Is work the highest value of American culture? What's the evidence?

3. To what extent is the misunderstanding between the Nez Percé and the whites a matter of language (definition)? Of tradition?

4. What is the Nez Percé's attitude toward the earth? What metaphor extends through and is elaborated within the whole passage?

CORRESPONDENCES

1. Review Woolf's perspective on work and create a conversation between her and Smohalla of the Nez Percé.

2. Review Kafka's perspective. What does it mean? To what extent does it reflect the sentiments expressed by Smohalla of the Nez Percé?

APPLICATIONS

1. "Men who work cannot dream and wisdom comes in dreams." Write a journal entry responding to Chief Smohalla. To what extent does involvement in work affect time for dreams?

2. Discuss with your group whether it is more important to make a lot of money or choose a profession for which you have a passion.

Life Stories

MICHAEL DORRIS

Michael Dorris (1945–1997) wrote fiction and essays about Native American life and social issues. He was educated at Georgetown University and Yale University and was a professor of Native American studies at Dartmouth College. His several publications, many of them co-authored with his wife, Louise Erdrich, include The Broken Cord *(1990), an account of his adopted son's struggle with fetal alcohol syndrome. Other publications include* Working Men *(1993) and* Paper Trail *(1994), from which "Life Stories" is taken. His last novel,* Cloud Chamber, *was published in 1997.*

IN MOST CULTURES, adulthood is equated with self-reliance and responsibility, yet often Americans do not achieve this status until we are in our late twenties or early thirties—virtually the entire average lifespan of a person in a traditional non-Western society. We tend to treat prolonged adolescence as a warm-up for real life, as a wobbly suspension bridge between childhood and legal maturity. Whereas a nineteenth-century Cheyenne or Lakota teenager was expected to alter self-conception in a split-second vision, we often meander through an analogous rite of passage for more than a decade—through high school, college, graduate school.

Though he had never before traveled alone outside his village, the Plains Indian male was expected at puberty to venture solo into the wilderness. There he had to fend for and sustain himself while avoiding the menace of unknown dangers, and there he had absolutely to remain until something happened that would transform him. Every human being, these tribes believed, was entitled to at least one moment of personal, enabling insight.

Anthropology proposes feasible psychological explanations for why this flash was eventually triggered: Fear, fatigue, reliance on strange foods, the anguish of loneliness, stress, and the expectation of ultimate success all contributed to a state of receptivity. Every sense was quickened, alerted to perceive deep meaning, until at last the interpretation of an unusual event—a dream, a chance encounter, or an unexpected vista—reverberated with metaphor. Through this unique prism, abstractly preserved in a vivid memory or song, a boy caught foresight of both his adult persona and of his vocation, the two inextricably entwined.

Today the best approximations that many of us get to such a heady sense of eventuality come in the performance of our school vacation jobs. Summers are intermissions, and once we hit our teens it is during these breaks in our structured regimen that we initially taste the satisfaction of remuneration that is earned, not merely doled. Tasks defined as *work* are not only graded, they are compensated; they have a worth that is unarguable because it translates into hard currency. Wage labor—and in the beginning, this generally means a confining, repetitive chore for which we are quickly over-qualified—paradoxically brings a sense of blooming freedom. At the outset, the complaint to a peer that business supersedes fun is oddly liberating—no matter what drudgery requires your attention, it is by its very required nature serious and adult.

At least that's how it seemed to me. I come from a line of people hard hit by the Great Depression. My mother and her sisters went to work early in their teens—my mother operated a kind of calculator known as a comptometer while her sisters spent their days, respectively, at a peanut factory and at Western Union. My grandmother did piecework sewing. Their efforts, and the Democratic Party, saw them through, and to this day they never look back without appreciation for their later solvency. They take nothing for granted. Accomplishments are celebrated, possessions are valuable, in direct proportion to the labor entailed to acquire them; anything easily won or bought on credit is suspect. When I was growing up we were far from wealthy, but what money we had was correlated to the hours some one of us had logged. My eagerness to contribute to, or at least not diminish, the coffer was countered by the arguments of those whose salaries kept me in school: My higher education was a sound group investment. The whole family was adamant that I have the opportunities they had missed and, no matter how much I objected, they stinted themselves to provide for me.

Summer jobs were therefore a relief, an opportunity to pull a share of the load. As soon as the days turned warm I began to peruse the classifieds, and when the spring semester was done, I was ready to punch a clock. It even felt right. Work in June, July, and August had an almost Biblical aspect: In the hot, canicular weather your brow sweated, just as God had ordained. Moreover, summer jobs had the luxury of being temporary. No matter how bizarre, how onerous, how off my supposed track, employment terminated with the falling leaves and I was back on neutral ground. So, during each annual three-month leave from secondary school and later from the university, I compiled an eclectic résumé: lawn cutter, hair sweeper in a barber shop, lifeguard, delivery boy, temporary mail carrier, file clerk, youth program coordinator on my Montana reservation, ballroom dance instructor, theater party promoter, night-shift hospital records keeper, human adding machine in a

Paris bank, encyclopedia salesman, newspaper stringer, recreation bus manager, salmon fisherman.

The reasonable titles disguise the madness of some of these occupations. For instance, I seemed inevitably to be hired to trim the yards of the unconventional. One woman followed beside me, step by step, as I traversed her yard in ever tighter squares, and called my attention to each missed blade of grass. Another client never had the "change" to pay me, and so reimbursed my weekly pruning with an offering culled from his library. I could have done without the *Guide to Artificial Respiration* (1942) or the many well-worn copies of Reader's Digest Condensed Books, but sometimes the selection merited the wait. Like a rat lured repeatedly back to the danger of mild electric shock by the mystique of intermittent reenforcement, I kept mowing by day in hopes of turning pages all night.

The summer I was eighteen a possibility arose for a rotation at the post office, and I grabbed it. There was something casually sophisticated about work that required a uniform, about having a federal ranking, even if it was GS-1 (Temp/Sub), and it was flattering to be entrusted with a leather bag containing who knew what important correspondence. Every day I was assigned a new beat, usually in a rough neighborhood avoided whenever possible by regular carriers, and I proved quite capable of complicating what would normally be fairly routine missions. The low point came on the first of August when I diligently delivered four blocks' worth of welfare checks to the right numbers on the wrong streets. It is no fun to snatch unexpected wealth from the hands of those who have but moments previously opened their mailboxes and received a bonus.

After my first year of college, I lived with relatives on an Indian reservation in eastern Montana and filled the only post available: Coordinator of Tribal Youth Programs. I was seduced by the language of the announcement into assuming that there existed Youth Programs to be coordinated. In fact, the Youth consisted of a dozen bored, disgruntled kids—most of them my cousins—who had nothing better to do each day than to show up at what was euphemistically called "the gym" and hate whatever Program I had planned for them. The Youth ranged in age from fifteen to five and seemed to have as their sole common ambition the determination to smoke cigarettes. This put them at immediate and on-going odds with the Coordinator, who on his first day naively encouraged them to sing the "Doe, a deer, a female deer" song from *The Sound of Music*. They looked at me, that bleak morning, and I looked at them, each boy and girl equipped with a Pall Mall behind an ear, and we all knew it would be a long, struggle-charged battle. It was to be a contest of wills, the hearty and wholesome vs. prohibited vice. I stood for dodge ball, for collecting bugs in glass jars, for arts and crafts; they had pledged a preternatural allegiance to sloth. The odds were not in my favor and each waking dawn I experienced the light-headedness of anticipated exhaustion, that thrill of giddy dissociation in which nothing seems real or of great significance. I went with the flow and learned to inhale.

The next summer, I decided to find work in an urban setting for a change, and was hired as a general office assistant in the Elsa Hoppenfeld Theatre Party Agency, located above Sardi's restaurant in New York City. The Agency consisted of Elsa Hoppenfeld herself, Rita Frank, her regular deputy, and me. Elsa was a gregarious Viennese woman who established contacts through personal charm, and she spent much of the time courting trade away from the building. Rita was therefore both my immediate supervisor and constant companion; she had the most incredible fingernails I had ever seen—long, carefully shaped pegs lacquered in cruel primary colors and hard as stone—and an attitude about her that could only be described as zeal.

The goal of a theater party agent is to sell blocks of tickets to imminent Broadway productions, and the likely buyers are charities, B'nai Briths, Hadassahs, and assorted other fund-raising organizations. We received commissions on volume, and so it was necessary to convince a prospect that a play—preferably an expensive musical—for which we had reserved the rights to seats would be a boffo smash hit.

The object of our greatest expectation that season was an extravaganza called *Chu Chem*, a saga that aspired to ride the coattails of *Fiddler on the Roof* into entertainment history. It starred the estimable Molly Picon and told the story of a family who had centuries ago gone from Israel to China during the diaspora, yet had, despite isolation in an alien environment, retained orthodox culture and habits. The crux of the plot revolved around a man with several marriageable daughters and nary a kosher suitor within 5,000 miles. For three months Rita and I waxed eloquent in singing the show's praises. We sat in our little office, behind facing desks, and every noon while she redid her nails I ordered out from a deli that offered such exotic (to me) delicacies as fried egg sandwiches, lox and cream cheese, pastrami, *tongue*. I developed of necessity and habit a telephone voice laced with a distinctly Yiddish accent. It could have been a great career. However, come November, *Chu Chem* bombed. Its closing was such a financial catastrophe for all concerned that when the following January one Monsieur Dupont advertised on the Placement Board at my college, I decided to put an ocean between me and my former trusting clientele.

M. Dupont came to campus with the stated purpose of interviewing candidates for teller positions in a French bank. Successful applicants, required to be fluent in *français*, would be rewarded with three well-paid months and a rent-free apartment in Paris. I headed for the language lab and registered for an appointment.

The only French in the interview was *Bonjour, ça va?*, after which M. Dupont switched into English and described the wonderful deal on charter air flights that would be available to those who got the nod. Round-trip to Amsterdam, via Reykjavik, leaving the day after exams and returning in mid-September, no changes or substitutions. I signed up on the spot. I was to be a *banquier*, with *pied-à-terre* in Montparnasse!

Unfortunately, when I arrived with only $50 in travelers checks in my pocket—the flight had cleaned me out, but who needed money since my paycheck started right away—no one in Paris had ever heard of M. Dupont.

Alors.

I stood in the Gare du Nord and considered my options. There weren't any. I scanned a listing of Paris hotels and headed for the cheapest one: the Hotel Villedo, $10 a night. The place had an ambiance that I persuaded myself was antique, despite the red light above the sign. The only accommodation available was "the bridal suite," a steal at $20. The glass door to my room didn't lock and there was a rather continual floor show, but at some point I must have dozed off. When I awoke the church bells were ringing, the sky was pink, and I felt renewed. No little setback was going to spoil my adventure. I stood and stretched, then walked to a mirror that hung above the sink next to the bed. I leaned forward to punctuate my resolve with a confident look in the eye.

The sink disengaged and fell to the floor. Water gushed. In panic I rummaged through my open suitcase, stuffed two pair of underwear into the pipe to quell the flow, and before the dam broke, I was out the door. I barreled through the lobby of the first bank *I passed, asked to see the director,* and told the startled man my sad story. For some reason, whether from shock or pity, he hired me at $1.27 an hour to be a cross-checker of foreign currency transactions, and with two phone calls found me lodgings at a commercial school's dormitory.

From eight to five each weekday my duty was to sit in a windowless room with six impeccably dressed people, all of whom were totaling identical additions and subtractions. We were highly dignified with each other, very professional, no *tutoyer*ing. Monsieur Saint presided, but the formidable Mademoiselle was the true power: she oversaw each of our columns and shook her head sadly at my American-shaped numbers.

My legacy from that summer, however, was more than an enduring penchant for crossed 7s. After I had worked for six weeks, M. Saint asked me during a coffee break why I didn't follow the example of other foreign students he had known and depart the office at noon in order to spend the afternoon touring the sights of Paris with the *Alliance Française*.

"Because," I replied in my halting French, "that costs money. I depend upon my full salary the same as any of you." M. Saint nodded gravely and said no more, but then on the next Friday he presented me with a white envelope along with my check.

"Do not open this until you have left the Société Générale," he said ominously. I thought I was fired for the time I had mixed up krøners and guilders, and, once on the sidewalk, I steeled myself to read the worst. I felt the quiet panic of blankness.

"Dear Sir," I translated the perfectly formed script. "You are a person of value. It is not correct that you should be in our beautiful city and not see it. Therefore we have amassed a modest sum to pay the tuition for a two-week afternoon program for you at the *Alliance Française*. Your wages will not suffer, for it is your assignment to appear each morning in this bureau and reacquaint us with the places you have visited. We shall see them afresh through your eyes." The letter had thirty signatures, from the Director to the janitor, and stuffed inside the envelope was a sheaf of franc notes in various denominations.

I rushed back to the tiny office. M. Saint and Mademoiselle had waited, and accepted my gratitude with their usual controlled smiles and precise handshakes. But they had blown their Gallic cover, and for the next ten days and then through all the days until I went home in September, our branch was awash with sightseeing paraphermalia. Everyone had advice, favorite haunts, criticisms of the *Alliance*'s choices or explanations. Paris passed through the bank's granite walls as sweetly as a June breeze through a window screen, and ever afterward the lilt of overheard French, a photograph of *Sacré Coeur* or the Louvre, even a monthly bank statement, recalls to me that best of all summers.

I didn't wind up in an occupation with any obvious connection to the careers I sampled during my school breaks, but I never altogether abandoned those brief professions either. They were jobs not so much to be held as to be weighed, absorbed, and incorporated, and, collectively, they carried me forward into adult life like overlapping stairs, unfolding a particular pattern at once haphazard and inevitable.

INTERPRETATIONS

1. Dorris begins an essay on summer jobs by contrasting how Native Americans and white cultures measure maturity. What examples in the first three paragraphs do you find particularly interesting? With what points, if any, did you disagree?

2. Dorris cites several personal experiences with summer jobs. How does he rate them? Did they contribute positively to his transitions from adolescence to adulthood? Cite specific examples to support your point of view.

3. Dorris changes tone several times in the essay. Cite at least three instances and show how he uses tone to enhance meaning.

4. What factors contributed to making his French experience "the best of all summers"?

5. Explain Dorris's concluding paragraph. How does it relate to his introduction? To the unity of his essay?

CORRESPONDENCES

1. How did Dorris's and Soto's experiences with summer jobs contribute to their maturity? Was there a particular summer job that despite its negative aspects had a positive effect on your personal growth? Explain.

2. Review Hilfiker's perspective on work and discuss its relevance to Dorris's essay. What relevance does it have for you? How would you differentiate between a job as opposed to a calling or vocation?

APPLICATIONS

1. Review paragraph 5 of Dorris's essay. To what economic class did his family belong? Characterize their attitudes toward work. To Dorris's education? To what extent is your family's economic situation and attitudes toward work and education similar to or different from his? Discuss these issues with your group and write a summary of your conversations.

2. Describe someone with whom you work who obviously likes or dislikes his or her job. How much does that person communicate this in performance and attitude? How do such attitudes affect the workplace? Be specific.

3. Review paragraphs 8 and 9 in which Dorris recalls his summer jobs as a temporary postal worker and as Coordinator of Tribal Youth Programs. Evaluate the effectiveness of using humor to describe two difficult experiences. What does Dorris communicate about himself through his account of both positions? Write a journal entry responding to these questions.

4. Using Dorris's title, "Life Stories," write an essay on one or two summer jobs that you would characterize as "rites of passage."

Why We Work

ANDREW CURRY

Andrew Curry is a professional journalist based in Germany (he speaks German and Polish). He was educated at the Georgetown University School of Foreign Service (B.S. in 1998) and the Stanford University Center for Russian and East European Studies (M.A. in 2000). He has written on contemporary issues for a variety of publications, such as The Washington Post, The Christian Science Monitor, The Miami Herald, *and* The Guardian. *Curry was general editor of the* Smithsonian *magazine from February 2004, to August 2005. "Why We Work" appeared first in* U.S. News and World Report *in 2003.*

SOME DO IT FOR LOVE. Others do it for money. But most of us do it because we have no other choice.

In 1930, W. K. Kellogg made what he thought was a sensible decision, grounded in the best economic, social, and management theories of the time. Workers at his cereal plant in Battle Creek, Michigan, were told to go home two hours early. Every day. For good.

The Depression-era move was hailed in *Factory and Industrial Management* magazine as the "biggest piece of industrial news since [Henry] Ford announced his five-dollar-a-day policy." President Herbert Hoover summoned the eccentric cereal magnate to the White House and said the plan was "very worthwhile." The belief: Industry and machines would lead to a workers' paradise where all would have less work, more free time, and yet still produce enough to meet their needs.

So what happened? Today, work dominates Americans' lives as never before, as workers pile on hours at a rate not seen since the Industrial Revolution. Technology has offered increasing productivity and a higher standard of living while bank tellers and typists are replaced by machines. The mismatch between available work and those available to do it continues, as jobs go begging while people beg for jobs. Though Kellogg's six-hour day lasted until 1985, Battle Creek's grand industrial experiment has been nearly forgotten. Instead of working less, our hours have stayed steady or risen—and today many more women work so that families can afford the trappings of suburbia. In effect, workers chose the path of consumption over leisure.

But as today's job market shows so starkly, that road is full of potholes. With unemployment at a nine-year high and many workers worried about losing their jobs—or forced to accept cutbacks in pay and benefits—work is hardly the paradise economists once envisioned.

Instead, the job market is as precarious today as it was in the early 1980s, when business began a wave of restructurings and layoffs to maintain its competitiveness. Many workers are left feeling insecure, unfulfilled, and under-appreciated. It's no wonder surveys of today's workers show a steady decline in job satisfaction. "People are very emotional about work, and they're very negative about it," says David Rhodes, a principal at human resource consultants Towers Perrin. "The biggest issue is clearly workload. People are feeling crushed."

The backlash comes after years of people boasting about how hard they work and tying their identities to how indispensable they are. Ringing cell phones, whirring faxes, and ever-present e-mail have blurred the lines between work and home. The job penetrates every aspect of life. Americans don't exercise, they work out. We manage our time and work on our relationships. "In reaching the affluent society, we're working longer and harder than anyone could have imagined," says Rutgers University historian John Gillis. "The work ethic and identifying ourselves with work and through work is not only alive and well but more present now than at any time in history."

It's all beginning to take a toll. Fully one third of American workers—who work longer hours than their counterparts in any industrialized country—felt overwhelmed by the amount of work they had to do, according to a 2001 Families and Work Institute survey. "Both men and women wish they were working about 11 hours [a week] less," says Ellen Galinsky, the institute's president. "A lot of people believe if they do work less they'll be seen as less committed, and in a shaky economy no one wants that."

The modern environment would seem alien to pre-industrial laborers. For centuries, the household—from farms to "cottage" craftsmen—was the unit of production. The whole family was part of the enterprise, be it farming, blacksmithing, or baking. "In pre-industrial society, work and family were practically the same thing," says Gillis.

The Industrial Revolution changed all that. Mills and massive iron smelters required ample labor and constant attendance. "The factory took men, women and children out of the workshops and homes and put them under one roof and timed their movements to machines," writes Sebastian de Grazia in *Of Time, Work and Leisure.* For the first time, work and family were split. Instead of selling what they produced, workers sold their time. With more people leaving farms to move to cities and factories, labor became a commodity, placed on the market like any other.

Innovation gave rise to an industrial process based on machinery and mass production. This new age called for a new worker. "The only safeguard of order and discipline in the modern world is a standardized worker with interchangeable parts," mused one turn-of-the-century writer.

Business couldn't have that, so instead it came up with the science of management. The theories of Frederick Taylor, a Philadelphia factory foreman with deep Puritan roots, led to work being broken down into component parts, with each step timed to coldly quantify jobs that skilled craftsmen had worked a lifetime to learn. Workers resented Taylor and his stopwatch, complaining that his focus on process stripped their jobs of creativity and pride, making them irritable. Long before anyone knew what "stress" was, Taylor brought it to the workplace—and without sympathy. "I have you for your strength and mechanical ability, and we have other men paid for thinking," he told workers.

The division of work into components that could be measured and easily taught reached its apex in Ford's River Rouge plant in Dearborn, Michigan, where the assembly line came of age. "It was this combination of a simplification of tasks . . . with moving assembly that created a manufacturing revolution while at the same time laying waste human potential on a massive scale," author Richard Donkin writes in *Blood, Sweat and Tears*.

To maximize the production lines, businesses needed long hours from their workers. But it was no easy sell. "Convincing people to work 9 to 5 took a tremendous amount of propaganda and discipline," says the University of Richmond's Joanne Ciulla, author of *The Working Life: The Promise and Betrayal of Modern Work*. Entrepreneurs, religious leaders, and writers like Horatio Alger created whole bodies of literature to glorify the work ethic.

The first labor unions were organized in response to the threat of technology, as skilled workers sought to protect their jobs from mechanization. Later, semi- and unskilled workers began to organize as well, agitating successfully for reduced hours, higher wages, and better work conditions. Unions enjoyed great influence in the early 20th century, and at their height in the 1950s, 35 percent of U.S. workers belonged to one.

Union persistence and the mechanization of factories gradually made shorter hours more realistic. Between 1830 and 1930, work hours were cut nearly in half, with economist John Maynard Keynes famously predicting in 1930 that by 2030 a 15-hour workweek would be standard. The Great Depression pressed the issue, with job sharing proposed as a serious solution to widespread unemployment. Despite business and religious opposition over worries of an idle populace, the Senate passed a bill that would have mandated a 30-hour week in 1933; it was narrowly defeated in the House.

Franklin Delano Roosevelt struck back with a new gospel that lives to this very day: consumption. "The aim . . . is to restore our rich domestic market by raising its vast consuming capacity," he said. "Our first purpose is to create employment as fast as we can." And so began the modern work world. "Instead of accepting work's continuing decline and imminent fall from its dominant social position, business-men, economists, advertisers, and politicians preached that there would never be 'enough,'" says University of Iowa Professor Benjamin Hunnicutt, author of *Work Without End: Abandoning Shorter Hours for the Right to Work*. "The entrepreneur and industry could invent new things for advertising to sell and for people to want and work for indefinitely."

The New Deal dumped government money into job creation, in turn encouraging consumption. World War II fueled the fire, and American workers soon found themselves in a "golden age"—40-hour work-weeks, plenty of jobs, and plenty to buy. Leisure was the road not taken, a path quickly forgotten in the postwar boom of the 1950s and 1960s.

Decades of abundance, however, did not bring satisfaction. "A significant number of Americans are dissatisfied with the quality of their working lives," said the 1973 report "Work in America" from the Department of Health, Education and Welfare. "Dull, repetitive, seemingly meaningless tasks, offering little challenge or autonomy, are causing discontent among workers at all occupational levels." Underlying the dissatisfaction was a very gradual change in what the "Protestant work ethic" meant. Always a source of pride, the idea that hard work was a calling from God dated to the Reformation and the teachings of Martin Luther. While work had once been a means to serve God, two centuries of choices and industrialization had turned work into an end in itself, stripped of the spiritual meaning that sustained the Puritans who came ready to tame the wilderness.

By the end of the '70s, companies were reaching out to spiritually drained workers by offering more engagement while withdrawing the promise of a job for life, as the American economy faced a stiff challenge from cheaper workers abroad. "Employees were given more control over their work and schedules, and "human relations" consultants and motivational speakers did a booming business. By the 1990s, technology made working from home possible for a growing number of people. Seen as a boon at first, telecommuting and the rapidly proliferating "electronic leash" of cell phones made work inescapable, as employees found themselves on call 24/7. Today, almost half of American workers use computers, cell phones, e-mail, and faxes for work during what is supposed to be non-work time, according to the Families and Work Institute. Home is no longer a refuge but a cozier extension of the office.

The shift coincided with a shortage of highly skilled and educated workers, some of whom were induced with such benefits as stock options in exchange for their putting the company first all the time. But some see a different explanation for the rise in the amount of time devoted to work. "Hours have crept up partly as a consequence of the declining power of the trade-union movement," says Cornell University labor historian Clete Daniel. "Many employers find it more economical to require mandatory overtime than hire new workers and pay their benefits." Indeed, the trend has coincided with the steady decline in the percentage of workers represented by unions, as the labor movement failed to keep pace with the increasing rise of white-collar jobs in the economy. Today fewer than 15 percent of American workers belong to unions.

In a study of Silicon Valley culture over the past decade, San Jose State University anthropologist Jan English-Lueck found that skills learned on the job were often brought home. Researchers talked to families with mission statements, mothers used conflict-resolution buzzwords with their squabbling kids, and engineers used flowcharts to organize Thanksgiving dinner. Said one participant: "I don't live life; I manage it."

In some ways, we have come full circle. "Now we're seeing the return of work to the home in terms of telecommuting," says Gillis. "We may be seeing the return of households where work is the central element again."

But there's still the question of fulfillment. In a recent study, human resources consultants Towers Perrin tried to measure workers' emotions about their jobs. More than half of the emotion was negative, with the biggest single factor being workload but also a sense that work doesn't satisfy their deeper needs. "We expect more and more out of our jobs," says Hunnicutt. "We expect to find wonderful people and experiences all around us. What we find is Dilbert."

INTERPRETATIONS

1. Curry's research indicates that although increasingly American workers have chosen material prosperity rather than personal time, they are still dissatisfied with their jobs. What explanations does he offer to explain this apparent contradiction?

2. How has technology (cell phones, e-mail, faxes) contributed to the concept of being on the job "at home as well as in the workplace"? To what extent do you agree with Curry that "we manage our time and work on our relationships"?

3. How has the role of trade unions changed over the decades? To what extent has their decline resulted in an increase in the number of hours Americans work each week?

4. Review paragraph 22 that focuses on Silicon Valley culture and the changes of the last decade. To what extent have they affected personal and family life adversely in your opinion?

CORRESPONDENCES

1. Review Terkel's perspective on work and discuss its relevance to Curry's essay. What evidence is there of "violence to the spirit as well as the body"? Explain.

2. Review Baker's perspective and discuss how Curry's essay contradicts Baker's prediction. To what extent do you balance work and leisure?

APPLICATIONS

1. Write a journal entry on your criteria for choosing a profession. Is it part of a dream that you would like to fulfill or do you view your choice as mainly pragmatic? How important is personal satisfaction?

2. Economic success has long been associated with the American dream. Discuss with your group your concepts of the American dream. How are they similar or different? How do they compare to those of your parents' generation?

3. A recent survey estimates that 20 percent of high earners in the United States are working more than sixty hours per week at tasks that include meeting tight deadlines, frequent travel, increased flow of work, and work-related social events on evenings and even weekends. Can you imagine being one of these people involved in what is now termed an "extreme job"? Discuss this issue with your group and summarize your findings.

Essential Work

JOHN PATTERSON

*John Patterson was born and raised in the San Francisco Bay Area. In 2006,
he moved to Queens, New York, and in 2007 enrolled in Queensborough Community College (CUNY). After graduation in 2009, he moved back to California to attend California State East Bay for a B.A. in English. He hopes to
continue on to graduate school in English and possibly teach English himself.*

AS A SPECIES WE HUMAN BEINGS are endowed with the unique ability to
judge things for ourselves, and we possess the longevity to outlive our
premature judgments. Shared across the entire world, from Hong Kong
to Houston, work is a large part of the human experience that usually
accompanies us from young adulthood into old age. Because of its vast
and serious nature, work often has a polarizing effect on minds. The
large majority of people seem to greet each workday with fear and
dread while others welcome work as a chance to put themselves to
good use.

In my life I have had the pleasure of knowing a few members of the
latter class of people, individuals that do not see the proposition of near
endless work as an impossible task but rather a continuously renewing
opportunity to use their energy and potential in a positive way.

The most useful piece of advice I was ever given came from my
grandfather and dealt with the topic of work. He said, "People should
enjoy their work because there is a good chance they will do it for the
rest of their lives." In my grandfather's life this was very much the case.
The forty-four-year length of his work life was spent with one single
company and in one single position. He was a steel worker in charge of
cutting large sheets of steel into smaller, more easily manageable strips.
In 1932, three short years after the Great Depression took hold of American life, he gratefully began working in the steel mill and didn't retire
until 1976, one year after the Vietnam War ended. He started working
when he was 18 and retired at age 62. One might think that a lifetime of
single-sighted diligence would wear a man out and prepare him for a
long break, but that was not how it happened with my grandfather.

Instead of resting or playing bingo, my grandfather employed his
time and his energies in strengthening our family. After my father died
my grandfather was a constant positive presence in my life. He was tire-
less in supporting my mother, my siblings, and me. And although some

distance lay between my house and my grandfather's house, I don't recall too many days without his hard work brightening our lives. Maybe he continued to stay busy because he had grown accustomed to working through the entire day, or perhaps it was because he enjoyed the deep sleep that only hard work can bring. More than anything else, I think that he was just too bored sitting around at home with nothing to do so he just shifted his attention from his job in the steel mill to his family.

Looking back on my own work life I see how my attitude toward work differs from his. I am the modern worker who is dissatisfied with the work world at large and who thinks that his time is worth immeasurably more than the few dollars he receives at the end of the week. I am neither thankful to work nor happy to be there. In a few of my jobs the only part of the day I enjoyed was the end, when I could escape the tedium and repetition.

In my short work career I have had a couple of jobs that I wasn't that into. On the West Coast I worked in a warehouse for an interior design company, moving furniture, and in an office for a plant nursery organizing files. On the East Coast I worked in a food distribution warehouse arranging boxes of food and I also worked in a property management office dealing with irate phone calls. Although these jobs didn't provide me with the ultimate direction for a long career, they did give me a good understanding of what I do not want to do with my fife. Armed with that knowledge, I am currently trying to turn one of my passions, literature, into a paying gig.

The decision seems simple enough, but that doesn't mean it is easy to make. For a time I thought that I wanted to become a surgeon. I have been the patient in many surgeries: one to repair my ruptured appendix, and a few to fix my broken right arm. I thought I would love to perform surgeries and remedy horrible situations for people. But, upon further inspection of what I would have to do to become a surgeon, I found that I needed to excel in school, take huge daunting examinations, then get into medical school.

After completion of four years of medical school I could be a resident making $41,000.00 per year for four years. My student loan would be around $250,000.00 and would begin compounding interest the moment I graduate from medical school. Trapped under a mountain of debt, the first few years of actually being a doctor are spent modestly. When you get out of the residency program you start getting paid a lot more than you were during residency. As a result of the debt you have incurred, you have to work more hours in order to get the money to pay off your student loan as quickly as possible. Some doctors have told me that it took them over ten years to pay off their student loans for medical school during years where they would work upwards of 100 hours per week.

After I learned the reality of becoming a medical doctor a major concern crept into my mind—if I became a doctor I would have no time with my family and no time for myself. I began thinking of becoming a Ph.D. doctor. I started thinking about becoming a college professor. I have always been interested in English and in sharing stories with people. I looked at the path to a position as a professor of English. After I finish my B.A. in English I can sign up for a Master's/Doctorate program where I can get both a Master's and a Ph.D. in English in six years. With a doctorate I can get a job teaching English in some college. Certain colleges even have systems where graduate students get introduced to teaching undergraduate students while they are getting their doctorates.

Hard work is an addiction that grows large under a repetitive routine. It is important, therefore, that the worker at the beginning of his service should look carefully at his chosen route on the roads ahead to decide what drives him and what can help guide him in his pursuit of happiness. For some, continuing education is the path toward a meaningful work life, while others choose their path straight out of high school. Making up your mind about what to do with your life is an individual choice and often takes many years of reflection to arrive at a solid conclusion. But, sadly, simply discovering the desired direction of your life is not enough. You need to secure the road to your goal and propel yourself down it.

I have learned through my experiences in life and through the example of my grandfather that work is necessary to any positive experience and that one's attitude and acceptance to face new challenges is truly what makes him great. And I feel deep inside myself that the essential work that must be done in a person's life is unpaid, difficult to find, and is not often advertised in the newspaper.

INTERPRETATIONS

1. Evaluate Patterson's first paragraph. What points does he raise that you agree or disagree with? What is the effect of including "Hong Kong to Houston"?

2. What portrait of his grandfather emerges in the first part of the essay? To what extent do you agree that "people should enjoy their work because there is a good chance they will do it for the rest of their lives"?

3. Patterson describes himself as a "modern worker who is dissatisfied with his work and the pay he receives." Does his profile fit yours and that of your friends with respect to work? Why or why not?

4. Review Patterson's description of the preparation and expense of becoming a doctor. Is it accurate? Is his intent to dissuade young people from choosing the medical profession? Did he convince you? Why or why not?

5. What do you think of Patterson's choice of becoming a college English professor? How effectively does he defend his choice?

6. Review Patterson's conclusion, particularly his last sentence. How would you define "essential work"?

CORRESPONDENCES

1. Create a journal entry on a conversation between Patterson and Colicino on the topic of work.

2. Review Voltaire's perspective and discuss its relevance to Patterson's grandfather's point of view on work.

APPLICATIONS

1. Create a profile of Patterson's grandfather that includes his philosophy with respect to work and family.

2. According to Patterson it is essential "to secure the road to your goal and propel yourself down it." Write a journal entry recording a period where you did just that. How has that decision influenced your work life?

3. Working with your group, conduct a survey of friends, family members, or co-workers about how their definitions of happiness and/or success changed over time. Write a summary of your findings.

Black Hair

GARY SOTO

Gary Soto was born April 12, 1952, in Fresno, California, to Manuel and Angie Soto, whose Mexican heritage was important in his upbringing. He graduated in 1974 from California State–Fresno, and in 1976 he received an M.A. in creative writing from the University of California at Irvine. Between 1979 and 1993 he taught English at the University of California at Berkeley, where he now lives, but he has been a full-time writer since 1992. He is the author of numerous volumes of poetry, among them The Elements of San Joaquin *(1977), a grim picture of Mexican-American life, and* Black Hair *(1985), which focuses on his friends and family. One of Soto's memoirs,* Living Up the Street: Narrative Recollections, *received a Before Columbus Foundation American Book Award in 1985. More recent publications have included a novel,* Amnesia in a Republican County *(2003), four young-adult novels (three of them in 2006 and 2007), a collection of stories,* Help Wanted *(2005), and two more collections of poems. Soto has produced a film and a libretto for the Los Angeles Opera. He also serves as Young People's Ambassador for the California Rural Legal Assistance and the United Farm Workers of America. "Black Hair" will, if you let it, take you back to the days when you were first learning how to look for a job. What memories do you have of those days?*

THERE ARE TWO KINDS OF WORK: One uses the mind and the other uses muscle. As a kid I found out about the latter. I'm thinking of the summer of 1969 when I was a seventeen-year-old runaway who ended up in Glendale, California, to work for Valley Tire Factory. To answer an ad in the newspaper I walked miles in the afternoon sun, my stomach slowly knotting on a doughnut that was breakfast, my teeth like bright candles gone yellow.

I walked in the door sweating and feeling ugly because my hair was still stiff from a swim at the Santa Monica beach the day before. Jules, the accountant and part owner, looked droopily through his bifocals at my application and then at me. He tipped his cigar in the ashtray, asked my age as if he didn't believe I was seventeen, but finally after a moment of silence, said, "Come back tomorrow. Eight-thirty."

I thanked him, left the office, and went around to the chain link fence to watch the workers heave tires into a bin; others carted uneven stacks of tires on hand trucks. Their faces were black from tire dust and when they talked—or cussed—their mouths showed a bright pink.

From there I walked up a commercial street, past a cleaners, a motorcycle shop, and a gas station where I washed my face and hands; before leaving I took a bottle that hung on the side of the Coke machine, filled it with water, and stopped it with a scrap of paper and a rubber band.

The next morning I arrived early at work. The assistant foreman, a potbellied Hungarian, showed me a timecard and how to punch in. He showed me the Coke machine, the locker room with its slimy shower, and also pointed out the places where I shouldn't go: The ovens where the tires were recapped and the customer service area, which had a slashed couch, a coffee table with greasy magazines, and an ashtray. He introduced me to Tully, a fat man with one ear, who worked the buffers that resurfaced the white walls. I was handed an apron and a face mask and shown how to use the buffer: Lift the tire and center, inflate it with a footpedal, press the buffer against the white band until cleaned, and then deflate and blow off the tire with an air hose.

With a paint brush he stirred a can of industrial preserver. "Then slap this blue stuff on." While he was talking a co-worker came up quietly from behind him and goosed him with the air hose. Tully jumped as if he had been struck by a bullet and then turned around cussing and cupping his genitals in his hands as the other worker walked away calling out foul names. When Tully turned to me smiling his gray teeth, I lifted my mouth into a smile because I wanted to get along. He has to be on my side, I thought. He's the one who'll tell the foreman how I'm doing.

I worked carefully that day, setting the tires on the machine as if they were babies, since it was easy to catch a finger in the rim that expanded to inflate the tire. At the day's end we swept up the tire dust and emptied the trash into bins.

At five the workers scattered for their cars and motorcycles while I crossed the street to wash at a burger stand. My hair was stiff with dust and my mouth showed pink against the backdrop of my dirty face. I then ordered a hotdog and walked slowly in the direction of the abandoned house where I had stayed the night before. I lay under the trees and within minutes was asleep. When I woke my shoulders were sore and my eyes burned when I squeezed the lids together.

From the backyard I walked dully through a residential street, and as evening came on, the TV glare in the living rooms and the headlights of passing cars showed against the blue drift of dusk. I saw two children coming up the street with snow cones, their tongues darting at the packed ice. I saw a boy with a peach and wanted to stop him, but felt embarrassed by my hunger. I walked for an hour only to return and discover the house lit brightly. Behind the fence I heard voices and saw a flashlight poking at the garage door. A man on the back steps mumbled something about the refrigerator to the one with the flashlight.

I waited for them to leave, but had the feeling they wouldn't because there was the commotion of furniture being moved. Tired, even more desperate, I started walking again with a great urge to kick things and tear the day from my life. I felt weak and my mind kept drifting because of hunger. I crossed the street to a gas station where I sipped at the water fountain and searched the Coke machine for change. I started walking again, first up a commercial street, then into a residential area where I lay down on someone's lawn and replayed a scene at home—my Mother crying at the kitchen table, my stepfather yelling with food in his mouth. They're cruel, I thought, and warned myself that I should never forgive them. How could they do this to me.

When I got up from the lawn it was late. I searched out a place to sleep and found an unlocked car that seemed safe. In the back seat, with my shoes off, I fell asleep but woke up startled about four in the morning when the owner, a nurse on her way to work, opened the door. She got in and was about to start the engine when I raised my head up from the backseat to explain my presence. She screamed so loudly when I said "I'm sorry" that I sprinted from the car with my shoes in hand. Her screams faded, then stopped altogether, as I ran down the block where I hid behind a trash bin and waited for a police siren to sound. Nothing. I crossed the street to a church where I slept stiffly on cardboard in the balcony.

I woke up feeling tired and greasy. It was early and a few street lights were still lit, the east growing pink with dawn. I washed myself from a garden hose and returned to the church to break into what looked like a kitchen. Paper cups, plastic spoons, a coffee pot littered on a table. I found a box of Nabisco crackers which I ate until I was full.

At work I spent the morning at the buffer, but was then told to help Iggy, an old Mexican, who was responsible for choosing tires that could be recapped without the risk of exploding at high speeds. Every morning a truck would deliver used tires, and after I unloaded them Iggy would step among the tires to inspect them for punctures and rips on the sidewalls.

With a yellow chalk he marked circles and Xs to indicate damage and called out "junk." For those tires that could be recapped, he said "goody" and I placed them on my hand truck.

When I had a stack of eight I kicked the truck at an angle and balanced them to another work area where Iggy again inspected the tires, scratching Xs and calling out "junk."

Iggy worked only until three in the afternoon, at which time he went to the locker room to wash and shave and to dress in a two-piece suit. When he came out he glowed with a bracelet, watch, rings, and a shiny fountain pen in his breast pocket. His shoes sounded against the asphalt. He was the image of a banker stepping into sunlight with millions on his mind. He said a few low words to workers with whom he was friendly and none to people like me.

I was seventeen, stupid because I couldn't figure out the difference between an F 78 14 and 750 14 at sight. Iggy shook his head when I brought him the wrong tires, especially since I had expressed interest in being his understudy. "Mexican, how can you be so stupid?" he would yell at me, slapping a tire from my hands. But within weeks I learned a lot about tires, from sizes and makes to how they are molded in iron forms to how Valley stole from other companies. Now and then we received a truckload of tires, most of them new or nearly new, and they were taken to our warehouse in the back where the serial numbers were ground off with a sander. On those days the foreman handed out Cokes and joked with us as we worked to get the numbers off.

Most of the workers were Mexican or black, though a few redneck whites worked there. The base pay was a dollar sixty-five, but the average was three dollars. Of the black workers, I knew Sugar Daddy the best. His body carried two hundred and fifty pounds, armfuls of scars, and a long knife that made me jump when he brought it out from his boot without warning. At one time he had been a singer, and had cut a record in 1967 called *Love's Chance*, which broke into the R and B charts. But nothing came of it. No big contract, no club dates, no tours. He made very little from the sales, only enough for an operation to pull a steering wheel from his gut when, drunk and mad at a lady friend, he slammed his Mustang into a row of parked cars.

"Touch it," he smiled at me one afternoon as he raised his shirt, his black belly kinked with hair. Scared, I traced the scar that ran from his chest to the left of his belly button, and I was repelled but hid my disgust.

Among the Mexicans I had few friends because I was different, a *pocho*[1] who spoke bad Spanish. At lunch they sat in tires and laughed over burritos, looking up at me to laugh even harder. I also sat in tires while nursing a Coke and felt dirty and sticky because I was still living on the street and had not had a real bath in over a week. Nevertheless, when the border patrol came to round up the nationals, I ran with them as they scrambled for the fence or hid among the tires behind the warehouse. The foreman, who thought I was an undocumented worker, yelled at me to run, to get away. I did just that. At the time it seemed fun because there was no risk, only a goodhearted feeling of hide-and-seek, and besides it meant an hour away from work on company time. When

---

[1]A derogatory term for Mexicans living in the United States who have forgotten their cultural heritage.

the police left we came back and some of the nationals made up stories
of how they were almost caught—how they out-raced the police. Some
of the stories were so convoluted and unconvincing that everyone
laughed *mentiras*,[2] especially when one described how he overpowered
a policeman, took his gun away, and sold the patrol car. We laughed
and he laughed, happy to be there to make up a story.

If work was difficult, so were the nights. I still had not gathered
enough money to rent a room, so I spent the nights sleeping in parked
cars or in the balcony of a church. After a week I found a newspaper ad
for room for rent, phoned, and was given directions. Finished with
work, I walked the five miles down Mission Road looking back into the
traffic with my thumb out. No rides. After eight hours of handling tires,
I was frightening, I suppose, to drivers since they seldom looked at me;
if they did, it was a quick glance. For the next six weeks I would try to
hitchhike, but the only person to stop was a Mexican woman who gave
me two dollars to take the bus. I told her it was too much and that no bus
ran from Mission Road to where I lived, but she insisted that I keep the
money and trotted back to her idling car. It must have hurt her to see me
day after day walking in the heat and looking very much the dirty Mexican to the many minds that didn't know what it meant to work at hard
labor. That woman knew. Her eyes met mine as she opened the car door,
and there was a tenderness that was surprisingly true—one for which
you wait for years but when it comes it doesn't help. Nothing changes.
You continue on in rags, with the sun still above you.

I rented a room from a middle-aged couple whose lives were a
mess. She was a school teacher and he was a fireman. A perfect setup,
I thought. But during my stay there they would argue with one another
for hours in their bedroom.

When I rang at the front door both Mr. and Mrs. Van Deusen
answered and didn't bother to disguise their shock at how awful I
looked. But they let me in all the same. Mrs. Van Deusen showed me
around the house, from the kitchen and bathroom to the living room
with its grand piano. On her fingers she counted out the house rules as
she walked me to my room. It was a girl's room with lace curtains, sce-
nic wallpaper of a Victorian couple enjoying a stroll, canopied bed, and
stuffed animals in a corner. Leaving, she turned and asked if she could
do laundry for me and, feeling shy and hurt, I told her no; perhaps the
next day. She left and I undressed to take a bath, exhausted as I sat on
the edge of the bed probing my aches and my bruised places. With a
towel around my waist I hurried down the hallway to the bathroom
where Mrs. Van Deusen had set out an additional towel with a tube of

[2]Lies.

shampoo. I ran the water in the tub and sat on the toilet, lid down, watching the steam curl toward the ceiling. When I lowered myself into the tub I felt my body sting. I soaped a wash cloth and scrubbed my arms until they lightened, even glowed pink, but still I looked unwashed around my neck and face no matter how hard I rubbed. Back in the room I sat in bed reading a magazine, happy and thinking of no better luxury than a girl's sheets, especially after nearly two weeks of sleeping on cardboard at the church.

I was too tired to sleep, so I sat at the window watching the neighbors move about in pajamas, and, curious about the room, looked through the bureau drawers to search out personal things—snapshots, a messy diary, and a high school yearbook. I looked up the Van Deusen's daughter, Barbara, and studied her face as if I recognized her from my own school—a face that said "promise," "college," "nice clothes in the closet." She was a skater and a member of the German Club; her greatest ambition was to sing at the Hollywood Bowl.

After awhile I got into bed and as I drifted toward sleep I thought about her. In my mind I played a love scene again and again and altered it slightly each time. She comes home from college and at first is indifferent to my presence in her home, but finally I overwhelm her with deep pity when I come home hurt from work, with blood on my shirt. Then there was another version: Home from college she is immediately taken with me, in spite of my work-darkened face, and invites me into the family car for a milkshake across town. Later, back at the house, we sit in the living room talking about school until we're so close I'm holding her hand. The truth of the matter was that Barbara did come home for a week, but was bitter toward her parents for taking in boarders (two others besides me). During that time she spoke to me only twice: Once, while searching the refrigerator, she asked if we had any mustard; the other time she asked if I had seen her car keys.

But it was a place to stay. Work had become more and more difficult. I not only worked with Iggy, but also with the assistant foreman who was in charge of unloading trucks. After they backed in I hopped on top to pass the tires down by bouncing them on the tailgate to give them an extra spring so they would be less difficult to handle on the other end. Each truck was weighed down with more than two hundred tires, each averaging twenty pounds, so that by the time the truck was emptied and swept clean I glistened with sweat and my T-shirt stuck to my body. I blew snot threaded with tire dust onto the asphalt, indifferent to the customers who watched from the waiting room.

The days were dull. I did what there was to do from morning until the bell sounded at five; I tugged, pulled, and cussed at tires until I was listless and my mind drifted and caught on small things, from cold sodas to shoes to stupid talk about what we would do with a million dollars. I remember unloading a truck with Hamp, a black man.

"What's better than a sharp lady?" he asked me as I stood sweaty on a pile of junked tires. "Water. With ice," I said.

He laughed with his mouth open wide. With his fingers he pinched the sweat from his chin and flicked at me. "You be too young, boy. A woman can make you a god."

As a kid I had chopped cotton and picked grapes, so I knew work. I knew the fatigue and the boredom and the feeling that there was a good possibility you might have to do such work for years, if not for a lifetime. In fact, as a kid I imagined a dark fate: To marry Mexican poor, work Mexican hours, and in the end die a Mexican death, broke and in despair.

But this job at Valley Tire Company confirmed that there was something worse than field work, and I was doing it. We were all doing it, from foreman to the newcomers like me, and what I felt heaving tires for eight hours a day was felt by everyone—black, Mexican, redneck. We all despised those hours but didn't know what else to do. The workers were unskilled, some undocumented and fearful of deportation, and all struck with an uncertainty at what to do with their lives. Although everyone bitched about work, no one left. Some had worked there for as long as twelve years; some had sons working there. Few quit; no one was ever fired. It amazed me that no one gave up when the border patrol jumped from their vans, baton in hand, because I couldn't imagine any work that could be worse—or any life. What was out there, in the world, that made men run for the fence in fear?

How we arrived at such a place is a mystery to me. Why anyone would stay for years is even a deeper concern. You showed up, but from where? What broken life? What ugly past? The foreman showed you the Coke machine, the washroom, and the yard where you'd work. When you picked up a tire, you were amazed at the black it could give off.

INTERPRETATIONS

1. "There are two kinds of work: one uses the mind and the other uses muscles." How effectively does Soto support this thesis in his essay? Cite evidence.

2. Soto catalogs his first day at work in great detail. How do his sensory and visual descriptions not only enhance his essay but also serve his purpose?

3. What role does Iggy play in Soto's summer work experience? How is Iggy different from his co-workers? Does Soto ever resolve his doubts about Iggy's "dignity"? Explain.

4. Why does Soto include the Van Duesens? Is it digressive or does it add another dimension to his narrative? Explain.

5. In paragraphs 29 and 30, Soto contrasts being a field worker with his summer in the tire factory. Although field work pays less, why is it better in his view than the tire factory?

6. Most writers use their conclusions to summarize their essays. Why does Soto conclude his essay with a series of questions? To what effect?

CORRESPONDENCES

1. Review Patterson's and Soto's introductions. What makes them effective? Are they equally provocative? Explain.

2. According to Shrank's perspective, the workplace performs the function of community. To what extent does Soto's experience refute this concept?

APPLICATIONS

1. If you involve yourself with hard labor, the kind that Soto has described in his essay, what kind of literacy is acquired? For a few minutes, do an activity that requires the use of your muscles. For example, you might run a few sprints, lift weights, work vigorously in the garden, or split firewood. As you engage in this activity, pay attention to the physical sensations you experience. Write a few paragraphs about what you felt and came to understand about your body and physical activity.

2. In the context of describing his summer job, Soto also focuses on the destructive effects of poverty. Write an analysis of the connections he makes between poverty and despair. How does poverty also contribute to emotional and intellectual paralysis?

3. Compare with your group your various experiences with summer jobs. Then focus on one that was particularly pleasant or unpleasant. What did you learn about yourself from this experience? Was it an effective rite of passage? Explain.

Work Hard—Quit Right!

THOMAS M. COLICINO

Thomas M. Colicino would like to thank all the educators, families, friends, and others that inspire and encourage his writing. Mr. Colicino is currently enrolled in Queensborough Community College, where he was majoring in science and mathematics but is now proud to be discovering where his true talents and interests lie. Mr. Colicino is reassured in learning that there is a Nobel Prize in Literature.

THERE IS A RATHER SHORT LIST of gainful jobs available if you have no experience. In my varied, short and somewhat storied career I have been a gymnastics coach, dishwasher, and coffee guru. It's painful how quickly these positions become indispensable. There's almost no form of promotion available, but there is pressure to work your difficult, thankless post—especially when you need the money.

I started teaching gymnastics in seventh grade and quit after eleventh grade. Overall this work experience was the best I have had, but it wasn't paid. The financial reward was that I did not have to pay for my own membership and there was always a generous take during the holidays, but as I grew older I needed more cash. My parents provided me with money as long as I did my chores. They loved making an honest working man out of me.

One common fault with an entry-level job besides the low pay is the absurdity of the hours. Dishwashing at a catering hall means busting your bones while everyone upstairs dances the night away. An average shift would be from six in the evening until two in the morning. I eventually took another job just to see the sun that couldn't shine through my windowless basement apartment.

I learned something about endurance and initiative working as a dishwasher. Having to brave the midnight winter chill in a soaking wet uniform, lugging what seemed like five-ton garbage bags full of refuse the same consistency and smell of vomit to an immense Dumpster tucked neatly out of sight along the side of the property, was inhumane. I grew to take the work as my own Olympiad. How quickly could I shovel a path to the Dumpster? How far could I heave the trash bag without it splitting open? Would I be able to sort and stack the dishes fast enough to keep the overwhelmed dishwasher chugging at a steady clip? The pressure and resulting exhaustion was gratifying and helped me sleep better than I can ever remember. The work did get me into shape, but I'm still waiting for my medal.

After leaving the catering hall for better hours, more pay and benefits, I was employed by a modest coffee corporation out of Seattle. Looking back, I learned to appreciate coffee and I drink it to this day. It was a prosperous six months for me. I saved a couple of thousand dollars, met some nice people and received an award for my diligent work. Everything was regimented and it was quite simple to learn the ropes and the recipes. My all time favorite chore, after walking around the block to take out the trash (how I longed for my Dumpster outside the catering hall!), was running around to the four or five neighborhood locations to stock up on what we just ran out of; oftentimes, it was paper bags, paper cups or plastic lids. But, seriously, preparing coffee compulsively and foolishly taking too many extra shifts for too little extra pay took its toll. In an ambitious way I wanted to make a career out of the job, but I was soon discouraged. After having a sit down with the boss who seemed more concerned about how my attitude affected the image of the store instead of how six months of hard work and dedication had burned me out momentarily, I used my noodle and quit the bean. Sometimes it's not about money. Sometimes you are down and out without a great source of income no matter how much experience you have. What in the world can you do?

Do not underestimate volunteering as a way to enrich your life. Volunteering allows you to be selfish. There's no money involved, no love lost. You can sincerely enjoy what you are doing. You shouldn't have to "just deal" with anything or anyone. I enjoy working with animals. Kittens, puppies, cats and dogs in pounds or shelters just need some affection and companionship. So it's easy to break the ice and have a great time. It's dirty work, but caring for living creatures that love you back is something I find fulfilling. Quitting a volunteer job is always your right, but working hard has its potential rewards. Earning a paid position doing something you are willing to do for free is difficult, but I can think of no better job in the world.

Despite the American urgency to make money, quitting a job is not anything uncommon or career ending. It is important to understand why you are moving on. Consider your financial needs, resources and responsibilities. Consider your dreams and your sanity. Don't let anyone call you irresponsible or careless. Prove through your dedication to a goal or principle that you are a steadfast and loyal individual. As a gymnastics coach there was a sense of community and the satisfying experience of passing on what I had learned to younger people. Yet the need for money eclipsed this wholesome exchange. I no longer had time I could donate. I needed to quit. While I was a dishwasher I knew it was not a career path, but I had a responsibility to pay rent and feed myself, something that could not be accomplished working there. And as a coffee guru I saw potential to have the stability of a full-time job and the money to live a fulfilling life, but there was little appeal to the work involved.

The best things in life are not free. At times you may need money, but no matter what you are doing you have to spend your time, patience and knowledge to get the job done. And always consider quitting in pursuit of a more prosperous future.

INTERPRETATIONS

1. With regard to his job as a dishwasher in a catering hall (paragraph 3), Colicino writes: "I eventually took another job just to see the sun that couldn't shine through my windowless basement apartment." What do you think he means by this? What rhetorical technique does he apply to make his point? Where else in the essay does he apply this strategy?

2. How would you summarize Colicino's experiences working at the coffee shop? What particular phrases capture your attention?

3. What main idea does Colicino present in his essay? Where does it appear? How might you summarize it in your own words?

CORRESPONDENCES

1. Toward the end of Narayan's essay, Venkat Rao writes a letter of resignation to his boss. Why does he intend to quit his job? How do these reasons correspond to Colicino's beliefs?

2. From what Colicino writes, do you think that he is more like John Patterson or Patterson's grandfather? What evidence from the essays are you able to find to support your opinions?

APPLICATIONS

1. Freewrite on your concept of work. Focus on the images and associations that the word evokes. Then write an essay defining what work means to you.

2. Have you ever quit a job where, like Colicino, you felt that doing so was a justifiable and necessary action? Write a narrative describing your situation and this experience. When you get to the part of your story where you quit, use details and dialogue to place a reader directly into the action. Try to make this exact moment your finest moment!

3. What characteristics were possessed by the best job you ever had? What qualities were present in the worst job you ever worked? Produce a chart that has the positives on one side of the page and the negatives on the other. Share your chart with the members of your peer group. After a discussion about the charts, arrive at a consensus concerning the top five positive qualities of employment and the five worst ones. Use this information to create two "want ads": one for the best job you can possibly imagine and a second one for the worst of all jobs.

Working Like a Dog

CHARLES NEUMAN

Charles Neuman has two dogs who love to swim. He enjoys outdoor activities with his three sons, playing jazz and classical piano, and building wooden boats. A self-described "friendly introvert," Neuman finds family life, even with all of its challenges, to be surprisingly invigorating. He gives credit to his wife, who is a special education teacher on Long Island, where Neuman and his family live. Neuman teaches physics and astronomy at Queensborough Community College (CUNY).

DOGS ARE NATURAL WORKERS. They like to do things. They can teach us a lot about our own work and about fulfilling our purpose.

Among the many heroes of the 9/11 terrorist attacks are the search and rescue dogs. Search and rescue dogs undergo extensive training to be able to locate live victims. When brought to a scene such as the destroyed Twin Towers in New York City, the dogs are ready for action. They climb through rough terrain and work for many hours without water or a break, using their skills to sniff out survivors while ignoring all other distractions.

After 9/11, stories began to surface that these dogs worked long shifts without success. The live victims were not to be found. To keep the dogs from becoming discouraged or depressed, dog handlers typically hide people as fake victims so that the dogs can fulfill their purpose and earn a reward such as playing with a toy. It must have been a surreal scene: The destruction, and then the dogs searching for, but not finding, victims. And amongst this desolation, the playful hide-and-seek games to keep the dogs feeling purposeful.

Like dogs, humans need to feel useful, to have something meaningful to do. It can be depressing if we feel we have no purpose, or if we feel that we cannot fulfill our purpose, and we may not be lucky enough to have someone to lift our spirits. Dogs teach us that when times are tough, we should keep sniffing. We never know what we will find. Maybe we do not have a purpose, or maybe we will stumble upon someone else's generosity to help us fulfill our destiny.

In Hebrew, the word for dog is כֶּלֶב ("ke-lev"), which means "like a heart" and implies a sense of loyalty. The Biblical character Caleb, whose name in Hebrew is כָּלֵב ("Ka-lev"), demonstrated his loyalty to his people and to his mission. When Moses led his people to the outskirts of the Land of Canaan, after a long journey through the wilderness, he sent Caleb and eleven others to spy out the Land. Ten people came back with negative reports that mirrored the prevalent whining, complaining, and defeatist attitudes. But Caleb and Joshua looked at the situation with a can-do attitude and brought back positive reports. Consequently they were rewarded by eventually being able to enter the Land they sought. Caleb represents the archetypal dog, as his name implies. Just like the search and rescue dogs, he kept at his job under trying circumstances. He remained focused on the job at hand and avoided being distracted by feelings of doom or defeat. Like Caleb, we can apply dog-like loyalty to our work and to our many missions in life. When we face challenges, we can choose not to whine and complain, and we can keep moving forward as Caleb did. Our reward may be a sense of a job well done, or perhaps something more concrete.

Dogs are good at their jobs because they are smart, but also because they are not *too* smart. They don't know the truth: that we are ultimately doomed. Our Sun will burn out in about five billion years. Even if planet Earth survives the dramatic increase in the Sun's size before it dies, there will be no hope for life on it. Actually, we are doomed long before that. In about 500 million years, our Sun will be too hot for our planet to support any life at all. Furthermore, there is no guarantee that humans will even make it that far. After all, the average life span of a mammalian species on Earth is about one million years.

But if a dog did know this, his intuition would lead him to the idea that we are part of a greater network of life in the universe. A dog might intuit, as scientists have concluded from probability studies, that there is likely life in many places in the universe, among the billions of solar systems in the billions of galaxies in the universe. With this information, a dog could ignore the distracting thoughts and go back to being a dog, which is what dogs do so well. And if we accessed our inner-dog, we, too, could see ourselves as part of a greater network and not as isolated workers with isolated problems. This solidarity could give us peace of mind that would allow us to focus on our jobs with dog-like determination and enthusiasm.

This idea of interconnectedness, that we are linked to everything in the universe, is not only a conclusion of modern physics but is also a central part of Buddhist philosophy. If a dog understood, even on some abstract level, that we are connected to life outside our world, it would be as if a dog had a Buddha nature. The question of the Buddha nature of a dog is not new. In Zen Buddhism, it is an enlightening experience to ponder a koan, a seemingly unsolvable riddle. Consider, for example, the question, "What is the sound of one hand clapping?" This question clearly does not make sense. The more we reflect on it, however, the more insight we may gain into the true nature of things. The idea is to use our intuitive mind rather than our rational mind. There is a famous Zen koan that consists of a question posed to the Zen master Zhaozhou: "Does a dog have a Buddha nature?" The koan includes Zhaozhou's one-word answer, which is to be the jumping-off point for insightful contemplation.

You do not have to be a Zen master to see evidence for a dog's Buddha nature. A dog lives in the moment. She can be completely relaxed in a comfortable nap, but if you get out her leash she will immediately spring into action. It takes me about a half hour, on a good day, to leave the house, but a dog can be ready in seconds. She might do one stretch first (typically the yoga pose "downward dog"), and then she's ready for a walk around the block or a marathon. Whatever comes her way, she can handle it. Wouldn't it be great if we could handle everything that comes our way in our work? Instead of reacting to each challenge at work, we could live in each moment and not have to label it as "good" or "bad." It just is. There would be no need to watch the clock or count the days until vacation or retirement. Each infinitesimal moment has infinite possibility.

Whether we think of a dog's nature as Buddha-like or not, we can learn from it. We can become more dog-like through practices such as meditation and yoga, or just by stopping every once in a while to look at the trees or to sniff the breeze. Or by appreciating a freshly painted fire hydrant. Whatever works.

Dogs are not just our best friends. They are our guides to life. We learn from dogs that our challenge in our work, and in all of our pursuits, is to be trained, to use our training for a worthy purpose, to be dedicated, to keep sniffing, and to take things as they come. Finally, we must not forget to take a nap every once in a while.

INTERPRETATIONS

1. How does Neuman employ *tone* in this essay? Is his use of tone consistent throughout or does it change in places? What examples might you provide to support your answer?

2. What examples does Neuman provide to convey his meaning? What are their sources?

CORRESPONDENCES

1. Research the colloquial meaning of the expression "working like a dog." Which essay best supports this original meaning, Curry's (p. 222) or Neuman's? Explain how the phrase "working like a dog" is approached by each writer.

2. Neuman maintains that dogs possess positive attitudes toward work. Which of these characteristics may be found in the narrator of Colicino's essay (p. 240)?

APPLICATIONS

1. Visit the Web sites below and read a few koans. When one **STRIKES** you, reflect on it for a few minutes. Then, write a journal entry that captures your thinking about the koan.

   http://www.chinapage.com/zen/koan1.html

   http://www.ibiblio.org/zen/cgi-bin/koan-index.pl

   http://www.ashidakim.com/zenkoans/zenindex.html

2. Make a list of those qualities dogs possess that would benefit a human being in the workplace. Pick the one that has the most meaning to you and that you already possess. Now, write a letter to a prospective employer explaining how this characteristic would benefit the organization and make you a more attractive candidate in a current or future work situation.

Forty-Five a Month

R. K. NARAYAN

R. K. Narayan (1906–2001) was one of India's most prolific writers. During his lifetime Narayan wrote 34 novels, which include: Swami and Friends *(1935),* The English Teacher *(1953),* The Printer of Malgudi *(1957),* The Guide *(1958),* The Man-Eater of Malgudi *(1961),* The Vendor of Sweets *(1967),* The Painter of Signs *(1976), and* A Tiger for Malgudi *(1983). Narayan's short-story collections include:* Malgudi Days *(1982) and* The Grandmother's Tale and Selected Stories *(1994). As you read Narayan's story, think about how you would have reacted in Rao's situation .*

In 1947, India declared its independence from the British, who had controlled most of that country for about 300 years. Colonial India had at the same time been partitioned into Pakistan and India, creating in the same year about 12 million Hindu and Muslim refugees, of whom about 200,000 were killed. Mohandas K. Gandhi (known as the Mahatma), the leader of Indian independence who had advocated nonviolent civil disobedience and abolition of the Untouchable caste, was assassinated the year after independence. The Congress Party dominated Indian politics for forty years (from Independence until late 1989) under Prime Ministers Jawaharlal Nehru, his daughter Indira Gandhi (no relation to Mohandas), and her son Rajiv Gandhi. The Nehru-Gandhi dynasty ended when Rajiv Gandhi lost the November 1989 election and was assassinated while campaigning two years later. His successors have faced an electorate that is more assertive and more impatient, a new divergence between state and society, increasing clashes between Hindus, Sikhs, and Muslims, and ongoing tensions between India and its neighbors, particularly Pakistan.

Indian culture, one of the oldest in the world, can be traced to at least 5,000 B.C. The founder of Buddhism lived in fifth-century India. In the third century B.C. Buddhism became the established religion; the native Hinduism revived, however, and eventually prevailed, and now claims well over three-quarters of the Indian population of 800 million.

SHANTA COULD NOT STAY IN HER CLASS any longer. She had done clay-modeling, music, drill, a bit of alphabets and numbers and was now cutting coloured paper. She would have to cut till the bell rang and the teacher said, "Now you may all go home," or "Put away the scissors and take up your alphabets—" Shanta was impatient to know the time. She asked her friend sitting next to her, "Is it five now?"

"Maybe," she replied.

"Or is it six?"

"I don't think so," her friend replied, "because night comes at six."

"Do you think it is five?"

"Yes."

"Oh, I must go. My father will be back at home now. He has asked me to be ready at five. He is taking me to the cinema this evening. I must go home." She threw down her scissors and ran up to the teacher. "Madam, I must go home."

"Why, Shanta Bai?"

"Because it is five o'clock now."

"Who told you it was five?"

"Kamala."

"It is not five now. It is—do you see the clock there? Tell me what the time is. I taught you to read the clock the other day." Shanta stood gazing at the clock in the hall, counted the figures laboriously and declared, "It is nine o'clock."

The teacher called the other girls and said, "Who will tell me the time from that clock?" Several of them concurred with Shanta and said it was nine o'clock, till the teacher said, "You are seeing only the long hand. See the short one, where is it?"

"Two and a half."

"So what is the time?"

"Two and a half."

"It is two forty-five, understand? Now you may all go to your seats—" Shanta returned to the teacher in about ten minutes and asked, "Is it five, madam, because I have to be ready at five. Otherwise my father will be very angry with me. He asked me to return home early."

"At what time?"

"Now." The teacher gave her permission to leave, and Shanta picked up her books and dashed out of the class with a cry of joy. She ran home, threw her books on the floor and shouted, "Mother, Mother," and Mother came running from the next house, where she had gone to chat with her friends.

Mother asked, "Why are you back so early?"

"Has Father come home?" Shanta asked. She would not take her coffee or *tiffin*[1] but insisted on being dressed first. She opened the trunk and insisted on wearing the thinnest frock and knickers, while her mother wanted to dress her in a long skirt and thick coat for the evening. Shanta picked out a gorgeous ribbon from a cardboard soap box in which she kept pencils, ribbons and chalk bits. There was a heated argument

---

[1]Midday snack.

between mother and daughter over the dress, and finally Mother had to give in. Shanta put on her favourite pink frock, braided her hair and flaunted a green ribbon on her pigtail. She powdered her face and pressed a vermilion mark on her forehead. She said, "Now Father will say what a nice girl I am because I'm ready. Aren't you also coming, Mother?"

"Not today."

Shanta stood at the little gate looking down the street.

Mother said, "Father will come only after five; don't stand in the sun. It is only four o'clock."

The sun was disappearing behind the house on the opposite row, and Shanta knew that presently it would be dark. She ran in to her mother and asked, "Why hasn't Father come home yet, Mother?"

"How can I know? He is perhaps held up in the office."

Shanta made a wry face. "I don't like these people in the office. They are bad people—"

She went back to the gate and stood looking out. Her mother shouted from inside, "Come in, Shanta. It is getting dark, don't stand there." But Shanta would not go in. She stood at the gate and a wild idea came into her head. Why should she not go to the office and call out Father and then go to the cinema? She wondered where his office might be. She had no notion. She had seen her father take the turn at the end of the street every day. If one went there, perhaps one went automatically to Father's office. She threw a glance about to see if Mother was anywhere and moved down the street.

It was twilight. Everyone going about looked gigantic, walls of houses appeared very high and cycles and carriages looked as though they would bear down on her. She walked on the very edge of the road. Soon the lamps were twinkling, and the passersby looked like shadows. She had taken two turns and did not know where she was. She sat down on the edge of the road biting her nails. She wondered how she was to reach home. A servant employed in the next house was passing along, and she picked herself up and stood before him.

"Oh, what are you doing here all alone?" he asked. She replied, "I don't know. I came here. Will you take me to our house?" She followed him and was soon back in her house.

Venkat Rao, Shanta's father, was about to start for his office that morning when a *jutka*[2] passed along the street distributing cinema handbills. Shanta dashed to the street and picked up a handbill. She held it up and asked, "Father, will you take me to the cinema today?" He felt unhappy at the question. Here was the child growing up without

[2]A two-wheeled horse-drawn carriage.

having any of the amenities and the simple pleasures of life. He had hardly taken her twice to the cinema. He had no time for the child. While children of her age in other houses had all the dolls, dresses and outings that they wanted, this child was growing up all alone and like a barbarian more or less. He felt furious with his office. For forty rupees[3] a month they seemed to have purchased him outright.

He reproached himself for neglecting his wife and child—even the wife could have her own circle of friends and so on: she was after all a grown-up, but what about the child? What a drab, colourless existence was hers! Every day they kept him at the office till seven or eight in the evening, and when he came home the child was asleep. Even on Sundays they wanted him at the office. Why did they think he had no personal life, a life of his own? They gave him hardly any time to take the child to the park or the pictures. He was going to show them that they weren't to toy with him. Yes, he was prepared even to quarrel with his manager if necessary.

He said with resolve, "I will take you to the cinema this evening. Be ready at five."

"Really! Mother!" Shanta shouted. Mother came out of the kitchen.

"Father is taking me to a cinema in the evening."

Shanta's mother smiled cynically. "Don't make false promises to the child—" Venkat Rao glared at her. "Don't talk nonsense. You think you are the only person who keeps promises—"

He told Shanta, "Be ready at five, and I will come and take you positively. If you are not ready, I will be very angry with you."

He walked to his office full of resolve. He would do his normal work and get out at five. If they started any old tricks of theirs, he was going to tell the boss, "Here is my resignation. My child's happiness is more important to me than these horrible papers of yours."

All day the usual stream of papers flowed onto his table and off it. He scrutinized, signed and drafted. He was corrected, admonished and insulted. He had a break of only five minutes in the afternoon for his coffee.

When the office clock struck five and the other clerks were leaving, he went up to the manager and said, "May I go, sir?" The manager looked up from his paper. "You!" It was unthinkable that the cash and account section should be closing at five. "How can you go?"

"I have some urgent private business, sir," he said, smothering the lines he had been rehearsing since the morning: "Herewith my resignation." He visualized Shanta standing at the door, dressed and palpitating with eagerness.

[3]The rupee is an Indian unit of money.

"There shouldn't be anything more urgent than the office work; go back to your seat. You know how many hours I work?" asked the manager. The manager came to the office three hours before opening time and stayed nearly three hours after closing, even on Sundays. The clerks commented among themselves, "His wife must be whipping him whenever he is seen at home; that is why the old owl seems so fond of his office."

"Did you trace the source of that ten-eight difference?" asked the manager.

"I shall have to examine two hundred vouchers. I thought we might do it tomorrow."

"No, no, this won't do. You must rectify it immediately."

Venkat Rao mumbled, "Yes, sir," and slunk back to his seat. The clock showed 5:30. Now it meant two hours of excruciating search among vouchers. All the rest of the office had gone. Only he and another clerk in his section were working, and of course, the manager was there. Venkat Rao was furious. His mind was made up. He wasn't a slave who had sold himself for forty rupees outright. He could make that money easily; and if he couldn't, it would be more honourable to die of starvation.

He took a sheet of paper and wrote: "Herewith my resignation. If you people think you have bought me body and soul for forty rupees, you are mistaken. I think it would be far better for me and my family to die of starvation than slave for this petty forty rupees on which you have kept me for years and years. I suppose you have not the slightest notion of giving me an increment. You give yourselves heavy slices frequently, and I don't see why you shouldn't think of us occasionally. In any case it doesn't interest me now, since this is my resignation. If I and my family perish of starvation, may our ghosts come and haunt you all your life—" He folded the letter, put it in an envelope, sealed the flap and addressed it to the manager. He left his seat and stood before the manager. The manager mechanically received the letter and put it on his pad.

"Venkat Rao," said the manager, "I'm sure you will be glad to hear this news. Our officer discussed the question of increments today, and I've recommended you for an increment of five rupees. Orders are not yet passed, so keep this to yourself for the present." Venkat Rao put out his hand, snatched the envelope from the pad and hastily slipped it in his pocket.

"What is that letter?"

"I have applied for a little casual leave, sir, but I think . . ."

"You can't get any leave for at least a fortnight to come."

"Yes, sir, I realize that. That is why I am withdrawing my application, sir."

"Very well. Have you traced that mistake?"

"I'm scrutinizing the vouchers, sir. I will find it out within an hour . . ."

It was nine o'clock when he went home. Shanta was already asleep. Her mother said. "She wouldn't even change her frock, thinking that any moment you might be coming and taking her out. She hardly ate any food; and wouldn't lie down for fear of crumpling her dress. . . ."

Venkat Rao's heart bled when he saw his child sleeping in her pink frock, hair combed and face powdered, dressed and ready to be taken out. "Why should I not take her to the night show?" He shook her gently and called, "Shanta, Shanta." Shanta kicked her legs and cried, irritated at being disturbed. Mother whispered, "Don't wake her," and patted her back to sleep.

Venkat Rao watched the child for a moment. "I don't know if it is going to be possible for me to take her out at all—you see, they are giving me an increment—" he wailed.

INTERPRETATIONS

1. Why do you think Narayan focuses on the daughter at the outset of the story?

2. "For forty rupees a month they seemed to have purchased him outright." Is this an accurate portrayal of Rao's situation? How does his personality contribute to his dissatisfaction at work?

3. Analyze the mother's role in the story. Does she share her husband's antipathy toward his job? How do you know?

CORRESPONDENCES

1. Dorris and Narayan focus on rights in the workplace from different vantage points and cultural perspectives. What conversation can you imagine them sharing?

2. Review Terkel's perspective on work and discuss its relevance to the texts by Narayan and Soto.

APPLICATIONS

1. Imagine yourself in Shanta's position and write a journal entry on your emotional responses to your father's broken promise.

2. Narayan's stories often reflect the conflict between tradition and individuality. How are both reflected in "Forty-five a Month"? Analyze the elements of the conflict.

3. Brainstorm with your group on images of power. Do you associate power with the workplace? In what context? Is it possible to have power within the constraints of the employee-employer relationship? Summarize the group's discussion.

4. In the story "Forty-five a Month," the plot seems to follow directly from the beginning to the end. Despite the hopes and expectations of both Shanta and a reader, Venkat Rao will not attend the cinema that evening. What, however, do you think would have happened if Rao had said his piece and left his resignation with his manager? How would this twist in plot affect not only what happens in the story but characterization, setting, and theme? After considering the possibilities, write your version of a section of the story that takes into account the twist in plot offered above. Try as best you can to match Nayaran's style and literary technique (e.g., attention to detail, use of dialogue, involvement of the narrator).

Free and Equal

LALITA GANDBHIR

Indo-American Lalita Gandbhir (b. 1938) works as a physician in the Boston area, where she has lived since coming to the United States in 1963. She has published stories in the Toronto South Asian Review, *the* Massachusetts Review, Spotlight, *and other journals, and she has published two collections of short stories in India. Before reading her short story, freewrite about your association with its title.*

RAMESH CAREFULLY STUDIED his reflection in the mirror hung in the hallway. His hair, shirt, tie, suit, nothing escaped his scrutiny. His tie seemed a little crooked, so he undid it and fixed it with slow deliberate movements. Then he reexamined the tie. A conservative shade of maroon, not too wide, not too narrow, just right for the occasion, for the image he wanted to project.

All of a sudden he was aware of two eyes staring at him. He turned to Jay, his little son. Jay sat on the steps leading to the second floor, his eyes focused on his father.

"Why are you staring at me?" Ramesh inquired.

"Going to work now?" Jay intimated the reason for the surprised stare.

Ramesh understood the reason behind Jay's confusion. He used to go to work dressed like this in the mornings. Jay had not seen him dressed in a suit in the evening.

For a moment Ramesh was proud of his son. "What a keen observer Jay is!" Ramesh thought to himself. "For six months I have not worked, yet he noticed a change in my old routine."

However, the implications behind the question bothered Ramesh.

"I am going to a job fair," he answered irritably and again attempted to focus on his tie.

"Can I come?" Jay promptly hurled a question in Ramesh's direction. To him a fair was a fun event. He had been to fairs with his mother before and did not wish to miss this one.

"Jay, this is not the kind of fair you are thinking of. This is a job fair."

"Do they sell jobs at job fairs?"

"Yes." Jay's question struck a sensitive spot. "No, they don't sell jobs. They are buyers. They shop for skills. It's me who is selling my skills. Unfortunately, it's a buyer's market."

The question stimulated Ramesh's chain of thought. "Is my skill for sale?" Ramesh wondered. "If that is true, then why did I dress so carefully? Why did I rehearse answers to imaginary questions from interviewers?"

"No, this job hunting is no longer a simple straightforward business transaction like it used to be when engineers were in demand. I am desperate. I am selling my soul. The job market is no longer a two-way street. I have no negotiating power. I just have to accept what I can get."

Ramesh pulled on his socks mechanically and longingly thought of the good old days like a sick old man thinking of his healthful youth.

Just ten years ago he had hopped from job to job at will. Money, interesting work, more responsibility, benefits, a whim for any reason that appealed to him, and he had switched jobs. Responding to advertisements was his hobby. Head hunters called him offering better and better situations. He went to job fairs casually dressed and never gave a second thought to his attire.

He had job offers, not one or two, but six or seven. The industry needed him then. It was so nice to be coveted!

Ramesh wiped his polished, spotless shoes with a soft cloth.

How carefree he used to be! He dressed like this every morning in five minutes and, yes, Jay remembers.

He never polished his shoes then. His hand moving the cloth on his shoes stood still for a minute. Yes, Rani, his wife, did it for him. Nowadays she seemed to do less and less for him. Why? He asked himself.

Rani had found a part-time job on her own when companies in the area had started to lay off engineers. She had not bothered to discuss the matter with him, just informed him of her decision. In a year she accepted a full-time slot. "How did she manage to receive promotions so soon?" Ramesh wondered.

Rani still ran the home and cared for their young children. Ramesh had seen her busy at all kinds of tasks from early morning until late at night.

Over the last three months she did less and less for Ramesh. She no longer did his laundry or ironing. She had stopped polishing his shoes and did not wait up for him when he returned late from job fairs.

"She is often tired," Ramesh tried to understand, but he felt that she had let him down, wronged him just when his spirit was sinking and he needed her most.

"She should have made an effort for the sake of appearance. It was her duty toward a jobless, incomeless husband."

He pushed all thoughts out of his mind.

He tied his polished shoes, dragged his heavy winter coat out of the closet, and picked up his keys.

"Tell your Ma that I have left," he ordered Jay, and closed the door without saying good-bye to Rani.

In the car, thoughts flooded his mind again.

Perhaps he made a mistake in coming to study abroad for his Master's in engineering. No! That was not the error. He should not have stayed on after he received his Master's. He should have returned home as he originally planned.

He intended to return, but unfortunately he attended a job fair after graduation just for fun and ended up accepting a job offer. A high salary in dollars converted into a small fortune in rupees, proved impossible to resist. He always converted dollars into rupees then, before buying or selling. He offered himself an excuse of short-term American experience and stayed on. The company that hired him sponsored him for a green card.

He still wanted to return home, but he postponed it, went for a visit instead and picked Rani from several prospective brides, married her and returned to the United States.

The trip left bitter memories, especially for Rani. He could not talk his mother out of accepting a dowry.

"Mother, Rani will earn the entire sum of a dowry in a month in the United States. A dowry is a hardship for her middle-class family. Let us not insist on it. Just accept what her family offers."

But Mother, with Father's tacit support, insisted. "You are my only son. I have waited for this occasion all my life. I want a proper wedding, the kind of wedding our friends and relatives will remember forever."

Ramesh gave in to her wishes and had a wedding with pomp and special traditional honors for his family. His mother was only partially gratified because she felt that their family did not get what was due them with her foreign returned son! The dowry, however, succeeded in upsetting Rani, who looked miserable throughout the ceremony.

"We will refund all the money once you come to the United States," Ramesh promised her. "It's a minor sum when dollars are converted to rupees."

Instead of talking in his conciliatory tone, Rani demanded, too harshly for a bride, "If it's a minor sum, why did you let your family insist on a dowry? You know my parents' savings are wiped out."

Over a few years they refunded the money, but Rani's wounds never healed and during fights she referred to the dowry spitefully.

Her caustic remarks did not bother Ramesh before, but now with her income supporting the family, they were beginning to hurt. "Write your mother that your wife works and makes up for part of the dowry her father failed to provide!" she had remarked once.

"Don't women ever forgive?" he had wondered.

"I am extra sensitive." He brushed off the pain that Rani's words caused.

The job fair was at a big hotel. He followed the directions and turned into a full parking lot. As he pulled into the tight space close to the exit, he glanced at the hotel lobby. Through the glass exterior wall, underneath a brightly lit chandelier, he could see a huge crowd milling in the lobby.

Panic struck him. He was late. So many people had made it there ahead of him. All applicants with his experience and background might be turned away.

Another car approached and pulled into the last parking space in the lot. The engine noise died and a man roughly his height and build stepped out, just as Ramesh shut his car door. Out on the walkway Ramesh heard a greeting.

"Hello, how are you?"

Ramesh looked up.

In the fluorescent lights his eyes met friendly blue eyes. He noticed a slightly wrinkled forehead and receding hairline, like his own.

"Hello," Ramesh responded.

The stranger smiled. "Sometimes I wonder why I come to these fairs. In the last six months I must have been to at least ten."

"Really? So have I!" He must have been laid off at the same time, Ramesh thought.

"We must have attended the same ones. I don't remember seeing you," the newcomer said.

"Too many engineers looking for a job—you know," Ramesh offered as explanation.

The pair had approached the revolving lobby doors. Ramesh had a strong urge to turn back and return home.

"Come on, we must try." The newcomer apparently had sensed the urge. "My name is Bruce. Would you like to meet me at the door in an hour? We will have a drink before we go home. It will—kind of lift my spirits."

"All right," Ramesh agreed without thinking and added, "I am Ramesh."

Bruce waited for Ramesh to step into the revolving door.

Ramesh mechanically pushed into the lobby. His heart sagged even further. "With persons like Bruce looking for a job, who will hire a foreigner like me?" he wondered. He looked around. Bruce had vanished into the crowd.

Ramesh looked at a row of booths set up by the side wall. He approached one looking for engineers with his qualifications. A few

Americans had already lined up to talk to the woman screening the applicants.

She looked at him and repeated the same questions she had asked applicants before him. "Your name, sir?"

He had to spell it. She made a mistake in noting it down. He had to correct her.

"Please fill out this application." He sensed a slight irritation in her voice.

"Thank you," he said. His accent seemed to have intensified. He took the application and retreated to a long table.

He visited six or seven booths of companies who might need—directly, indirectly, or remotely—someone of his experience and education; challenge, benefit package, location, salary, nothing mattered to him anymore. He had to find a job.

An hour and a half later, as he approached the revolving door, he noticed Bruce waiting for him.

During the discussion over drinks, he discovered that Bruce had the same qualifications as himself. However, Bruce had spent several years wandering around the world, so he had only four years of experience. Ramesh had guessed right. Bruce had been laid off the same time as himself.

"It's been very hard," Bruce said. "What little savings we had are wiped out and my wife is fed up with me. She thinks I don't try hard. This role reversal is not good for a man's ego."

"Yes," Ramesh agreed.

"I may have to move but my wife doesn't want to. Her family is here."

"I understand."

"I figure you don't have that problem."

"No. You must have guessed I'm from India."

After a couple of drinks they walked out into an empty lobby and empty parking lot.

Two days later Bruce called. "Want to go to a job fair? It's in Woodland, two hundred miles from here. I hate to drive out alone." Ramesh agreed.

"Who will hire me when Americans are available?" he complained to Rani afterward.

"You must not think like that. You are as good as any of them," Rani snapped. "Remember what Alexander said."

Ramesh remembered. Alexander was a crazy history student with whom he had shared an apartment. Rani always referred to Alexander's message.

Ramesh had responded to an advertisement on his university's bulletin board and Alexander had answered the phone.

"You have to be crazy to share an apartment with me. My last roommate left because he could not live with me."

"What did you do? I mean, why did he leave?" Ramesh asked.

"I like to talk. You see, I wake up people and tell them about my ideas at night. They call me crazy Alexander . . ."

"I will get back to you." Ramesh put the receiver down and talked to the student who had moved out.

"You see, Alexander's a nut. He sleeps during the day and studies at night. He's a history buff. He studies revolutions. He wakes up people just to talk to them, about theories, others' and his own! He will offer to discount the rent if you put up with him."

Short of funds, Ramesh moved in with Alexander.

Much of Alexander's oratory bounced off Ramesh's half-asleep brain, but off and on a few sentences made an impression and stuck in his memory.

"You must first view yourself as free and equal," Alexander had said.

"Equal to whom?"

"To those around you who consider you less than equal . . ."

"Me? Less than equal?"

"No! Not you, stupid. The oppressed person. Oppression could be social, religious, foreign, traditional."

"Who oppressed me?"

"No! No! Not you! An imaginary oppressed person who must first see himself as the equal of his oppressors. The idea of equality will ultimately sow seeds of freedom and revolution in his mind. That idea is the first step. You see . . . stop snoring . . . That's the first step toward liberation."

Soon Ramesh walked like a zombie.

In another month, he too moved out.

After his marriage he told Rani some of his conversations with Alexander.

"Makes sense," she said, looking very earnest.

"Really! You mean you understand?" Rani's reaction amazed Ramesh.

"Yes, I do. I am an oppressed person, socially and traditionally. That's why my parents had to come up with a dowry."

A month went by and Ramesh was called for an interview.

Bruce telephoned the same night. He and some other engineers he knew had also been called. Had Ramesh received a call, too?

Ramesh swallowed hard. "No, I didn't." He felt guilty and ashamed. He had lied to Bruce, who was so open, friendly, and supportive, despite his own difficulties.

Ramesh's ego had already suffered a major trauma. He was convinced that he would not get a job if Americans were available and he did not wish to admit to Bruce later on, "I had an interview, but they didn't hire me." It was easier to lie now.

The interview over, Ramesh decided to put the job out of his mind. His confidence at a low ebb, he dared not hope.

Three weeks went by and he received a phone call from the company that interviewed him. He had the job.

"They must have hired several engineers," Ramesh thought, elated.

Bruce called again. "I didn't get the job. The other guys I know have also received negative replies."

The news stunned Ramesh. He could not believe that he had the job and the others did not. As he pondered this, he realized he owed an embarrassing explanation to Bruce. How was he going to tell him that he had the job?

As Bruce jabbered about something, Ramesh collected his courage.

"I have an offer from them," he stated in a flat tone and strained his ear for a response.

After a few unbearable seconds of silence, Bruce exclaimed, "Congratulations! At least one of us made it. Now we can all hope. I know you have better qualifications."

Ramesh knew that the voice was sincere, without a touch of the envy he had anticipated.

They agreed to meet Saturday for a drink, a small celebration, Bruce suggested.

"Rani, I got the job. The others didn't." Ramesh hung up the receiver and bounded up to Rani.

"I told you, you are as good as any of them," Rani responded nonchalantly and continued to fold laundry.

"Maybe . . . possibly . . . they needed a minority candidate," Ramesh muttered.

Rani stopped folding. "Ramesh," she said as her eyes scanned Ramesh's face, "You may have the job and the knowledge and the qualifications, but you are not free and equal."

"What do you mean?" Ramesh asked.

INTERPRETATIONS

1. Alexander, for all his eccentricities, is portrayed as the voice of wisdom. How does his "message" of free and equal relate to the problems of job seeking? To the problems of competition between foreign and native-born job seekers? To the problem of dowries?

2. How realistic is Bruce's lack of resentment that Ramesh got a job? How well does the story make us believe in Ramesh's "better qualifications"?

3. From your own experience, what is the usual relationship between two candidates competing in a limited job market? Do they confide in each other or share tips? Does the first one to get a job feel guilty?

CORRESPONDENCES

1. Soto and Gandbhir discuss how one's job affects self-respect. Which examples did you find most convincing?

2. What was Gandbhir's purpose in writing this story? Is she trying to show human nature in action, or to entertain, or to persuade? How does her purpose compare with Narayan's?

APPLICATIONS

1. "You may have the job and the knowledge and the qualifications, but you are not free and equal." Discuss Rani's assessment of her husband. Is it possible for Ramesh to be "free and equal" in the United States? Why or why not?

2. Discuss with your group your images of success. To what extent do they involve economic prosperity? Your self-image? Is it possible for everyone to be successful? Do individual strivings for success affect communal values? How?

3. Discuss with your group issues of discrimination in the workplace involving race, gender, disabilities, and/or seniority. What suggestions would you make to cope with these situations?

The Knowing Eye

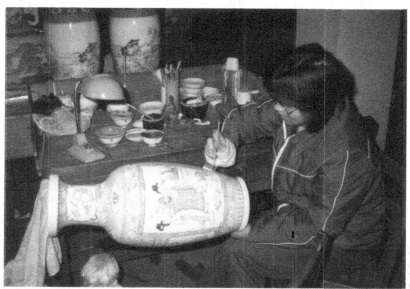

Zack Rutkin

READING IMAGES

1. What kinds of work are the people in the photographs doing? In general, are cultural values placed upon the work that people do? Explain your answers to these questions.

2. In the future, would you like to work by yourself or with people? What are the advantages and disadvantages of each work situation? How may you use each photograph to reinforce what you have stated?

MAKING CONNECTIONS

1. What relationships do you find among these photographs? How does each one reflect work?

2. In "Black Hair," Gary Soto writes about his observations and feelings when working in a tire shop. How do you think the worker in the fish market would relate to Soto's essay?

Mackenzie Lawrence

Suzanna Konecky

WORDS AND IMAGES

1. Examine all three photographs. What would these people say about the job they are doing? Write a journal entry that addresses this question from the perspective of each person depicted. Use visual cues present in the foreground and background to help you to account for the context of each photograph. What similarities and differences do you notice in your three journal entries?

2. There is a saying that a picture is worth a thousand words. Pick one photograph and write an essay that expresses your thoughts about it. Be sure to create a focused essay, using a clear thesis statement and body paragraphs to support it.

Additional Writing Topics

1. Gandbhir notes the attitude toward affirmative action in the workplace. Review her comments. Then conduct an informal survey by interviewing several people affected by affirmative action programs. Summarize your findings.

2. Have you, like Dorris, had experiences that resembled his wilderness quest? How did they help you better understand yourself and your talents? Write an essay describing these experiences and how they helped shape your identity and vocational goals.

3. Review Sayers's perspective on work and test its validity by interviewing people you know in various occupations on their attitudes toward working and the workplace. What conclusions did you reach? Write an analysis based on their responses.

4. Recent sociological surveys indicate that overworked parents in the United States are unable to provide a sense of family and community for their children. Discuss this with your group. How is it pertinent to the concept of latchkey children? How would you classify that lifestyle and its effects on family life? What solutions can you think of?

5. Working with your group, construct your own Bill of Rights for a changing workplace. You might consider such issues as:

   Drug testing

   Health benefits

   Retirement plans

   Child care

   Flexible hours

   Promotional opportunities

   Tuition reimbursement for upgrading skills

   Write a brief rationale for the inclusion of each item in your "Bill."

6. Is there a career that has captured your imagination that you would like to pursue? Do you dream of being a musician, talk show host, archaeologist, or lawyer? Write an essay explaining what draws you to this career. How do you intend to make it a reality?

7. Reflect on your reasons for pursuing your education. To what extent are they related to your professional goals? Are your goals market driven or based on personal preference? Write a journal entry on these issues.

CHAPTER

6

Traditions

T HE IDEA OF TRADITION or heritage is inherent in most definitions of culture. A culture incorporates the shared knowledge, expectations, and beliefs of a group of people. The human imagination has always been captivated by the idea of the past and its connections to the present. Stories from the oral traditions of ancient cultures as well as our own evoke the powers and mysteries of the past by re-creating a time in which myths, fables, legends, and archetypes dictated the values of human actions within the community. The ritual of orality—of storytelling—was an integral part of communal life, as tribe members from the oldest to the youngest listened to, recalled, or retold stories about creation, good and evil, war and peace, life and death.

Folklore also helps explain human relationships, hopes, fears, and dreams. Folktales and myths are not culturally or ethically bound as people from all over the world use them to explain their cultures, traditions, and social customs.

In the United States we tend to value the new over the old; to seek solutions to problems that often involve breaking with the past. Thus it should be no surprise that our attitude toward roots and traditions is ambivalent: We want it, but we want to be free of it; we love part of the tradition but hate part of it. Tradition is both past and future, both history and destiny. Thus it is essential that we engage in conversations with one another about our own traditions and those of other, older cultures.

It is no accident that several texts in this chapter come out of a very old culture: Bantu, Mayan, Native American, Northern European, Chinese, and Indian. Our purpose is to explore the significance of these traditions—both our own and those of others. These opening texts demonstrate the universal importance of traditions but also celebrate their diversity. They show how essential it is to converse about an astonishing

267

variety of traditions including rituals, ceremonies, and customs, as well as symbols, ideals, and emotions. Consequently, intracultural and intercultural conversations often end in argument. You can see such arguments variously in progress in Yael Yarimi's reflections on the importance of cultural mourning, and in "The Algonquin Cinderella," where the focus is on the cruelty and violence of older sisters to their younger sibling, and in the more contemporary "Cinderella's Stepsisters" that cites examples of "the violence that women do to each other: professional violence, competitive violence, emotional violence."

When dialogue stops—when tradition is unquestioningly accepted or revered—it can stifle, maim, or even kill. So, at least, suggests John King Fairbank as he looks at footbinding, a thousand-year-old custom that only ended in the last century. In "The Lottery," a cautionary tale set in a New England village in the 1940s, Shirley Jackson also suggests that blind adherence to custom can be destructive, even deadly. A similar point is made by Mark Fineman in his factual account of a tradition obsessed in his 1970s essay "Stone-Throwing in India: An Annual Bash."

Participation in conversations about your own traditions and those of other cultures can be challenging, even disturbing, since it may involve new ways of listening and seeing. It invites you to suspend judgment and avoid making unfavorable comparisons by looking at the value of a people and their culture through a different lens. Although it is impossible to be totally free of ethnocentrism, we hope that the overheard conversations in this chapter will deepen your appreciation of cultural pluralities.

Perspectives

History has a way of intruding upon the present.

—Louise Erdrich

Every man, every woman, carries in head and mind the image of the ideal place, the right place, the one true home, known or unknown, actual or visionary.

— Edward Abbey

Contemporary man has rationalized the myths, but he has not been able to destroy them.

—Octavio Paz

I was born a thousand years ago, born in the culture of bows and arrows . . . born in an age when people loved the things of nature, and spoke to it as though it had a soul.

—Chief Dan George

The past is a foreign country: they do things differently there.

—L. P. Hartley

I have found that life persists in the midst of destruction, and therefore, there must be a bigger law than that of destruction.

—Mohandas K. (Mahatma) Gandhi

The position of women in a society provides an exact measure of the development of that society.

—Gustav Geiger

Memory is the diary that we all carry about with us.

—Oscar Wilde

Tradition is a guide and not a jailor.

—W. Somerset Maugham

True places are not found on maps.

—Herman Melville

To everything there is a season, and a time to every purpose under the heaven: a time to be born, and a time to die; a time to plant, and a time to pluck up that which is planted; a time to kill, and a time to heal; a time to break down, and a time to build up; a time to weep, and a time to laugh; a time to mourn, and a time to dance; a time to cast away stones, and a time to gather stones together; a time to embrace, and a time to refrain from embracing; a time to get, and a time to lose; a time to keep, and a time to cast away; a time to rend, and a time to sew; a time to keep silence, and a time to speak; a time to love, and a time to hate; a time of war, and a time of peace. What profit hath he that worketh in that wherein he laboreth?

—Ecclesiastes 3:1–10

History is the present. That's why every generation writes it anew. But what most people think of as history is its end product, myth.

—E. L. Doctorow

We do not remember days, we remember moments.

—Cesare Pavese

We have to do with the past only as we can make it useful to the present and the future.

—Frederick Douglass

We want to remain curious, startled, provoked, mystified, and uplifted. We want to glare, gaze, gawk, behold, and stare. We want to be given opportunities to change, and ultimately we want to be told that we can become kings and queens, or lords of our own destinies. We remember wonder tales and fairy tales to keep our sense of wonderment alive and to nurture our hope that we can seize possibilities and opportunities to transform ourselves and our worlds.

—Jack Zipes

Memory is something we reconstruct, something we create. Memory is a story we make up from snatches of the past.

—Lynne Sharon Schwartz

Myths are public dreams, dreams are private myths.

—Joseph Campbell

Each act of creation shall leave you humble, for it is never as great as your dream and always inferior to that most marvelous dream of God which is nature.

—Gabriela Mistral

Gratitude is the heart's memory.

—French Proverb

To be ourselves we must have ourselves—possess, if need be
repossess, our life-stories. We must "recollect" ourselves, recollect the
inner drama, the narrative, of ourselves. A man needs such a narrative,
a continuous inner narrative, to maintain his identity, his self.

—Oliver Sachs

Where I come from, the words that are most highly valued are those
which are spoken from the heart, unpremeditated and unrehearsed.
Among the Pueblo people, a written speech or statement is highly
suspect because the true feelings of the speaker remain hidden as he
reads words that are detached from the occasion and the audience.

—Leslie Marmon Silko

I do not wish my house to be walled on all sides and my windows
stuffed. I want the cultures of all lands to be blown about my house as
freely as possible.

—Mahatma Ghandi

APPLICATIONS

1. Wilde and Schwartz comment on the relationship between mem-
    ory and identity as well as its importance in the rituals of story-
    telling. Discuss their perspectives with your group. To what extent
    is it true that we all have stories to tell?

2. Analyze the points of view expressed in three perspectives on
    aspects of traditions. On what functions of traditions do they
    focus? What do they suggest about the roles of traditions? Do you
    agree that our attitude toward tradition is ambivalent? Write an
    essay using these questions as a framework.

3. To what extent do stories help us to know who we are? Is there a
    story that made an impression on you as a child? Summarize this
    story for your group and analyze the reasons for its effect.

Here are two different stories about how the world was created. The first is a legend from the Bantu, a diverse black people inhabiting a large part of southern Africa south of the Congo and speaking many languages (including Zulu and Swahili) and dialects. The second is the opening of the Popol Vuh, the sacred saga of the Quiché, a branch of the great Mayan civilization. The Quiché Maya live in what is now western Guatemala.

In the Beginning: Bantu Creation Story

AFRICAN LEGEND

IN THE BEGINNING, in the dark, there was nothing but water. And Bumba was alone.

One day Bumba was in terrible pain. He retched and strained and vomited up the sun. After that light spread over everything. The heat of the sun dried up the water until the black edges of the world began to show. Black sandbanks and reefs could be seen. But there were no living things.

Bumba vomited up the moon and then the stars, and after that the night had its light also.

Still Bumba was in pain. He strained again and nine living creatures came forth: the leopard named Koy Bumba, and Pongo Bumba the crested eagle, the crocodile, Ganda Bumba, and one little fish named Yo; next, old Kono Bumba, the tortoise, and Tsetse, the lightning, swift, deadly, beautiful like the leopard; then the white heron, Nyanyi Bumba, also one beetle, and the goat named Budi.

Last of all came forth men. There were many men, but only one was white like Bumba. His name was Loko Yima.

The creatures themselves then created all the creatures. The heron created all the birds of the air except the kite. He did not make the kite. The crocodile made serpents and the iguana. The goat produced every beast with horns. Yo, the small fish, brought forth all the fish of all the seas and waters. The beetle created insects.

Then the serpents in their turn made grasshoppers, and the iguana made the creatures without horns.

Then the three sons of Bumba said they would finish the world. The first, Nyonye Ngana, made the white ants; but he was not equal to the task, and died of it. The ants, however, thankful for life and being, went searching for black earth in the depths of the world and covered the barren sands to bury and honour their creator.

Chonganda, the second son, brought forth a marvellous living plant from which all the trees and grasses and flowers and plants in the world have sprung. The third son, Chedi Bumba, wanted something different, but for all his trying made only the bird called the kite.

Of all the creatures, Tsetse, lightning, was the only troublemaker. She stirred up so much trouble that Bumba chased her into the sky. Then mankind was without fire until Bumba showed the people how to draw fire out of trees. "There is fire in every tree," he told them, and showed them how to make the firedrill and liberate it. Sometimes today Tsetse still leaps down and strikes the earth and causes damage.

When at last the work of creation was finished, Bumba walked through the peaceful villages and said to the people, "Behold these wonders. They belong to you." Thus from Bumba, the Creator, the First Ancestor, came forth all the wonders that we see and hold and use, and all the brotherhood of beasts and man.

Quiché-Mayan Creation Story

QUICHÉ-MAYAN LEGEND

BEFORE THE WORLD WAS CREATED, Calm and Silence were the great kings that ruled. Nothing existed, there was nothing. Things had not yet been drawn together, the face of the earth was unseen. There was only motionless sea, and a great emptiness of sky. There were no men anywhere, or animals, no birds or fish, no crabs. Trees, stones, caves, grass, forests, none of these existed yet. There was nothing that could roar or run, nothing that could tremble or cry in the air. Flatness and emptiness, only the sea, alone and breathless. It was night; silence stood in the dark.

In this darkness the Creators waited, the Maker, Tepeu, Gucumatz, the Forefathers. They were there in this emptiness, hidden under green and blue feathers, alone and surrounded with light. They are the same as wisdom. They are the ones who can conceive and bring forth a child from nothingness. And the time had come. The Creators were bent deep around talk in the darkness. They argued, worried, sighed over what was to be. They planned the growth of the thickets, how things would crawl and jump, the birth of man. They planned the whole creation, arguing each point until their words and thoughts crystallized and became the same thing. Heart of Heaven was there, and in the darkness the creation was planned.

Then let the emptiness fill! they said. Let the water weave its way downward so the earth can show its face! Let the light break on the ridges, let the sky fill up with the yellow light of dawn! Let our glory be a man walking on a path through the trees! "Earth!" the Creators called. They called only once, and it was there, from a mist, from a cloud of dust, the mountains appeared instantly. At this single word the groves of cypresses and pines sent out shoots, rivulets ran freely between the round hills. The Creators were struck by the beauty and exclaimed, "It will be a creation that will mount the darkness!"

INTERPRETATIONS

1. In the Bantu story "The creatures themselves then created all the creatures": Fish produced fish, birds produced birds (except for the predatory kite), and so on. How "scientific" is this explanation?

2. Why is there almost no explanation of Bumba's identity (other than his being white and "the Creator, the First Ancestor") or of his sickness? Are such details better omitted? Can you supply the missing explanation?

3. In the Bantu story what purpose does the retching incident serve? What tone does it set?

4. What is the purpose of the Bantu story?

5. How important in the Quiché creation story is language?

6. In the Quiché story what are the Creators' main attributes? How are they demonstrated in the story?

7. What seems to be the Creators' main motive in creating "a man" in the Quiché story?

8. Interpret the last sentence of the Quiché story. What explanation does it provide for the Creation?

CORRESPONDENCES

1. Review the perspective from Ecclesiastes. Compare the concepts in Ecclesiastes with those in the Bantu and Quiché stories. Which account do you prefer? How do they differ in implication?

2. Compare the tones and meanings of the two creation stories.

APPLICATIONS

1. Working in your group, discuss the roles and function of creation texts. Why is it important to become aware of different cultural explanations of the origins of the natural world? Analyze the significance of the motifs of light and darkness in both creation stories. What do they suggest about the nature of good and evil?

2. Review Zipes's perspective and write an essay in which you seek to persuade your audience of the importance of preserving a sense of wonder about yourself and the world. Be specific.

3. Write an essay discussing the importance of storytelling in your family. Have any of the stories become family traditions? What elements account for their popularity? How have the stories affected your sense of identity and that of your family?

Footbinding

JOHN KING FAIRBANK

*John King Fairbank (1907–1991) was born in South Dakota and received
degrees from Harvard and Oxford universities. He was the director emeritus
of Harvard's East Asian Research Center and enjoyed a distinguished career
in the field of Asian studies. His numerous books on China include* Modern
China: A Bibliographical Guide to Chinese Works, 1898–1937 *(1950);*
The United States and China *(1971);* Chinabound: A Fifty-Year Memoir
(1983); and China Watch *(1987). Before reading Fairbank's essay, consult a
dictionary for a definition of footbinding.*

*China, one of the world's oldest civilizations (dating at least to 5000 B.C.)
with a fifth of the world's population (about a billion inhabitants), has had a
tumultuous history, especially in the last two centuries. For thousands of years,
beginning with the Shang Dynasty (about 1500–1000 B.C.), a succession of
dynasties ruled China and expanded Chinese political and cultural domination
of East Asia. In 1644 a foreign invader, the Manchus, established the Ch'ing
Dynasty without destroying the underlying culture. The nineteenth century
was a time of increasing stagnation and rebellion. European powers took advantage of internal strife to take control of large parts of the country. The country
became a republic in 1912, but lost much of its territory to the Japanese, both
before and during World War II. The People's Republic of China was declared in
1949 under the leadership of Mao Zedong, by which time footbinding—but not
its effects—had vanished. In the excerpt that follows, Fairbank describes the rise
of the custom of footbinding in the tenth century, details its mechanics and its
influence on domestic life, and advances reasons for its longevity.*

OF ALL THE MANY UNEXPLORED FACETS of China's ancient history, the subjection of women has been the least studied. Women were fitted into the
social and cosmic order (which were a continuum) by invoking the principles of Yang and Yin. All things bright, warm, active, male, and dominant were Yang while all things dark, cold, passive, female, and yielding
were Yin. This dualism, seen in the alternation of night and day or the
contrast of the sun and moon, was a ready-made matrix in which
women could be confined. The subjection of women was thus a sophisticated and perfected institution like the other Chinese achievements, not
a mere accident of male biceps or female childbearing as might be more
obviously the case in a primitive tribe. The inequality between the sexes
was buttressed with philosophical underpinnings and long-continued

social practices. Symbolic of woman's secondary status was her bridal night: she expected to be deflowered by a stranger, a husband selected by her family whom she had never seen before. Even though the facts may often have been less stark, the theory was hard-boiled.

Out of all this complex of theory and custom by which the Chinese world was given an enduring and stable order, the most neglected aspect is the institution of footbinding. This custom arose at court in the tenth century during the late T'ang and spread gradually among the upper class during the succeeding Sung period. By the Ming and Ch'ing eras after 1368 it had penetrated the mass of the Han Chinese population. It became so widespread that Western observers in the nineteenth century found it almost universal, not only among the upper class but throughout the farming population.

Footbinding spread as a mark of gentility and upper-class status. Small feet became a prestige item to such an extent that a girl without them could not achieve a good marriage arrangement and was subjected to the disrespect and taunts of the community. In short, bound feet became *de rigueur,* the only right-thinking thing to do for a daughter, an obligation on the part of a mother who cared about her daughter's eventual marriage and success in life. The bound foot was a must. Only tribal peoples and exceptional groups like the Manchu conquerors or the Hakka Chinese migrant groups in South China or finally the mean people, that lowest and rather small group who were below the social norms of civility, could avoid binding their daughters' feet.

The small foot was called a "golden lotus" or "golden lily" (*chin-lien*) and was much celebrated in poems and essays by male enthusiasts. Here is the early Sung poet Su Tung-p'o (1036–1101):

Anointed with fragrance, she takes lotus steps;
Though often sad, she steps with swift lightness.
She dances like the wind, leaving no physical trace.
Another stealthily but happily tries on the palace style,
But feels such distress when she tries to walk!
Look at them in the palms of your hands, so wondrously
small that they defy description.

The Sung philosophers stressed women's inferiority as a basic element of the social order. The great Chu Hsi (1130–1200) codified the cosmology of China as magistrally as his near contemporary Thomas Aquinas (d. 1274) codified that of Western Christendom. When he was a magistrate in Fukien province, Chu Hsi promoted footbinding to preserve female chastity and as "a means of spreading Chinese culture and teaching the separation of men and women."

By the Ming period the overwhelming majority of Han Chinese women all over the country had artificially small feet. The Manchu emperors many times inveighed against it in hortatory edicts, but to no avail. Male romanticizing on the subject continued unabated as in this poem of the fourteenth century:

> Lotus blossoms in shoes most tight,
> As if she could stand on autumnal waters!
> Her shoe tips do not peek beyond the skirt,
> Fearful lest the tiny embroideries be seen.[1]

There can be no doubt that footbinding was powered by a sexual fetish. Chinese love manuals are very specific about the use of bound feet as erogenous areas. All the different ways of taking hold of the foot, rubbing it with the hands, and using the mouth, tongue, and lips are explicitly catalogued. Many cases are recorded with the verisimilitude of high-class pornography. Meanwhile, the aesthetic attractiveness of the small shoes with their bright embroidered colors was praised in literature, while the tottering gait of a bound-foot woman was considered very fetching as a symbol of feminine frailty, which indeed it was. In fact, of course, bound feet were a guarantee of chastity because they kept women within the household and unable to venture far abroad. Lily feet, once formed, could not be unlocked like a chastity belt. By leaving only men able-bodied, they ensured male domination in a very concrete way.

Thus the prevalence of footbinding down to the 1920s, while the movement against it began only in the 1890s, vividly index the speed and scope of China's modern social revolution. This may be less comprehensible to white American males than to white women, or especially to black Americans, for Chinese women within the present century have had an emancipation from veritable slavery.

While footbinding is mentioned in so many foreign books about China, it is usually passed by as a curious detail. I don't think it was. It was a major erotic invention, still another achievement in Chinese social engineering. Girls painfully deformed themselves throughout their adolescence in order to attract desirable husbands who, on their part, subscribed to a folklore of self-fulfilling beliefs: for example, that footbinding made a vagina more narrow and muscular and that lotus feet were major foci of erotic sensitivity, true erogenous zones, a net addition of 50 percent to the female equipment. Normal feet, we are now

---

[1]Howard Levy, *Chinese Footbinding: The History of a Curious Erotic Custom* (New York: Walton Rawls, 1966), p. 47.

told by purveyors of sexual comfort, are an underdeveloped area sensually, but one must admit they are a bit hard to handle—whereas small lotus feet could be grasped, rubbed, licked, sucked, nibbled, and bitten. The garrulous Jesuit Father Ripa, who spent a decade at the court of K'ang-hsi in the early 1700s, reported that "Their taste is perverted to such an extraordinary degree that I knew a physician who lived with a woman with whom he had no other intercourse but that of viewing and fondling her feet."[2] Having compacted all their nerve endings in a smaller area, golden lilies were far more sensitive than, for example, the back of the neck that used to bewitch Japanese samurai. After all, they had been created especially for male appreciation. When every proper girl did it, what bride would say that her sacrifice, suffering, and inconvenience were not worth it? A bride without small feet in the old China was like a new house in today's America without utilities—who would want it? Consequently in the 1930s and '40s one still saw women on farms stumping about on their heels as they worked, victims of this old custom.

A girl's foot was made small, preferably only three inches long, by pressing the four smaller toes under the sole or ball of the foot (plantar) in order to make it narrower. At the same time it was made shorter by forcing the big toe and heel closer together so that the arch rose in a bowed shape. As a result the arch was broken and the foot could bear no weight except on the heel. If this process was begun at age five, the experience was less severe than if a little girl, perhaps in a peasant household, had been left with normal feet until age eight or ten so that she could be of more use in the household.

> When I was seven [said one woman to Ida Pruitt], my mother . . . washed and placed alum on my feet and cut the toenails. She then bent my toes toward the plantar with a binding cloth ten feet long and two inches wide, doing the right foot first and then the left. She . . . ordered me to walk but when I did the pain proved unbearable. That night . . . my feet felt on fire and I couldn't sleep; mother struck me for crying. On the following days, I tried to hide but was forced to walk on my feet . . . after several months all toes but the big one were pressed against the inner surface . . . mother would remove the bindings and wipe the blood and pus which dripped from my feet. She told me that only with removal of the flesh could my feet become slender . . . every two weeks I changed to new shoes.

[2]Fortunato Prandi, ed. and trans., *Memoirs of Father Ripa* (London: John Murray, 1855), p. 58.

Each new pair was one-to-two-tenths of an inch smaller than the previous one . . . In summer my feet smelled offensively because of pus and blood; in winter my feet felt cold because of lack of circulation . . . four of the toes were curled in like so many dead caterpillars . . . it took two years to achieve the three-inch model . . . my shanks were thin, my feet became humped, ugly and odoriferous.[3]

After the first two years the pain lessened. But constricting the feet to a three-inch size was only the beginning of trouble. By this time they were very private parts indeed and required daily care, washing and manicuring at the same time that they had to be kept constantly bound and shod night and day. Unmanicured nails could cut into the instep, bindings could destroy circulation, blood poisoning or gangrene could result. Massage and applications of hot and cold water were used to palliate the discomfort, but walking any distance remained difficult. It also produced corns on the bent-under toes, which had to be pared with a knife. Once deformed to taste, bound feet were of little use to stand on. Since weight was carried entirely on the heels, it had to be constantly shifted back and forth. Since the bound foot lacked the resilience of a normal foot, it was a tiring and unsteady support.

Footbinding, in short, had begun as an ostentatious luxury, which made a girl less useful in family work and more dependent on help from others. Yet, once the custom had spread among the populace, lotus feet were considered essential in order to get a good husband. Marriages, of course, were arranged between families and often by professional matchmakers, in whose trade the length of the lily foot was rated more important than beauty of face or person. When the anti-footbinding movement began at the end of the nineteenth century, many mothers and daughters, too, stubbornly clung to it to avoid the public shame of having large feet. The smallness of the foot, in short, was a source of social pride both to the family and to the victim. First and last one may guess that at least a billion Chinese girls during the thousand-year currency of this social custom suffered the agony of footbinding and reaped its rewards of pride and ecstasy, such as they were.

There are three remarkable things about footbinding. First, that it should have been invented at all—it was such a feat of physio-psychosociological engineering. Second, that once invented it should have spread so pervasively and lasted so long among a generally

---

[3]Ida Pruitt, *A Daughter of Han: The Autobiography of a Chinese Working Woman* (New Haven: Yale University Press, 1945), p. 22.

humane and practical-minded farming population. We are just at the beginning of understanding this phenomenon. The fact that an upper-class erotic luxury permeated the peasantry of Old China, for whom it could only lower productivity, suggests that the old society was extraordinarily homogeneous.

Finally, it was certainly ingenious how men trapped women into mutilating themselves for an ostensibly sexual purpose that had the effect of perpetuating male domination. Brides left their own homes and entered their husband's family in the lowest status, servants of their mothers-in-law. Husbands were chosen for them sight unseen, and might find romance in extra-marital adventures or, if they could afford it, bring in secondary wives. But a woman once betrothed, if her husband-to-be died even as a child, was expected to remain a chaste widow thereafter. Mao remarked that "women hold up half the sky," but in the old China they were not supposed to lift their heads. The talent that one sees in Chinese women today had little chance to grow and express itself. This made a weak foundation for a modern society.

INTERPRETATIONS

1. What is Fairbank's purpose in describing "the principles of Yang and Yin"? How does this relate to the topic of footbinding? Does the intellectual theory (Yang-Yin) really explain any important aspects of Chinese behavior? Or is it a rationalization? A pretext? An emblem?

2. According to Fairbank, "there are three remarkable things about footbinding." What are they and why are they significant?

3. What examples can you give of elaborate psychological or other theories in contemporary America that have the aura of science or intellect but really explain very little? Do these theories affect our society for good or for ill, or do they simply remain in the realm of theory? If you find they have practical effects on people's behavior, what effects?

CORRESPONDENCES

1. Review the Douglass perspective on traditions. How does it apply to the selection by Fairbank? To what extent was footbinding "useful" in the culture of its day?

2. Review the Geiger perspective. How does it apply to "Footbinding"? To which other selections in this chapter is it also relevant? In what way?

APPLICATIONS

1. Fairbank estimates that "at least a billion Chinese girls during the thousand-year currency of this social custom suffered the agony of footbinding . . ." What does Fairbank's essay suggest about reevaluating the custom?

2. What is the general relationship between tradition and individual desires? For example, are the traditional ethnic or tribal costumes you are familiar with calculated to promote individual beauty (or sex appeal) or the beliefs and values of the tribe or collective? Write an essay responding to these questions with specific examples.

3. A fetish is an inanimate object or charm thought to possess magical powers such as good luck or protection from evil. In psychiatry, fetishism is associated with an abnormal sexual attraction to an inanimate object such as a shoe. What associations do you and your group have with fetishes or fetishism? Summarize your discussion.

4. In "Footbinding," Fairbank writes about the physical subjugation of women. Do you think that such practices continue to exist? Check the following Web sites for information that you might use to formulate an argument.

    http://www.towson.edu/%7Eloiselle/foot.html

    http://outlawtv.com/333/016.htm

    http://www.nefilim.de/addfiles/myth/nephilim/articles/cranial_deformation.htm

The Algonquin Cinderella

NATIVE AMERICAN MYTH

The small Algonquin tribe of Canada was one of the first with whom the French formed alliances. Because of their mingling with whites, little remains of Algonquin culture. Their name, however, came to be used to designate other nearby tribes, and their language family (known as Algonquian) is one of the most widespread of all North American Indian languages, extending from New Brunswick to the Rocky Mountains. Among Indian languages in the Algonquian stock are the Arapaho, the Cheyenne, the Blackfoot, the Potawatami, the Ottawa, the Passamaquoddy, the Penobscot, the Delaware, and the Cree. Record your memory of the first fairy tale that impressed you as a child.

THERE WAS ONCE A LARGE VILLAGE of the MicMac Indians of the Eastern Algonquins, built beside a lake. At the far end of the settlement stood a lodge, and in it lived a being who was always invisible. He had a sister who looked after him, and everyone knew that any girl who could see him might marry him. For that reason there were very few girls who did not try, but it was very long before anyone succeeded.

This is the way the test of sight was carried out: at evening-time, when the Invisible One was due to be returning home, his sister would walk with any girl who might come down to the lakeshore. She, of course, could see her brother, since he was always visible to her. As soon as she saw him, she would say to the girls:

"Do you see my brother?"

"Yes," they would generally reply—though some of them did say "No."

To those who said that they could indeed see him, the sister would say:

"Of what is his shoulder strap made?" Some people say that she would enquire:

"What is his moose-runner's haul?" or "With what does he draw his sled?"

And they would answer:

"A strip of rawhide" or "a green flexible branch," or something of that kind.

Then she, knowing that they had not told the truth, would say:
"Very well, let us return to the wigwam!"

When they had gone in, she would tell them not to sit in a certain place, because it belonged to the Invisible One. Then, after they had helped to cook the supper, they would wait with great curiosity, to see him eat. They could be sure that he was a real person, for when he took off his moccasins they became visible, and his sister hung them up. But beyond this they saw nothing of him, not even when they stayed in the place all the night, as many of them did.

Now there lived in the village an old man who was a widower, and his three daughters. The youngest girl was very small, weak and often ill: and yet her sisters, especially the elder, treated her cruelly. The second daughter was kinder, and sometimes took her side: but the wicked sister would burn her hands and feet with hot cinders, and she was covered with scars from this treatment. She was so marked that people called her *Oochigeaskw*, the Rough-Faced-Girl.

When her father came home and asked her why she had such burns, the bad sister would at once say that it was her own fault, for she had disobeyed orders and gone near the fire and fallen into it.

These two elder sisters decided one day to try their luck at seeing the Invisible One. So they dressed themselves in their finest clothes, and tried to look their prettiest. They found the Invisible One's sister and took the usual walk by the water.

When he came, and when they were asked if they could see him, they answered: "Of course." And when asked about the shoulder strap or sled cord, they answered: "A piece of rawhide."

But of course they were lying like the others, and they got nothing for their pains.

The next afternoon, when the father returned home, he brought with him many of the pretty little shells from which wampum was made, and they set to work to string them.

That day, poor Little Oochigeaskw, who had always gone barefoot, got a pair of her father's moccasins, old ones, and put them into water to soften them so that she could wear them. Then she begged her sisters for a few wampum shells. The elder called her a "little pest," but the younger one gave her some. Now, with no other clothes than her usual rags, the poor little thing went into the woods and got herself some sheets of birch bark, from which she made a dress, and put marks on it for decoration, in the style of long ago. She made a petticoat and a loose gown, a cap, leggings and a handkerchief. She put on her father's large old moccasins, which were far too big for her, and went forth to try her luck. She would try, she thought, to discover whether she could see the Invisible One.

She did not begin very well. As she set off, her sisters shouted and hooted, hissed and yelled, and tried to make her stay. And the loafers around the village, seeing the strange little creature, called out "Shame!"

The poor little girl in her strange clothes, with her face all scarred, was an awful sight, but she was kindly received by the sister of the Invisible One. And this was, of course, because this noble lady understood far more about things than simply the mere outside which all the rest of the world knows. As the brown of the evening sky turned to black, the lady took her down to the lake.

"Do you see him?" the Invisible One's sister asked.

"I do, indeed—and he is wonderful!" said Oochigeaskw.

The sister asked:

"And what is his sled-string?"

The little girl said:

"It is the Rainbow."

"And, my sister, what is his bow-string?"

"It is the Spirit's Road—the Milky Way."

"So you *have* seen him," said his sister. She took the girl home with her and bathed her. As she did so, all the scars disappeared from her body. Her hair grew again, as it was combed, long, like a blackbird's wing. Her eyes were like stars; in all the world there was no other such beauty. Then, from her treasures, the lady gave her a wedding garment, and adorned her.

Then she told Oochigeaskw to take the *wife's* seat in the wigwam; the one next to where the Invisible One sat, beside the entrance. And when he came in, terrible and beautiful, he smiled and said:

"So we are found out!"

"Yes," said his sister. And so Oochigeaskw became his wife.

INTERPRETATIONS

1. Why does Oochigeaskw succeed where her sisters failed?

2. What explanation does the story offer or imply for Oochigeaskw's ability to see the Invisible One? How is this ability related to Oochigeaskw's persecuted position in the family?

3. How do the clothes Oochigeaskw makes or assembles for herself indicate a reverence for tradition? What effect do you think this reverence might have on her success in winning the Invisible One?

4. What part do moccasins play in the story?

CORRESPONDENCES

1. Compare the Native American version of the Cinderella story with the standard version you read as a child. What motifs do they have in common? How do they differ?

2. Review Chief Dan George's perspective on nature and discuss its relevance to "The Algonquin Cinderella."

APPLICATIONS

1. Write a contemporary version of a favorite childhood fairy tale and analyze the significance of your changes. To what extent do they reflect your values?

2. Is there anything positive to be learned from the Cinderella story? What does it teach about sibling rivalry? How might identifying with Cinderella be helpful to some children?

3. From ancient times to the present, poets and lyricists have used nature as their subject. Share with your group a favorite poem or lyric about nature. What aspects of nature emerged in the various texts? To what extent were the writers' attitudes toward nature influenced by their cultural backgrounds?

Cinderella's Stepsisters

TONI MORRISON

Toni Morrison (b. 1931) received the Nobel Prize for Literature in 1993, the first American woman to win the award since Pearl Buck in 1938, and the first African-American woman ever to win the award. Born in Lorain, Ohio, she received a B.A. in English from Howard University and an M.A. from Cornell University. Morrison made her debut as a novelist in 1970 with The Bluest Eye. *Her other novels include* Sula *(1973),* Song of Solomon *(1977),* Tar Baby *(1981),* Beloved *(1987),* Jazz *(1992), and* Paradise *(1998). Morrison's most recent novel,* Love, *was published in 2003. Four publications with her son, Slade Morrison, retellings for children of Aesop's fables, were collected in 2005 into one volume,* Who's Got Game? Three Fables, *which was followed by two more juvenile titles with her son. Morrison has received the National Book Critics Circle Award, the American Academy and Institute of Arts and Letters Award, the Pulitzer Prize, and the Robert F. Kennedy Award. She has taught at several universities, among them Princeton University since 1989 as professor of the humanities. Before reading Morrison's remarks to a Barnard College graduating class on the conflict between ambition and the nurturing sensibility, search your memory for times in your own life when these two drives competed.*

LET ME BEGIN BY TAKING YOU BACK A LITTLE. Back before the days at college. To nursery school, probably, to a once-upon-a-time time when you first heard or read, or, I suspect, even saw "Cinderella." Because it is Cinderella that I want to talk about; because it is Cinderella who causes me a feeling of urgency. What is unsettling about that fairy tale is that it is essentially the story of a household—a world, if you please—of women gathered together and held together in order to abuse another woman. There is, of course, a rather vague absent father and a nick-of-time prince with a foot fetish. But neither has much personality. And there are the surrogate "mothers," of course (god- and, step-), who contribute both to Cinderella's grief and to her release and happiness. But it is her stepsisters who interest me. How crippling it must have been for those young girls to grow up with a mother, to watch and imitate that mother, enslaving another girl.

I am curious about their fortunes after the story ends. For contrary to recent adaptations, the stepsisters were not ugly, clumsy, stupid girls with outsize feet. The Grimm collection describes them as "beautiful and fair in appearance." When we are introduced to them they are beautiful, elegant women of status, and clearly women of power. Having watched and participated in the violent dominion of another woman, will they be any less cruel when it comes their turn to enslave other children, or even when they are required to take care of their own mother?

It is not a wholly medieval problem. It is quite a contemporary one: feminine power when directed at other women has historically been wielded in what has been described as a "masculine" manner. Soon you will be in a position to do the very same thing. Whatever your background—rich or poor—whatever the history of education in your family—five generations or one—you have taken advantage of what has been available to you at Barnard and you will therefore leave both the economic and social status of the stepsisters *and* you will have their power.

I want not to *ask* you but to *tell* you not to participate in the oppression of your sisters. Mothers who abuse their children are women, and another woman, not an agency, has to be willing to stay their hands. Mothers who set fire to school buses are women, and another woman, not an agency, has to tell them to stay their hands. Women who stop the promotion of other women in careers are women, and another woman must come to the victim's aid. Social and welfare workers who humiliate their clients may be women, and other women colleagues have to deflect their anger.

I am alarmed by the violence that women do to each other: professional violence, competitive violence, emotional violence. I am alarmed by the willingness of women to enslave other women. I am alarmed by a growing absence of decency on the killing floor of professional women's worlds. You are the women who will take your place in the world where *you* can decide who shall flourish and who shall wither; you will make distinctions between the deserving poor and the undeserving poor; where you can yourself determine which life is expendable and which is indispensable. Since you will have the power to do it, you may also be persuaded that you have the right to do it. As educated women the distinction between the two is first-order business.

I am suggesting that we pay as much attention to our nurturing sensibilities as to our ambition. You are moving in the direction of freedom and the function of freedom is to free somebody else. You are moving toward self-fulfillment, and the consequences of that fulfillment should be to discover that there is something just as important as you are and that just-as-important thing may be Cinderella—or your stepsister.

In your rainbow journey toward the realization of personal goals, don't make choices based only on your security and your safety. Nothing is safe. That is not to say that anything ever was, or that anything worth achieving ever should be. Things of value seldom are. It is not safe to have a child. It is not safe to challenge the status quo. It is not safe to choose work that has not been done before. Or to do old work in a new way. There will always be someone there to stop you. But in pursuing your highest ambitions, don't let your personal safety diminish the safety of your stepsister. In wielding the power that is deservedly yours, don't permit it to enslave your stepsisters. Let your might and your power emanate from that place in you that is nurturing and caring.

Women's rights is not only an abstraction, a cause; it is also a personal affair. It is not only about "us"; it is also about me and you. Just the two of us.

INTERPRETATIONS

1. How much of the Cinderella fairy tale do you remember from childhood? Why is Morrison particularly interested in the stepsisters? What contemporary relevance does she find in their story?

2. "I am alarmed by the violence that women do to each other: professional violence, competitive violence, emotional violence." What examples does Morrison cite to support her statement? To what extent do you agree with her?

3. What distinction does Morrison make between "masculine" and "feminine" power? Do men and women think differently about competition, ambition, and success? Explain.

CORRESPONDENCES

1. Review Gandhi's perspective and discuss its application to Morrison's text.

2. Morrison's purpose is to persuade. How would you characterize her tone? How do her purpose and tone compare with that of "The Algonquin Cinderella"?

APPLICATIONS

1. Discuss with your group Morrison's comments in paragraph 7 about safety and security. How plausible is it that "power emanates from that place in you that is nurturing and caring"?

2. Write an essay analyzing the implications of Morrison's conclusion. Be specific.

3. Write an essay about a character in a fairy tale that you identified with, or rejected, as a child. What factors determined your responses? In retrospect, was the experience negative or positive? Cite reasons.

4. What do you think Cinderella herself would reply to Toni Morrison? Write a letter from Cinderella to Morrison that addresses issues that are raised in "Cinderella's Stepsisters."

Seven Days of Mourning

YAEL YARIMI

Yael Yarimi was born in Qiryat Eqron, Israel, a daughter of Jews of Yemenite descent. Like the majority of the sabras (first generation who were born in the new land), Yael had a communication problem with the old generation, who tried to practice the culture they had brought with them. The gaps that were created among the generations were very common in the country in which they lacked identity. Naturally, Yael pursued the Western lifestyle, the dominant one in Israel, and deserted the one of her ancestors, since the latter seemed to her obsolete. Yael rediscovered the richness of her roots only after she arrived in the United States in the late 1980s, when she reexamined her heritage.

In this essay, she expresses both appreciation and regret for the ignorance she had toward her heritage. She dedicates this essay to her parents Shalom and Yona ("peace" and "dove"), who endured many great ordeals when they came to the Holy Land. Going through a similar experience in America, Yael can now profoundly realize the high price her parents paid for their passage from the familiar to the strange. This is her way of thanking them for raising her with pride and confidence in spite of all the difficulties.

Tuesday

Dear Diary,

It is eleven p.m. I hear unclear words coming from the next room. It is as if Mom and Dad entered an unfamiliar state and are speaking in a strange language . . . Among these odd words I can only understand one sentence Mom just said: "We must call everybody and inform them about the funeral time" . . . Now I hear my father crying. Oh my God! This is the first time in my life I have ever heard him crying just like us—the children.

I WAS TWELVE and too young to digest the significance of my grandfather's death. However, I was bothered with the notion that I would never see him again. I couldn't sleep. Constantly hiding my diary under the pillow, I remember trying to strangle my weeping under the blanket. Threatening pictures emerged and floated in my mind.

290

I cannot forget the scene: our front yard that was also our playground, turned overnight into a huge black tent made of strong, plastic canvas sheet and a great number of supporting rods. Strange people were unloading dozens of long tables and benches into the tent.

By the afternoon, all my relatives, neighbors and some other people had already arrived. Naturally, the men formed into a big rectangular pattern and began praying in loud voices, while the women were transferring large cooking pots from our house to the back of the tent. There, they installed a giant cooking stove which could be big enough for an army division. These volunteer ladies looked as if they were in a hurry. They worked so skillfully, that one might have thought that their lives depended on it.

We—the children—were running around between the legs and were scolded with blaming fingers. We were asked to be quiet. "This is not a time for joy" rebuked one of the ladies while holding my little brother by his ear. He was then sent away promising to keep quiet. Everything had happened very fast.

My father's eyes were an unforgettable sight. As the son of the deceased, my father was sitting on the ground, in one of the tent corners. Suddenly, he seemed so old, so infirm. My father, who was naturally a strong man, a towering figure, changed before my eyes into a helpless man with a saddened feeling of inner rage.

Not far from the men, in another corner, the mourning women were sitting on the ground as well. In the center of them, a woman I had never seen before was mourning in a heartbreaking wailing voice and caused all the other women to cry with her. I still remember her holding a square handkerchief with one hand on her forehead in a way that covered her entire face. Accompanying her sad songs, she then moved her upper body from side to side in a steady rhythm. Her mourning songs were interrupted by her outcries after every two stanzas that described my grandfather. I could see my grandmother's pleading facial expression as if she was trying to stop these words from being said.

I then was wondering how the mourning woman could cry and sob in such an honest way as if she knew my grandfather. I also could not understand why she had to add more agony to the already sad situation.

Dear Diary,

I hate Aunt Rina, I hate her so much. She had no right to push me and ask me to help the working ladies . . . I feel so sad today . . . I couldn't enter the cemetery this afternoon; Mom says that women with periods are not clean; therefore I couldn't be present when my grandfather was buried. It is so corny . . . Grandpa,

I know you hear me. I know you are watching me from heaven . . . This is a mad house. Mom says its going to be like that every day for the next seven days . . . My friend Sara, remember her?, the one you used to call "The Russian"?, she says they never cooked for funerals . . . She says our funeral is like camping. You would have been proud of me if you heard what a lecture I gave her about us, about our dream that came true; to be in the land of the Jews, about all the things you used to tell me.

I am still astonished each time I recall the dedication of the Yemenite Jewish Community during the Shiva—the seven days of mourning in Jewish tradition in which all the community has to console and help the family to get over the loss.

All men rose at dawn and were praying three times a day. After each prayer, meals were served, in a religious ceremony, first to the men, then to the mourning women and last to the congregation. Deep, stiff, plastic dishes were filled with soup and meat in the Yemenite style. Scattered pita breads were laid along the tables by the side of small round dishes that contained a spicy dip called *hilba*—made of herbs. Hilba is used to flavor the soup. People then were eating with their hands, and there were no conversations during the eating time.

Dear Diary,
    It has been a couple days that people are sleeping in my house. Everywhere I turn I encounter people, it's as if my house has turned into a hostel . . . Today it is an important day that's why I marked it in red ink. Today I have received my very first kiss.
    Eddie, my cousin and I climbed the lemon tree in our back yard and kissed . . . I love him so much . . . Dad must not know; he will kill me, like the time he beat me when I played with Eric.

I closed the diary, which had aged with the years. I held it to my bosom and allowed myself to cry. I can still feel the pain and the insult of the blows I received from my father. It was eighteen years ago, but I still remember him saying outrageously "Kiss is a half intercourse," then came a second round of blows.

Knocking on the door, my husband woke me up from the journey to my past. "Everybody is leaving," he shouted. "Hurry up." I wore a black dress with a black scarf as is customary at mourning in my family.

By the time we arrived at the cemetery, my grandmother had already been buried. Women were spread out on the grave, yelling and pulling their hair. Grandmother was eighty-nine years old when she died. I was so sorry that distance did not enable me to see her before.

Living in the Diaspora, I find myself torn apart between the home I am trying to establish with my American husband, and the great, rich and embracing tradition I have left in my land of birth. I miss the togetherness, the caring and the warmth among my people so much that I sometimes contemplate leaving everything I have accomplished here and just returning to my roots, to the familiar, and running away from the ambiguous coldness I feel in America.

Entering the tent, my husband and I were sitting on the benches, in front of the same old tables, listening to the same heartbreaking weeping but this time from a different lady.

A new generation of kids in our family were laughing and running around happy for the opportunity that brought them all together. Some of the traditional rituals will probably vanish among the new generation of Yemenite Jews in Israel, but in appearance only. I believe the essential tradition will remain forever.

INTERPRETATIONS

1. How do you feel about the custom of a leader causing "all the other women to cry with her" even though the leader didn't know Yarimi's grandfather? What purpose does it serve?

2. Why do you think food has such an important place in these ceremonies? How common in other traditions is this attention to food?

3. Does moving away from one's home or native land strengthen or weaken the importance of tradition? What examples can you provide from your own experience?

4. What is added to this narrative by seeing most of it from the point of view of a twelve-year-old?

CORRESPONDENCES

1. Review Schwartz's perspective on memory and discuss its application to "Seven Days of Mourning." What do the journal entries reveal about the narrator's memories? What is Yarimi's purpose in linking her grandfather's death to the present?

2. The Algonquin Cinderella and Yarimi both focus on the impor-
    tance of ritual and the preservation of traditions. To what extent
    do you agree that preserving both adds dimension to individual
    and communal living? What examples can you cite?

APPLICATIONS

1. Discuss with your group Yarimi's ambivalence about living in the
    Diaspora. Should she run away from the "ambiguous coldness of
    America"? What consensus did you reach?

2. Are all of Yarimi's memories pleasant? What portrait of her father
    emerges in her journal? What do the entries reveal about the
    writer?

3. How important are mourning rituals in your culture? Are pre-
    scribed gender roles involved? Is the food served part of the rituals?
    Will you teach your children these customs? Why or why not?

4. On page 291, Yael Yarimi describes the scene at her house follow-
    ing her grandfather's funeral. What sights do you see? Make a
    drawing that takes into account your interpretation of Yarimi's
    work. Pay attention to color as well as content and composition.

New (and Improved?) Delhi

GAUTAM BHATIA

Gautam Bhatia (b. 1952) is an architect and critic who lives in New Delhi. He graduated in fine arts and did his postgraduate work in architecture at the University of Pennsylvania. He has a way with titles, as you can see from the following article, which was first published in The New York Times Maga-zine *in 2006, and from the titles of his books. He published three in 1994:* Laurie Baker: Life, Works, Writings *(about an English architect who came to India and wrote* Laurie Baker's Mud *[1993]);* Silent Spaces and Other Stories of Architecture; *and* Punjabi Baroque and Other Memories of Architecture. A Short History of Everything: A Novel *followed in 1998,* Eternal Stone *in 2000,* Comic Century: An Unreliable History of the 20th Century *in 2004, and* MUD the House *(with Vishwajyoti Ghosh) in 2006. If you should write an essay called "New (and Improved?) York or New (and Improved) Orleans, what aspect of the place would you emphasize?*

ONE EVENING A FEW YEARS AGO, I found myself on the road that heads south out of Delhi, in the city's fastest-developing suburb: Qutab Enclave. The area along the road was one big construction site. Many new structures sat between piles of rubble, and workers milled around concrete mixers on brown hot ground, half dug, half built. Pigs and stray dogs strolled near new plate-glass outlets for Reebok, Benetton and Levi's.

As the head of a small architecture practice in Delhi, I had just made a routine visit to the site of a house under construction nearby when I decided to take a look at the newly-erected head-quarters of a leading software company. This was one of the first so-called e-buildings in India—what its makers described as intelligent, user-friendly architecture. In my own practice, I try to conform to the ideals of hand craft, low cost and no maintenance, and having just examined the hand-applied mud plaster of the house I was working on, the idea of a peek into a high-tech extreme machine seemed all the more intriguing.

I parked in the vast lot and made my way toward a composition of polished stone and beveled glass. Built of Italian marble and erected with American and French technologies under South Korean supervision, it was truly global architecture. It was also perhaps eight times as expensive as the most expensive building in India. But a structure that has intelligence and the ability to interact with its user was one of a kind among the dumb, unfriendly buildings of old India.

Nearing the entrance, a sensor alerted a mechanism in the base of the glass door that it might soon have to open. I stood under a concealed camera for a few seconds, while my picture was beamed to an electronic control center somewhere inside, and it informed the circuit in the door that I should be allowed to pass. Sure enough, the door opened. A simple device worth probably 22 lakhs, now about 50,000 U.S. dollars, had eliminated the need for a human Haryanvi guard at $110 per month.

Inside the lobby I stood in virtual darkness, looking for a light switch and hoping that the command center would measure my distress and send down a light. For a long while nothing happened. I stepped cautiously, hoping that the floor was real and not an e-floor. Once I reached the elevators, light flooded in as if all the switches had been flicked on at once. Rubbing my eyes, I hoped again that the command center would sense my distress and turn off a few lights; but no. Still, this complicated light circuitry that I imagine cost $50,000 was worth it: it defrayed the cost of a 60-watt bulb left on throughout the night and paid for itself in a mere 120 years.

Before long, I heard the white noise of all six elevators racing down to pick me up. But after the lobby experience, I wasn't too keen on getting into an e-lift and opted to climb nine floors by an old-fashioned set of steps. Upstairs, I was met by the building representative, who narrated the benefits of technology as if memorized from a brochure, explaining that the double-glass wall had microlouvers and heat sensors inserted in the glass—at the cost of about $700,000. "During hot days, the entire south wall is protected without any expenditure of human energy."

I wanted to say that in my parents' time they used reed mats that could just be rolled down when it got too hot. Instead I said, "That's nice," and looked through the glass at all the virtually free human energy around the road below: the thousands of underpaid laborers who had helped erect the building. It was clear that the world had embarked on a new adventure. In India, like everywhere else, building had become a device to display forms of new abundance and make them available to a growing market of consumers. One client of mine, a farmer turned garment exporter, wanted me to re-create Thomas Jefferson's Monticello on a suburban lot. Another, the owner of a Mumbai shipping company, asked me to design a house he saw in a film.

Back outside, I began driving home across a landscape of multiplex cinemas and shimmering plate-glass malls. All around me, a younger breed of professionals were attacking projects with the impatience of lucrative business deals—seeking to align their work with the idea of India as an industrial power. I thought of the house I was working on, its mud walls and brick courtyard, the kind even Mahatma Gandhi would have approved of. According to Gandhi, the ideal Indian house is built of materials and skills harnessed nearby.

For my client, a banker who had spent a working life all over the world, this new home was a symbolic return to traditional India. For me, the important thing was simply to go to my study each day, pull out a 6B pencil and spend time at the drawing board, trying for something timeless.

INTERPRETATIONS

1. Why does Bhatia visit the building he describes? What does he discover about it?
2. How does Bhatia use comparison and contrast in his essay? What specific examples support your answer?
3. Explain the tone that Bhatia chooses for this essay. Why do you think that this choice is appropriate or inappropriate?
4. What do you think Bhatia's main point is? Where is it most clearly stated?

CORRESPONDENCES

1. Review Hartley's perspective and discuss its relevance to Bhatia's attitudes toward the past.
2. Review Ghandi's perspective. To what extent is it antithetical to the house under construction that Bhatia visits? To your ideal house?

APPLICATIONS

1. Imagine that you live in a cluster of houses that all have a similar structure or that share a related theme. Suddenly a developer decides to build a home that is radically different and that compromises the integrity of the neighborhood. Write a letter to your Zoning Commission that argues for or against the project. Select a tone appropriate to your purpose, topic, and audience, and articulate specific supporting arguments.

2.   What is something that you are able to do both by hand and by using a machine? Write a comparison and contrast essay that not only explains the process of making the object using both methods, but that also explains the subtleties and/or implications of using each system.

3.   Describe a typical home in a country that you either lived in or visited. Accompany this verbal description with architectural drawings or photographs.

Share your description and drawings with the members of your group. What is the relation between form and function? What features of the house reflect the culture or traditions present in the place where it stands?

The Lottery

SHIRLEY JACKSON

Shirley Jackson (1919–1965) was born and raised in California. In 1933, she moved with her family to Rochester, New York, where she briefly attended the University of Rochester. Notable publications include the novel Hangsaman *(1951) and the play* We Have Always Lived in the Castle *(1962). In "The Lottery" (1948), a frequently anthologized piece, Jackson scrutinizes scapegoating. Record in your journal your associations with "scapegoating."*

THE MORNING OF JUNE 27TH was clear and sunny, with the fresh warmth of a full-summer day; the flowers were blossoming profusely and the grass was richly green. The people of the village began to gather in the square, between the post office and the bank, around ten o'clock; in some towns there were so many people that the lottery took two days and had to be started on June 26th, but in this village, where there were only about three hundred people, the whole lottery took less than two hours, so it could begin at ten o'clock in the morning and still be through in time to allow the villagers to get home for noon dinner.

The children assembled first, of course. School was recently over for the summer, and the feeling of liberty sat uneasily on most of them; they tended to gather together quietly for a while before they broke into boisterous play, and their talk was still of the classroom and the teacher, of books and reprimands. Bobby Martin had already stuffed his pockets full of stones, and the other boys soon followed his example, selecting the smoothest and roundest stones; Bobby and Harry Jones and Dickie Delacroix—the villagers pronounced this name "Dellacroy"—eventually made a great pile of stones in one corner of the square and guarded it against the raids of the other boys. The girls stood aside, talking among themselves, looking over their shoulders at the boys, and the very small children rolled in the dust or clung to the hands of their older brothers or sisters.

Soon the men began to gather, surveying their own children, speaking of planting and rain, tractors and taxes. They stood together, away from the pile of stones in the corner, and their jokes were quiet and they smiled rather than laughed. The women, wearing faded house dresses and sweaters, came shortly after their menfolk. They greeted one another and exchanged bits of gossip as they went to join their husbands. Soon the women, standing by their husbands, began to call to their children, and the children came reluctantly, having to be called four or five times. Bobby Martin ducked under his mother's grasping hand and ran, laughing, back to the pile of stones. His father spoke up sharply, and Bobby came quickly and took his place between his father and his oldest brother.

The lottery was conducted—as were the square dances, the teenage club, the Halloween program—by Mr. Summers, who had time and energy to devote to civic activities. He was a round-faced, jovial man and he ran the coal business, and people were sorry for him, because he had no children and his wife was a scold. When he arrived in the square, carrying the black wooden box, there was a murmur of conversation among the villagers, and he waved and called, "Little late today, folks." The postmaster, Mr. Graves, followed him, carrying a three-legged stool, and the stool was put in the center of the square and Mr. Summers set the black box down on it. The villagers kept their distance, leaving a space between themselves and the stool, and when Mr. Summers said, "Some of you fellows want to give me a hand?" there was a hesitation before two men, Mr. Martin and his oldest son, Baxter, came forward to hold the box steady on the stool while Mr. Summers stirred up the papers inside it.

The original paraphernalia for the lottery had been lost long ago, and the black box now resting on the stool had been put into use even before Old Man Warner, the oldest man in town, was born. Mr. Summers spoke frequently to the villagers about making a new box, but no one liked to upset even as much tradition as was represented by the black box. There was a story that the present box had been made with some pieces of the box that had preceded it, the one that had been constructed when the first people settled down to make a village here. Every year, after the lottery, Mr. Summers began talking again about a new box, but every year the subject was allowed to fade off without anything's being done. The black box grew shabbier each year; by now it was no longer completely black but splintered badly along one side to show the original wood color, and in some places faded or stained.

Mr. Martin and his oldest son, Baxter, held the black box securely on the stool until Mr. Summers had stirred the papers thoroughly with his hand. Because so much of the ritual had been forgotten or discarded, Mr. Summers had been successful in having slips of paper substituted for the chips of wood that had been used for generations. Chips of wood, Mr. Summers had argued, had been all very well when the village was tiny, but now that the population was more than three hundred and likely to keep on growing, it was necessary to use something that would fit more easily into the black box. The night before the lottery, Mr. Summers and Mr. Graves made up the slips of paper and put them in the box, and it was then taken to the safe of Mr. Summers's coal company and locked up until Mr. Summers was ready to take it to the square next morning. The rest of the year, the box was put away, sometimes one place, sometimes another; it had spent one year in Mr. Graves's barn and another year underfoot in the post office, and sometimes it was set on a shelf in the Martin grocery and left there.

There was a great deal of fussing to be done before Mr. Summers declared the lottery open. There were the lists to make up—of heads of families, heads of households in each family, members of each household in each family. There was the proper swearing-in of Mr. Summers by the postmaster, as the official of the lottery; at one time, some people remembered, there had been a recital of some sort, performed by the official of the lottery, a perfunctory, tuneless chant that had been rattled off duly each year; some people believed that the official of the lottery used to stand just so when he said or sang it, others believed that he was supposed to walk among the people, but years and years ago this part of the ritual had been allowed to lapse. There had been, also, a ritual salute, which the official of the lottery had had to use in addressing each person who came up to draw from the box, but this also had changed with time, until now it was felt necessary only for the official to speak to each person approaching. Mr. Summers was very good at all this; in his clean white shirt and blue jeans, with one hand resting carelessly on the black box, he seemed very proper and important as he talked interminably to Mr. Graves and the Martins.

Just as Mr. Summers finally left off talking and turned to the assembled villagers, Mrs. Hutchinson came hurriedly along the path to the square, her sweater thrown over her shoulders, and slid into place in the back of the crowd. "Clean forgot what day it was," she said to Mrs. Delacroix, who stood next to her, and they both laughed softly. "Thought my old man was out back stacking wood," Mrs. Hutchinson went on, "and then I looked out the window and the kids was gone, and then I remembered it was the twenty-seventh and came a-running." She dried her hands on her apron, and Mrs. Delacroix said, "You're in time, though. They're still talking away up there."

Mrs. Hutchinson craned her neck to see through the crowd and found her husband and children standing near the front. She tapped Mrs. Delacroix on the arm as a farewell and began to make her way through the crowd. The people separated good-humoredly to let her through; two or three people said, in voices just loud enough to be heard across the crowd, "Here comes your Missus, Hutchinson," and "Bill, she made it after all." Mrs. Hutchinson reached her husband, and Mr. Summers, who had been waiting, said cheerfully, "Thought we were going to have to get on without you, Tessie." Mrs. Hutchinson said, grinning, "Wouldn't have me leave m'dishes in the sink, now, would you, Joe?" and soft laughter ran through the crowd as the people stirred back into position after Mrs. Hutchinson's arrival.

"Well, now," Mr. Summers said soberly, "guess we better get started, get this over with, so's we can go back to work. Anybody ain't here?"

"Dunbar," several people said. "Dunbar, Dunbar."

Mr. Summers consulted his list. "Clyde Dunbar," he said. "That's right. He's broke his leg, hasn't he? Who's drawing for him?"

"Me, I guess," a woman said, and Mr. Summers turned to look at her. "Wife draws for her husband," Mr. Summers said. "Don't you have a grown boy to do it for you, Janey?" Although Mr. Summers and everyone else in the village knew the answer perfectly well, it was the business of the official of the lottery to ask such questions formally. Mr. Summers waited with an expression of polite interest while Mrs. Dunbar answered.

"Horace's not but sixteen yet," Mrs. Dunbar said regretfully. "Guess I gotta fill in for the old man this year."

"Right," Mr. Summers said. He made a note on the list he was holding. Then he asked, "Watson boy drawing this year?"

A tall boy in the crowd raised his hand. "Here," he said. "I'm drawing for m'mother and me." He blinked his eyes nervously and ducked his head as several voices in the crowd said things like "Good fellow, Jack," and "Glad to see your mother's got a man to do it."

"Well," Mr. Summers said, "guess that's everyone. Old Man Warner make it?"

"Here," a voice said, and Mr. Summers nodded.

A sudden hush fell on the crowd as Mr. Summers cleared his throat and looked at the list. "All ready?" he called. "Now, I'll read the names—heads of families first—and the men come up and take a paper out of the box. Keep the paper folded in your hand without looking at it until everyone has had a turn. Everything clear?"

The people had done it so many times that they only half listened to the directions; most of them were quiet, wetting their lips, not looking around. Then Mr. Summers raised one hand high and said, "Adams." A man disengaged himself from the crowd and came forward. "Hi, Steve," Mr. Summers said, and Mr. Adams said, "Hi, Joe." They grinned at one another humorlessly and nervously. Then Mr. Adams reached into the black box and took out a folded paper. He held it firmly by one corner as he turned and went hastily back to his place in the crowd, where he stood a little apart from his family, not looking down at his hand.

"Allen," Mr. Summers said, "Anderson . . . Bentham."

"Seems like there's no time at all between lotteries any more," Mrs. Delacroix said to Mrs. Graves in the back row. "Seems like we got through with the last one only last week."

"Time sure goes fast," Mrs. Graves said.

"Clark . . . Delacroix."

"There goes my old man," Mrs. Delacroix said. She held her breath while her husband went forward.

"Dunbar," Mr. Summers said, and Mrs. Dunbar went steadily to the box while one of the women said, "Go on, Janey," and another said, "There she goes."

"We're next," Mrs. Graves said. She watched while Mr. Graves came around from the side of the box, greeted Mr. Summers gravely, and selected a slip of paper from the box. By now, all through the crowd there were men holding the small folded papers in their large hands, turning them over and over nervously. Mrs. Dunbar and her two sons stood together, Mrs. Dunbar holding the slip of paper.

"Harburt . . . Hutchinson."

"Get up there, Bill," Mrs. Hutchinson said, and the people near her laughed.

"Jones."

"They do say," Mr. Adams said to Old Man Warner, who stood next to him, "that over in the north village they're talking of giving up the lottery."

Old Man Warner snorted. "Pack of crazy fools," he said. "Listening to the young folks, nothing's good enough for *them*. Next thing you know, they'll be wanting to go back to living in caves, nobody work any more, live *that* way for a while. Used to be a saying about 'Lottery in June, corn be heavy soon.' First thing you know, we'd all be eating stewed chickweed and acorns. There's *always* been a lottery," he added petulantly. "Bad enough to see young Joe Summers up there joking with everybody."

"Some places have already quit lotteries," Mrs. Adams said.

"Nothing but trouble in *that*," Old Man Warner said stoutly. "Pack of young fools."

"Martin." And Bobby Martin watched his father go forward. "Overdyke . . . Percy."

"I wish they'd hurry," Mrs. Dunbar said to her oldest son. "I wish they'd hurry."

"They're almost through," her son said.

"You get ready to run tell Dad," Mrs. Dunbar said.

Mr. Summers called his own name and then stepped forward precisely and selected a slip from the box. Then he called, "Warner."

"Seventy-seventh year I been in the lottery," Old Man Warner said as he went through the crowd. "Seventy-seventh time."

"Watson." The tall boy came awkwardly through the crowd. Someone said, "Don't be nervous, Jack," and Mr. Summers said, "Take your time, son."

"Zanini."

After that, there was a long pause, a breathless pause, until Mr. Summers, holding his slip of paper in the air, said, "All right, fellows." For a minute, no one moved, and then all the slips of paper were opened. Suddenly, all the women began to speak at once, saying, "Who is it?" "Who's got it?" "Is it the Dunbars?" "Is it the Watsons?" Then the voices began to say, "It's Hutchinson. It's Bill." "Bill Hutchinson's got it."

"Go tell your father," Mrs. Dunbar said to her older son.

People began to look around to see the Hutchinsons. Bill Hutchinson was standing quiet, staring down at the paper in his hand. Suddenly, Tessie Hutchinson shouted to Mr. Summers, "You didn't give him time enough to take any paper he wanted. I saw you. It wasn't fair!"

"Be a good sport, Tessie," Mrs. Delacroix called, and Mrs. Graves said, "All of us took the same chance."

"Shut up, Tessie," Bill Hutchinson said.

"Well, everyone," Mr. Summers said, "that was done pretty fast, and now we've got to be hurrying a little more to get done in time." He consulted his next list. "Bill," he said, "you draw for the Hutchinson family. You got any other households in the Hutchinsons?"

"There's Don and Eva," Mrs. Hutchinson yelled. "Make *them* take their chance!"

"Daughters drew with their husbands' families, Tessie," Mr. Summers said gently. "You know that as well as anyone else."

"It wasn't *fair*," Tessie said.

"I guess not, Joe," Bill Hutchinson said regretfully. "My daughter draws with her husband's family, that's only fair, And I've got no other family except the kids."

"Then, as far as drawing for families is concerned, it's you," Mr. Summers said in explanation, "and as far as drawing for households is concerned, that's you, too. Right?"

"Right," Bill Hutchinson said.

"How many kids, Bill?" Mr. Summers asked formally.

"Three," Bill Hutchinson said. "There's Bill, Jr., and Nancy, and little Dave. And Tessie and me."

"All right, then," Mr. Summers said. "Harry, you got their tickets back?"

Mr. Graves nodded and held up the slips of paper. "Put them in the box, then," Mr. Summers directed. "Take Bill's and put it in."

"I think we ought to start over," Mrs. Hutchinson said, as quietly as she could. "I tell you it wasn't *fair*. You didn't give him time enough to choose. *Every*body saw that."

Mr. Graves had selected the five slips and put them in the box, and he dropped all the papers but those onto the ground, where the breeze caught them and lifted them off.

"Listen, everybody," Mrs. Hutchinson was saying to the people around her.

"Ready, Bill?" Mr. Summers asked, and Bill Hutchinson, with one quick glance around at his wife and children, nodded.

"Remember," Mr. Summers said, "take the slips and keep them folded until each person has taken one. Harry, you help little Dave." Mr. Graves took the hand of the little boy, who came willingly with him up to the box. "Take a paper out of the box, Davy," Mr. Summers said. Davy put his hand into the box and laughed. "Take just *one* paper," Mr. Summers said. "Harry, you hold it for him." Mr. Graves took the child's hand and removed the folded paper from the tight fist and held it while little Dave stood next to him and looked up at him wonderingly.

"Nancy next," Mr. Summers said. Nancy was twelve, and her school friends breathed heavily as she went forward, switching her skirt, and took a slip daintily from the box. "Bill, Jr.," Mr. Summers said, and Billy, his face red and his feet overlarge, nearly knocked the box over as he got a paper out. "Tessie," Mr. Summers said. She hesitated for a minute, looking around defiantly, and then set her lips and went up to the box. She snatched a paper out and held it behind her.

"Bill," Mr. Summers said, and Bill Hutchinson reached into the box and felt around, bringing his hand out at last with the slip of paper in it.

The crowd was quiet. A girl whispered, "I hope it's not Nancy," and the sound of the whisper reached the edges of the crowd.

"It's not the way it used to be," Old Man Warner said clearly. "People ain't the way they used to be."

"All right," Mr. Summers said. "Open the papers. Harry, you open little Dave's."

Mr. Graves opened the slip of paper and there was a general sigh through the crowd as he held it up and everyone could see that it was blank. Nancy and Bill, Jr., opened theirs at the same time, and both beamed and laughed, turning around to the crowd and holding their slips of paper above their heads.

"Tessie," Mr. Summers said. There was a pause, and then Mr. Summers looked at Bill Hutchinson, and Bill unfolded his paper and showed it. It was blank.

"It's Tessie," Mr. Summers said, and his voice was hushed. "Show us her paper, Bill."

Bill Hutchinson went over to his wife and forced the slip of paper out of her hand. It had a black spot on it, the black spot Mr. Summers had made the night before with the heavy pencil in the coal-company office. Bill Hutchinson held it up and there was a stir in the crowd.

"All right, folks," Mr. Summers said. "Let's finish quickly."

Although the villagers had forgotten the ritual and lost the original black box, they still remembered to use stones. The pile of stones the boys had made earlier was ready; there were stones on the ground with the blowing scraps of paper that had come out of the box. Mrs. Delacroix selected a stone so large she had to pick it up with both hands and turned to Mrs. Dunbar. "Come on," she said. "Hurry up."

Mrs. Dunbar had small stones in both hands, and she said, gasping for breath, "I can't run at all. You'll have to go ahead and I'll catch up with you."

The children had stones already, and someone gave little Davy Hutchinson a few pebbles.

Tessie Hutchinson was in the center of a cleared space by now, and she held her hands out desperately as the villagers moved in on her. "It isn't fair," she said. A stone hit her on the side of the head.

Old Man Warner was saying, "Come on, come on, everyone." Steve Adams was in the front of the crowd of villagers, with Mrs. Graves beside him.

"It isn't fair, it isn't right," Mrs. Hutchinson screamed and then they were upon her.

INTERPRETATIONS

1. What do the villagers mean by "fairness"? What is implied by the fact that the only villager to complain about the lottery's consequences is Tessie Hutchinson?

2. Why does Jackson use a flat, reportorial style to describe an event that would normally be headline news? Consider the role of irony in this story.

3. How important is it that the story is set in roughly contemporary New England? How, for example, would its influence differ if the story were set in Aztec Mexico, a culture that routinely practiced human sacrifice?

4. The tradition here depicted brings summary execution or reprieve. What traditions do we participate in that have life-or-death consequences, in either the short or the long run?

Stone-Throwing in India: An Annual Bash

MARK FINEMAN

Mark Fineman (1952–2003) had a varied career in journalism after receiving his degree from Syracuse University: he worked for The Chicago Sun-Times; *the* Allentown, Pennsylvania, Call-Chronicle; The Philadelphia Inquirer; *and the* Los Angeles Times. *He won several awards, including the Overseas Press Club Award in 2001, a National Headliners Award in 1991, an American Society of Newspaper Editors Award for deadline writing in 1987, and a George Polk Award in 1985. To what extent do you find Fineman's title engaging? Is there anything unusual about it?*

PANDHURNA, INDIA —To most of the 45,000 seemingly normal residents of this sleepy little town on the banks of the River Jam, Anil Sambare is nothing more than a spoilsport.

To some, he is something worse. A troublemaker, some say. An idealistic radical, according to others. Some even think him a traitor to his hometown.

And all because the twenty-seven-year-old high school teacher has dedicated his life to stopping his entire town from going completely berserk once a year in a frenzied festival of destruction—a daylong event in which thousands of people try to stone each other to death in the name of fun, tradition and, now, stardom.

The annual event is called the Gotmaar Festival—literally, "stone-hitting"—and it is an ancient Pandhurna tradition, unique and brutal even by Indian standards.

No one here remembers exactly how ancient it is, although older people say that it dates back at least three centuries. And no one knows exactly why they do it every year, year after year, despite scores of deaths and thousands of injuries, although the myth behind it is a compelling one.

All the Pandhurnans really know for sure is that once a year, on the day of the new moon in the Hindu month of Sharawan, when the drums start beating along the River Jam, the time for the madness has begun again.

Within minutes, thousands of male Pandhurnans, ranging in age from six to sixty, many of them deeply scarred or limping from festivals of years past, divide into two groups, gather their huge piles of stones on opposite sides of the river and, for the next six-and-a-half hours, try to kill, maim and mangle as many fellow townsfolk as they can.

When sunset comes, and the drumbeat stops, the two sides drop their rocks, come together, shake hands, nurse each other's wounds and return to the peaceful monotony of rural Indian life.

This year, the Gotmaar carnage, which took place two weeks ago, left four dead and 612 injured. But there were a few new twists this year that speak volumes about India's struggle to enter the modern age.

First, there was Anil Sambare and his signature drive to end the carnage, which drew the ire of almost everyone. Second, this is an election year in India, which meant that Sambare's signature campaign was doomed to failure. And finally, there was the introduction of a new evil, videotape equipment, which is likely to ensure that Pandhurna's sado-masochistic ritual will continue for many years to come.

The story of the Pandhurnans and their bizarre, ancient rite of stoning is a living illustration of the paradoxes of a modern-day India, as well as a freeze-frame glimpse at the ironies and distortions resulting from Indian Prime Minister Rajiv Gandhi's five-year-old pledge to modernize rural India.

Pandhurna, in central Madhya Pradesh state, is hardly what one would call a backwater. In many ways it is a model of Rajiv Gandhi's rural modernization plan.

There are 10,000 television sets in Pandhurna, 340 telephones and even 100 videocassette players. More than ninety percent of the homes have electricity. Everyone has access to clean drinking water. Unemployment is under five percent, and there are even beauty parlors doing booming business.

"There is just this one little thing that sets us apart," said Bhargao Pandurang Bhagwatkar, who has taught in the local high school for the last forty-one years. "We all know it is barbaric. It is a kind of madness. And it has no reason at all. But it has been with us since Day 1, and, on that day every year, we just cannot help ourselves."

Day 1, as myth has it, was sometime in the 1600s, according to local historians, police and other local officials, who say they and their predecessors have been trying to stop it every year for the last half-century.

On Day 1, it seems, Pandhurna's brutal battle began as a love story.

"The way the old ones tell it," town official M. M. Singh explained, "a boy from the Pandhurna side of the river eloped with a girl from the village on the other side, which was then known as Sawargaon but since has merged into Pandhurna.

"As the amorous young couple was trying to flee across the river, the Sawargaon people began throwing stones at them. The Pandhurnans heard about this and quickly ran to the river bank, where they began stoning the Sawargaons.

"The couple, of course, died in the cross-fire. And it's on the spot where they died that the people now put the tree every year."

"The tree?" the stranger asked.

"Oh, the tree. The tree is the main object of the game."

The Pandhurnans who actually play "the game," which is what everyone here except Sambare calls the annual stoning battle, explained that the tree is cut the day before the festival from a special grove of flame trees beside a temple to the Hindu god of destruction, which is where legend states that the mythical young couple first met.

The tree is then "planted" in the middle of the River Jam, and the object of "the game" is to chop down the tree with an ax, without, of course, getting stoned to death in the process.

Enter the videotape.

Unlike previous years, in which an average of two or three Pandhurnans were stoned to death during the festival, the four deaths this year were from drowning.

"These boys had climbed the tree, and were posing for the camera," Sambare explained. "They were so preoccupied with the video camera, they didn't see the stones coming. They got hit in the head, fell into the river and drowned."

Sambare knows what he's talking about. He lives on Stone-hitting Road, in a riverfront house with a view of the battle zone. And he jumped into the river and saved four other "players" from the same fate this year, getting hit in the back with stones in the process.

But that's not why Sambare is so committed to ending the carnage of Gotmaar. It's not even because his uncle was stoned to death twenty-seven years ago, or because he cannot stop his own younger brother from joining in—"imagine, my own brother bought five different outfits and changed clothes five times during the stone-hitting this year because he wanted to look good for the camera."

"No, I am fighting this because it is a perversion, because it is barbaric and because it puts all of India in a very poor light," said Sambare, who has a masters degree in mathematics.

"This is not a game. This is madness. And now, with this videotape, there is all of a sudden a renewed interest in joining in. Everyone wants to show off their bravado."

Enter Rajiv Gandhi's high-tech revolution.

The videotape was the government's idea. And the local police actually paid 5,000 rupees (about $300) in government funds to a local video contractor to film the festival this year.

"The idea was to minimize the killing," said Krishna Kohle, the enterprising Pandhurnan who got the video contract. "It was, how do you call it, a compromise."

For decades, local officials said, the authorities have attempted to end the festival. Two years ago, the police even opened fire on the festival, killing two Pandhurnans, in an attempt to end it after a passing constable was accidentally stoned to death.

"I myself have seen too many deaths and very much want this madness to end," said Dr. Ratan Singhvi, a local physician who is Pandhurna's equivalent of mayor and the local head of Gandhi's ruling Congress-I party.

"I have seen people with eyes bulging out, ears sheared off, noses broken, teeth shattered, skulls and legs fractured to bits. But we've never been able to stop it. My God, the people like it.

"Of course, an additional problem is these people are all dead drunk when they're playing the game, and the game gives them a good excuse to get drunk. They look forward to it all year long."

Enter politics.

"The people of Pandhurna, you see, are very sentimental about this festival," Singhvi said. "And such things are very important to our local voters. Had we stopped the Gotmaar this year, for example, the Congress Party definitely would be sent away in the next elections. So what we did instead was try to cut down on the deaths—we banned the slingshot."

Called *gofans*, the handmade slingshots came into vogue two years ago and clearly escalated the conflict. They turned the stones into speeding bullets, tripling the death toll and ultimately forcing the police to step in. The *gofan* was outlawed. And, in an effort to enforce that ban, police hired the video man to film violators for prosecution.

"I guess it backfired," said Kohle, who conceded he is now making a tidy profit renting out copies of the Gotmaar video to townspeople who want to relive their moments of bravery and endurance.

INTERPRETATIONS

1. Explain the myth that serves as the catalyst for the town's annual stone-hitting event.

2. "This is not a game. This is madness. And now with this videotape, there is all of a sudden a renewed interest in joining in." To what extent do you agree with Sambare? How has the video camera affected the stone-hitting activities?

3. What are Sambare's reasons for protesting against his town's tradition? Do you think he will succeed? To what extent is he foolish to try?

CORRESPONDENCES

1. Review the Maugham perspective on traditions and explain its meaning. How does it apply to the texts by Jackson and Fineman?

2. Imagine a conversation between Anil Sambare and *one* of the characters depicted in Shirley Jackson's short story "The Lottery" (e.g., Old Man Warner, Mrs. Hutchinson, Mr. Summers). What would these two people say to each other? Write down the conversation that you think they would have. Try to extend this discourse for twenty lines.

APPLICATIONS

1. A symbol is something that stands for something else. In Jackson's story, a reader may look at the lottery, the black box, or Old Man Warner as signifying something more than a literal meaning.

2. Select a work that you have already written. How might you use a symbol to represent an idea that you are discussing? What modifications must you make in your piece to accommodate your use of this symbol? Once you consider these questions, revise your essay to include your symbolic treatment of your topic.

3. When Jackson's story was first published in *The New Yorker* in 1948, she received hundreds of letters from people "who wanted to know where these lotteries were held, and whether they could go there and watch." Discuss with your group what the responses to "The Lottery" reveal about human nature. What is your response?

4. By showing how familiar the process of each event is to the townspeople involved, what are the authors implying about traditions, mass psychology, and social pressure? To what extent does your group's response to this question compare with that of other groups in your class?

5. Review the titles of the texts by Jackson and Fineman. What are your associations with a lottery or an annual bash? What images do the words evoke? How do these underscore the ironies in both titles?

The Losing Champion

RAMON MENDEZ JR.

Ramon Mendez Jr. is a former Queensborough Community College student with a passion for boxing. In his essay "The Losing Champion" Mendez Jr. not only allows the reader to get an up close and personal glimpse into what it takes to fulfill a dream of participating in competitive boxing but also shows the importance of having the right person in your corner with you.

I GREW UP LOVING THE SPORT of boxing. My father was in the 1982 Golden Gloves in New York. My uncle who now resides in Puerto Rico was also in the Golden Gloves. Both were finalist and semi-finalist in their respective weight classes. It's pretty safe to say boxing runs in the family. I didn't really grasp the sport of boxing at a young age; I mostly saw it on television or read about it in magazines. I was small and skinny and I looked like I would shatter into pieces if I was hit with a jab. I never made it public to anyone that I would like to try or even pursue boxing. I just kept the desire to box and train all bottled up inside.

I got older and still did not make any so-called "progress" in my boxing career. That is until I became friends with a couple of guys about the same age as me, who happened to be novice boxers. I saw how physically fit and defined they were, and I knew that was how I wanted to look. I didn't want to be in my thirties and have a big gut looking like I was seven months pregnant. I wanted to get my body into shape and take myself from being an average teenage boy to a better-than-average boxer. We ran four miles each morning and assisted each other with exercise techniques, each challenging one another in friendly competition. This grueling regimen lasted for a couple of months, but quickly ended when I realized they weren't in it for the same reasons I was.

They had reached a plateau they had no desire exceeding. They each had been to a place I was desperately trying to reach, and once I realized that training became something I did alone. With my iPod tied to my arm, I jogged and exercised till dusk, not stopping until the street lights came on. After continuous workouts my body began to show results. My arms, stomach and calf muscles began to define and slightly protrude outward, giving me a nice boxer's physique. Training for seven months I was a solid one-hundred-and-forty-seven-pound welterweight.

Seeing my body progress over time really put a smile on my face. I had wanted to tell my father of my newfound passion, but was afraid he would dismiss it as a teenage fling, which I would surely get over. In a way I was scared of not getting acceptance by someone who had participated in the actual sport. "Acceptance or no acceptance," I told him one night, and scrunched my face together as I impatiently waited for his response. He paused for a moment and gave a smile, a smile I couldn't quite describe even until this day.

He stared at me almost as if I was a walking mirror, a mirror in which he was seeing his younger self. He nodded his head in agreement and finally said, "Well, it took you long enough." That night we watched his old boxing tapes, and he explained each round to me second by second with his flamboyance and great enthusiasm. He bobbed his head left and right on the sofa, yelling at the referee through the television. He was re-living the experience, a point in his life he cherished dearly. From this point forward, with the help and guidance of my father, the dream and desire to box was that much closer.

He bought me a nice heavy duty punching bag and put it up in the garage. I practiced every day on my stance, my jab and my left hook. Boxing was a passion that was dormant inside of him, a passion I seemed to have awoken. He would stand beside me each session as I trained tirelessly. Once in a while I would glance over and see him throwing punches in the air as if he was hitting the bag. I remember thinking of the stories he would tell me of his amateur fights back in the day, and how he would run to the gym after desperately trying to get me to eat my baby food, a battle most parents face with toddlers. I used that as a great motivational tool to strive to accomplish what my uncle and father had. I unleashed a flurry of punches on the bag, displaying my one-two combinations and my unperfected left hook.

There I was under the supervision of a trained boxer, displaying all I had, bobbing, weaving and shifting my feet. My father made it clear that I needed to know the art of boxing first, or there would be harsh consequences in the ring. He helped me on my breathing and how to stay composed in a fight, and stressed that fighting with anger and frustration would only drain me out, costing me the fight or possible injury. Two months' training with him, the moves and techniques became second nature. Day in and day out I practiced under the scorching summer's sun. Throwing jab after jab until the sweat poured down from my face and back, there was no quitting. I had a goal, and no matter what, my mind was set on accomplishing it. I gradually moved to my father's old jump rope.

At first it was a terror to get used to and often left me with marks on my legs and back, but who said it would be easy? Like everything else I got accustomed to it and it became a breeze. My father would put on the radio and have me jump rope until a full song had finished. I can still hear the whipping sound the rope made as it sliced through the air. The days I spent in the garage brought me and my father closer together. He was passing down a family tradition that we had. The way he taught me and the ways he explained the techniques I could see in his eyes that the burning desire to box was still there.

When I entered my first qualifying match I was extremely nervous. I had butterflies in my stomach weeks before the fight even took place. I spent most of my nights tossing and turning, playing out what I thought would happen during the bout. I can remember so vividly the morning of my actual match. I was as always rudely awakened by my father's obnoxiously loud electric razor. He was getting himself ready for his son's first match, but I was not at all excited. I had doubts on winning the fight and, to be honest, I was kind of scared.

We finally made our way to the match. To see all those people there was nerve wracking but also pleasing. I had worked hard to get to this point and now I was physically there. We retired to the back room, anxiously waiting for our match to begin. I began to warm up and throw jabs freely in the air, my father watching from afar. I could hear the crowd from the long narrow hallway, cheering and yelling at the top of their lungs. For a moment I envisioned I was in an HBO pay-per-view bout, fighting for a championship belt.

Within a few minutes I was standing on the opposite side of the ring from my opponent, our eyes and body language trying to intimidate each other. The noise from the crowd slowly dimmed in my ears until it was a soft, faint muffle of whispers and cheers. Everything died out except the precise instructions my father was yelling from the sidelines. Before I knew it the bell rang and it was on. I jabbed and weaved my way through round one, and unleashed an arsenal of combos and punches in the remaining rounds. My opponent was quicker than I expected and capitalized whenever he got a chance. The fight lasted its full length, a solid three rounds.

I didn't win that fight that I trained so hard for, but I learned a great deal in the process. I realized the passion and the art one must have to succeed in such a sport. Practice makes perfect like the old saying goes, and as a learner of repetition I can assure you that saying holds more truth than we give it credit for. I realized I had a passion for boxing just as my father before me and feel fortunate to have had him in my corner when it was my turn to lace up the gloves. Hopefully, one day I will be able to pass down my knowledge and love for boxing to my children as my father did to me.

INTERPRETATIONS

1. How does Mendez's opening paragraph set the scene for his entire essay? What basic themes does he introduce that appear later in the piece?

2. Mendez writes that boxing was a family tradition. Where in the essay do you think this idea is expressed? Cite specific examples.

CORRESPONDENCES

1. Choose the Perspective (pages 269–271) that you think best sums up the spirit of Mendez's essay. Explain how the quotation relates to the narrative.
2. In the essay "Footbinding," Fairbank discusses a traditional Chinese method to increase a woman's attractiveness. Where in his essay does Mendez mention his concern with his physique? How do *you* feel about fitting into someone else's vision of what a person is supposed to look like?
3. In "Seven Days of Mourning," Yarimi writes about her experiences with a religion-based tradition. How does a tradition that is codified compare with one that is not? That is, how is the family tradition written about by Mendez similar to or different from one that is prescribed by a religion, ethnic group, or nation? Do you think that one of these types of traditions is inherently more powerful and meaningful than the other? Why or why not?

APPLICATIONS

1. Vince Lombardi, a famous professional football coach, once said, "Winning isn't everything, it's the only thing." What do you think of this quotation? How would Mendez respond to it in view of his own experiences? After you have had time to formulate your own answers to these questions, discuss your thoughts with your groupmates. What conclusions does your group come to? As a group, write a brief response to Lombardi.
2. In his narrative, Mendez describes the process he engaged in to become a boxer. Using *time* (chronological order) to organize a sequence of events and actions, he takes the reader through his first moments considering becoming a boxer, his training, and the end of his career as an active participant in the sport.

   Write a process/analysis essay where you trace your engagement in an activity. You might relate how you came to be a musician, a computer gamer, an entrepreneur, a scientist, or a chef. As you tell your story, be careful to mark time to show your progress while analyzing and explaining your personal development. If you, like Mendez, have family involvement in this area, try to include reflections that demonstrate this family tradition.

The Knowing Eye

FreeStockPhotos.com

READING IMAGES

1. What is happening in these photographs? What is familiar to you? What is unfamiliar? To what extent are you able to relate to what is depicted in each photograph?

2. What is the relationship between the setting of each photograph and the people or person in it? How has the photographer chosen to use backgrounds and foregrounds?

Lu Feng

MAKING CONNECTIONS

1. Which photograph do you think best applies to the Shirley Jackson story "The Lottery"? Explain your answer fully.

2. What kinds of traditions are depicted by these photographs? How are these types represented in the essays of this chapter?

WORDS AND IMAGES

1. What music do you think would be listened to by the dancer in the second photograph? What details in the image help you to make this determination? Try to locate an example of this music and listen to it. Next, write a description of this music that includes how it makes you feel and what it helps you to think about.

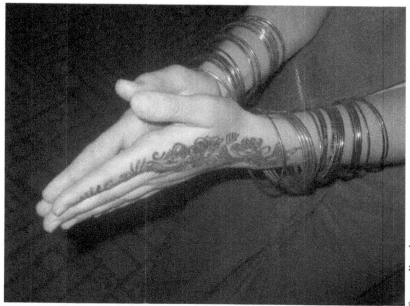

Suzanna Konecky

2. What is a sacred tradition that you or your family participate in? What is a secular tradition that you uphold? Write an essay about these traditions, how they are similar to and different from each other.

Additional Writing Topics

1. Many writers in this chapter recall aspects of their family's traditions—weddings, funerals, and religious customs. Focus on a ritual that you would like to record, and do so from a cross-generational or a cross-cultural perspective. Interview members of your family and extended family on their memories and associations. Write an account of these recollections that illustrates and explains their importance.

2. In the Cinderella tales and Fairbank's "Footbinding," various traditions (or magic powers) are used to confine women, to control them in some way(s). In every case, women escape the controls or turn them, at least in part, to their advantage. Discuss for these works the advantages and consolations that women in these cultures find even in their arduous and rigidly ordered lives. What qualities of human nature do they reveal, and are the qualities common to both men and women, or not?

3. All cultures observe holidays of national or international importance. What functions do these observances serve? Write an essay about the holidays your family celebrates and the rituals you observe. How "traditional" are these observances—and your role in them?

4. Write a journal entry on what you know about your own roots. What else would you like to discover about them? Which members of your immediate and extended family might you consult? What sources—letters, journals, family photographs—might be useful? After compiling information from these various sources, write a narrative essay on what you discovered about your origins.

5. Several writers in this chapter recall and describe a place at a moment when a major truth comes into focus for them. Recall some major awakening in your past life—love, death, religion, hatred—and then describe briefly but exactly the place where the awakening occurred so that your mood is also evident.

6. Review Erdrich's perspective on the relation between past and present. How do the texts in this chapter support her theory that "history has a way of intruding upon the present"? To what extent do you agree with her point of view?

7. According to Cesare Pavese, "We do not remember days, we remember moments." Freewrite about a moment of special significance for

you. Then expand on the memory and its importance in a fully developed essay. Why do you remember it so vividly? What do you remember? How might you best explain its effects on you?

8. Past experiences—their own or others—are important to Yarimi and Bhatia. Does the fact that each essay is about a particular culture and its traditions have any relevance to the writer's purpose? Have you had a similar experience that could be valuable to record? Before beginning, decide whether your purpose is to inform or persuade.

CHAPTER

7

Cultural Encounters

Peaceful encounters among cultures take many forms: treaties, trade, tourism, art exhibits, drama, movies, dance, student exchanges, exchange of scientific information, world fairs, conferring of awards and honors like the Nobel Prizes, sports events, musical events, conferences, emergency and other aid, cooperation in law enforcement, the United Nations. In general these encounters please, intrigue, or interest us. Variety enhances—in food, dress, language, religion, art, celebrations, government. However, as the Senegalese folktale that begins this chapter implies, there is another side to human nature, and it is bleak. People may be so fond of their vested arrangements, so afraid that change will be for the worse, that they prefer falsehood to truth. Exposure to other cultures, the sifting of truth, the juxtaposition of another's knowledge and our ignorance, for example, are sometimes more than we can stand: "Better the devil we know than the devil we don't" expresses an enduring attitude that quickly surfaces when cultures compete rather than complement. Such clashes exact a price and take various forms.

Are our encounters with people affected by our culture? Indeed they are. "The American Dream," for example, is more than a slogan adorning a T-shirt; it is a shorthand expression of a widespread belief among Americans that freedom, social justice, and improvement in material standards are desirable and possible for all. But lack of awareness of cultural differences or the assumptions of one cultural group that another is inferior often results in encounters that are patriotic power struggles. Although the United States continues to be a nation of immigrants (a recent survey reported that almost 80 percent of New York City's population is comprised of immigrants) in search of that dream, many groups have felt excluded from the right to equality promised in the Declaration of Independence of 1776. They are challenging the monocultural concept that was first expressed in Hector St. Jean de Crevecoeur's 1781 statement that "individuals of all nations are melted down in a new race of men" and which has shaped the collective consciousness of North America for almost two centuries.

In fact, several new metaphors have been offered to replace that of the melting pot. Asian American writer Bharti Mukherjee proposes that a "fusion chamber," in which elements interact but do not melt, has become more appropriate to describe the new multiracial democracy of the twenty-first century. African American novelist Toni Morrison concurs: "We have to acknowledge that the thing we call 'literature' is pluralistic now, just as society ought to be." Isabelle de Courtivron, professor of language and literature at the Massachusetts Institute of Technology, goes further in a recent article. "I think one can surely belong to a gender, a country, a language, a culture, a religion, a race,— or to several of each—without having to make consistently unilateral identifications with any of them."

Several personal encounters in this chapter involve personal and cultural reevaluations. Garrett Hongo, for example, in "Fraternity" struggles with the "punishment" and "exclusion" of racism inflicted by members of his own and another ethnic group, as well as the personal rejection of his Portuguese girlfriend. In "Passion and the Dream," Linda Stanley records how a jury in Queens, New York, had to reexamine their concepts of immigrants as well as their ideas about the American dream, and Emma Wunsch contrasts her personal and communal experiences in Brooklyn with the adjustments she made in moving to New Hampshire. Ariela Rutkin-Becker describes her personal and cultural transformations as a college student in Cairo resulting from her friendships with Mona, Mohamad, and Mahmoud.

As you read the cultural encounters in this chapter, consider how factors such as race, ethnicity, and social class have contributed to or detracted from your own position in American society. You might also consider what changes you may have to make in your own presuppositions as you forge your individual identity in the multicultural world of the twenty-first century.

Perspectives

A Sengalese poet said "In the end we will conserve only what we love. We love only what we understand, and we will understand only what we are taught." We must learn about other cultures in order to understand, in order to love, and in order to preserve our common world heritage.

—Yo-Yo Ma

The United States, by its very nature, by its very development, is the essence of diversity. It is diverse in its geography, population, institutions, technology; its social, cultural, and intellectual modes. It is a society that at its best does not consider quality to be monolithic in form or finite in quantity, or to be inherent in class. Quality in our society proceeds in large measure out of the stimulus of diverse modes of thinking and acting; out of the creativity made possible by the different ways in which we approach things; out of diversion from paths or modes hallowed by tradition.

—Arturo Madrid

Culture is that which binds men together.

—Ruth Benedict

The greatest distance between people is not space but culture.

—Jamake Highwater

People and their cultures perish in isolation, but they are born or reborn in contact with other men and women, with men and women of another culture, another creed, another race. If we do not recognize our humanity in others, we will not recognize it in ourselves.

—Carlos Fuentes

As long as you keep a person down, some part of you has to be down there to hold him down, so it means you cannot soar as you otherwise might.

—Marian Anderson

Man is an animal suspended in the webs of significance which he himself has created. I take culture to be those webs.

—Clifford Geertz

I speak to the black experience, but I am always talking about the human condition—about what we can endure, dream, fail at, and still survive.

—*Maya Angelou*

No man is an island, intire of it selfe; every man is a peece of the Continent, apart of the maine; if a Clod bee washed away by the Sea, Europe is the lesse, as well as if a Promontorie were, as well as if a Mannor of thy friends or of thine owne were; any man's death diminishes me, because I am involved in Mankinde; And therefore never send to know for whom the bell tolls; It tolls for thee.

—*John Donne*

Americans are wedded by proximity to a common culture.

—*Richard Rodriguez*

Culture regulates our lives at every turn. From the moment we are born until we die there is, whether we are conscious of it or not, constant pressure upon us to follow certain types of behavior that other men have created for us.

—*Clyde Kluckhohn*

It is a terrible, an inexorable, law that one cannot deny the humanity of another without diminishing one's own; in the face of one's victim one sees oneself.

—*James Baldwin*

Where justice is denied, where poverty is enforced, where ignorance prevails and where any one class is made to feel that society is in an organized conspiracy to oppress, rob and degrade them, neither persons nor property will be safe.

—*Frederick Douglass*

There are two ways of spreading light: to be the candle or the mirror that receives it.

—*Edith Wharton*

There is wisdom in turning as often as possible from the familiar to the unfamiliar; it keeps the mind nimble, it kills prejudice, and it fosters humor.

—*George Santayana*

We travel, initially, to lose ourselves; and we travel, next, to find ourselves.

—*Pico Iyer*

It's that same old, same old story. We all have an immigrant ancestor, one who believed in America, and who, daring or duped, took sail.

—*Fae Myeene Ng*

The alien resident mourns even as she chooses to abandon. Her memory, like her guilt and early love, is involuntary but her choice of the United States is willful.

—*Shirley Geok-lin Lim*

As social equality spreads there are more and more people who, though neither rich nor powerful enough to have much hold over others, have gained or kept enough wealth and enough understanding to look after their own needs. Such folk owe no man anything and hardly expect anything from anybody. They form the habit of thinking of themselves in isolation and imagine that their whole destiny is in their own hands.

Thus, not only does democracy make men forget their ancestors, but it also clouds their view of their descendants and isolates them from their contemporaries. Each man is forever thrown back on himself alone, and there is danger that he may be shut in the solitude of his own heart.

—*Alexis de Tocqueville*

The only way to make sure people you agree with can speak is to support the rights of people you don't agree with.

—*Eleanor Holmes Norton*

APPLICATIONS

1. Discuss Madrid's perspective on the United States. To what extent do you agree with his point of view? Consider how aspects of other cultures including food, fashion, music, or movies influence your daily life. Is it possible to appreciate multiculturalism without losing cultural identity?

2. Select two perspectives with which you disagree and, in your journal, record and analyze the reasons for your point of view.

3. The perspectives of Ng and Lim focus on aspects of the immigrant experience. Review them with your group and summarize your discussion in your journal.

The Falsehood of Truth

SENEGALESE MYTH

Senegal is a republic in western Africa that gained independence from France in 1960. Explain the paradox in the title of the Senegalese myth.

FENE-FALSEHOOD AND DEUG-TRUTH started out on a journey one day.

Fene-Falsehood said, "Everyone says that the Lord loves truth better than falsehood, so I think that you had better do all the talking for us."

Deug-Truth agreed, and when they came to a village, Deug-Truth greeted the first woman they met and asked if they could have a drink. She gave them a filthy bowl full of lukewarm water and then sat down in the doorway of her hut and began to eat a big meal of rice. While the two travelers were still there, the woman's husband came home and asked for his supper.

"It's not ready," replied the woman insolently.

The husband then turned to the two strangers who were watching and asked, "What would you say about a woman like that?"

"I would say that she is the worst wife I have seen in a long time. It's bad enough for her not to be hospitable to strangers, but it is really disgraceful when she doesn't feed her own husband," replied Deug-Truth. Fene-Falsehood didn't say a word.

The woman became furious and began to yell and scream louder than either of the two travelers had ever heard anyone scream before. "Are you going to stand by and let these strangers insult me!" she screamed to her husband. "If so, I will go home to my father and you will have to raise a bride-price for a new wife."

Then the husband, too, became angry and chased the two strangers out of town.

So Deug and Fene continued their travels and next came to a village where they found several children dividing up a bull that had just been slaughtered. They thought that this was rather strange, for it was the custom that meat was always divided by the head-man. While they were still watching, they saw the chief come up and take a very poor share of meat which the children handed him. The chief saw the two strangers and asked, "Who do you think is the leader in this village?"

Fene said nothing but Deug immediately answered, "It seems to me that these children must be the leaders of this village, for they are dividing the meat."

The chief immediately became angry and chased them out of that village.

As they continued to walk along, Fene said to Deug, "It is said that the Lord loves you the best, but I am beginning to wonder if man is not rather different from God. It seems to me that men do not like you very well. I think I will try my luck at the next village."

At the next village, they found that all the people were weeping because the favorite wife of the king had just died. Fene thought for a minute and then said, "Go tell the king that a man is here who can raise people from the dead."

Soon Fene was brought before the king and said, "I will raise your wife from the dead if you will give me half of your fortune."

The king immediately agreed and Fene had a hut built above the family grave. The king and all of the people waited outside and listened to the strange noises. First they heard huffing and panting and strange chants, but then they began to hear Fene talking loudly as if he were arguing. Finally he burst out of the door and slammed it shut—holding it tightly.

"Oh, dear," he said, "you did not tell me that your whole family was buried in there. When I woke your wife up, your father and your grandfather both came out too. I thought I had better check before I let them all out."

The king and his advisers began to look frightened, for the king's father had been a very cruel king and the new king and his friends had given his death a little assistance.

"I think you had better leave them all," said the king. "We would have a lot of trouble here with three kings."

"Well, it's not that easy," said Fene slyly. "Your father has offered me half of his property to let him out. I am certainly not going to send him back for nothing."

"I will still give you half of my property," said the desperate king. "Just get rid of them all."

So Fene received half of the king's fortune and concluded that while truth might have the favor of God, falsehood was the best way to get ahead with men.

INTERPRETATIONS

1. Are the incidents along the journey effective illustrations of the moral? To what institutions does falsehood apply? How do you respond to the choices made by the husband and the king?

2. The Senegalese myth is an allegory about abstractions like false-hood and truth. What associations do you have with myths or fables? What expectations do characters based on abstractions set up?

3. What does this fable teach about human attitudes toward absolutes like truth and falsehood? Are they relevant only to Sene-galese culture? Explain.

The Wise Rogue

JEWISH FOLKTALE AS TOLD BY MOSES GASTER

The editor of A Harvest of World Folk Tales *describes the origins of "The Wise Rogue" as follows:*

> *The keynotes of Jewish folk story are wisdom, humor, and piety, and its favorite form is the parable. It is plainly the product of a society that was in its early days priestly and in its later days persecuted. Rare are the mighty, muscular heroes (Samson was one, of course, but David against Goliath and Judith against Holofernes seem much more characteristic); nor are there any authentic fire-breathing dragons or broom-riding witches. The heroes of the Jews are wise kings, learned rabbis, or rogues who live by their wits; their dragons are the Devil and the Temptations; their witches are those who have historically oppressed them. Even their humor is of a wordly wise or satiric sort; and their sillies, the Wise Men of Helm, are not so much numskulls as absent-minded philosophers, men whose heads are filled with more than is commonly useful.*

A MAN WHO WAS ONCE CAUGHT stealing was ordered by the king to be hanged. On the way to the gallows he said to the governor that he knew a wonderful secret, and it would be a pity to allow it to die with him, and he would like to disclose it to the king. He would put a seed of a pomegranate in the ground, and through the secret taught to him by his father he would make it grow and bear fruit overnight. The thief was brought before the king, and on the morrow the king, accompanied by the high officers of state, came to the place where the thief was waiting for them. There the thief dug a hole and said, "This seed must be put in the ground only by a man who has never stolen or taken anything which did not belong to him. I being a thief cannot do it." So he turned to the vizier who, frightened, said that in his younger days he had retained something which did not belong to him. The treasurer said that in dealing with large sums he might have entered too much or too little, and even the king owned that he had kept a necklace of his father's. The thief then said, "You are all mighty and powerful and want nothing, and yet you cannot plant the seed, whilst I who have stolen a little because I was starving am to be hanged." The king, pleased with the ruse of the thief, pardoned him.

INTERPRETATIONS

1. "The king, pleased with the ruse of the thief, pardoned him." Usually people do not enjoy being tricked; what was different about this case? How would you have felt if the trick had been played on you?

2. What does this story imply about the relationship between justice and mercy?

3. What is the tone of this story? How does it affect the meaning?

CORRESPONDENCES

1. In folk literature, the trickster is the antithesis of the cultural hero, and his role is to destabilize the status quo by introducing the unexpected. How does the trickster function in both the Senegalese and the Jewish fables?

2. Review the Geertz perspective. What does it mean? How does it relate to "The Wise Rogue"? What does the story imply?

APPLICATIONS

1. The folktale, in contrast to literature, which is transmitted through written texts, is communicated orally primarily through memory and tradition. Create a folktale with your group members. Before beginning, decide on the moral you wish to communicate and think of humorous ways to include it.

2. Do you think of yourself as an idealist or a realist? An optimist or pessimist? Introvert or extrovert? Honest or dishonest? Are these categories adequate or too absolute to be accurate? Write a short essay on your attitude toward labeling.

3. What do the Senegalese and the Jewish stories suggest about success? Are rogues likely to achieve success? What examples can you think of? Discuss these questions in your group and record your conclusions.

Fraternity

GARRETT HONGO

Garrett Hongo was born in 1951 in Hawaii to Japanese-American parents and grew up in Los Angeles. He received an M.F.A. at the University of California at Irvine. Hongo's publications include Bandits Down Highway 99 *(1978), with Lawson Inada and Alan Lau;* The River of Heaven *(1988), which was the Lamont Poetry Selection of The Academy of American Poets and a finalist for the Pulitzer Prize; and* Yellow Light *(1982). His most recent book,* Volcano: A Memoir of Hawaii, *from which the following essay was excerpted, was published in 1995. Hongo told* Contemporary Authors *that a large part of his writing was "a quest for ethnic and familial roots, cultural identity and poetic inspiration." He is the recipient of numerous fellowships. He is currently professor of creative writing at the University of Oregon at Eugene. Before reading Hongo's essay, record in your journal your definition of fraternity.*

IT WAS HIGH SCHOOL IN GARDENA. I was in classes mostly with Japanese American kids—*kotonks*. Mainland Japanese, their ethnic pet name originated, during the war, with derisive Hawaiian GIs who thought of the sound of a coconut being hit with a hammer. Sansei *kotonks* were sons and daughters of the Nisei *kotonks* who had been sent off to the concentration camps during World War II. School was tepid, boring. We wanted cars, we wanted clothes, we wanted everything whites and blacks wanted to know about sex but were afraid to tell us. We "bee-essed" with the black kids in the school parking lot full of coastal fog before classes. We beat the white kids in math, in science, in typing. We ran track and elected cheerleaders. We *ruled*, we said. We were dumb, teeming with attitude and prejudice.

Bored, I took a creative writing class with an "academically mixed" bunch of students. There were Chicanos, whites, a black woman, and a troika of Japanese women who sat together on the other side of the room from me. They said nothing—*ever*—and wrote naturalistically correct *haiku*. Suddenly among boisterous non-Japanese, I enjoyed the gabbing, the bright foam of free talk that the teacher encouraged. An aging man in baggy pants that he wore with suspenders, he announced he was retiring at the end of the year and that he wanted no trouble, that he was going to read "Eee-bee White" during our hour of class every day, that we were welcome to read whatever we wanted so long as we gave him a list ahead of time, and that we could talk as much as we wanted so long as we left him alone. We could read, we could write, we could jive each other all class long. It was freedom. And I took advantage.

I sat next to a Chicano my age named Pacheco and behind a white girl a class younger than me named Regina. Behind us was a curly-headed white guy who played saxophone in the marching band. He'd been in academic classes with me, the only Caucasian among Japanese, a Korean, and a few Chinese. He was a joker, and I liked him, but usually stayed away—we didn't fraternize much across the races, though our school was supposed to be an experiment in integration.

Gardena H. S. wasn't so much a mix or blend as a mosaic. Along with a few whites and blacks, Japanese were in the tough, college-prep, "advanced placement" scholastic track. Most whites and blacks were in the regular curriculum of shop, business skills, and a minimum of academic courses. The "dumb Japs" were in there with them. And the Chicanos filled up what were called the *remedial* classes, all taught imperiously only in English, with no provision for language acquisition. We were a student body of about three thousand, and we walked edgily around each other, swaggering when we could, sliding the steel taps on our big black shoes along the concrete outdoor walkways when we wanted to attract a little attention, making a jest of our strut, a music in the rhythm of our walking. Blacks were bused in from Compton; the whites, Japanese, and Chicanos came from around the town. Girls seemed to me an ethnic group of their own too, giggling and forming social clubs, sponsoring dances, teaching some of us the steps.

Crazes of dress moved through our populations—for Chicanos: woolen Pendletons over thin undershirts and a crucifix; big low-top oxfords; khaki work trousers, starched and pressed; for the *bloods*: rayon and satin shirts in metallic "fly-ass" colors; pegged gabardine slacks; cheap moccasin-toed shoes from downtown shops in L.A.; and for us *Buddhas*: high-collar Kensingtons of pastel cloths, A-tapered "Racer" slacks, and the same moccasin shoes as the bloods, who were our brothers. It was crazy. And *inviolable*. Dress and social behavior were a code one did not break for fear of ostracism and reprisal. Bad dressers were ridiculed. Offending speakers were beaten, tripped walking into the john, and set upon by gangs. They *wailed* on you if you fucked up. A girl was nothing except pride, an ornament of some guy's crude power and expertise in negotiating the intricacies of this inner-city semiotic of cultural display and hidden violence. I did not know girls.

I talked to Regina, saying "white girl" one time. She told me not to call her that, that she was *Portuguese* if anything, that I better *know* that white people were *always* something too. From vague memories of Hawaii, I reached for the few words in *Portuguese* that I knew, I asked her about the sweet bread her mother baked, about heavy donuts fried in oil and rolled in sugar. I said *bon dea* for "good day" to her. I read the books she talked about—Steinbeck, Kesey, Salinger, and Baldwin. Her mother brought paperbacks home from the salon she worked in, putting up other women's hair—*rich* women's. We made up our reading list from books her mother knew. I wanted desperately to impress her, so I began to write poetry too, imitating some melancholy rock and country-and-western lyrics. She invited me to her house after school. It was on the way, so I walked her home. It became a practice.

Her father was a big, diabetic man from Texas. With his shirt off, he showed me how he shot himself with insulin, poking the needle under the hairy red skin on his stomach, working it over the bulge of fat around his belly. He laughed a lot and shared his beer. There were other guys over too—white guys from the football team, a Filipino, and one other Japanese guy who played left tackle. They were tough, raucous, and talked easily, excitedly. I stood alone in the front yard one day, holding a soft drink in my hand, the barbecue party going on around me. Regina and her mother were baking bread inside. No one knew exactly what was going on, and I was still trying to pretend all was casual.

I took photographs of her. We had a picnic on the coast by the lighthouse near Marineland, on the bluffs over the Pacific. It was foggy, mist upon us and the tall, droopy grasses in the field we walked through, but we made do. She wrapped herself in the blanket she'd brought for us to sit on. We were in the tall grasses of the headlands far from the coast road. She posed. I changed lenses, dropping film canisters, other things. She waved to me, unbuttoning the blouse she was wearing, her body full of a fragrance. The warm, yeasty scent of her skin smelled like bread under bronze silk.

We couldn't be seen together—not at the private, car-club-sponsored Japanese dances out in the Crenshaw District, not at the whites-dominated dances after school in the high school gym. Whites did not see Buddhas, and Buddhas did not see bloods. We were to stay with our own—*that* was the code—though we mixed some in the lunch line, in a few classes, on the football field, and in gym. We segregated ourselves.

Regina and I went to the Chicano dances in El Monte. Pacheco introduced us to them. Regina, tanned Portuguese, passed for Chicana, so long as she kept her mouth shut and her lashes long. Pacheco showed her what skirts to wear, his quick hands fluttering through the crinolines and taffetas in her closet at home. He advised me to grow a mustache and let my black hair go long in the back, to slick it down with pomade and to fluff it up in front, then seal it all in hair spray. I bought brown Pendletons and blue navy-surplus bell-bottoms. I bought hard, steel-toed shoes, We learned trots and tangos. We learned *cuecas* and polkas. We *passed, ese,* and had a good time for a couple of months.

One day, Regina got hurt. She was stopped by one of the football players at the beach. She was stepping onto a bus when he came up behind her and grabbed her arm. She tried to twist away, and the arm snapped. She crumpled. Everyone ran. She rode in a friend's car to the hospital that day and had the arm set. She didn't call me.

I heard about it after school the next day, crossing the street against the light. It was summer, and I was taking classes while Regina spent her days at the beach. I'd see her weekdays, stopping at her house on the way home. I was going to her when, just outside the gates of our school, a guy I knew taunted me with the news. He was Japanese, and it was strange to hear him say anything about Regina. I hadn't realized anyone from my crowd knew about us.

I wanted to run the rest of the way to her house. I crossed over a rise of bare earth, then down to a bedded railway—a strip line so that scrap steel and aluminum could be shipped from the switching stations and railyards downtown to steel and aeronautical factories near our school. Brown hummocks rose above eye level and masked the track of crossties, steel rails, and the long bed of gravel. I was set upon there by a troop of Japanese boys. A crowd of them encircled me, taunting, then a single gangly fellow I recognized from gym class executed most of the blows. They beat me, grinding my face in the gravel, shouting epithets like *inu* ("dog"), *cow-fucker*, and *paddy-lover*.

I've seen hand-sized reef fish, in a ritual of spawning, leave their singular lairs, gathering in smallish, excitable schools—a critical mass—and, electrified by their circling assembly, suddenly burst the cluster apart with sequences of soloing, males alternating, pouncing above the finning group, clouding the crystalline waters above the circle with a roll of milt.

All spring and summer, I'd been immune, unaware of the enmity of the crowd. I hadn't realized that, in society, humiliation is a force more powerful than love. Love does not exist in society, but only between two, or among a family. A kid from Hawaii, I had undergone no real initiation in shame or social victimization yet and maintained an arrogant season out of bounds, imagining I was exempt. It was humiliating to have been sent to Camp. The Japanese American community understood their public disgrace and lived modestly, with deep prohibitions. I was acting outside of this history. I could cross boundaries, I thought.

But I was not yet initiated into the knowledge that we Japanese were *not* like anyone else, that we lived in a community of violent shame. I paid for my naïveté with a bashing I still feel today, with cuts that healed with scars I can still run my fingers along. I can still taste the blood, remember the split skin under the mustache on my upper lip, and feel the depth of an anger that must have been *historical, tribal*, arising from fears of dissolution and diaspora.

Separated societies police their own separations. I was hated one day, and with an intensity I could not have foreseen. I was lifted by my clothes, the hands of my schoolmates at the nape of my shirt collar and the back of the waistband of my trousers, and I was hurled against the scrawny trunk of a little jacaranda tree and beaten there, fists cracking against my arms as I tried to cover my face, thumping along my sides and back, booted feet flailing at my legs. I squirmed, crawled, cried out. And I wept. Out of fear and humiliation and a psychic wounding I understand only now. I was *hated*. I was high and needed lowering. My acts were canceled. Regina was canceled. Both by our own peoples, enacting parallel vengeances of their own, taking our bodies from us.

Our trystings were over, and, later that summer, Regina simply moved away. Her father was retiring, she said, and had found a nice trailer park up by Morro Bay. She wouldn't see me before she left. I had to surprise her at a Laundromat one Saturday. She gave me a paperback book. She laughed, made light of everything, but there was a complete *fear* of me that I felt from her, deeply, one I had not felt before—at least, it had never registered. *Race*. It is an exclusion, a punishment, imposed by the group. I've felt it often since. It is a fear of *fraternity*. A fraternity that is forbidden. I wept, but let her go.

INTERPRETATIONS

1. In paragraph 1, Hongo describes his ethnic group. What portrait does he create?

2. "Gardena H. S. wasn't so much a mix or blend as a mosaic." What evidence supports his thesis?

3. "Dress and social behavior were a code one did not break for fear of ostracism and reprisal." What evidence resonates with your experiences in high school?

4. List the highlights of Hongo's relationship with Regina. Why does he devote so much space to this experience?

5. Hongo's brutal beating by his Japanese classmates was traumatic. Characterize your response to this incident.

CORRESPONDENCES

1. Review Fuentes's perspective on cultural interactions. To what extent do you agree with it? What conversation on this subject can you imagine Hongo and Fuentes sharing?

2. Review Santayana's perspective and show how Hongo's experience refutes it.

APPLICATIONS

1. Brainstorm about "fraternity." What images and associations does it evoke? What new meanings does Hongo's memoir create?

2. Discuss with your group Hongo's concept that "in society humiliation is a force more powerful than words." How does his concept of community compare to yours? Have you ever been punished for "crossing boundaries"?

3. Hongo describes race as "an exclusion," "a punishment," and a "fear of fraternity." Write an essay on your definition of race, supporting it as does Hongo with examples from your own experience.

4. In "Fraternity," Hongo tells a powerful story of his attempt to cross cultural boundaries. What story do you think Regina would tell? Create two journal entries written by Regina. Let the first one address her thoughts and feelings about culture before meeting Hongo. Direct the second entry to her thoughts and feelings after meeting him.

Passion and the Dream

LINDA STANLEY

Linda Stanley is a professor of English at Queensborough Community Col-lege in New York City, where she teaches many recent immigrants. She has a Ph.D. in comparative literature from New York University, and for many years has been interested in, and has published on, the changing responses of people in other countries to the American experience as F. Scott Fitzgerald portrays it in The Great Gatsby. *Brainstorm on your associations with Stanley's title. To what extent is it appropriate?*

RESIDENTS OF QUEENS, NEW YORK, we are on jury duty, and, as juries do, we find a lot in common. We learn early that most of us are Catholic, with a couple of Protestants and one Orthodox Jew for some variety. Almost all are college graduates (two teachers, two engineers, a copy editor, a nurse, a personnel officer, a sales manager), and each sex and age group are equally represented. Irish, English, Danish, French, German, Croatian, Cuban, Polish, Romanian, Italian, Austrian, African-American—we are representative of early, for the most part European, immigrations to Queens. With only one exception, we are at least second-generation Americans, and some of us go much further back.

Each day we spend most of our time together outside the court-room, either surrounding the table in the cramped closet of a jury room or, for at least an hour and a half each day, eating lunch together. We tell stories. Stories about childhood games, of what we were doing during the Vietnam War, of parenthood and grandparenthood, of travels, of sports and other leisure activities, of jobs, of events in the news. The stories form a fragile bond between us and keep us going for the two weeks, one day and one night of being almost constantly together.

Controversial topics, like the current trial of the four policemen accused of the Rodney King beating,[1] are treated as newstories and not as topics for discussion. Those who are Republicans are matched by an equal number of Democrats, the young men drink alcohol while the

---

[1] According to Wikipedia, Rodney King is a Black American who in 1991 "was the victim of police brutality." An incident in which the police struck King repeatedly with their batons was videotaped by a bystander and the footage of the incident was aired around the world. A resulting public outrage raised tensions between the black community and the Los Angeles Police Department. Two officers were sent to prison while two others were acquitted.

middle aged feel the need to work out, and the single women are matched by the married and so we are careful. We know all Americans do not agree, and we do not want disharmony. By their sheer existence, our stories relieve us of our discomfort at being thrust in this situation. We also find pleasure in their content, and we laugh constantly.

We find varying degrees of pleasure in discussing the case. Some object to our doing so because the judge has admonished us not to. To ignore the courtroom is impossible because, next to the stories, we have the case in common. But our discussions are tangential to the issue of guilt as we admire the appearance of the young, female assistant district attorney, express wariness about the sternness of the judge, evaluate the cut of the defendant's suits, and relive the hilarity of the account of one of the witnesses. We do not feel we are prematurely closing our own minds or those of others through these discussions.

We discover early that the ethnic makeup of this defendant, plaintiff and witnesses represents much of the current immigration to Queens. The defendant and his brother, who witnesses for him, are Egyptian; his wife is from Ecuador; another witness is from India. Only one witness, from Greece, represents an earlier nationality on the scene, but he too is a first-generation American.

We on the jury are gradually gripped by the intensity of both the defendant and his wife. At first, we feel sorry for the wife, who sobs her way through her testimony. Too, we feel annoyed when the judge points out that the defendant does not have to testify because, as he tells us, in the American system the defendant is considered innocent and need not defend himself. Rather, he explains, it is up to the prosecution to prove he is guilty. Well, we think, that seems arrogant on the part of someone with so many charges of reckless endangerment against him. Our sympathies are with his wife, the tearful wife.

But when the defendant testifies, our sympathies slowly shift. An intense and nervous man, he blinks constantly. He also weeps. When the assistant district attorney finally gets up to cross-examine him, we wonder, with surprise, how she can ever hope to destroy such agonized testimony.

The passions are what move us. We cannot be told the reasons why the alleged crime has taken place, we can be told only the facts. The truth is denied us, but we can imagine their stories. They have come from so far with so many hopes to this city, the possessors of the same brave American Dream that all immigrants to America have dreamed. We know that he went first to Italy to learn to cook Italian food, perhaps knowing that Egyptian food is not in demand in America, and has prospered, now owning a medallion cab and a house. She has left behind a mother and a sister in Ecuador whom she returns to with her three children when all is not well between her and her Egyptian. Even when she comes back to New York, she leaves the children behind where they learn Spanish, a language their father cannot speak. The command of English of this pair is not conducive to easy communication and, we think, this has perhaps complicated their difficulties.

But their passion for their children is communicated in a universal language. His tears are for the children he had not been allowed to see for nine months, hers are for the terror of his taking them one pleasant Sunday morning in May on the street outside her new home in Queens.

We know that we will have to agree that what he has done is illegal. We have also discussed with disapproval how many Latin American women leave their children behind when coming to work in New York. We are suspicious of their actions, but we are not suspicious of their passions. Despite, or perhaps because of what we hear and know of many Americans' seeming callousness towards the fate of their own children, we are gripped by what these people so freely communicate to us about their love of their "babies."

Because of the many charges against the defendant, a unanimous decision does not come easily. We are taken to a hotel to be sequestered overnight. We eat dinner together and share rooms. For the first time, we share stories of significant events and people in our lives, of parents who have died and of the distress of their deaths. Breakfast finds us valued friends.

Back in the jury room, we unanimously decide we do not want to find him guilty of all charges. Yes, he hit his wife with a meat tenderizer when she protested his taking the children and, yes, he sped through the neighborhood with the three children held only by the arms of another person in the two-seater van, but we see his face even as we deliberate, and we cannot find him guilty of reckless endangerment in the first degree. He loves those children and is not callously indifferent to their fates. We settle on reckless endangerment in the second degree as well as to the assault charge and proceed to the courtroom.

There, the verdict is read by our foreman, a religious person who feels great sympathy for the defendant. The defendant, of course, is not aware of the foreman's agony as he begins to agonize himself. He shields his face with his hand and cries. His brother, who is present, cries also. When his lawyer asks for a poll of our votes, we have difficulty concentrating as each charge is read, and we must collect our thoughts occasionally before answering. Many of us feel tears welling up in our own eyes.

In the jury room once again, we feel the intensity of the experience keenly. We are very aware that we have supported each other through a difficult time. We make plans to meet again. We ask our court officer if all juries feel such intense camaraderie, and he can think of only one.

Fifteen minutes later, we prepare to leave the courthouse for the last time. As we pass through the lobby outside the courtroom, the defendant's brother stands weeping still.

Their passion has touched us profoundly. In losing their bright new world, they have shared with us the passions of an old world that they have been unable to leave behind. We have thought of inviting the defendant and his family to our reunion. We want them to understand what has transpired during the trial, that the dream is behind us all in its raw, most innocent form but that regeneration is possible. In a way that they can probably neither understand nor appreciate, they have made it possible for us.

INTERPRETATIONS

1. Why do you think Stanley implies that members of a jury always "find a lot in common"? From your own experience, do people thrown together always discover that they share common interests? To what extent does the essay suggest that, more than most groups, serving on jury duty might heighten common bonds?

2. What do we learn about the jurors from the essay? Why do they discuss stories rather than controversial issues? To what extent do you agree that the characteristics they have in common might have been overwhelmed by their political, marital, and sexual differences?

3. "The passions are what move us." How does the author build up to this statement? To what extent might the courtroom procedure of allowing only facts pertinent to the case encourage juries to interpret for themselves the "truth" of the case and to react to emotions expressed?

4. To what extent, based on the evidence Stanley presents, do you agree with the jury's decision to settle for "reckless endangerment in the second degree"? How convincing a rationale has she built for this lesser verdict?

5. Explain the meaning of the last paragraph of the essay. What "dream" does the author refer to? Why does this dream need regeneration and how does the author think the defendant and his wife have provided it?

CORRESPONDENCES

1. To what extent does Stanley's essay support Rodriguez's perspective that "Americans are wedded by proximity to a common culture"?

2. Is Stanley's purpose to inform or persuade? Is the tone of her essay similar to that of Hongo? Explain.

APPLICATIONS

1. Discuss the effect on our national life of the language barrier between many Americans. Is there, as the author suggests, a "universal language" that permits Americans to communicate with even the most recent immigrants?

2. To what extent do you think second- and third-generation Americans are generally as sympathetic to new immigrants as this jury is? How might you have responded as a member of the jury?

3. Alienation from the mainstream is a recurrent theme in several texts in this chapter. If you are a person of color who has felt like an outsider, write an analysis of that experience. If you are Caucasian and have felt excluded in a group, analyze the causes and effects in a brief essay.

4. Who is America? Check the following Web sites to learn the composition of inhabitants of the United States. Then, compare your findings to the jury described by Stanley in her essay.

   http://factfinder.census.gov

   http://www.socccd.cc.ca.us/ref/almanac/demographics/uspop.htm

   http://quickfacts.census.gov/qfd/index.html

On Leaving New York

EMMA WUNSCH

Emma Wunsch has an M.F.A. from Brooklyn College and has published short fiction in the anthology The Best of the Bellevue Review, Lit, Fugue, Passages North, Natural Bridge, *and* The Brooklyn Review. *From 2002 to 2008, she taught composition and creative writing at Brooklyn College. She currently lives in New Hampshire with her husband and daughter.*

WHEN MY HUSBAND, Nick, called to tell me that he thought his interview at a small liberal arts college in New Hampshire had gone well, I was happy for him since he'd worked hard preparing for the interview. I went to bed soon after he called; I was six months pregnant and tired easily. But I woke at 3:00 AM with my heart pounding. My god, I thought, I'm going to have to leave Brooklyn.

I wasn't surprised when the college called a few days later with the official job offer. I couldn't imagine leaving Brooklyn, but I also knew we couldn't stay; not only were we going to have a baby, but opportunities to teach college-level photography were few and far between. Like it or not, after spending the last six years living in and loving Brooklyn, I was New Hampshire bound.

Brooklyn was the first place I'd lived as an adult where I felt at home. There were so many things I loved about the Borough of Kings: the almost frenetic energy at Juniors—*the* place to have cheesecake; the intense conversations you could have with someone you'd just met about where the best pizza really was; listening to all the Russian conversations at Brighton Beach; getting free ice cream at ten o'clock in the morning when a new ice cream shop opened; simply looking at all the people on whatever subway car I happened to be on. I had many happy, only-in-New-York memories that were based in Brooklyn. Like the time back when we were dating when Nick and I went on a really long walk to go to a Hungarian cafe. When we finally got there, we discovered there was a party going on. At first we were disappointed that we'd walked so far only to be turned away, but then we discovered that it was a birthday party for the cafe, which meant free goulash for all! Then there was seeing one of my favorite authors buying toothpaste in the local drugstore. And I'll never forget the time that Nick and I watched a man playing the trumpet while driving a bright red El Camino into the Lincoln Tunnel.

The week after Nick signed a year contract with his new college, everything about Brooklyn seemed to make me cry. Walking around our neighborhood, then deciding where to go out to dinner, made me sad because Nick had said in our new town there were just two restaurants, both with only standard American fare. Where was I going to get falafel or bi bim bop or pad see ew? The takeout menus fell out of their folder one evening and I got weepy because there was no takeout in our new town. I teared up walking to the subway because in New Hampshire, I'd have to drive. No longer would I be able to nap, read, or just zone out listening to my iPod while someone else got me where I needed to go. I felt especially sad that I'd have to leave my teaching job. For six years, I'd taught at Brooklyn College; I felt lucky to have students from right around the block in Midwood, to ones from China, Trinidad, the Ukraine, Japan, and Guyana. I kept thinking about the weekend we'd driven up to see our new town. We'd driven around the town center, referred to as The Green, dozens of times and hadn't seen anyone. I had a million friends in Brooklyn, maybe more.

At the end of August, three weeks after our daughter Georgia was born, our new family of three headed north. Life was very hard, but that was more about our baby who got up every two hours than anything specifically to do with New Hampshire. During those first few weeks I was so tired that I missed sleep more than I missed Brooklyn.

But although there wasn't a wide range of restaurants in town, there was a group for new mothers. Every Thursday, for two months, Georgia and I dutifully attended the meetings. At around six weeks, when she still wouldn't nap, it was the women there who gave me advice: "Drive to Kmart, buy the cheapest swing they have, put her in it, and crank it up. Then she'll sleep." Desperate, I took their advice and went in my new car to buy the swing. Driving home, the new swing secure in the trunk, I had to admit it was beautiful out. It was the peak of fall and I'd never seen such foliage; the enormous blue sky, the surrounding lush green mountains, and leaves that seemed like they were in Technicolor, made me feel like I was in a car commercial or movie set. Pulling into the driveway, I wondered what would have happened if I was still in Brooklyn. I'm sure I would've gotten the same advice, but it would have been nearly impossible to have both the swing and the baby on the subway. And although the leaves do change in New York, it pales in comparison to the beauty of it up here.

Although I missed the variety of shops in Brooklyn, as the weeks passed I discovered there was more going on in my town that I thought. I got my watch fixed at the local jewelry store, bought nursing tops and swaddles at the Women's Health Resource Center, strollered Georgia through the gallery/community art center, and got her birth certificate framed at the local frame/art supply store. One evening, after we'd lived in New Hampshire for several months, I thought about all I'd done that day in town, which included taking a mommy-and-me yoga class, pushing our daughter on the baby-swing on the town green, donating used clothing to the local second-hand store, depositing checks, buying a new bike helmet, and picking up tickets to see a band that was coming to play at the town's opera house. I was amazed at how much more there was here than I'd originally thought.

While I missed my old friends in Brooklyn, I met a few women through the mothers' group who eventually became new friends. Although there wasn't a ton of racial diversity in the area, I discovered that many of the people I met came from different socio-economic backgrounds and were smart, lively, and engaging. I met a high school physics teacher, an academic reference librarian, an event planner, and a woman who had worked at Planned Parenthood. These women helped me navigate the area and also clued me into activities I wouldn't have known about. Thanks to them, the three of us indulged in free ice cream cones at Dairy Day, watched ox pulling at The Old Timer's Fair, and went to a sugar shack to watch the process of turning sap into maple syrup. I was even invited to start attending Brain Exchange Meetings. Once a month a group of women from their early twenties to late sixties would meet and brainstorm about one another's problems or concerns. I had never done anything like this in Brooklyn, and I looked forward to attending the meetings each month.

Other things that I've discovered that I like about New Hampshire include: not having to wait in long lines in the bank or post office, wide, practically empty aisles in grocery stores even at peak times, the long sunsets of spring and summer, the blue winter skies, driving on the highway for miles without seeing another car, being able to make a reservation at *the* area restaurant the day before, and going to the weekly Farmer's Market on The Green during the summer and early fall.

Of course living in New Hampshire hasn't been easy. I missed having my family close by and having a lot of choices of where to shop. Winters here are really long and there were days when it was too cold to go outside and Georgia and I would get stir-crazy. During these seemingly endless afternoons, I would fantasize about moving back to New York. But I know that even in Brooklyn there would be long afternoons indoors with a fussy baby. On a trip back to New York, I really appreciated the variety of foods that were available to me, but I also discovered that it was a lot easier to pack the car with the stroller, diaper bag, and booster seat than to carry everything on the subway. I miss seeing and hearing all the different languages and races in New York, but that doesn't mean that I can't enjoy meeting new people, I might not be able to get Ethiopian food here, but I found very good sushi and Korean food just one town away.

Over the course of the last year I've learned that just because I miss New York doesn't mean I can't be happy living someplace else.

One thing won't ever change though: I will *always* be a Yankee fan and although it might be difficult, Nick and I are going to work really hard to make sure Georgia, who will probably be spending her formative years in Red Sox country, is one too.

INTERPRETATIONS

1. Characterize the tone of Wunsch's essay. Is it effective? Why or why not?

2. Is there a turning point in the essay? Where did you realize that the move to New Hampshire was not going to be as bad as she had anticipated?

3. Wunsch is careful to include many examples of the contrasts she sets up. Which did you find most effective? Least effective? Explain.

4. Wunsch chose to focus on place to discuss her conflicts about leaving New York. Given the elements of her story (leaving an enjoyable life because of a spouse's career), can you think of other conflicts—like gender roles—that she might have focused on?

5. The essay concludes with a reference to baseball, a subject she hasn't previously mentioned. Is this ending effective? Why or why not?

CORRESPONDENCES

1. Review Lawrence's perspective on place and discuss its relevance to "On Leaving New York." What new things does Wunsch discover about herself?

2. Review Santayana's perspective and discuss its relevance to Wunsch's essay. How did Wunsch "grow" as a result of moving to New Hampshire?

APPLICATIONS

1. Wunsch writes that Brooklyn was the firsr place she lived as an adult where she felt at home. Write a journal entry describing a place where you felt at home.

2. Wunsch's move turned out to be better than she first thought. Describe a move in your life that turned out to be disappointing. What did you learn from this experience?

3. Wunsch chose a series of contrasts as the framework for her essay. Describe your leaving one place for another using a different technique.

The Man I Killed

TIM O'BRIEN

Tim O'Brien was born in 1946 in Austin, Minnesota, and grew up in Wor-
thington, in the same state. He was drafted into the Vietnam War shortly
after receiving a B.A. from Macalester College. After returning from two
years in the service, O'Brien began postgraduate studies at Harvard. His war
memoir If I Die in a Combat Zone, Box Me Up and Ship Me Home *was*
named Outstanding Book of 1973 by The New York Times. *It was one of*
the earliest books about Vietnam by a combatant. The novel Going after
Cacciato *(1978), also based on O'Brien's war experiences, won the National*
Book Award. The Things They Carried *(1990, republished in 2004, from*
which the following selection is taken) is a collection of fictitious war stories,
although O'Brien gave his storyteller the name "Tim O'Brien." O'Brien's
other novels include Northern Lights *(1975),* The Nuclear Age *(1985),* In
the Lake of the Woods *(1994), which received the James Fenimore Cooper*
Prize from the American Society of Historians, and Tomcat in Love *(1998).*
His latest novel is July, July *(2002). "Ultimately what matters," O'Brien*
told an interviewer for Bookreporter.com, "is not 'fact' versus 'fiction,' but
rather the power of a good story, well told, to squeeze the reader's heart." Does
"The Man I Killed" squeeze your heart?

HIS JAW WAS IN HIS THROAT, his upper lip and teeth were gone, his one
eye was shut, his other eye was a star-shaped hole, his eyebrows were
thin and arched like a woman's, his nose was undamaged, there was a
slight tear at the lobe of one ear, his clean black hair was swept upward
into a cowlick at the rear of the skull, his forehead was lightly freckled,
his fingernails were clean, the skin at his left cheek was peeled back in
three ragged strips, his right cheek was smooth and hairless, there was
a butterfly on his chin, his neck was open to the spinal cord and the
blood there was thick and shiny and it was this wound that had killed
him. He lay face-up in the center of the trail, a slim, dead, almost dainty
young man. He had bony legs, a narrow waist, long shapely fingers.
His chest was sunken and poorly muscled—a scholar, maybe. His
wrists were the wrists of a child. He wore a black shirt, black pajama
pants, a gray ammunition belt, a gold ring on the third finger of his
right hand. His rubber sandals had been blown off. One lay beside him,
the other a few meters up the trail. He had been born, maybe, in 1946
in the village of My Khe near the central coastline of Quang Ngai

Province, where his parents farmed, and where his family had lived for several centuries, and where, during the time of the French, his father and two uncles and many neighbors had joined in the struggle for independence. He was not a Communist. He was a citizen and a soldier. In the village of My Khe, as in all of Quang Ngai, patriotic resistance had the force of tradition, which was partly the force of legend, and from his earliest boyhood the man I killed would have listened to stories about the heroic Trung sisters and Tran Hung Dao's famous rout of the Mongols and Le Loi's final victory against the Chinese at Tot Dong.[1] He would have been taught that to defend the land was a man's highest duty and highest privilege. He had accepted this. It was never open to question. Secretly, though, it also frightened him. He was not a fighter. His health was poor, his body small and frail. He liked books. He wanted someday to be a teacher of mathematics. At night, lying on his mat, he could not picture himself doing the brave things his father had done, or his uncles, or the heroes of the stories. He hoped in his heart that he would never be tested. He hoped the Americans would go away. Soon, he hoped. He kept hoping and hoping, always, even when he was asleep.

"Oh, man, you fuckin' trashed the fucker," Azar said. "You scrambled his sorry self, look at that, you *did*, you laid him out like Shredded fuckin' Wheat."

"Go away," Kiowa said.

"I'm just saying the truth. Like oatmeal."

"Go," Kiowa said.

"Okay, then, I take it back," Azar said. He started to move away, then stopped and said, "Rice Krispies, you know? On the dead test, this particular individual gets A-Plus."

Smiling at this, he shrugged and walked up the trail toward the village behind the trees.

Kiowa kneeled down.

"Just forget that crud," he said. He opened up his canteen and held it out for a while and then sighed and pulled it away. "No sweat, man. What else could you do?"

Later, Kiowa said, "I'm serious. Nothing *anybody* could do. Come on, stop staring."

The trail junction was shaded by a row of trees and tall brush. The slim young man lay with his legs in the shade. His jaw was in his throat. His one eye was shut and the other was a star-shaped hole.

Kiowa glanced at the body.

[1]The Trung sisters led a Vietnamese rebellion against Chinese rule in A.D. 40; Tran Hung Dao repelled a Mongol attack in 1287; Le Loi defeated the Chinese in 1426.

"All right, let me ask a question," he said. "You want to trade places with him? Turn it all upside down—you *want* that? I mean, be honest."

The star-shaped hole was red and yellow. The yellow part seemed to be getting wider, spreading out at the center of the star. The upper lip and gum and teeth were gone. The man's head was cocked at a wrong angle, as if loose at the neck, and the neck was wet with blood.

"Think it over," Kiowa said.

Then later he said, "Tim, it's a *war*. The guy wasn't Heidi—he had a weapon, right? It's a tough thing, for sure, but you got to cut out that staring."

Then he said, "Maybe you better lie down a minute."

Then after a long empty time he said, "Take it slow. Just go wherever the spirit takes you."

The butterfly was making its way along the young man's forehead, which was spotted with small dark freckles. The nose was undamaged. The skin on the right cheek was smooth and fine-grained and hairless. Frail-looking, delicately boned, the young man would not have wanted to be a soldier and in his heart would have feared performing badly in battle. Even as a boy growing up in the village of My Khe, he had often worried about this. He imagined covering his head and lying in a deep hole and closing his eyes and not moving until the war was over. He had no stomach for violence. He loved mathematics. His eyebrows were thin and arched like a woman's, and at school the boys sometimes teased him about how pretty he was, the arched eyebrows and long shapely fingers, and on the playground they mimicked a woman's walk and made fun of his smooth skin and his love for mathematics. The young man could not make himself fight them. He often wanted to, but he was afraid, and this increased his shame. If he could not fight little boys, he thought, how could he ever become a soldier and fight the Americans with their airplanes and helicopters and bombs? It did not seem possible. In the presence of his father and uncles, he pretended to look forward to doing his patriotic duty, which was also a privilege, but at night he prayed with his mother that the war might end soon. Beyond anything else, he was afraid of disgracing himself, and therefore his family and village. But all he could do, he thought, was wait and pray and try not to grow up too fast.

"Listen to me," Kiowa said. "You feel terrible, I know that."

Then he said, "Okay, maybe I *don't* know."

Along the trail there were small blue flowers shaped like bells. The young man's head was wrenched sideways, not quite facing the flowers, and even in the shade a single blade of sunlight sparkled against the buckle of his ammunition belt. The left cheek was peeled back in three ragged strips. The wounds at his neck had not yet clotted, which made him seem animate even in death, the blood still spreading out across his shirt.

Kiowa shook his head.

There was some silence before he said, "Stop *staring*."

The young man's fingernails were clean. There was a slight tear at the lobe of one ear, a sprinkling of blood on the forearm. He wore a gold ring on the third finger of his right hand. His chest was sunken and poorly muscled—a scholar, maybe. His life was now a constellation of possibilities. So, yes, maybe a scholar. And for years, despite his family's poverty, the man I killed would have been determined to continue his education in mathematics. The means for this were arranged, perhaps, through the village liberation cadres, and in 1964 the young man began attending classes at the university in Saigon, where he avoided politics and paid attention to the problems of calculus. He devoted himself to his studies. He spent his nights alone, wrote romantic poems in his journal, took pleasure in the grace and beauty of differential equations. The war, he knew, would finally take him, but for the time being he would not let himself think about it. He had stopped praying; instead, now, he waited. And as he waited, in his final year at the university, he fell in love with a classmate, a girl of seventeen, who one day told him that his wrists were like the wrists of a child, so small and delicate, and who admired his narrow waist and the cowlick that rose up like a bird's tail at the back of his head. She liked his quiet manner; she laughed at his freckles and bony legs. One evening, perhaps, they exchanged gold rings.

Now one eye was a star.

"You okay?" Kiowa said.

The body lay almost entirely in shade. There were gnats at the mouth, little flecks of pollen drifting above the nose. The butterfly was gone. The bleeding had stopped except for the neck wounds.

Kiowa picked up the rubber sandals, clapping off the dirt, then bent down to search the body. He found a pouch of rice, a comb, a fingernail clipper, a few soiled piasters, a snapshot of a young woman standing in front of a parked motorcycle. Kiowa placed these items in his rucksack along with the gray ammunition belt and rubber sandals.

Then he squatted down.

"I'll tell you the straight truth," he said. "The guy was dead the second he stepped on the trail. Understand me? We all had him zeroed. A good kill—weapon, ammunition, everything." Tiny beads of sweat glistened at Kiowa's forehead. His eyes moved from the sky to the dead man's body to the knuckles of his own hands. "So listen, you best pull your shit together. Can't just sit here all day."

Later he said, "Understand?"

Then he said, "Five minutes, Tim. Five more minutes and we're moving out."

The one eye did a funny twinkling trick, red to yellow. His head was wrenched sideways, as if loose at the neck, and the dead young man seemed to be staring at some distant object beyond the bell-shaped flowers along the trail. The blood at the neck had gone to a deep purplish black. Clean fingernails, clean hair—he had been a soldier for only a single day. After his years at the university, the man I killed returned with his new wife to the village of My Khe, where he enlisted as a common rifleman with the 48th Vietcong Battalion. He knew he would die quickly. He knew he would see a flash of light. He knew he would fall dead and wake up in the stories of his village and people.

Kiowa covered the body with a poncho.

"Hey, you're looking better," he said. "No doubt about it. All you needed was time—some mental R&R."

Then he said, "Man, I'm sorry."

Then later he said, "Why not talk about it?"

Then he said, "Come on, man, talk."

He was a slim, dead, almost dainty young man of about twenty. He lay with one leg bent beneath him, his jaw in his throat, his face neither expressive nor inexpressive. One eye was shut. The other was a star-shaped hole.

"Talk," Kiowa said.

INTERPRETATIONS

1. How does the opening paragraph of O'Brien's story set up the pages that follow?

2. Who are Azar and Kiowa? What do they want O'Brien to do? Why?

3. Why does O'Brien, the writer, include the paragraphs of narration in his story? What do these paragraphs tell you about Tim, the soldier?

4. What facts does the narrator of the story absolutely *know* about the man he killed? What does he *surmise*?

CORRESPONDENCES

1. To what extent do you identify with the narrators in "Fraternity" and "The Man I Killed." Explain your answer.

2. Are Hongo and O'Brien seeking to persuade or inform their readers? How would you distinguish between the tone of each text?

APPLICATIONS

1. What do you learn about war from O'Brien's story? What preconceptions about war has this story changed? Within your small discussion group, talk with your classmates about the ideas you had about war before reading this story and those you formed after reading it. Write a journal entry about what you have learned as a result of this exploration.

2. "War is hell." Do you think that this maxim is true or false? Write an essay that explores fully your response to this statement.

3. O'Brien's story seems to end unresolved. What do you think he is feeling when the story concludes? Why doesn't he say anything to Kiowa? If you found the ending to be unsatisfying, rewrite the last several paragraphs after reflecting on the previous questions. Alternatively, pick up the action after a period of three months and continue the story in a way that presents your thoughts about the previous questions.

Child of the Lot

ARIELA RUTKIN-BECKER

Ariela Rutkin-Becker's journey as a Near Eastern Studies major in college led her to Egypt for a semester abroad in Spring 2008, where she lived in an apartment with seven other American students. She hopes to return to the corner of Ibrahim Naguib and Qasr El-Ainy streets to visit Mona, Mohamad, and Mahmoud in the near future. This piece is dedicated to all children with a penchant toward irreverence, no matter what the circumstances seem to dictate. And to their mothers, who open their homes to a foreigner with a generosity that transcends time and language.

IF EGYPT IS CONSIDERED *"Umm Al-Dunya,"* Mother of the World, then Mohamad is her child. His ambiguous living situation tied with our hazy Charabic (Charades/Arabic) conversations with him helped to compound the relationship on both sides: it was a relationship, as my suitemate Caitlin put it, "shrouded in mystery." How could it not be? His parents were a mystery—he always seemed to associate with a group of older men. (These men, with the exception of one who photographed us when we were playing with Mohamad, defied the odds of aggressively commenting on our appearances and every move, and instead were quite civil in our limited exchange of pleasantries.) His day-to-day life was a mystery; our suspicion that he lived in a shack in the parking lot across the street from our apartment was confirmed only at the very end of our stay, and I am still unsure how he got to school each day, though I was assured that he was indeed in pre-kindergarten of some sort.

In our interactions, though, Mohamad handled himself in the most self-assured manner for a four-year-old, and everyone around him ate it up. He would stand—drowning and proud—in his little *gellabiya* (a simple, traditional Arab garment, worn by men primarily in the house), a seven-layer cake of dirt on every epidermal surface, a fanfare of flies following his every move, and wave to us almost every time our taxi pulled up in front of his lot. He would then run to snatch the water bottle from whichever of us *ignabeya* (foreigners) was invariably holding one at the time, and run away drinking it up with a deliberateness that made me both pity and admire him. Indeed, this brazen act was never punished by us or by his family. His general penchant toward irreverence was sporadically reprimanded—like when he would jump on the bed and punch his older brother Mahmoud—but normally ignored or entertained, like when

352

we brought over a house plant as a gift the last night for dinner and Mohamad forcefully swung it around outside in the lot, unaware of his striking similarity to an American cowboy, draining it of all its water until the plant itself practically begged for rest.

We accidentally found Mohamad's match one day in a tiger puppet. My roommate Lindsey and I had just come home from a violin perform-ance at the opera house and passed by Mohamad standing by the lot upon our return. Still dressed up in our fancy garb, we ran upstairs and quickly returned with the first of a series of gifts: a tiger puppet that had been given to Lindsey on her birthday by a friend. Mohamad, delighted, kept asking "Azay?" How? How does this work? Lindsey showed him how she put her hand inside, and when she made the mouth move, it must have seemed magical to the young boy who squealed with delight. A modern-day Pinocchio moment, happening in Cairo, Egypt. I think Mohamad's inability to manipulate the toy himself by virtue of his tiny hands—we kept telling him "I'ma enta akbar, when you are bigger, just wait, have patience!"—just made it seem that much more magical. Funny how inaccessibility can do that sometimes.

• • •

The woman whom we eventually discovered to be Mohamad's mother, Mona, came to the big city as a young woman, probably for the prospect of marrying and to live a "better life." Many nights were spent pondering that concept, whether a shack in the middle of a rural area is somehow lesser than a shack in the middle of Cairo, what opportunities if any were afforded her now that she wouldn't have had in her birth-place. She, like practically every Egyptian we met, was fascinated by technological devices. While I sat and marveled at the fact that Mona had her own mobile phone when her family was living in a shack at the side of a parking lot, Mona and Mahmoud (Mohamad was banned from this activity) would take turns experimenting with my digital camera. It fas-cinated them how my camera could take a fluid moment and turn it still.

• • •

That's what my entire experience in Cairo felt like—a fluid moment turned still. My life as an American university student halted, re-centered around a different way of being. And so it seemed with the city of Cairo itself: frenetic on the surface, but a fixed, unchanging socioeconomic land-scape for a soul in Mohamad's situation.

Someone walking down the street, for example, might stroll between two corners: one with a looming billboard of a sunglass-clad President Mubarak, proclaiming his allegiance to the tenets of Islam; the other featuring a (relatively) seductive singer, advertising her next

European-produced album. Between those two corners, our passerby might observe men in the middle of prayer, a USAID-sponsored metal detector, a rally supporting Palestinian rights, cars honking out victory cheers following a Misr soccer game, veiled women being jeered by street guards, or all of the above. That same person, having observed all of this loud, hectic action, might be oblivious to the entrenched social lines: lines which carve out Mona's position as a parking lot monitor as a rather favorable one. I wonder if Mohamad himself sees—or will see—all the activity bubbling under the surface or will only notice their ensuing trails of dust. Will he make the reverse choice of his mother and retreat from Cairo for a quieter existence one day? If he decides to remain in Cairo, will he be able to participate in any activity that is not determined by the class he was born into?

• • •

Mona served us something that resembled cow brains that last night, the night we brought over the plant. I struggled over this, knowing on the one hand that consuming red meat after eleven years of not eating it would undoubtedly leave me wretchedly ill the next day on my flight back to New York: especially this red meat, on to which Mohamad had transferred some of his fly contingency. On the other hand, I felt that denying her offer would be improper and even impossible. I would have been satisfied eating just the fava beans, which were prepared as a side dish. As I scrambled in my head for how I would explain this to Mona, I remembered how functional I once believed the word *"nabateya,"* vegetarian, would be. It was one of the first words I inquired about in Arabic class, but now I think it is only one that foreigners use.

After all, what does the average Egyptian know about the distinctions that Americans make almost subconsciously? Would the pressure of entering a grocery store in the US delight Mohamad—or would it ravage his spirit? Would he be entertained, or worryingly perplexed by this new world? Could he decode its funny-sounding language: *"double fiber honey wheat English muffins," "cage-free grade A eggs," "100% lactose free fat free ultra-pasteurized Vitamin A & D milk," "0 grams trans fat multigrain pretzel sticks," "organic free-farmed Alaskan salmon"*? Even if the four-year-old boy could understand each word literally, would he be able to comprehend the preciseness of this language when taken all together?

In Egypt, the stakes were quite different. It's not a matter of non-fertilized or fertilized turnips, anti-oxidant or extra pulp orange juice: food is literally a matter of life or death. In the short five months that I was in Egypt, twelve people were killed by desperate patrons on bread lines. By the time we were leaving, food prices had practically doubled from what they were at the time of our arrival. The average Egyptian, associating this inflation with a stagnant government, might ask the same questions Mohamad would about his tiger puppet: *"Azay?"* How is this happening? How can I get this to work? But Mohamad was satisfied with our answer to wait until he got bigger. I don't know how much longer the Egyptian people, and hungry people in every country, can wait, how much longer they can tolerate being told to wait.

• • •

That night in the lot, the complexities of the world around me came to life in a single instant as I debated about the beef. It struck me that there I was, my last night in Egypt, but this was one of my first authentically-Egyptian experiences. Mona's generosity in serving us this barely-affordable meat was derived from the purest of motives, her curiosity sincere, not a touristic design.

Given her genuineness, I still wonder if I should have made a different decision from the cost-benefit-derived one that came as the beef was, seemingly in slow-motion, set down in front of me: I would not eat Mona's meat. As I came to this guilt-ridden decision, I realized that I would have to reject the meat sneakily; Mona was not going to relent. While she went to the sink to wash off some fruit, I took a couple of small pieces of meat from the bowl, excused myself into the parking lot, and dumped them in a corner. Selfish, yes; wasteful, yes; but I could not think of another option. The morsels of beef all-too-quickly became covered by the dust of Cairo, the dust of that parking lot, and I headed back into the shack.

• • •

I asked Mona that night if Mohamad understood that I was leaving to go back to the USA. She told me yes, that he was *za'alan*, very upset. I'm still not convinced that he quite understood, but Mona gave me her phone number and my Child of the Lot gave me a kiss on the cheek and a bigger *maa'salama* than usual. Lindsey and I walked across the street to our apartment, not quite full yet.

I could have gone for some more beans.

INTERPRETATIONS

1. Rutkin-Becker uses the phrase "shrouded in mystery" to describe her relationship with Mohamad. What else do you think is "shrouded in mystery"? When answering this question, consider carefully the frames of reference (see Glossary) invoked by the various participants in the action.

2. How does Rutkin-Becker's use of description and her choice of words affect you as a reader? What particular words or phrases can you locate to support your opinion?

CORRESPONDENCES

1. In what ways does the "Falsehood of Truth" (p. 326) help to explain the narrator's actions when she is served the meat prepared by Mona? What would Deug and Fene have done?

2. In the essays by Rutkin-Becker and Wunsch (p. 342), both narrators have moved to new locales. How do their experiences in these new environments compare? Which Perspective (pp. 323–325) do you think best applies to each?

3. Examine the photograph on page 367 that was taken by Rutkin-Becker. What do you learn from it that was not evident when reading the essay? What information is enhanced? Is, as the old saying goes, a picture worth a thousand words? Explain fully your answers to these questions.

APPLICATIONS

1. Is there a food that you cannot or will not eat? Imagine that this food is being served to you by the parents of someone that you know and care about. How would you handle the situation? Write out this scene as a play, using stage directions and dialogue.

2. To better understand Mohamad one must better understand Egypt. In addition to what you have learned about this nation from the essay, how do the following Web sites affect your understanding of "Child of the Lot"? In a reading-journal entry, explain how what you learn impacts your comprehension of the piece.

   http://www.state.gov/r/pa/ei/bgn/5309.htm

   http://www.unicef.org/infobycountry/egypt_statistics.html

3. It is clear from the essay that Rutkin-Becker's experiences in Cairo were powerful. How do you think she felt on the plane ride back to the United States? Write a song or poem that you think expresses her feelings. If you choose to write a song, try to capture some of the musical flavor of the region. The following Web sites contain samples you may listen to.

   http://www.focusmm.com/egypt/eg_musmn.htm

   http://www.layalisharqmusic.co.uk/raqs_sharqi_samples.htm

Literacy Narratives

Gloria Naylor and Kenneth Woo focus on the paradoxes of language. Naylor reveals the potential of language to wound, even destroy, whereas Woo discovers finally that words can create and liberate the self. As you reflect on their experiences, think about your encounters with language in the community and in other cultures. How do their cultural and educational experiences compare with yours? When did you first realize that words have the potential to imprison and liberate the self?

What's in a Name?

GLORIA NAYLOR

Gloria Naylor was born in 1950 in New York City to parents who were share-croppers from Mississippi. She was, from her earliest years, a prodigious reader. After high school she worked as a missionary for the Jehovah's Witnesses from 1968 to 1975. After 1975 Naylor worked as a switchboard opera-tor, pursued writing, and received a B.A. from Brooklyn College in English. She was greatly influenced by black women novelists such as Toni Morrison, Zora Neale Hurston, and Alice Walker. Naylor earned an M.A. in Afro-American studies at Yale in 1983. Her first novel, The Women of Brewster Place *(1982), won a National Book Award and was adapted as a miniseries, produced by Oprah Winfrey. Naylor's other novels include:* Linden Hills *(1985),* Mama Day *(1988),* Bailey's Cafe *(1990), and* The Men of Brew-ster Place *(1998). While reading Naylor's essay, which begins with theoreti-cal remarks about language and soon turns to narrative examples, ask yourself how the two sections complement each other.*

LANGUAGE IS THE SUBJECT. It is the written form with which I've managed to keep the wolf away from the door and, in diaries, to keep my sanity. In spite of this, I consider the written word inferior to the spoken, and much of the frustration experienced by novelists is the awareness that whatever we manage to capture in even the most transcendent passages falls far short of the richness of life. Dialogue achieves its powers in the dynamics of a fleeting moment of sight, sound, smell and touch.

I'm not going to enter the debate here about whether it is language that shapes reality or vice versa. That battle is doomed to be waged whenever we seek intermittent reprieve from the chicken and egg dispute. I will simply take the position that the spoken word, like the written word, amounts to a nonsensical arrangement of sounds or letters without a consensus that assigns "meaning." And building from the meanings of what we hear, we order reality. Words themselves are innocuous; it is the consensus that gives them true power.

I remember the first time I heard the word nigger. In my third-grade class, our math tests were being passed down the rows, and as I handed the papers to a little boy in back of me, I remarked that once again he had received a much lower mark than I did. He snatched his test from me and spit out that word. Had he called me a nymphomaniac or a necrophiliac, I couldn't have been more puzzled. I didn't know what a nigger was, but I knew that whatever it meant, it was something he shouldn't have called me. This was verified when I raised my hand, and in a loud voice repeated what he had said and watched the teacher scold him for using a "bad" word. I was later to go home and ask the inevitable question that every black parent must face— "Mommy, what does 'nigger' mean?"

And what exactly did it mean? Thinking back, I realize that this could not have been the first time the word was used in my presence. I was part of a large extended family that had migrated from the rural South after World War II and formed a close-knit network that gravitated around my maternal grandparents. Their ground-floor apartment in one of the buildings they owned in Harlem was a weekend mecca for my immediate family, along with countless aunts, uncles and cousins who brought along assorted friends. It was a bustling and open house with assorted neighbors and tenants popping in and out to exchange bits of gossip, pick up an old quarrel or referee the ongoing checkers game in which my grandmother cheated shamelessly. They were all there to let down their hair and put up their feet after a week of labor in the factories, laundries and shipyards of New York.

Amid the clamor, which could reach deafening proportions—two or three conversations going on simultaneously, punctuated by the sound of a baby's crying somewhere in the back rooms or out on the street—there was still a rigid set of rules about what was said and how. Older children were sent out of the living room when it was time to get into the juicy details about "you-know-who" up on the third floor who had gone and gotten herself "p-r-e-g-n-a-n-t!" But my parents, knowing that I could spell well beyond my years, always demanded that I follow the others out to play. Beyond sexual misconduct and death, everything else was considered harmless for our young ears. And so among the anecdotes of the triumphs and disappointments in the various workings of their lives, the word nigger was used in my presence, but it was set within contexts and inflections that caused it to register in my mind as something else.

In the singular, the word was always applied to a man who had distinguished himself in some situation that brought their approval for his strength, intelligence or drive:

"Did *Johnny* really do that?"

"I'm telling you, that nigger pulled in $6,000 of overtime last year. Said he got enough for a down payment on a house."

When used with a possessive adjective by a woman—"my nigger"—it became a term of endearment for husband or boyfriend. But it could be more than just a term applied to a man. In their mouths it became the pure essence of manhood—a disembodied force that channeled their past history of struggle and present survival against the odds into a victorious statement of being: "Yeah, that old foreman found out quick enough—you don't mess with a nigger."

In the plural, it became a description of some group within the community that had overstepped the bounds of decency as my family defined it: Parents who neglected their children, a drunken couple who fought in public, people who simply refused to look for work, those with excessively dirty mouths or unkempt households were all "trifling niggers." This particular circle could forgive hard times, unemployment, the occasional bout of depression—they had gone through all of that themselves—but the unforgivable sin was a lack of self-respect.

A woman could never be a "nigger" in the singular, with its connotation of confirming worth. The noun girl was its closest equivalent in that sense, but only when used in direct address and regardless of the gender doing the addressing. "Girl" was a token of respect for a woman. The one-syllable word was drawn out to sound like three in recognition of the extra ounce of wit, nerve or daring that the woman had shown in the situation under discussion.

"G-i-r-l, stop. You mean you said that to his face?"

But if the word was used in a third-person reference or shortened so that it almost snapped out of the mouth, it always involved some element of communal disapproval. And age became an important factor in these exchanges. It was only between individuals of the same generation, or from an older person to a younger (but never the other way around), that "girl" would be considered a compliment.

I don't agree with the argument that use of the word nigger at this social stratum of the black community was an internalization of racism. The dynamics were the exact opposite: the people in my grandmother's living room took a word that whites used to signify worthlessness or degradation and rendered it impotent. Gathering there together, they transformed "nigger" to signify the varied and complex human beings they knew themselves to be. If the word was to disappear totally from the mouths of even the most liberal of white society, no one in that room was naïve enough to believe it would disappear from white minds. Meeting the word head-on, they proved it had absolutely nothing to do with the way they were determined to live their lives.

So there must have been dozens of times that the word "nigger" was spoken in front of me before I reached the third grade. But I didn't "hear" it until it was said by a small pair of lips that had already learned it could be a way to humiliate me. That was the word I went home and asked my mother about. And since she knew that I had to grow up in America, she took me in her lap and explained.

INTERPRETATIONS

1. Naylor writes that "words themselves are innocuous; it is the consensus that gives them true power." Do you agree with this position? Can you think of an example that supports it?

2. What are the effects of juxtaposing the rich multiple meanings of "nigger" in African-American culture with the derogatory label of the third grader? How does this juxtaposition support meanings being dependent upon context?

APPLICATIONS

1. Describe a time when you heard a familiar word in a new way.

2. In her opening paragraph, Naylor distinguishes between the *written* and the *spoken* word. To what extent do these different terms represent differences in *literacy*? Explain your answer.

3. What kind of literacy is the child in Naylor's narrative exposed to and forced to engage in? When was there a time in your life that you were thrown into the adult world and a new type of literacy? What kind of literacy were you confronted with? How did you begin to negotiate this new literacy?

4. What kind of literacy is being described and exemplified in paragraphs 4 through 13? As she becomes more aware of this type of literacy, what distinctions does Naylor come to understand?

Konglish

KENNETH WOO

I NEVER REALLY LIKED TO WRITE. Whenever I thought of English, or English class, there was only one word that popped into my head: essays. I always felt this feeling of nausea, "got to finish the essay by a certain date and what in the world am I supposed to write." I constantly saw myself as a science and math "buff" (majoring in computer science) and viewed English as an obstacle. I would think to myself, "why must I keep learning how to write, isn't the knowledge I already know enough to get by?" But there are a few instances in my life in which writing greatly affected my life, changing the way I perceived the art form of a brush (the pen) painting emotions on a blank white canvas (paper).

Moving from Flushing, New York to Douglaston was going to be a huge alteration in my life. Though I was only in second grade, I dreaded the thought of moving. What I feared the most was attending a new school: beady little eyes from strangers gazing at me because I was the new kid on the block. It was like those nightmares where I find myself standing naked in front of a laughing audience. The school I attended (P.S. 94) was one of the most academic achieving schools in the city, being number one or two in every imaginable category.

I remembered I had a poem to write about something that was close to your heart. I thought to myself, "I'm in the second grade, how am I supposed to write a poem?" I really thought a second grader writing a poem was outrageous. But I had no choice, and the poem was due the next day. So I sat in my miniature desk and tried to cook up something worthy since this was my first assignment at school. All of a sudden I thought about my grandfather. I had no idea what he looked like (since he died before I was born), what his favorite dish was; my grandfather was basically a stranger to me. So my pen started to dance and I called the poem, "I Wonder." I handed the poem to my teacher and waited for the poem to be marked. When the class received their poems back, I didn't receive back the piece I wrote. "Did I do something wrong? Great, what a great first impression." I never had the guts to ask her what happened to my poem, so I did what my father always said to do when in doubt: keep your lips shut. So I kept my lips shut. By the end of the class, I heard, "Ken, can you stay after school? I want to talk to you about your poem." What did I write in that poem? Was it wrong to write about my grandfather? I remembered my hands were sweating like bullets and my legs couldn't help but shake.

I approached the teacher cautiously, as if she were the enemy over the war line. I waited for my educator to shoot and assassinate my poem. "Yes, Mrs. Nazarro?" She leaned over my shivering body and said, "This is one of the best poems I ever read in my entire life. I read this piece in front of my Queens College lecture, and half the audience fell into tears. Ken, you have a gift—a gift of writing."

What my teacher said hit me like a ton of bricks. I couldn't understand what she was saying. I didn't want to write the poem, I didn't even feel like I put effort into it. But I kept all my emotions in and replied, "Thank you, Mrs. Nazarro." This was the first time I ever accomplished a writing experience, and I didn't like the feeling. I felt a sort of embarrassment, feeling "cheesed out." For some reason or another, I took this writing skill I had and shoved it deep into my soul, never seeing it again. I didn't see this ability to write until fifteen years later.

Time went by, from essays here and boring compositions there, and I finally graduated high school. When I attended SUNY Albany, I registered my classes so that I wouldn't have to take an English course for a while. After a semester, my mother decided it was time for me to go to the motherland, Korea. I didn't think much of the trip "What's the big deal?" I thought going to summer school would have been a lot more productive in using my time but I had no say. So I jumped on a 747 and twelve hours later, ended up in this strange land they called the Land of the Morning Calm.

When my feet first touched Kimpo Airport, I was stunned and in awe. I never had seen a place where everyone was Korean. It took my eyes a while to get adjusted to, and I stared at the passengers that walked by. After my gazing, I took the next train to Korea University. At this university, I had registered for two courses, Business Management and Structure of Korea, and Introduction to Korean. I was really excited about the business course, but oh no, not Korean. Thinking about having to take a Korean course reminded me of the English courses I was forced to take.

For the first couple of weeks, we only attacked the basic stuff. From vowels to consonants, I felt like I was back in kindergarten. Han-gul (the Korean alphabet) is pretty much a simple concept to follow. It's basically our alphabet but circles and slashes are the A's, B's, and C's. The challenging part of the language, like English, is the numerous vocabulary words that had to be learned. Quickly, the Han-gul dictionary became a friend. When I was in Korea, it was hard. Everyone around me talked Korean while I struggled trying to say, "Hello, my name is Kenneth Woo, and how are you doing today?"

For lunch, I would walk to the local McDonald's. I preferred to eat there more than the local native cuisine because Ronald McDonald reminded me of home. I clearly remembered the first time I stepped in, as if it happened yesterday. I attempted to read the red and yellow alien language that gawked into my eyes. "What does that say?" I stood there for an eternity trying to figure out what it said when it finally whacked me. I was staring at Big Mac, only it was in the Korean alphabet. I suddenly noticed how much trouble I was in.

There was only one thing left to do—to conquer what I didn't know. I attacked the books and studied the Korean language as if my life depended on it (at the time, my survival in the country did rely on it). From the alphabet and days of the week, to learning their way of grammatical structure, it was a challenge I did not believe I could accomplish. However after some time, I was getting the hang of the language. I knew the consonants and vowels forwards and backwards, and was able to read the whole McDonald's menu.

Attending classes wasn't a problem. Most of the students never attended because they would get so drunk and wasted the night before, still drunk when they woke up. Wednesday was a problem for me. During the other days of the week I had classes and on the weekends I stayed at a relative's house, but Wednesday was a killer. I usually stayed in my room, smoking a cigarette as each minute passed by. Then one day in my dorm room, I approached a flier that read, "Free Brush-Painting classes on Wednesday . . . Rm 101 1:00 P.M." I decided to be brave and attend the mysterious class. When I walked in, there was one thing I noticed: I was the only male. This didn't bother me at all since a couple of my classmates looked attractive but I questioned myself what I was doing there. I ended up staying and I saw a dorky, black-dressed (like the WWF wrestler Undertaker), slothful man with a clean brush. He introduced himself as Mr. Lim, Master of the Brush. I chuckled at the title and waited for my lesson. Like the Korean language class, we went over the basic brush stroking techniques and went over some of the Chinese characters. What amazed me the most was how hard it was to hold an authentic Asian character brush. The tip was wide yet pointy, short yet heavy. The proper grip of the brush is the ambitious part. It's like when a person first approaches a billiard table and has no idea how to hold the cue stick.

Following a few practices, the Master of the Brush instructed that we had to paint our name in Chinese characters with a couple of words describing ourselves. I thought about the task and had a notion to make a poem out of the assignment. So I worked on the poem and brushed it out on the thin rice paper and handed it in to Mr. Lim. He read what I wrote and stared into my eyes. He replied, "Wow, this is a great poem, simple but deep. You have a talent. Your brushstrokes are another thing, but your poetry. God . . ." I snatched my piece and responded that I had to go eat lunch. I was enraged, I had no idea why. What he said made my blood pump. I knew it was the part about me having a talent. I didn't care about my techniques as a brushpainter, I could have cared less. But how can a typical Korean-American have a gift of writing poems, it made no sense to me. Once again I was determined to keep my talent buried within myself, forever.

I walked outside and it was so humid that the sun had a hard time peeking through the smog. Sweat was pouring out my pores like Niagara Falls and I wanted to go to a cool, air-conditioned place. I went to my spot (McD's) and ordered a No. 3 combo, super-sized. I sat by the window and ate gradually. As people walked by, I would stare at them thinking about where they were going, what part of Korea they were from, if they had a romance going. Then something caught my eye. Across the street there was an elderly woman with a mid-sized shopping cart packed with things, from clothing to a rice-cooker. This was the only homeless person I had seen in my native land since my feet touched here. I was in shock, not because she was homeless, but the way people on the street treated her. They passed by, as if she were a parking meter. She would shake a noiseless cup and hear no coins rattling. I stepped outside and lit my cigarette, trying to ignore the situation. I pondered to myself, "It was none of my business."

I flicked my cigarette and at the moment two guys approached the helpless grandmother and yelled in Korean, "What a disgrace to our country. Get the fuck off my land." They laughed and walked away. From across the street I saw two little droplets of water stream down her powerless face. My gut told me to do something, so I walked over and told her that it was all right. I reached into my pockets and gave her 50,000 won (equivalent to thirty American dollars) and told her it was a token from my heart. Then like my pores from the heat, her eyes started streaming with water like a broken faucet and she kept thanking me. She then uttered out of nowhere, "Don't close your soul, leave it open and share it among other people. It's a gift." I didn't think much of what she said assuming that she was drunk. I informed her that crying and gratitude were not needed and walked away. As my feet marched down the street, I heard the words of thank you all the way to my dorm.

This situation brought the Socrates out of me. Philosophical questions started to burn my cranium. How can a country like Korea ignore the unfortunate? I decided to talk to my aunt about what had happened and she told me the naked truth. She said that even though Korea excelled from the rubbles of the Korean War, the country still has a lot to do. The country has no social security, no welfare, and doesn't care for the people who need aid the most. I thought to myself, "how can a

Third World country that turned into a First World forget about the helpless?" Then I told her what the homeless woman said to me about my soul. My aunt paused, then slowly she said, "People like that know what they are talking about. Americans might think they are crazy, but here, they are the wisest. Consider what she said and open your soul." I felt like I was in an episode of the "Twilight Zone." What in the world is everyone talking about? Is the kimchee or the rice getting to their heads? I left the question unanswered and just looked forward to touching down on Uncle Sam's land.

The plane ride was exhausting and my parents were all over me. They showered their kisses on my weak pale face, and I returned the love. I arrived home and the whole family was exhausted. The lights turned out, but I had a problem called jet lag. So I unpacked and walked around my house. I stumbled upon an old Reebok box and opened the ancient treasure chest. The cloud of dust cleared and I found ratty old papers. It was a box filled with my old school work. It had my "A" paper on World War II, the 100I received on those ridiculous spelling tests, and then "BAM." Under all the debris, I found my spirit, "I Wonder." I thought I was dreaming and pinched my arms a couple of times. It was reality, and I took the poem to a light source and read it out loud. Wow, this brought back memories. It then hit me like a freight train. This was my breath of life, my soul. What Mrs. Nazarro, Mr. Lim, the homeless grandmother, and my aunt were talking about was in this poem. My special gift is writing broken sentences into funny stanzas to express my emotions. This was my soul and my talent. I remembered what the poor grandmother said and smiled.

I woke up my mom and handed her the poem. She read the poem and her face shined. She hugged me and I left the room so she could continue her beauty sleep. I walked outside my abode and lit a cancer stick. I looked at the weak full moon and the beautiful dawn sky. I then closed my eyes, unlocked the door to my soul, and threw the key into the sun. I don't need the key. From now on, there were going to be visitors in and out reading my talent.

INTERPRETATIONS

1. Woo's narrative reflects on his journey to creativity from second grade to his second year in college. Why was he so reluctant to pursue his poetic self? What impresses you most about his journey?

2. Woo now thinks of words as being powerful enough to unlock the door to his soul. How does he explain this transformation? How do you respond to his metaphor?

APPLICATIONS

1. Imagine having the opportunity to talk with Woo. What would you ask him? What literacy experience would you share with him?

2. What kinds of literacy does the author encounter? Present specific examples from the essay to support your views.

3. Why is the homeless person presented in paragraphs 13–14 important to Woo? What kind of literacy does she represent to the author?

4. How does Woo use the concept of literacy as a theme in this essay? How do your experiences with literacy help you to understand your own life? Explain your answers fully.

The Knowing Eye

Ariela Rutkin-Becker

READING IMAGES

1. At first glance, it might be difficult to discern the cultural encounter taking place in each photograph. What specific details show the encounter? What historical knowledge is useful to help you to see the cultural encounter as it applies to each photograph?

2. How do you feel when you see these photographs? How do they register a level of emotional energy?

Amanda Stellman

MAKING CONNECTIONS

1. How do these photographs relate to ones that you have seen previously? In particular, review the images presented in "Family and Community," "Work," and "Traditions" (chapters 2, 5, and 6).

2. Which essays in this chapter seem to match these photographs best? What similarities do you notice between text and image?

Mackenzie Lawrence

WORDS AND IMAGES

1. How do you think the setting (place, time, atmosphere, mood) of each photograph is related to the cultural encounter being depicted? Freewrite your answer to this question for all three paragraphs. Next, select the photograph that you find to be most intriguing and use comparison and contrast to describe your observations. Be sure to include specific references to the phtograph.

2. If you were creating a slide show for one of these photographs, what kind of music might accompany it? Produce a story board for the slides, explaining what influenced your musical selections. Provide specific examples from your soundtrack.

Additional Writing Topics

1. As college campuses become more ethnically diverse, how might administrators, faculty, staff, and students work together to create a climate of inclusiveness that enhances educational, social, personal, and cultural encounters? Interview a cross section of the college community on this issue. What suggestions did they make? What responsibilities are they willing to assume? Write a summary of your findings for your campus or local newspaper.

2. In the context of the American Dream, analyze how Hongo and Stanley explore the themes of immigration, exile, and displacement. Take into account generational as well as cultural differences.

3. Write a visual description of a place that you know well. Use spatial order to help your reader see it as you do or once did. Decide on the spatial pattern that you wish to use before beginning. Use comparison if appropriate.

4. Write about a group you participated in recently. Analyze how the group members interact with one another. By what means do they communicate with one another? How do they handle disagreement or friction? Write an essay on what you learned about group relations.

5. Lack of awareness of cultural differences or the assumption by one cultural group that another is inferior results in interactions that are painful power struggles. Apply this thesis to any three selections in this chapter.

6. Although "the melting pot" is the traditional metaphor associated with the immigrant experience in the United States, many sociologists now believe that "the fusion chamber" is a more accurate description of current cultural interacting. Contrast the implications of both terms and, using any three essays in this chapter, justify your choice of metaphor.

7. Who are you? Create a pie chart that accurately represents your cultural heritage. When you have finished, write an essay that describes and explains your thoughts about each section of your pie.

8. To what extent do you agree that in spite of our enormous ethnic diversity and the hyphenated identity of the children of most immigrant parents, we are on the whole shaped by a common culture.

9. Review Iyer's perspective on travel and analyze its relevance to any three cultural interactions in this chapter.

8

Popular Culture

I N PREVIOUS CHAPTERS WE EXPLORED the degree to which our identities, relationships, education, and careers are influenced by the many people in our private and public worlds. In this chapter we will focus on another instrument for shaping our thoughts and behavior: popular culture. Traditionally, as we have seen, cultures are social. They inculcate human achievements, particularly those that serve the good of the people. The world of culture is a world in which values are realized and conserved. What then is popular culture? "Popular"may be defined as "in relation to the general public, the majority," and the culture it encompasses includes media images of contemporary life and culture. Popular culture is dynamic, transitory, and an initiator of change. Through sophisticated technology it introduces us to worlds far from our local communities, enlarging our perspectives of cultural realities at home and abroad. Popular culture also creates a commonality that cuts across traditional barriers of geography, language, education, economics, ethnicity, and class.

The essays in this chapter reflect aspects of popular culture you encounter daily in magazines, television, films, and music, and when you use a cell phone or computer. As you analyze each medium individually and in your groups, you will be asked to think critically about issues in contemporary culture and to develop an awareness of the extent to which the medium not only influences our ideas but often directs our daily actions, including how to "talk," what music to listen to, films to see, television programs to watch, and games to play.

The influences of film and television are all-pervasive. No consideration of the forces that have helped shape the history of the century could ignore the impact of the media. From the birth of film, movies have—among other things—documented events and informed our ideas of romantic love, physical beauty, heroism, and personal and national identity. Culturally, they have exposed us not only to subcultures and countercultures within the United States but throughout the world.

Films are the focus of two texts in this chapter. In "Why Does Wall-E Listen to Broadway Musicals?" Martín Kutnowski reflects upon the pervasive influence of movies and music to portray the poignancy of Wall-E's humanity including his deep sense of loss. Kutnowski also explores Wall-E's ability to think and feel, and juxtaposes the robot's awareness of these human traits against our own seemingly diminishing capacity to think and feel independently as we rely more on technology. In "Why We Crave Horror Movies" Stephen King discusses how movies, and in particular horror movies, allow us to feed our baser instincts without acting on them. As King explains, the audiences captivated by horror films represent all of us to a degree, as we must "keep the gators fed."

Today, new technologies compete for our attention, in our homes, at school, and in the workplace. Cell phones, BlackBerrys, iPods, electronic gaming systems, and computers have all made significant changes to the way we work and play. In "The Pleasures of the Text," Charles McGrath explores the world of text messaging, whose homophones, emoticons, and acronyms have enabled us to live and love through a cell phone keypad. In direct competition with television and movies for our leisure time, the personal computer has made possible a new venue for entertainment: the video game. John Misak, in his essay "Is That Video Game Programming You?" explores videogaming and videogamers. Questions of game content and control are central to this new medium.

Our growing dependence on technology in modern popular culture is also explored by authors Sherry Turkle and Katherine Larios. In "Too Much Technology," Larios suggests that relying on new technology as the sole source of gaining knowledge or exploring the world around us leaves only a shallow impression on both mind and memory. Turkle's essay, "Can You Hear Me Now," questions the authenticity of connecting to each other in the digital world. Does our easy ability to connect to each other instantaneously and regardless of distance increase or decrease the intimate aspect of human connectedness?

Perhaps the aspect of popular culture that has most influenced the values of the present generation is music. Tom Lee, in "A Timeless Culture," initially addresses the concept of popular culture and then extends his analysis to consider what transforms a popular work into a "classic." James Geasor ("Whatever Happened to Rock 'n' Roll?") and Todd Craig (". . . well, if you can't hold the torch . . . then why pass it . . . ?") both work with this second idea: Geasor's focus is on rock and roll music and Craig centers his attention on hip-hop. These three essays work together, and we have treated them as a mini-unit. You will find the Correspondence questions for all three readings at the end of Craig's essay.

In sum, the icons and images of popular culture pervade all aspects of contemporary culture, nationally and globally. Critical analyses of the texts in this chapter should provide catalysts for your evaluation of the issues they address, as well as their impact on your life.

Perspectives

Two out of every three adults in the United States say they fidget, fuss, take furtive glances in windows and mirrors, and study other people's reaction to the way they look. It is not overstating it to report that a solid majority of the American people are close to being obsessed with their physical appearance.

—Louis Harris

Resigning one's self to living off the table scraps of the American Century is what twentystuff culture is all about. It's about recycling anger into irony, pain into poses.

—Walter Kirn

The image is freedom, words are prison.

—Jean Luc Godard

The success of modern advertising, its penetration into every corner of American life, reflects a culture that has itself chosen illusion over reality.

—Jack Solomon

Movies are still the most seductive and powerful of artistic mediums, manipulating us with ease by a powerful combination of sound and image.

—Jessica Hagendorn

All objects, all phases of culture are alive. They have voices. They speak of their history and interrelatedness. And they are talking at once.

—Camille Paglia

I am my body.

—Marge Piercy

In America, the photographer is not simply the person who records the past but the one who invents it.

—Susan Sontag

We now have a whole culture based on the assumption that people know nothing and so anything can be said to them.

—Stephen Vizinczey

The lowest form of popular culture—lack of information, misinformation, and a contempt for the truth or the reality of most people's lives—has overrun real journalism. Today, ordinary Americans are being stuffed with garbage.

—Carl Bernstein

Piercing is a return to flesh as fashion—and a revitalized rite of passage.

—D. James Romero

It is easier to understand a nation by listening to its music than by learning its language.

—Anonymous

What's swinging in words? If a guy makes you tap your foot and if you feel it down your back, you don't have to ask anybody if that's good music or not. You can always feel it.

—Miles Davis

In the hip-hop community, it's about how real are you, or how strong can you be, and really my music just reflects me. If you can accept me, then you can accept my music.

—Nick Cannon

The thing about hip-hop is that it's from the underground, ideas from the underbelly, from people who have mostly been locked out, who have not been recognized.

—Russell Simmons

Hip-hop is supposed to uplift and create, to educate people on a larger level and to make a change.

—Doug E. Fresh

Along with the idea of romantic love, she was introduced to another—physical beauty. Probably the most destructive ideas in the history of human thought. Both originated in envy, thrived in insecurity, and ended in disillusion. In equating physical beauty with virtue, she stripped her mind, bound it, and collected self-contempt by the heap. She forgot lust and simple caring for. She regarded love as possessive mating, and romance as the goal of the spirit. It would be for her a well-spring from which she would draw the most destructive emotions, deceiving the lover and seeking to imprison the beloved, curtailing freedom in every way.

—Toni Morrison

The truest expression of a people is in its dances and its music. Bodies never lie.

—*Agnes de Mille*

Movies are not a good source of role models or heroes. It appears that the majority of today's films focus on violence and crime. Since we live in a nation where crime is the cause of many social problems that exist, I do not think that portraying criminals and violent characters as heroes is good for children. By doing this, the film industry tells the audience that violent people are admirable and that their values should be embraced. I feel there should be more positive role models in movies and on television so that young people can actually have someone to look up to who represents positive values.

—*Celeste Armenti*

If Poe were alive, he would not have to invent horror; horror would invent him.

—*Richard Wright*

APPLICATIONS

1. Review the perspectives on movies and discuss each with your group. On what issues did you agree and disagree?

2. The perspectives of Harris and Morrison focus on the preoccupation with physical beauty in contemporary American culture. To what extent do you and your group members disagree with their points of view? Compose three perspectives of your own on the topic.

3. Is piercing as important as clothing in constructing identity? Does it also make a statement about individuality or is it a reflection of conformity to current fashion trends? Discuss these issues in a short essay.

The Pleasures of the Text

CHARLES MCGRATH

Charles McGrath (b. 1947 in Boston) was deputy editor of The New Yorker *from 1974 to 1997, when he became book review editor for* The New York Times. *He is currently a writer at large for* The Times, *appearing frequently in* The New York Times Magazine, *in which the following essay was published in January 2006. McGrath received a B.A. (summa cum laude) from Yale in 1968. He is the editor of* Books of the Century: A Hundred Years of Authors, Ideas and Literature *(1998) and (with David McCormick)* The Ultimate Golf Book: A History and a Celebration of the World's Greatest Game *(2002). Before you read, make a list of the pros and cons of texting. Do you find McGrath using any of your pros or cons? Which predominate? Does the essay need updating?*

THERE USED TO BE AN AD ON SUBWAY CARS, next to the ones for bail bondsmen and hemorrhoid creams, that said: "if u cn rd ths u cn gt a gd job & mo pa." The ad was promoting a kind of stenography training that is now extinct, presumably. Who uses stenographers anymore? But the notion that there might be value in easily understood shorthand has proved to be prescient. If u cn rd these days, and, just as important, if your thumbs are nimble enough so that u cn als snd, you can conduct your entire emotional life just by transmitting and receiving messages on the screen of your cellphone. You can flirt there, arrange a date, break up and—in Malaysia at least—even get a divorce.

Shorthand contractions, along with letter-number homophones ("gr8" and "2moro," for example), emoticons (like the tiresome colon-and-parenthesis smiley face) and acronyms (like the ubiquitous "lol," for "laughing out loud"), constitute the language of text-messaging—or txt msg, to use the term that txt msgrs prefer. Text-messaging is a refinement of computer instant-messaging, which came into vogue five or six years ago. But because the typical cellphone screen can accommodate no more than 160 characters, and because the phone touchpad is far less versatile than the computer keyboard, text-messaging puts an even greater premium on concision. Here, for example, is a text-message version of "Paradise Lost" disseminated by some scholars in England: "Devl kikd outa hevn coz jelus of jesus&strts war. pd'off wiv god so corupts man (md by god) wiv apel. devi stays serpnt 4hole life&man ruind. Woe un2mnkind."

As such messages go, that one is fairly straightforward and unadorned. There is also an entire code book of acronyms and abbreviations, ranging from CWOT (complete waste of time) to DLTBBB (don't let the bedbugs bite). And emoticonography has progressed way beyond the smiley-face stage, and now includes hieroglyphics to indicate drooling, for example (:-) . . .), as well as secrecy (:X), Hitler (/.#( ) and the rose (@$);-). Keep these in mind; we'll need them later.

As with any language, efficiency isn't everything. There's also the issue of style. Among inventive users, and younger ones especially, text-messaging has taken on many of the characteristics of hip-hop, with so much of which it conveniently overlaps—in the substitution of "z" for "s," for example, "a," for "er" and "d" for "th." Like hip-hop, text-messaging is what the scholars call "performative"; it's writing that aspires to the condition of speech. And sometimes when it makes abundant use of emoticons, it strives not for clarity so much as a kind of rebus-like cleverness, in which showing off is part of the point. A text-message version of "Paradise Lost"—or of the prologue, anyway—that tries for a little more shnizzle might go like this: "Sing hvnly mewz dat on d :X mtntp inspyrd dat shephrd hu 1st tot d chozn seed in d begnin hw d hvn n erth @$);- outa chaos."

Not that there is much call for Miltonic messaging these days. To use the scholarly jargon again, text-messaging is "lateral" rather than "penetrative," and the medium encourages blandness and even mindlessness. On the Internet there are several Web sites that function as virtual Hallmark stores and offer ready-made text messages of breathtaking banality. There are even ready-made Dear John letters, enabling you to dump someone without actually speaking to him or her. Far from being considered rude, in Britain this has proved to be a particularly popular way of ending a relationship—a little more thoughtful than leaving an e-mail message but not nearly as messy as breaking up in person—and it's also catching on over here.

Compared with the rest of the world, Americans are actually laggards when it comes to text-messaging. This is partly for technical reasons. Because we don't have a single, national phone company, there are several competing and incompatible wireless technologies in use, and at the same time actual voice calls are far cheaper here than in most places, so there is less incentive for texting. But in many developing countries, mobile-phone technology has so far outstripped land-line availability that cellphones are the preferred, and sometimes the only, means of communication, and text messages are cheaper than voice ones. The most avid text-messagers are clustered in Southeast Asia, particularly in Singapore and the Philippines.

There are also cultural reasons for the spread of text-messaging elsewhere. The Chinese language is particularly well-suited to the telephone keypad, because in Mandarin the names of the numbers are also close to the sounds of certain words; to say "I love you," for example, all you have to do is press 520. (For "drop dead," it's 748.) In China, moreover, many people believe that to leave voice mail is rude, and it's a loss of face to make a call to someone important and have it answered by an underling. Text messages preserve everyone's dignity by eliminating the human voice.

This may be the universal attraction of text-messaging, in fact: it's a kind of avoidance mechanism that preserves the feeling of communication—the immediacy—without, for the most part, the burden of actual intimacy or substance. The great majority of text messages are of the "Hey, how are you, whassup?" variety, and they're sent sometimes when messenger and recipient are within speaking distance of each other—across classrooms, say, or from one row of a stadium to another. They're little electronic waves and nods that, just like real waves and nods, aren't meant to do much more than establish a connection—or disconnection, as the case may be—without getting into specifics.

"We're all wired together" is the collective message, and we'll signal again in a couple of minutes, not to say anything, probably, but just to make sure the lines are still working. The most depressing thing about the communications revolution is that when at last we have succeeded in making it possible for anyone to reach anyone else anywhere and at any time, it turns out that we really don't have much we want to say.

INTERPRETATIONS

1. According to McGrath, why do people use text messaging? Where does he state these reasons?

2. What conclusion does McGrath come to regarding text messaging? Explain why you agree or disagree with these ideas.

3. How does this essay's title, "The Pleasures of the Text," represent McGrath's viewpoint? How does the title itself represent the writer's tone?

CORRESPONDENCES

1. Review some of the literacy narratives presented previously (Alexie, page 72; Madera, page 77; Marshall, page 185; Cremona, page 195; Naylor, page 357; Woo, page 361). Which of these narratives in your opinion, is most clearly allied with, or anticipates, text-messaging? What type of literacy is recalled by text messaging (see page 10)? Explain your answers.

2. What do you think McGrath would say about interactive ("live") videogame play, where gamers communicate electronically with others as they play? How might McGrath address the form and content of the ongoing conversations?

3. How is text-messaging, as described by McGrath, an expression of popular culture? What specific arguments does Tom Lee ("A Timeless Culture") make that best apply to text messaging?

APPLICATIONS

1. Write a text message that you would send to a friend. Now write this message in formal English, perhaps embellishing the original message. Which version do you think best conveys your meaning to your audience? Explain your answer fully in an essay that makes reference to McGrath's.

2. "If u cn rd this," check out the following Web sites:

   http://www.snopes.com/language/apocryph/cambridge.asp

   http://www.bisso.com/ujg_archives/000224.html

   http://www.computeruser.com/resources/dictionary/emoticons.html

   http://www.environmental-studies.de/SIM-Card/SMS/SMS-glossary/sms-glossary.html

2a. What have you learned about literacy from these Web sites? Write down your own definition of literacy. How does your definition compare with one that you find in the dictionary?

2b. What have you learned about a human being's ability to read? How do these ideas inform your understanding of literacy? Provide specific examples from the Web sites above in your analysis essay.

3. Write (or translate) a poem or song into the language of text messaging. Add emoticons to represent your reactions to the work in appropriate places.

   Now, share your poem, including the in-text responses, with your group. How well were your groupmates able to understand your poem? Did they have reactions similar to yours in the same places as you?

   Discuss the poems submitted by all members of your group. What conclusions have you come to regarding translating in general?

Can You Hear Me Now?

SHERRY TURKLE

Sherry Turkle is Abby Rockefeller Mauzé Professor of the Social Studies of Science and Technology in the Program in Science, Technology, and Society at MIT and the founder (2001) and current director of the MIT Initiative on Technology and Self, a center of research and reflection on the evolving connections between people and artifacts. Professor Turkle received a joint doctorate in sociology and personality psychology from Harvard University and is a licensed clinical psychologist.

Professor Turkle has written numerous articles on psychoanalysis and culture and on the "subjective side" of people's relationships with technology, especially computers. She is engaged in active study of robots, digital pets, and simulated creatures, particularly those designed for children and the elderly as well as in a study of mobile cellular technologies. Profiles of Professor Turkle have appeared in such publications as The New York Times, Scientific American, *and* Wired Magazine. *She is a featured media commentator on the effects of technology for CNN, NBC, ABC, and NPR, including appearances on such programs as* Nightline *and* 20/20. *For further information about professor Turkle and links to her published works, visit the MIT Web site at http://web.mit.edu/sturkle/www/.*

Thanks to technology, people have never been more connected—or more alienated.

I HAVE TRAVELED 36 hours to a conference on robotic technology in central Japan. The grand ballroom is Wi-Fi enabled, and the speaker is using the Web for his presentation. Laptops are open, fingers are flying. But the audience is not listening. Most seem to be doing their e-mail, downloading files, surfing the Web or looking for a cartoon to illustrate an upcoming presentation. Every once in a while audience members give the speaker some attention, lowering their laptop screens in a kind of digital curtsy.

In the hallway outside the plenary session attendees are on their phones or using laptops and PDAs to check their e-mail. Clusters of people chat with each other, making dinner plans, "networking" in that old sense of the term—the sense that implies sharing a meal. But at this conference it is clear that what people mostly want from public space is to be alone with their personal networks. It is good to come together physically, but it is more important to stay tethered to the people who define one's virtual identity, the identity that counts. I think of how Freud believed in the power of communities to control and subvert us, and a psychoanalytic pun comes to mind: "virtuality and its discontents."

The phrase comes back to me months later as I interview business consultants who seem to have lost touch with their best instincts for how to maintain the bonds that make them most competitive. They are complaining about the BlackBerry revolution. They accept it as inevitable, decry it as corrosive. Consultants used to talk to one another as they waited to give presentations; now they spend that time doing e-mail. Those who once bonded during limousine rides to airports now spend this time on their BlackBerrys. Some say they are making better use of their "downtime," but they argue their point without conviction. This waiting time and going-to-the-airport time was never downtime; it was work time. It was precious time when far-flung global teams solidified relationships and refined ideas.

We live in techno-enthusiastic times, and we are most likely to celebrate our gadgets. Certainly the advertising that sells us our devices has us working from beautiful, remote locations that signal our status. We are connected, tethered, so important that our physical presence is no longer required. There is much talk of new efficiencies; we can work from anywhere and all the time. But tethered life is complex; it is helpful to measure our thrilling new networks against what they may be doing to us as people.

Here I offer five troubles that try my tethered soul.

THERE IS A NEW STATE OF THE SELF, ITSELF

By the 1990s the Internet provided spaces for the projection of self. Through online games known as Multi-User Domains, one was able to create avatars that could be deployed into virtual lives. Although the games often took the forms of medieval quests, players admitted that virtual environments owed their holding power to the opportunities they offered for exploring identity. The plain represented themselves as glamorous; the introverted could try out being bold. People built the dream houses in the virtual that they could not afford in the real. They took online jobs of responsibility. They often had relationships, partners and even "marriages" of significant emotional importance. They had lots of virtual sex.

These days it is easier for people without technical expertise to blend their real and virtual lives. In the world of Second Life, a virtual world produced by Linden Lab, you can make real money; you can run a real business. Indeed, for many who enjoy online life, it is easier to express intimacy in the virtual world than in rl, that being real life. For those who are lonely yet fearful of intimacy, online life provides environments where one can be a loner yet not alone, have the illusion of companionship without the demands of sustained, intimate friendship.

Since the late 1990s social computing has offered an opportunity to experiment with a virtual second self. Now this metaphor doesn't go far enough. Our new online intimacies create a world in which it makes sense to speak of a new state of the self, itself. "I am on my cell . . . online . . . instant messaging . . . on the Web"—these phrases suggest a new placement of the subject, wired into society through technology.

ARE WE LOSING THE TIME TO TAKE OUR TIME?

The self that grows up with multitasking and rapid response measures success by calls made, e-mails answered and messages responded to. Self-esteem is calibrated by what the technology proposes, by what it makes easy. We live a contradiction: Insisting that our world is increasingly complex, we nevertheless have created a communications culture that has decreased the time available for us to sit and think, uninterrupted. We are primed to receive a quick message to which we are expected to give a rapid response. Children growing up with this may never know another way. Their experience raises a question for us all: Are we leaving enough time to take our time on the things that matter?

We spend hours keeping up with our e-mails. One person tells me, "I look at my watch to see the time. I look at my BlackBerry to get a sense of my life." Think of the BlackBerry user watching the BlackBerry movie of his life as someone watching a movie that takes on a life of its own. People become alienated from their own experience and anxious about watching a version of their lives scrolling along faster than they can handle. They are not able to keep up with the unedited version of their lives, but they are responsible for it. People speak of BlackBerry addiction. Yet in modern life we have been made into self-disciplined souls who mind the rules, the time, our tasks. Always-on/always-on-you technology takes the job of self-monitoring to a new level.

BlackBerry users describe that sense of encroachment of the device on their time. One says, "I don't have enough time alone with my mind"; another, "I artificially make time to think." Such formulations depend on an "I" separate from the technology, a self that can put the technology aside so as to function apart from its demands. But it's in conflict with a growing reality of lives lived in the presence of screens, whether on a laptop, palmtop, cell phone or BlackBerry. We are learning to see ourselves as cyborgs, at one with our devices. To put it most starkly: To make more time means turning off our devices, disengaging from the always-on culture. But this is not a simple proposition, since our devices have become more closely coupled to our sense of our bodies and increasingly feel like extensions of our minds.

Our tethering devices provide a social and psychological Global Positioning System, a form of navigation for tethered selves. One television producer, accustomed to being linked to the world via her cell and Palm (nasdaq: PALM - news - people) handheld, revealed that for her, the Palm's inner spaces were where her self resides: "When my Palm crashed it was like a death. It was more than I could handle. I felt as though I had lost my mind."

THE TETHERED ADOLESCENT

Kids get cell phones from their parents. In return they are expected to answer their parents' calls. On the one hand this arrangement gives teenagers new freedoms. On the other they do not have the experience of being alone and having to count on themselves; there is always a parent on speed dial. This provides comfort in a dangerous world, yet there is a price to pay in the development of autonomy. There used to be a moment in the life of an urban child, usually between the ages of 12 and 14, when there was a first time to navigate the city alone. It was a rite of passage that communicated, "You are on your own and responsible. If you feel frightened, you have to experience these feelings." The cell phone tether buffers this moment; with the parents on tap, children think differently about themselves.

Adolescents naturally want to check out ideas and attitudes with peers. But when technology brings us to the point where we're used to sharing thoughts and feelings instantaneously, it can lead to a new dependence. Emotional life can move from "I have a feeling, I want to call a friend," to "I want to feel something, I need to make a call." In either case it comes at the expense of cultivating the ability to be alone and to manage and contain one's emotions.

And what of adolescence as a time of self-reflection? We communicate with instant messages, "check-in" cell calls and emoticons. All of these are meant to quickly communicate a state. They are not intended to open a dialogue about complexity of feeling. (Technological determinism has its place here: Cell calls get poor reception, are easily dropped and are optimized for texting.) The culture that grows up around the cell phone is a communications culture, but it is not necessarily a culture of self-reflection—which depends on having an emotion, experiencing it, sometimes electing to share it with another person, thinking about it differently over time. When interchanges are reduced to the shorthand of emoticon emotions, questions such as "Who am I?" and "Who are you?" are reformatted for the small screen and flattened out in the process.

VIRTUALITY AND ITS DISCONTENTS

The virtual life of Facebook or MySpace is titillating, but our fragile planet needs our action in the real. We have to worry that we may be connecting globally but relating parochially.

We have become virtuosos of self-presentation, accustomed to living our lives in public. The idea that "we're all being observed all the time anyway, so who needs privacy?" has become commonplace. Put another way, people say, "As long as I'm not doing anything wrong, who cares who's watching me?" This state of mind leaves us vulnerable to political abuse. Last June I attended the Webby Awards, an event to recognize the best and most influential Web sites. Thomas Friedman won for his argument that the Web had created a "flat" world of economic and political opportunity, a world in which a high school junior in Brooklyn competes with a peer in Bangalore. MySpace won a special commendation as the year's most pathbreaking site.

The awards took place just as the government wiretapping scandal was dominating the press. When the question of illegal eavesdropping came up, a common reaction among the gathered Weberati was to turn the issue into a nonissue. We heard, "All information is good information" and "Information wants to be free" and "If you have nothing to hide, you have nothing to fear." At a pre-awards cocktail party one Web luminary spoke animatedly about Michel Foucault's idea of the panopticon, an architectural structure of spokes of a wheel built out from a hub, used as a metaphor for how the modern state disciplines its citizens. When the panopticon serves as a model for a prison, a guard stands at its center. Since each prisoner (citizen) knows that the guard might be looking at him or her at any moment, the question of whether the guard is actually looking—or if there is a guard at all—ceases to matter. The structure itself has created its disciplined citizen. By analogy, said my conversation partner at the cocktail hour, on the Internet someone might always be watching; it doesn't matter if from time to time someone is. Foucault's discussion of the panopticon had been a critical take on disciplinary society. Here it had become a justification for the U.S. government to spy on its citizens. All around me there were nods of assent.

High school and college students give up their privacy on MySpace about everything from musical preferences to sexual hang-ups. They are not likely to be troubled by an anonymous government agency knowing whom they call or what Web sites they frequent. People become gratified by a certain public exposure; it is more validation than violation.

SPLIT ATTENTION

Contemporary professional life is rich in examples of people ignoring those they are meeting with to give priority to online others whom they consider a more relevant audience. Students do e-mail during classes; faculty members do e-mail during meetings; parents do e-mail while talking with their children; people do e-mail as they walk down the street, drive cars or have dinner with their families. Indeed, people talk on the phone, hold a face-to-face meeting and do their e-mail at the same time. Once done surreptitiously, the habit of self-splitting in different worlds is becoming normalized. Your dinner partner looks down with a quick glance and you know he is checking his BlackBerry.

"Being put on pause" is how one of my students describes the feeling of walking down the street with a friend who has just taken a call on his cell. "I mean I can't go anywhere; I can't just pull out some work. I've just been stopped in midsentence and am expected to remember, to hold the thread of the conversation until he wants to pick it up again."

Traditional telephones tied us to friends, family, colleagues from school and work and, most recently, to commercial, political and philanthropic solicitations. Things are no longer so simple. These days our devices link us to humans and to objects that represent them: answering machines, Web sites and personal pages on social networking sites. Sometimes we engage with avatars who anonymously stand in for others, enabling us to express ourselves in intimate ways to strangers, in part because we and they are able to veil who we really are. Sometimes we engage with synthetic voice-recognition protocols that simulate real people as they try to assist us with technical and administrative issues. We order food, clothes and airline tickets this way. On the Internet we interact with bots, anthropomorphic programs that converse with us about a variety of matters, from routine to romantic. In online games we are partnered with "nonplayer characters," artificial intelligences that are not linked to human players. The games require that we put our trust in these characters that can save our fictional lives in the game. It is a small jump from trusting nonplayer characters—computer programs, that is—to putting one's trust in a robotic companion.

When my daughter, Rebecca, was 14, we went to the Darwin exhibition at the American Museum of Natural History, which documents his life and thought and somewhat defensively presents the theory of evolution as the central truth that underpins contemporary biology. At the entrance are two Galápagos tortoises. One is hidden from view; the other rests in its cage, utterly still. "They could have used a robot," Rebecca remarks, thinking it a shame to bring the turtle all this way when it's just going to sit there. She is concerned for the imprisoned turtle and unmoved by its authenticity. It is Thanksgiving weekend. The line is long, the crowd frozen in place and my question, "Do you care that the turtle is alive?" is a welcome diversion. Most of the votes for the robots echo Rebecca's sentiment that, in this setting, aliveness doesn't seem worth the trouble. A 12-year-old girl is adamant: "For what the turtles do, you didn't have to have the live ones." Her father looks at her, uncomprehending: "But the point is that they are real."

When Animal Kingdom opened in Orlando, populated by breathing animals, its first visitors complained they were not as "realistic" as the animatronic creatures in other parts of Disney World. The robotic crocodiles slapped their tails and rolled their eyes; the biological ones, like the Galápagos tortoises, pretty much kept to themselves.

I ask another question of the museumgoers: "If you put in a robot instead of the live turtle, do you think people should be told that the turtle is not alive?" Not really, say several of the children. Data on "aliveness" can be shared on a "need to know" basis, for a purpose. But what are the purposes of living things?

Twenty-five years ago the Japanese realized that demography was working against them and there would never be enough young people to take care of their aging population. Instead of having foreigners take care of their elderly, they decided to build robots and put them in nursing homes. Doctors and nurses like them; so do family members of the elderly, because it is easier to leave your mom playing with a robot than to leave her staring at a wall or a TV. Very often the elderly like them, I think, mostly because they sense there are no other options. Said one woman about Aibo, Sony (nyse: SNE - news - people)'s household-entertainment robot, "It is better than a real dog. . . . It won't do dangerous things, and it won't betray you. . . . Also, it won't die suddenly and make you feel very sad."

Might such robotic arrangements even benefit the elderly and their children in the short run in a feel-good sense but be bad for us in our lives as moral beings? The answer does not depend on what computers can do today or what they are likely to be able to do in the future. It hangs on the question of what we will be like, what kind of people we are becoming as we develop very intimate relationships with our machines.

INTERPRETATIONS

1. The subtitle of Turkle's essay, "Thanks to technology, people have never been more connected—or more alienated," appears to be a contradiction in terms. If technology is allowing us to be more easily connected, how is it making us more alienated? What is your reaction to this statement? Use evidence from the text to agree or disagree with Turkle's assessment.

2. Turkle raises the issue of how much privacy we have when we are on our computers. She points out that when we connect to the digital world we may unwittingly be allowing others to infringe on our personal freedoms. For example, to what extent are you concerned that when you are on the Internet someone might always be tracking the Web sites you visit and the products you purchase? How safe do you feel when you are surfing the Internet?

APPLICATIONS

1. Sit down in a busy public place for half an hour (a mall, playground, coffee shop) and observe the kinds of communication people are engaged in. Keep track, for example, of how many people are listening to iPods, talking on cell phones, texting, or using laptops. How many people are engaged in face-to-face conversation?

   What conclusions can you draw from your notes? In a research report, write about your observations and what you think they indicate. Include additional research sections to explain the hypothesis you are testing, the procedures you followed, and the data you collected.

2. Turkle writes: "To make more time means turning off our devices, disengaging from the always-on culture."

   Now is the time for you to go "cold turkey"! For as long as you can stand to, keep away from your screen life! Remove yourself from computers, cell phones, TVs, iPods, videogames, and any other device that connects you to a world outside of yourself. Once you have cut yourself off from all external communication, create a series of journal entries that document your thoughts and feelings about this experience as well as any philosophical musings you might have about the nature of communication in your life and in the modern world. After your last entry, indicate the duration of this enterprise.

Too Much Technology?

KATHERINE LARIOS

Katherine Larios has lived in Queens, New York, her whole life and hopes to spend many more years there. She enjoys being involved on the local level and spent a decade volunteering in her community. She graduated with honors from Queens College, earning a B.A. in history, and Katherine plans to continue studying at CUNY in order to earn a graduate degree. She has worked at Queensborough Community College in New York for several years and in many capacities. Most recently she has been working as a CUNY office assistant, but she can also be found tutoring history and English.

IN THIS GLOBAL WORLD we have the ability to educate ourselves in new ways. With all of the new technologies, we have the ability to instantly reach out toward knowledge of distant places: we can take a virtual tour of the Hagia Sophia, view the Great Wall of China from space, learn various words and phrases in any language we'd like, find out the latest Paris fashions, watch the scariest Japanese horror movie, argue politics with someone in Germany and someone in Brazil simultaneously, and essentially learn anything from anywhere at any time. Is it no wonder, then, that we spend as much time with these technologies as we do, that we rely on them for everything from recreational interests to immediate information to communication? Why not? Why would we look anywhere else? It's just so easy.

The most direct consequence of our preoccupation with technology is that we can obtain huge quantities of information, among other things, with astonishing ease. Of course, we are completely comfortable with that. But if we become too comfortable, will we be prepared to handle the range of repercussions further down the road? Are we perhaps already too comfortable?

Learning is a process; one that starts with curiosity, proceeds to questions, and as information is absorbed, becomes knowledge. But information can sit in the brain for a long time, forever in some cases, without becoming knowledge, for it lacks consideration and understanding. Learning takes both time and patience.

Of course, in an Internet age when information comes quickly, what is the lag time for understanding? How complete can understanding truly be when it comes from the quick touch of a button rather than from effort or experience? Do we even bother with understanding anymore? Or do we just satisfy ourselves that we "know" something and consider that enough?

Although there is an incredible amount of information on the Internet, there is also a real disparity between the quantity and the quality of that information, and when the emphasis on quantity supersedes quality, the deeper the hollow of our thoughts. By making things effortless, we unwittingly sacrifice quality. It might seem that the end result is the same, but a process without effort changes everything. We would still have a final product, but there will be no connection to it—we might not even understand the work that we did.

Of course, learning is more than informational knowledge. Skills, including social skills, are learned. By denying ourselves the opportunities to learn through experience, we weaken our ability to make personal improvements and we also weaken our ability to improve our social skills through personal contact.

I wonder, now that we are almost completely preoccupied with electronic technologies, what other skills are falling into disuse? What other senses are being muted? As we veer off toward preferring the unnatural to the natural, it would behoove us to keep in mind that the consequences of this will also be unnatural. For example, humans have already deadened most of their sense of smell, through several factors, including the decline in our usage of the actual ability to discern objects using our sense of smell and also the masking of scents with chemicals, gaseous pollution, and perfumes. Luckily, we probably no longer need to depend on our sense of smell as much as we once did. But if we were, let's say, to get lost in the woods and had to forage for our food, we would likely starve to death. Most humans are no longer capable of detecting (or knowing) which foods are poisonous and which are edible.

Another example of an unnatural consequence is particularly evident with social interaction, which was once a vital source of human learning. In an ironic twist, we have now become so comfortable with technology that we have somehow managed to isolate ourselves from the people surrounding us. We are insulated from external reality by all of these technologies. How common is it to see a group of friends walking down the street *together*, though strangely, they seem to ignore one another? Each prefers a separate, electronic conversation via texting over a face-to-face verbal discussion.

Instant images or information can never truly replace experience, because if it is not real to us, we lose its meaning as well as any personal affiliation with that particular information. Our memories of what we learned won't be complete and we will remain disconnected from the information we've received.

This disconnection between our dependence on instant information/ communication and true understanding is dangerous, since without understanding, we risk ignorance and indifference. The ease with which a lack of understanding can lead to prejudice is real and should not be over-looked as a potential consequence. We must be on guard and preserve ourselves from this risk. We cannot assume that visiting blogs and texting people through electronic devices is the same thing as speaking to them personally. Electronic interaction hides subtleties that can be essential to understanding. Even with personal interaction, picking up subtleties is a skill that requires honing, and must be learned before we become trained enough to have it translate instinctively.

Besides, isn't learning supposed to be a challenge? It actually *has* to be a challenge; when things are too easy, we learn nothing. It just passes through us, without touching us in any way, because there is no achievement without effort. For example, professional athletes first put in a lot of strenuous work to train their bodies for endurance and agility before and during the countless hours spent practicing the skills of the game. Achievement does not come easy; it requires a prolonged and sustained struggle. If we had never learned to fall, we'd have never learned to walk.

When things become too easy for us, and when we get used to things becoming too easy, we tend to forget to try. Unfortunately, this is problematic for us on a number of levels, but has some real repercussions for the way we learn. It seems as though learning is becoming endangered as our efforts become more non-existent. As a result, our knowledge, too, becomes ghost-like.

We must all be vigilant, and make sure that we do not let our aloofness fade into indifference, or let our effort become lackadaisical. We must reach out to others and ask them about their lives, their cultures, and their perspectives. We must share our stories and experiences with them. We must tear our eyes away from our electronics every now and then and look around us. Technology is good, and we should continue to use it as a supplement. We should, however, never rely *only* on technology for our learning or our way of life. At least, we should never stop thinking and questioning, just because it has been made so easy for us to do so.

INTERPRETATIONS

1. What is your reaction to the title of the essay? What do you consider to be the advantages and/or disadvantages of having so much information readily accessible on your computer?

2.   How does Larios view the effect that technology is having on both our ability to develop social skills and stay connected to the natural world around us? Do you agree or disagree with her argument? If you agree with Larios, elaborate on her ideas by giving your own examples to further your stance on the issues. If you disagree, give specific examples of how technology is furthering our ability to develop social skills and allowing us to keep in harmony with the natural world.

CORRESPONDENCES

1.   Compare and contrast the essays by Larios and Turkle in order to gain a further understanding of how each author views the effects of technology on modern societies. In what ways do the authors agree or disagree about our growing dependence on technology? Cite examples from both texts to justify your answer.

2.   In each of their essays Turkle and Larios are making a statement about how technology is influencing popular culture yet we are not all born into the same culture. Are Turkle and Larios viewing technology and popular culture from a distinctly American or Western slant? How does your cultural experience with technology either agree or disagree with one or both writers? Explain.

APPLICATIONS

1.   As Larios suggests in her opening paragraph, "Why not" use technologies for all that they are worth? For example, young people today—and you may have experienced this yourself—typically have to learn basic mathematical facts such as multiplication tables. Many children ask, when confronted with this assignment, "Why do we have to memorize when we can just use a calculator?" Imagine yourself the parent of a child who has just asked this question. Write a letter to your child's teacher explaining your views about this subject. In your letter, try to incorporate both your experiences as a child as well as those from later life.

2.   In her essay, Larios argues that technology may affect learning. Try the following exercise.

Using a pen and paper, freewite for five minutes. (Write as quickly as you can without stopping, and write whatever comes to mind. See the glossary definition of freewriting on p. 429.) How did you experience this freewriting session? Was it easy to do or was it difficult? Were your ideas all over the place or were you focused upon one particular topic? Did you like or dislike doing the freewriting? How often did you find yourself correcting mistakes as you wrote?

Now use a computer to freewrite for five minutes. After completing this session ask yourself the questions appearing above; however, also consider how using this writing tool compares with writing by hand. Last, after carefully rereading both freewritings, consider how the *medium* that you use to write may be related to *what* you have written. Create a journal entry using either writing technology explaining what you have learned.

3. Larios writes: "Besides, isn't learning supposed to be a challenge? It actually *has* to be a challenge; when things are too easy, we learn nothing. It just passes through us, without touching us in any way, because there is no achievement without effort."

What in your life have you had to work hard at to learn? In a narrative essay tell your story of this experience, explaining carefully *what* you learned as well as *how* you learned it.

Is That Video Game Programming You?

JOHN MISAK

John Misak (b. 1970) teaches English at Queensborough Community College and the New York Institute of Technology. He has written for several gaming magazines and is an editor at Gamesworld Network. Many of his articles have focused on the impact of games on gamers and society as a whole. He is the author of four mystery novels: Soft Case, Time Stand Still, All in a Row, *and also* Death Knell, *which was published in 2007.*

THE GRAVEL UNDERFOOT crunches just a bit louder than you hoped, as you try to quietly position yourself to take out the enemy perched high on his watchpost. Crouched down alongside the barracks, you check your ammunition. With a sigh, you count four rounds for your silenced machine gun. Sure, you have over a hundred AK-47 rounds, but you might as well go and sound the security alarm instead of firing that thunderous weapon. You have to make those four rounds count. The guard seems content to stare off into space, unaware of your presence and your intention to stop his breathing permanently. A quick view in the binoculars confirms his exact position. A light breeze kicks up some dust and you use all of your willpower to hold in a cough. You feel the sweat on your hands as you raise the machine gun, recheck your aim, and squeeze off the remaining rounds in a quick burst. The gun throbs into your shoulder. Your target goes down, and you experience a satisfying thrill. Your elation is cut short, however, by the realization that you forgot about the guard in the check station. He reminds you of this by putting a few piercing rounds in your side. You're dead.

The above, on first read, may appear violent. In a time of war and fear of war, reading about machine guns and stealth kills seems out of place. Glorifying violence, even that of heroes fighting in a war, just isn't done anymore. John Wayne's dead, along with George C. Scott and Lee Marvin, and Arnold just doesn't do that sort of thing any more. Violence, and the glorification of it, seems to have crept into the background of society.

Unless you are a gamer.

That's right, the exchange above did not take place in Iraq or Afghanistan. There's a good chance something like it took place next door or in your own living room. Usually it happens on a computer screen or television. There's a lot of button mashing and gamepad fiddling, and sometimes some yelling and screaming. But, at first glance, the participants do not seem violent. Now it's gone mobile. You can kill someone with a device smaller than a paperback or even with your phone. Killing's a global business, and as it appears, business is good. Billions of dollars good. With more to come.

Maybe you've done it yourself, put a bullet in someone's digital brain. People you know have killed, and they have reveled in it. Is this technology gone too far? Not only are we killing on the screen but with today's processing power we can learn the intricacies of a high-tech weapon. We know the kickback of a .45 caliber handgun. We know the best place to aim for is not the head but the heart because it is an easier target. Information normally given out only in Basic Training or the police academy is not only readily available but known by civilians. What's more, it's not just nameless computer generated enemies on the TV screen we're killing. It's little Bobby down the block, or perhaps even a college professor from the Midwest. Either way, they have identities. They have hopes and dreams and families. And a gamer's goal is to kill them.

Gamers are being sought after with constant legislative attempts to calm down their hobby. Fists are being pounded on podiums and places like Columbine are mentioned with anger and purpose. Video game violence is spilling into real life. The line between fantasy and reality is blurred and people are dying because of it. Little Bobby is using weapons. Little Bobby knows the blast radius of a grenade. Little Bobby goes on killing rampages and loves it. His mother has drawn the line, an anti-gaming activist says with a sneer, so he can only experience killing a police officer at his friend's house. His mother won't allow *that* sort of activity to grace her widescreen TV. She has morals and strict behavioral guidelines for little Bobby.

A few months later, a group of outcast teenagers lock and load and sweep through their high school, killing everyone in their path. On their computers are violent videogames. It turns out the kids re-enacted a level from one of the games. They followed it to the letter, using all they learned in the game to kill more efficiently. No headshots here. If only they had never played these games, all of their innocent classmates would still be alive. If they never used a pipe bomb in the video game *Duke Nukem* how would they have ever known what one was? They would never have turned violent if not for the bloody images on their computer screens.

Or would they have?

Saying the games caused the killing takes a logical leap many are not willing to make. In a sense, it is a form of profiling. To say that the killers' video game habit fed their murderous rampage means that all gamers have that rampage inside waiting to come out. It means Little Bobby is a killer in waiting. It is only a matter of time.

I've been around videogames pretty much since their inception. I've played them, reviewed them for magazines, even learned a little bit about making them. My first gaming experience was playing PONG in the arcade. I then upgraded to a home system with bad graphics. It wasn't until my family bought an Apple computer that I was introduced to real gaming. The first PC game I played involved going into a dungeon and killing monsters to get to an evil wizard. The game was called *Wizardry*. I kept stats of my characters' proficiency at killing. My mother thought nothing of it, though she preferred I spend more time outside. I told her putting out the garbage covered that. So, instead of playing ball and getting tanned outside, I was pasty white and sweated over the well-being of my characters.

That game specifically developed my love of videogames. The graphics were paltry and sparse, so the entire story and action took place in my head. I imagined the dank, acrid smell of the dungeon as I led my party of characters down its entrance. I never saw a picture of my characters but I knew what they looked like. They had their own personalities. That was, wow, over twenty years ago, and I can still see them. Other games offered me the same level of imagination. Could they have helped me become a fiction writer? Writing, above all else, takes imagination. A car pinstriper once told me he couldn't find employees to do his job. When I guessed it was because he couldn't find someone with steady hands, he shook his head. "I can *teach* anyone that. It's the eye for the lines of the car that is rare." The same goes for fiction, in a way. Anyone can learn grammar and structure; imagination is the real requirement of a creative writer. These games exercised that part of my brain and strengthened it. Now, with dazzling graphics, they don't develop imagination so much. Now they help in an even tougher area, the sense of place. This is always one of the toughest things to teach a new writer. So, for me, video games didn't make a mass murderer, but instead a writer. My writing might not win any prizes, but to say it is murderous is a bit much, I think. Torturous for some, perhaps, but they have little taste in fiction I've decided.

The question that begs to be asked is, does digital violence desensitize us to real world violence? Those that argue for this say that watching explosions and gunfire make it more acceptable to our brain in real life. I disagree, and strongly. I defy someone who has experienced a real bomb blast to say that my Xbox re-creates it perfectly. (I am sure Microsoft wants us to think so.) Also, not only have I played violent video games, I watched Tom and Jerry annihilate each other on television. Rambo single-handedly took on entire armies on the silver screen when I was a kid. My cousin introduced me to the odd thrill of blowing up plastic army men with firecrackers. Mom never let me do that but I did watch in awe. I've never gotten violent with anyone. In fact, I probably got myself out of such instances more than anyone I know. I could never hunt. I could never shoot someone, even in anger. I might want to strangle the random bad driver, but that's about it. Digital violence has not affected my life. Maybe I am a rare case.

What about boys playing with army men or G.I. Joe? Last time I checked, Joe doesn't make floral arrangements or study math. No, he blows things up, and with efficiency. With millions of Joes sold over the years, I would venture to say he hasn't made someone kill. Well, I am sure there is some wacko out there who followed the murderous commands coming from his refrigerator, but let's just say I think the line here melds with sanity. Going across the mall with a machete and a rifle takes a certain lack of sanity. Thinking you are the main character from *Grand Theft Auto* and trying to shoot at police goes in the same box, the one labeled "Nuts." I hesitate to say it but it needs to be said; normal people don't do these things whether they play video games or not. And by normal, I mean functional. If you go to church in a clown suit carrying a chicken, you need not apply.

We do have to take into account that *some* people are affected. The movie *Money Train* led to the mimicking of killing a subway token clerk. A few football players from Long Island died by lying on the yellow line of a highway because they saw it done in *The Program*. Touchstone pictures and their parent company, Disney, took the scene out of the movie. Someone surely sees a correlation. Or, perhaps more correctly, someone was worried about the bottom line. Dead teenagers don't go to the movies. Neither do their parents.

Of course, along with the sanity idea comes intelligence, or the lack thereof. I don't think I need to tell anyone that plopping yourself down in the middle of a highway is stupid. If I do, then the movie or video game or television show isn't to blame. A person like that might be apt to put a plastic bag over his or her head. Call me Darwinian but this smacks of survival of the fittest. The fittest, or the smartest, don't lie down on a highway. Someone please let me know if I missed a memo on that.

A more compelling argument might be the relationship I mentioned earlier between the Columbine killers and the video game *Doom*. This is the constant mention by those people pounding their fist on the podium. They digitally killed and they killed in reality. Surely one leads to the other. Because we can't tell who is impressionable enough to make this leap, should we ban these games to save people? Would the Columbine killers have done nothing if they hadn't played the game? The answer, at best, is elusive. It becomes personal. If you play these games you want them to stick around. If you don't, there exists a dark mysterious aura around them. Video game killers *could* be a dangerous breed and the only way to protect society is to not have them get the gratification from them. Preeminently wipe out bad behavior at the earliest indication of it, a la *Minority Report*. Wait, that didn't work out too well, did it?

If we stop these violent games, in my opinion, then we need to wipe out violent movies. And, if people get ideas from movies and games, then what of the murder mysteries we read? As a mystery writer myself, one of my jobs is to think of new and creative ways for a character to get away with murder. Therefore, my novels might be informational to a murderer in training. My books, and the four or so people who read them, must go. Can't have people watching *CSI* either. Someone might learn something there. Violent cartoons? They're no good. You might have Little Bobby dropping an anvil on his brother. Anvils, though not readily available, are dangerous to kids. Somewhere, some kid has his eyes on a 100 pound anvil for his little brother. Save the whales but eliminate the anvils, *CSI*, violent movies, and whatever else might give someone an idea how to off someone.

Stated that way this all seems drastic. Most people don't want the government telling them what to do too often. People also don't want young children exposed to excessive violence. Firing a rifle in a WWII video game re-enactment is one thing. Killing police officers wantonly in *Grand Theft Auto* might be something else. Think about it the next time you are at the video game store. Did the company create a game that has violence in the storyline or are they cashing in on unnecessary violence? Right now, the government isn't making the decision for us. Tomorrow might be another story. The podium-pounders are hard at work to convince the government to get involved.

For now, the choice is ours. Keep the games out of Little Bobby's hands, sure. No kid should be able to play a game like *Grand Theft Auto* and its ilk. I question whether anyone should be able to play a game centered around killing police officers and prostitutes. If you want to make a difference, use the best power you have in our society, your wallet. Gaming is a billion dollar industry and growing. The game companies are pumping out more and more violent games. They think that's what gamers want. If you agree, buy them. If you don't, don't. This is democracy at its finest. Using your buying power is like casting a vote in the booth. The only difference is, this vote really counts. The corporate bigwigs don't rely on confusing ballots, just dollars and cents.

INTERPRETATIONS

1. After reading only the first paragraph of Misak's essay, what do you think will come next? Why do you think Misak has chosen to begin his essay in this way?

2. What is Misak's primary argument? What evidence does he supply to convince you?

3. How does Misak's choice of language help to convey his meaning and retain a reader's interest? Find five images, allusions, or descriptive details that catch your attention. Explain how you respond to each of these items.

4. What good does Misak see in video games?

CORRESPONDENCES

1. How do you think video games represent popular culture, as written about by Lee (page 401)? Explain your answer, referring to both Lee and Misak.

2. According to Misak, why do people play violent video games? How are these reasons related to why people watch horror movies, as analyzed by King (page 418)?

APPLICATIONS

1. Misak states that some people are asking the government to prevent the sale of violent video games. Do you think that censorship is the best solution to the perceived problem? Create a formal argumentation and persuasion essay that defends your position. At some point in your composing process, probably when you are satisfied that you have set down your primary arguments, review the examples and exact language you use in your essay. Review how Misak uses language and imagery in his essay.

2. Do you like to play video games? Freewrite for five minutes about your answer to this question. Next, create a list of those reasons that appear in your freewriting. What examples can you generate to support each reason in your list? Finally, select a few primary reasons and their examples as the basis for a formal essay. When you write your introduction, how might you begin with a situation that will grab a reader's interest?

3. With the members of your peer group, decide on a movie that you will all see independently over the weekend. After you view the film, write a journal entry that responds to Misak's question about video games: "Did the company create a game that has violence in the storyline or are they cashing in on unnecessary violence?"

   In your next class session, each group member should read his or her journal entry. What ideas does the group have in common? What answer might the group provide to Misak's question in relation to the film they have seen, written about, and discussed?

A Timeless Culture

TOM LEE

Tom Lee (b. 1988) is a graduate of Sewanhaka High School in Floral Park, New York. Tom enjoys playing the sax, guitar, and piano. He is majoring in music at Queens College.

POP CULTURE IS TODAY, always has been, and always will be an immense part of our lives. We are aware of its existence; we are aware of its unavoidable effect on us; we are even aware of our society's sometimes-dangerous obsession with it. All the same, pop culture remains at the acme of importance in our culture. While writing this essay, I found myself focusing on mainstream pop culture vs. the lesser-known factions of it, and debated which one is better. However, I realize now that pop culture of any type is merely a reaction to another type or a combination of two or more others. So, what purpose in society does popular culture fill?

Pop culture brings to attention or combats certain political or social issues so that, possibly, somebody with more power can do something about it. In the early nineties art world, a lot of emphasis was placed on the theme of surveillance, the idea that people were not able to do anything unobserved. In the seventies, particularly 1977, the counter culture movement reached its peak with the punk rock explosion. Punk rock had very anti-establishment morals. This was so partly because of the disgust with the awesome power of government at the time, the other part being that the people involved were the children of the baby boomers who were abandoned and lost in the mediocrity of families with a large number of children. During the sixties, rampant in the world of literature, authors would write short stories about environmental issues such as mankind's harmful effect on the Earth. For example Rachel Carson wrote *Silent Spring* to point out the pollution problem that people were causing.

Even in music earlier than the seventies, genres have been created to oppose accepted values of the time. For example, post WWII music, inversely with the animosity of the war, had a very light, happy feel to it. American songwriters like Glenn Miller and the Andrews Sisters produced happy upbeat love songs such as "Don't Sit Under the Apple Tree," and "I'll Be with You in Apple Blossom Time." This change didn't only appear in America in the later years of the big band era and swing's evolution into solo singers, but it was also evident in other countries, such as Jamaica and its birth of ska. Jamaican songwriters like Byron Lee and the Dragonnaires conceived this idea as a way to evoke unity in the world. Social issues, too, have always been addressed in popular culture. Langston Hughes, a black poet during the Harlem Renaissance, empowered black people and gave them pride despite the strong prejudices that existed at the time.

Popular culture, no matter what it is, is usually a direct commentary on an idea and has a definite beginning and a definite end. Once the idea that is being commented on is addressed, the idea is supposed to fizzle out. However, in each generation of pop culture there are always a few timeless survivors. So, what is it that makes something timeless? What is the perfectly disjunct vision that separates Toni Morrison from Stephen King; the picture-perfect image that separates Ansel Adams from the paparazzi; what is that perfect fifth that separates The Beatles and Public Enemy? Is there even one definitive reason that something will remain with us throughout history? Is it written in the stars, the decided fate of the gods, or is it simply just good publicity?

It's on the tip of your tongue, but you can't give it a name. You don't know how to explain it, but you have a sixth sense that always knows when something is going to simply fade away. Of course, pop culture, quite obviously, affects kids first and foremost. Unfortunately, this inherent sixth sense is absent in the adolescent (for those of you who thought that Hanson or 'N Sync were going to last) breathing life into the commercial industry. Not to worry, as the old saying goes "with age comes reason,"and, as the reasonable can vouch for, with reason comes clarity of judgment. The reasonable can easily distinguish a classic from a flavor of the week . . . usually. The things that become classics, I find, are the ones that create clichés. By this I mean the ones that create something so innovative and different that everybody tries to mimic it. For example Charlotte Bronte, Pablo Picasso, and even Louis Armstrong all shaped their fields of expertise and created fresh new ideas. I take depth into account as well. Have you ever heard a song, saw a painting or read a novel months or years after you had first encountered it? Have you ever seen an entire universe of underlying subtleties that you hadn't noticed; taken a new interpretation of it; or simply just relived a moment in your life that you had forgotten about? That is depth. If you have experienced depth, you've probably stumbled upon a classic.

Traditional ideas are continuously revamped. Most people, and this has always been true, attempt to recapture the past. They want it to be "like the good old days," "the way mom and pop used to do it," "classic," "retro," or "old school." Nowadays especially, it is a growing trend in clothing (the "vintage look"), music (the reintroduction of classical instruments and the use of old songs in beats), art (the modern day replications of classic works), and movies (the remakes of old movies with new directors) to re-create ideas of the past. Of course, how can we not forget VH1 reality shows which bring old pop culture idols back into the limelight and shows like "I Love the 80s" and "Best Week Ever" which talk about both past and current pop culture alike? One doesn't find it ironic that the electronic downloading of music is at its peak, and at the same time more and more people have been going to live music concerts, and, yes, vinyl records have been reintroduced into the market. Technology designed merely to mimic the object it replaces never fully manages to deliver the same impact.

Human beings seem to have this fascination with the things of the past that have become dated. It gives us a nostalgic feeling and allows us to connect with our historical roots. It is human nature to strive for the past and attempt to reinvent what we once had: it is the great themes of the past such as the permanence of nature, the eternal plight between knowledge and ignorance, or the power of human emotion, that are always seen in the timeless artists. Despite the fact that these themes are often seen as cliché, it takes a true artist to just, in the words of TV fashion personality, Tim Gunn, "make it work." The universality of these themes allows human beings from any time, any place, any nationality, or social class to connect with the pool of humanity's collective unconscious.

INTERPRETATIONS

1. Lee ends his opening paragraph with the question: "So, what purpose in society does popular culture fill?" What answers does he provide in his essay? Where are they stated?

2. What do you think Lee means by his use of the term "popular culture"? What is your definition of this term? What is the dictionary definition of it?

3. In the final paragraphs of his essay, Lee theorizes about why people are interested in popular culture. What reasons does he provide? Explain why you agree or disagree with his analysis.

APPLICATIONS

1. Lee asks in paragraph 4, "So, what is it that makes something timeless?" What movies or music groups were popular when you were younger, say between the ages of ten and thirteen? Select one

of those that you revered and write a journal entry about your memories of this film or group and how you felt about it/them at the time. (Try to get yourself back into that same mind-set you had as a young teenager!)

Sometime in the next few days, view that film or listen to the music of that group again. Write another journal entry about your feelings and reactions.

Now, in a formal essay, attempt to define "popular culture" and establish those qualities found in films or movies that last, that are timeless. Use your two journal entries to formulate your definition and your analysis.

2. Write a letter in which you try to convince a friend that a new and popular musician or actor has the stuff of stardom. Explain your reasons carefully, and provide specific details and examples.

Whatever Happened
to Rock 'n' Roll?

JAMES GEASOR

James Geasor was born in Brooklyn, New York, in 1958. After more than twenty-two years in the printing business, he decided to pursue a degree in English education. James graduated with honors from Queensborough Community College (CUNY) in 2007 and graduated cum laude from Hofstra University in 2009. He is presently pursuing his M.A. in English literature at Hofstra University. For as long as he can remember, James has had an active interest in music that embraces many genres and cultures. He has attended innumerable concerts over the last four decades, seeing live and in concert such artists as The Beatles, Isaac Stern, Peter Hammill, the Rolling Stones, The Beach Boys, Focus, the Grateful Dead, Marc-Andre Hamelin, Bob Marley, David Bowie, Murray Perahia, Billy Taylor, Nirvana, Wu-Tang Clan, John Williams, Gang of Four, Buddy Rich, Black Sabbath, Chick Corea, Linkin Park, U2, and Talking Heads. He lives in Westbury, New York, with his son, Bryan.

THE SUMMER OF 1964 was my first personal experience with rock 'n' roll. I was six years old when my father packed me and five of my siblings into the family station wagon and took us to see the Beatles at Forest Hills Tennis Stadium one late August evening. Although only a child at the time, I was raised in a home that had a steady background of music and constant chatter, with what seemed an endless parade of visiting friends and relatives. As for the concert itself, I don't recall much other than there was an awful lot of hysterical screaming and that you couldn't hear much of the music. Countless girls would rush the stage only to be bear-hugged, lifted, and carried off by an obviously beleaguered security force. Although witness to a phenomenon that would only grow larger in the ensuing years, I didn't come to appreciate until much later that by the end of the decade the Beatles, and a few other up and coming rock bands, would change the face of popular culture in the Western Hemisphere. And change popular culture not only in music, but in fashion, art, political awareness, and attitude. By the late 1960s, the Civil Rights Movement and Vietnam War had become signposts for the maelstrom of youthful discontent, and the music of that generation would become the voice that helped them articulate their fears and concerns about their future and the future of the American psyche.

Between 1963 and 1970, the year they disbanded, the Beatles had released more than fifteen studio albums, many of which sold in the millions. But I'm not writing this in praise of the prolific songwriting talents of John Lennon and Paul McCartney. Rather, I wish to point out that the Beatles were one of the first musical groups who wrote songs about social issues and the human condition, and in doing so would create an intimate relationship with their audience. This artist and listener relationship was something that other rock groups would begin to emulate. In a sense they charted the course that many other groups would follow. Bands like the Grateful Dead, the Rolling Stones, and the Who would have long careers that their fans could follow along with, and it would create an intimacy which would allow their fans to grow with them. This feeling of belonging to something progressive and meaningful helped create a culture that hitherto was missing from the popular music scene. The admiration went as far as copying their hair styles, clothing, social discourse, and attitude.

But the prior mentioned break-up of the Beatles brought an end to a certain aura of the popular culture they had spawned. Part of the culture of the 1960s was the experimentation with drugs. At that time, rock music in particular was inextricably linked to the drug culture. Marijuana, LSD, barbiturates, and other even harder drugs had become part of a cultural phenomenon that ostensibly allowed those participating in this shared experience to expand their minds and free themselves of their perceived socially indoctrinated inhibitions. In the end it cost many people either their lives or a life of addiction and misery, and many famous musicians lost their lives to the overdose of drugs or to alcohol addiction, all in the attempt to "break on through to the other side."

As popular culture in America began to adjust to the changing political climate and burgeoning technological advancements of the 1970s, rock music began to change along with it. By the second half of the 1970s, disco and punk rock had burst onto the scene, and both had a rather weakening effect on the culture of rock music and popular culture in general. Where 60s bands like the Beatles and the Grateful Dead emphasized, to a certain degree, social and political awareness, punk rock preached anarchy and disillusionment. As for disco, the mindless strains of vacuous, pointless music, along with a vial of high-quality cocaine, was all that was needed to feel part of a culture that was void of anything significant, other than dancing the night away. Although bands like the Rolling Stones and the Grateful Dead carried on, their output became uneven, and obligations to recording contracts forced their creative energies to wax and wane to the point that even some of their die-hard fans began to question their commitment. Some artists who began their careers in the 1970s, such as Bruce Springsteen and

Billy Joel, did carry on the tradition of growing as artists within their music, and both released albums that contained songs about social and political awareness along with artistic merit. But as the 1980s began, the influence of technology would begin to change rock music and popular culture unlike anything before.

Although Bob Moog created his music synthesizer in the early 1960s, and certain late 60s and early 70s rock bands utilized its other-worldly sounds to great effect, its high cost kept it out of the hands of the average musician. By the early 1980s, other manufacturers began producing synthesizers that were more affordable. The electronic sounds and synthetic drum beats that began percolating on the air-waves ushered in a new type of rock music and a changing trend in popular culture. Up until the 1980s, the electric guitar was the undis-puted, instantly recognizable sound of rock 'n' roll. The advent of cheaper keyboards and the start of what was to become known as sequencing allowed musicians to "program" their songs using drum machines and keyboard synthesizers. Although some bands used both guitars and synthesizers, by the end of the 80s the synthesizer was the predominant instrument in popular music. The electronic based popu-lar music that carried over into the 90s was becoming dance oriented, rock music in general was starting to lose its focus, and many subcate-gories of popular music began to emerge.

A simple search on the Internet revealed more than one hundred of these subcategories of popular music. Death metal, speed metal, hard core, grunge, hip-hop, trip-hop, rap, trance, dance, electronica, dub, club, alternative, Christian . . . the list seemed endless. With the advent of sampling (where "artists" sample, or copy, small phrases of other people's music then twist it, i.e., string it together via sequencing, into something they can legally put their name on), technology had now begun to empower people whose musical talent was, at best, suspect. The growing cult of celebrity in the 90s had now completely blurred the lines as to what music had come to represent in its relationship with popular culture. Nowadays, it is not uncommon to find "musicians" using nothing more than laptop computers and maybe a keyboard sequencer to enthrall the crowds. Actual musical instruments are almost nowhere to be found, and the majority of music being piped out to the audience is pre-sampled and pre-sequenced prior to the concert. While there are artists who use sampling for effect rather than pure con-tent, and they can still retain that elusive spark of originality, technol-ogy (particularly the computer) has now created a vast overkill and bewildering amount of music that basically has no value other than as distractive entertainment. The energy and thrill of seeing a talented group of musicians perform live, warts and all, seems a thing of the past. Most popular music concerts today resemble aerobics videos with a soundtrack of sterile music, lip-synched vocals, and performers who care more about image and choreography than musical content.

And that is the underlying current of popular music and culture in the twenty-first century. Back in the 60s and through the early part of the 70s, artists and musicians helped define the segment of popular culture they wished to reach. In today's music, the opposite is true. Musicians and artists try to keep up with the fickle, changing trends of popular culture to stay afloat and in the public eye. To their dismay most up and coming artists, within a matter of months, wind up as flotsam and jetsam washed up on the shores of the vast coastline of popular culture. It seems that today's popular music and culture simply lacks curiosity. And that's not a dangerous thing, it's just kind of sad.

It takes time to nurture a talent and create a unique form of expression that others can identify with. And hopefully as your talent grows, your audience stays with you and eagerly awaits what you have to say both musically and lyrically with great anticipation. Unfortunately, in today's cultural climate of instant gratification and shortened attention spans, even artists that do have the ability to commit to long term artistic views have to deal with the uncertain and unsteady opinions of popular demand. And to the artists who turn a blind eye to public opinion and forge their own careers out of sheer will and artistic integrity, I applaud you one and all. But it seems there's not much of that going on anymore.

I'm not one who longs for the good old days of rock 'n' roll. I like to see trends and people change and grow, they just have to have meaning and direction, and that's what appears to be lacking in modern culture and music. As for the Beatles, I did like their music, but they were far from my favorite band and they weren't much of a musical influence on me personally. But what they represented as songwriters and their influence in changing popular culture in their time is something I understand and respect. If that six-year-old boy could have seen what was to come of popular music and culture in the 21st century, even he would have asked, "Whatever happened to rock 'n' roll?"

INTERPRETATIONS

1. In his title, Geasor asks, "Whatever Happened to Rock 'n' Roll?" What explanations does he provide to answer this question?

2. What writing techniques does Geasor use to organize his ideas and retain reader interest? Which do you find to be most effective?

3. According to Geasor, what contributions did the Beatles make to popular culture? To what extent do you agree with his opinions?

APPLICATIONS

1. Geasor begins his essay with his recollection of attending a Beatles concert when he was six years old. What is the first musical event that you remember going to? What was most memorable about this event to you?

   Write a first-person narrative about this experience that captures the moment. Remember to pay particular attention to your five senses in recalling specific details. Bring your reader into the scene itself!

2. How do you think history will judge the era of popular culture written about by Geasor? Create a chart that lists both the positives and negatives of "rock 'n' roll" as presented by him. Now create a formal essay that argues for either a positive or negative historical assessment.

. . . well, if you can't hold the torch . . . then why pass it . . .?[1]

TODD CRAIG

Todd Craig is a native of Queens, New York—a product of Ravenswood and Queensbridge Housing projects. As an alumnus of the scholarship program A Better Chance, Inc., Todd holds a B.A. from Williams College and an Ed.M. from Harvard Graduate School of Education. Todd's research interests are hip-hop culture and pedagogy, multimodality in the English composition classroom, and creative writing pedagogy. He has been a DJ for over a decade and a creative writer with various publications of poetry and fiction, and awards including the Rockefeller Brothers Fellowship and the 2008 Academy of American Poets Prize at St. John's University. Todd is presently completing his Doctor of Arts degree; his dissertation will examine hip-hop pedagogy and the function of the hip-hop DJ in the English composition classroom.

ONE DAY I WAS AT WORK talking to one of my students by the name of Jose. Jose is a deejay, and since we share this common interest, at any given time, you could catch the two of us talking about music and the climate of hip-hop as it stands right now in 2006. In one of our various conversations, we got on the topic of the new Ghostface album "Fishscale."

"Yo son, how you like that new Ghost?" was the natural question I had.

"Eh, its aight . . . "

"What?!? It's aight?"

"Yeah, its aight, but I don't think its one of Ghost's illest albums."

From this point in the conversation, I began to fill the role of hip-hop historian. But it was in the midst of this conversation I began to really think about the climate of hip-hop music, especially in 2006. What was most disconcerting to me was that this had been a similar response to the one I received when talking about Busta Rhymes's latest effort entitled "The Big Bang." What bothered me most was in a musical world where all people want to do as listeners is lean back, lean with it and rock with it, or even shoulder lean while consuming some chicken noodle soup with a soda as a beverage on the side, the next

---

[1]Busta Rhymes featuring Q-Tip and Chauncey Black, "You Can't Hold the Torch," *The Big Bang,* Aftermath/Interscope Records, copyright 2006.

410

generation coming of age in hip-hop are only concerned with listening to what they've been programmed to like. Meanwhile, veteran artists like Ghostface, Busta Rhymes, and many more who have been integral to the foundation of hip-hop are not getting the credit they deserve for their albums musically, specifically because they have made a conscious decision to NOT do what's "hot." Instead, while everyone else went left, they went right, and decided to make something we rarely see these days: a "classic" album.

This really hurts my feelings because of where I stand when it comes to hip-hop. Because when it comes to the music, I grew up in it, and was fortunate enough to experience what many people categorize as the "golden era" of hip hop, the mid-90s, where the focus was on the music as opposed to money and sales. See, I stand as a hip-hop understudy, a historian of sorts through listening to and analyzing the music. In my youth, every Sunday when I got my allowance, I ran to QP's fleamarket after Sunday school to purchase the next and newest hip-hop album on cassette tape. And as Biggie so eloquently put it "I let my tape rock 'til my tape pop."[2] I've been a deejay since 1990, and was buying records before then. So growing up, I didn't just listen to hip-hop— I studied it. I'm a vinyl enthusiast and hip-hop purist, dedicated to the sound and qualities of great music. Unfortunately that is turning into vintage music given the state of the game at this point.

Now, there are a number of ways that one could go about this conversation. For example, one could very easily make the argument that I, in my age of thirty-two a.k.a. Gen X'er gone grown-up, have gotten to the same point that my elders got to when I was younger: that being "Boy, you think that's good music . . . that ain't music . . . they got that song from this older record . . . When I was coming up, we listened to *music* . . . boy, you don't know the type of music we used to listen to . . . *that* was *music* . . . that crap you listening to, is garbage!" I hated that argument back then, so to avoid hypocrisy, I try hard not to make that argument now.

I'd rather go a different angle; see, hip-hop music is one of the first cultures that comes both with and out of the music that has gone from the "underground" subculture to actually overtake what we know as mainstream popular culture. It's really one of the first times we see grandkids learning to dance to the same genre of music their parents listen to at the same time those parents are listening to and sharing with *their* parents . . . all simultaneously. Thus the question for me is rooted in intellectual thought; mainly, how has this game we call hip-hop

---

[2]The Notorious B.I.G., "Juicy," *Ready to Die.* Bad Boy Entertainment/Arista Records, copyright 1994.

changed musically? And I've always said to myself, "At the point where I listen to the radio and the popular 'Old School at Noon' shows are all my favorite songs, I'll know I'm old." So in thinking about this, I've merely decided to just look at the difference in the music between now and what might be considered the crux of the golden era: January of 1994 to December, 1996. Given the fact that I can look back on hip-hop for a decade and have formative memories is interesting in and of itself given when I was growing up, hip-hop was a "faze that'll soon die out" or "a fad" like the thousands if not millions of one-year one-hit wonder songs it's generated. Now, McDonald's and Dunkin Donuts, Starbucks, Jeep and Sprite have all used elements of hip-hop in their advertising schemes. Even Volkswagen is throwing up Ws, and shouting "Vee Dub": all elements of hip-hop slang, language and culture.

For me, as a hip-hop fan and deejay, the best time for this music was encapsulated by the following albums: Nas's first album "Illmatic"; Mobb Deep's second album "The Infamous" (even though most people think it's the first album because they missed "Juvenile Hell"); Notorious B.I.G.'s first album "Ready to Die"; and finally Wu-Tang Clan's own Raekwon the Chef's first solo album "Only Built 4 Cuban Linx." What became apparent to me was when I asked the question "Give me your top ten albums between the years of January 1994 to December 1995," no one I asked could give me just ten. However, when asking about the albums of today, the usual response was "Todd, I don't even really listen to hip-hop like that anymore" or "the game's changed so much, I can't even give you ten quality albums." No one could give me only ten albums from a decade prior because of the oversaturation of good quality hip-hop music during that time. This was a time in hip-hop music when the focus was on making quality music. And because the music and culture at that time were evolving, all forms were heard and accepted based on the criteria of creativity, originality and sound quality. This artistry held true for both the lyrics and music. Whether it was in the lyrics, which showed creativity through subject matter—specifically gauged by use of mental brainwork to decipher the words—or with production that stemmed from Jazz, Soul, Blues, Latin, Funk loops or even R&B remakes with live instruments (check Stevie J. and The Roots), the ultimate goal and endeavor of the artist(s) involved was primarily focused on making good music. It wasn't necessarily about the trend or what was popular, it was in fact about going against the grain.

Part of that very clearly comes from the hunger of some of these artists, some leaving troublesome situations in order to find a better way of life in the music. As well, while some may argue that this was the time in which rap changed from the conscious pro-black lyrics and visuals to the "gangsterization" of rap, I look at it differently. Rap music has always been that subculture people have wanted to belong to and understand. You can easily make the argument that part of the shift in popular culture in regards to music entails being included in that new style, that mystery music, language and dress—and being able to fully understand what it means and from where it emanates. This was the sentiment of hip-hop music during these years. The walk, talk and dress of rappers, b-boys and hip-hoppers were similar to the DaVinci Code—complex to unravel but necessary to understand. But even then, there was so much more to understand; and not only was the music exclusive, but it was highly balanced. For every O.D.B., you had A Tribe Called Quest. For Smif-N-Wessun you had Common. For Boot Camp and D.I.T.C.,[3] you had Native Tongues and Digable Planets. For Gangstarr and Brand Nubian, you had 2Pac and CNN. There was such balance musically, it was all too easy to switch and shift gears in order to consume a balanced "hip-hop diet"; I could wake up grimy for breakfast to "The Infamous," have a pensive lyrical lunch with The Roots, then straddle both sides with dinner and dessert over Jeru.

And even for that era of the genre where the lyrics became more violent, it was far from glorification; it was, in fact, a lyrical war report. Essentially, what C-SPAN, CNN, MSNBC, and BBC are for news, hip-hop music was the news report for our people: the urban inner-city disenfranchised youth who see hundreds of black men murdered on a daily basis but never get to see their friends on the news. What ABC, CBS and NBC wouldn't give us on the news, artists like Nas, Mobb Deep, Capone and Noriega, Black Moon, Gangstarr and Wu-Tang Clan would give us in three minutes and thirty seconds or sometimes more. And really, if you listen to the songs and are immersed in the music of that time, you could realize like I do: there was always a message that came with this violent depiction of life. The message, was indeed, don't go *that* way. Unfortunately, the stereotype says that the music has influenced the youth to lead lives of crime. Interestingly enough, the main character in the new Volkswagen commercial is "throwing up" a W in a way that could be construed as a gang sign—somehow though, we as a society don't necessarily label that as negative reinforcement of the stereotype, right? And never once, as a society, have we thought about the simple question: What does it mean that we know through music that a certain part of society lives like this? Do we begin to change the way people live, or do we turn a blind eye to it in order to let the negativity perpetuate itself across generations of particular races and cultures? (Because isn't the saying that "life imitates art" and not vice-versa?)

---

[3]Diggin' In The Crates Crew—Hip-Hop rapper/producer team featuring: Lord Finesse, Fat Joe, Show and A.G., O.C., BuckWild, Big L.

Now in 2006, we have reached the era where hip-hop is no longer the subculture, but is indeed popular culture. We see it on a daily basis in the fashion choices of youth, the words they choose to speak in everyday language, and the shift in lifestyle. And now, the music, which was at the forefront of the culture then, can be looked at as secondary, as it is engrossed in the corporate world of big business. Hip-hop is no longer new, and with the loss of this mysterious newness, gone are the days of the balance that was prevalent in the music over a decade ago. Coupled with the monetary success and super-star status of many rappers turned actors, fashion designers, company CEOs, and entrepreneurs, there has been a shift in the music, because everyone wants to be a rapper and make money. But not everyone wants to make good music first and foremost. This can obviously be linked to the incorporation of hip-hop as big business in terms of sales for record executives throughout the industry. And as unfortunate as it is, it has taken place how it has for just about every form of African-American music and culture: it has been appropriated by a larger system that is not concerned with the roots and fundamental teachings and lessons of hip-hop, but instead merely with reaching kids to make more sales to make more money, cash bigger checks for the companies who can write even smaller checks to the artists who make and have made the system work for them in a way no one thought it would. Thus, for these artists to make all the money, someone else has to get a cut. And with this appropriation through big business, hip-hop has translated to the youth of today in a way it never spoke to us. For now, the focus is not on the love of the game, the culture or even the music, it's on making money, selling millions of records, counting BBS radio spins and tracking SoundScan sales. The absence of the love for the music has corrupted what was once a pure culture. It has shifted the focus from the purely idealistic love of the music to the fiscally business-driven materialistic desire of more money, more money . . . and—more money!

It's clear to me that a decade ago, we—specifically, members of hip-hop culture—educated children on the diversity of life, because if hip-hop is culture, we educated through a unique form of cultural diversity. We were not only shown how to be conscious and pensive, but we were also taught to be strong or "hard" and given examples of how *both* lifestyles played themselves out. The diversity was intrinsically infused within the music, simply because the range of content within the music was so overwhelming, accessible, and apparent. With hip-hop now, however, we educate kids on being only thugs and gangsters, and reaping the spoils without any major work. We are not primarily infusing morals or even reporting, but instead now, we are brainwashing . . . in the worst way. Because all we are telling kids is that this is what you need to be to be "that dude" or "that nigguh."[4] Through a majority of the music now, youth are subliminally told "you wanna shine shorty, you gotta go at it like this . . ." But how is a 14 or 15-year-old teenager who lives in an urban inner-city environment supposed to afford foreign cars and SUVs, chrome 24+ inch tire rims, platinum and diamond chains and rings, bracelets and watches, and the latest and greatest in technology?

Nowadays, there's very little in the music to balance the scales as much as there was a decade ago. Unfortunately now, there's only one path and vantagepoint musically based on the financial gain of the corporate culture that has appropriated and commodified hip-hop, and made big business of what once was our own unique movement and underground culture. And yes, I know, it goes down with every generational change—in fact, this is probably where my age comes in and plays a role in my analysis. But with hip-hop now spanning multiple generations, at bare minimum, we can begin to see the effects of how such significant changes to both the music and culture are really taking place and essentially affecting our youth and generations beyond them. So with this in mind, this historical viewpoint is indeed critical, as it has the potential to allow us to possibly anticipate or even predict the future trends using knowledge of the past, based on the history's ironic cyclical nature.

For me, the conversation culminated in a discussion I had with hip-hop producer Alchemist. As we were talking about this subject, he brought up an interesting point: "we are now in an era, with Jay droppin' an album, where a parent and son can listen to the same thing. But youth culture by nature is designed for rebellion, for kids to NOT want to like and listen to what their parents like. So now what's gonna happen to hip-hop?" Even though every hip-hop fan felt a loss when Jay-Z, rapper turned President of Def Jam Records, claimed retirement. However, Jay has made a comeback, creating a long time buzz within the hip-hop industry for the release of his new album, "Kingdom Come." While we have seen in hip-hop music a time where two to three generations are listening to the same genre of music, this can indeed be a time where they are all listening to the *same* artist, the *same* album—the *same* exact music. But youth culture indeed functions off the premise of rebellion. It is an ironic twist of fate that can and will truly be a test and testament to hip-hop music and culture as we know it. Because essentially, you are left in one of two places. The first shows two to three generations coming together what could be a monumental moment for not

---

[4]And how this word has changed from such a negative connotation to an acceptable greeting and categorization of people, I will never truly understand!

only hip-hop as a music, but also as an art form and culture that has truly weathered the storm in outlasting the infamous test of time. The second, there is discord amongst the youth and the different generations, and a rebellion to what could be considered "good music" in order to preserve this specific premise of youth culture. It could potentially swing us back into an era where the only hip-hop music that'll be tolerated is good quality music, or swing us further into the dark side of what I do like to refer to as "something else." I guess only time and an album release date can tell . . .[5]

I've always promoted the simple fact that history does repeat itself, and in order to truly know where you are going, at some point you have to look back to see exactly where you've been. So I'd be all the more happy for the pendulum to swing back to the right as opposed to the extreme left it sits on for our culture now. But to me, it's really always been just as simple as this: can we get back to the days where the love was truly for the music and the preservation of the culture and artistry?

Idealistic?

Of course.

Optimistic?

Without question.

Hopelessly romantic?

Let's allow time to call judgment on that one.

My request: focus strictly on the music . . . and the love of it. Because the money will always follow behind that lost, yet retrievable and obtainable goal—

The classic album.

INTERPRETATIONS

1. How would you characterize Craig's writing style? Use specific examples from the essay to support your interpretation.

2. How does Craig portray the "golden era" of hip-hop? Where in the essay are these qualities presented?

3. In paragraph 12, Craig discusses the connection between hip-hop music and politics. What specific arguments does he make? Explain why you agree or disagree with him.

4. According to Craig, what messages about life and the world are now being conveyed by hip-hop artists?

---

[5]Jay-Z sold over 600,000 albums in his first week. This amidst the climate of the majority of artists trying to sell 1,000,000 albums in a quarter.

CORRESPONDENCES

1. In his essay, Craig addresses the state of hip-hop then and now. How are his perceptions similar to and/or different from James Geasor's views of rock and roll?

2a. In their essays, Craig, Lee, and Geasor all consider the relationship between popular culture and the political climate of the time. What historical period is discussed by each writer? How does each period's popular music reflect its historical/political moment?

2b. How does today's popular music represent what is happening in your world today?

3. Tom Lee defines a "classic" as "something so innovative and different that everybody tries to mimic it." How do Geasor and Craig apply this definition to the kinds of popular music they write about? What characterizes classic rock and roll and hip-hop?

APPLICATIONS

1. Choose a current song, album, or music video that you think will transcend popular culture and become a "classic." Write an essay explaining why you think your selection will accomplish this feat. In framing your argument, think about the historical, sociological, and personal arguments used by Lee, Geasor, and Craig in their essays. Try to apply such a long view to the subject of your essay.

2. When does an artifact of popular culture (a song, painting, movie, or book) become a classic? Create a conversation that Lee, Geasor, and Craig might have in response to this question. Use quotations from their essays as much as possible, so that it seems that they are actually talking to each other. Have each writer "speak" at least four times.

Why We Crave Horror Movies

STEPHEN KING

Stephen King (b. 1947 in Portland, Maine) is one of the best-selling novelists of our time and is famous worldwide for his horror fiction. He graduated from the University of Maine in 1970 and began writing short stories to supplement his teaching salary. Carrie *(1974), King's first novel, was a phenomenal success in both print and on the screen. His works have often been made into successful movies, among them* Stand By Me *(1986),* The Shawshank Redemption *(1994), and* The Green Mile *(1999). Among King's many other novels are* The Shining *(1977),* Pet Sematary *(1983) (made into a movie in which King himself played), and* Misery *(1989). His most recent books are* Blaze *(2007),* Duma Key *(2008), and* Under the Dome *(2009). King writes every day, often on two books simultaneously, with the exceptions of Christmas, the Fourth of July, and his birthday. His bibliography lists well over forty volumes. He has won many awards, among them the Bram Stoker Award of the Horror Writers Association in 2008 for* Duma Key *and the short-story collection* Just After Sunset *(2008). As you read "Why We Crave Horror Movies," number the reasons King gives for our liking horror movies and note whether you agree or disagree.*

I THINK THAT WE'RE ALL MENTALLY ILL; those of us outside the asylums only hide it a little better—and maybe not all that much better, after all. We've all known people who talk to themselves, people who sometimes squinch their faces into horrible grimaces when they believe no one is watching, people who have some hysterical fear—of snakes, the dark, the tight place, the long drop . . . and, of course, those final worms and grubs that are waiting so patiently underground.

When we pay our four or five bucks and seat ourselves at tenth-row center in a theater showing a horror movie, we are daring the nightmare.

Why? Some of the reasons are simple and obvious. To show that we can, that we are not afraid, that we can ride this roller coaster. Which is not to say that a really good horror movie may not surprise a scream out of us at some point, the way we may scream when the roller coaster twists through a complete 360 or plows through a lake at the bottom of the drop. And horror movies, like roller coasters, have always been the special province of the young; by the time one turns 40 or 50, one's appetite for double twists or 360-degree loops may be considerably depleted.

We also go to re-establish our feelings of essential normality; the horror movie is innately conservative, even reactionary. Freda Jackson as the horrible melting woman in *Die, Monster, Die!* confirms for us that no matter how far we may be removed from the beauty of a Robert Redford or a Diana Ross, we are still light-years from true ugliness.

And we go to have fun.

Ah, but this is where the ground starts to slope away, isn't it? Because this is a very peculiar sort of fun indeed. The fun comes from seeing others menaced—sometimes killed. One critic has suggested that if pro football has become the voyeur's version of combat, then the horror film has become the modern version of the public lynching.

It is true that the mythic, "fairytale" horror film intends to take away the shades of gray . . . It urges us to put away our more civilized and adult penchant for analysis and to become children again, seeing things in pure blacks and whites. It may be that horror movies provide psychic relief on this level because this invitation to lapse into simplicity, irrationality and even outright madness is extended so rarely. We are told we may allow our emotions a free rein . . . or no rein at all.

If we are all insane, then sanity becomes a matter of degree. If your insanity leads you to carve up women like Jack the Ripper or the Cleveland Torso Murderer, we clap you away in the funny farm (but neither of those two amateur-night surgeons was ever caught, heh-heh-heh); if, on the other hand your insanity leads you only to talk to yourself when you're under stress or to pick your nose on the morning bus, then you are left alone to go about your business . . . though it is doubtful that you will ever be invited to the best parties.

The potential lyncher is in almost all of us (excluding saints, past and present; but then, most saints have been crazy in their own ways), and every now and then, he has to be let loose to scream and roll around in the grass. Our emotions and our fears form their own body, and we recognize that it demands its own exercise to maintain proper muscle tone. Certain of these emotional muscles are accepted—even exalted—in civilized society; they are, of course, the emotions that tend to maintain the status quo of civilization itself. Love, friendship, loyalty, kindness— these are all the emotions that we applaud, emotions that have been immortalized in the couplets of Hallmark cards and in the verses (I don't dare call it poetry) of Leonard Nimoy.

When we exhibit these emotions, society showers us with positive reinforcement; we learn this even before we get out of diapers. When, as children, we hug our rotten little puke of a sister and give her a kiss, all the aunts and uncles smile and twit and cry, "Isn't he the sweetest little thing?" Such coveted treats as chocolate-covered graham crackers often follow. But if we deliberately slam the rotten little puke of a sister's fingers in the door, sanctions follow—angry remonstrance from parents, aunts and uncles; instead of a chocolate-covered graham cracker, a spanking.

But anticivilization emotions don't go away, and they demand periodic exercise. We have such "sick" jokes as, "What's the difference between a truckload of bowling balls and a truckload of dead babies?" (You can't unload a truckload of bowling balls with a pitchfork . . . a joke, by the way, that I heard originally from a ten-year-old.) Such a joke may surprise a laugh or a grin out of us even as we recoil, a possibility that confirms the thesis: If we share a brotherhood of man, then we also share an insanity of man. None of which is intended as a defense of either the sick joke or insanity but merely as an explanation of why the best horror films, like the best fairy tales, manage to be reactionary, anarchistic, and revolutionary all at the same time.

The mythic horror movie, like the sick joke, has a dirty job to do. It deliberately appeals to all that is worst in us. It is morbidity unchained, our most base instincts let free, our nastiest fantasies realized . . . and it all happens, fittingly enough, in the dark. For those reasons, good liberals often shy away from horror films. For myself, I like to see the most aggressive of them—*Dawn of the Dead*, for instance—as lifting a trap door in the civilized forebrain and throwing a basket of raw meat to the hungry alligators swimming around in that subterranean river beneath.

Why bother? Because it keeps them from getting out, man. It keeps them down there and me up here. It was Lennon and McCartney who said that all you need is love, and I would agree with that.

As long as you keep the gators fed.

INTERPRETATIONS

1. An effective introduction should capture the reader's interest. Review King's first paragraph. What is his thesis? What evidence does he offer to support? Do you agree or disagree with his point of view? Did he gain your attention? Why or why not?

2. What are King's three main reasons for the popularity of horror movies? Which did you find most convincing?

3. What is King's purpose in writing this essay? Is he mainly seeking to inform or does he want also to persuade his reader? Explain.

CORRESPONDENCES

1. Review Wright's perspective on horror and discuss its application to King's essay.

2.   Review Armenti's perspective on movies. What conversation can you imagine him having with Stephen King? To what extent does Armenti's point of view on movies reflect yours?

APPLICATIONS

1.   Many of King's novels, including *The Shining* (1980), *Pet Sematary* (1989), or *Sleepwalkers* (1992), have been adapted for the screen. View one of them and write two paragraphs responding to King's comment that "Horror isn't a hack market now, and never was. The genre is one of the most delicate known to man, and it must be handled with great care and more than a little love."

2.   Review paragraphs 12–14 and write a journal entry agreeing or disagreeing with King's thesis.

3.   King writes in paragraph 12: "The mythic horror movie, like the sick joke, has a dirty job to do. It deliberately appeals to all that is worst in us." To what extent do you agree or disagree? Does King's claim describe why you like horror movies? What other reasons are there? Write a brief essay explaining your point of view.

Why Does Wall-E Listen to Broadway Musicals?

MARTIN KUTNOWSKI

Martin Kutnowski is a composer, writer, and teacher. His music has firm roots in the tonal idiom, often mixing references to the musical past with folk materials of his native country, Argentina. His articles are about music, popular media, and the adventure of teaching and learning. Currently the Director of the Fine Arts Program at St. Thomas University in Fredericton, New Brunswick, Kutnowski has also taught at City University of New York, the Aspen Music Festival, and Conservatorio Manuel de Falla in Buenos Aires. More information can be obtained at www.contrapunctus.com.

WALL-E (PIXAR, 2008) tells anew the story of Robinson Crusoe. His is not the kind of exile that happens when one leaves, but when one is left behind.

Wall-E sticks to a routine that organizes his existence, compacting garbage in rectangular bricks and piling it up in huge skyscraper-shaped pyramids, oblivious to the desolate landscape, cannibalizing and recycling parts of dead robots as he goes along, even finding time, at the end of the work day, to watch old movies on an iPod before going to sleep. The pyramids are an iconic allusion to extinguished cultures, but the irony is that these, unlike those in Giza or Teotihuacan, are not made of noble stone but decomposing household and industrial waste.

Like Spielberg's *Artificial Intelligence* (2001), *Wall-E* reflects on the possible extinction of the human species, and gives a new spin to Darwinian evolution. The intriguing, nostalgic, and resigned idea, as stated at the beginning of the film, is that machines will outperform (in many ways they already do), outlive (in many ways they already do), and in the end, replace us in the evolutionary chain. But will they also cause our demise?

Not if they are like Wall-E. Akin to a loyal pet on steroids, Wall-E embodies the best of what makes us humans, with none of the aggressive traits that unfortunately also characterize us. Like a hobbyist in his garage, Wall-E neatly organizes his newly found treasures: a gas cigarette lighter, a Rubik cube, a wheel cover to be used as a hat. . . . Here's the confirmation that Wall-E is not just a quasi-human robot. Yes, he has anthropomorphic features (a head, a set of incredibly expressive eyes explicitly reminiscent of Pixar's opening logo, a pair of arms), and yes, he demonstrates intelligence, compassion, curiosity, and even the instinct for survival, common to all living creatures. But, of all things, he is a collector, a sentimentalist. It's no surprise that he watches *Hello Dolly* every night. Later on, the arrival of Eve—like the arrival of Friday to Robinson's island—relieves Wall-E's loneliness. Louis Armstrong singing *La Vie en Rose* conveys Wall-E's happiness and dreamy mood when he and Eve are getting to know each other. Throughout the movie, and particularly because there is practically no verbal dialogue, the music is what clinches Wall-E's humanity, while also reminding us of what's been lost.

Mirroring the diversity of human society, the arrival of Wall-E and Eve to the mother ship further complicates the polyphony of individuals who comprise the machine community. There are kind robots, stubborn robots, funny robots, generous robots, evil robots, and so on. By the time we meet real humans in the story, we realize that they have become not much more than amorphous blubber, their useless bodies spread on high-tech reclining chairs because their ever-shrinking bone mass cannot sustain them on two feet any longer. These downgraded humans can only be fed and entertained, which offers a great contrast against the real dimension—heroic—of Wall-E. He is not just a thinking robot, one that enjoys listening to Broadway songs at that, but one that thinks for himself and is willing to risk his life in a Quixotic quest for love—the more painfully impractical and non-machine-like idea of all. In other words, Wall-E has *feelings*. Does it mean that he also has . . . a soul?

Indeed, it's clear that he does, and it's not hard to see why a company that makes computers would want to persuade us that machines have a soul. That's the reason why Wall-E wakes up with the same distinctive sound tag of an Apple computer—that famously radiant C major chord. If computers had a soul, we could love them as true equals, and they would love us back. (Apparently, Mac, iPod, and iPhone owners feel that way already.) As shown in *Toy Story* (1995), Pixar's very first feature-length computer-animated movie, children's toys do have a soul, and not just after midnight like the steadfast tin soldier, but full time. The theme song by Randy Newman, nominated as best original song for the 1995 Academy Award, "You've Got a Friend in Me," hints at the same idea: a toy—and also a computer, which is a toy for grown-up children after all—can be a true friend. This friendship just keeps giving, but one cannot escape the recursive nature of the statement: a computer animates a movie about toys that talk.

Maybe Pixar is just taking its mandate a tad literally—the Latin root of the word "animation" is *anima*, which means "soul." Once it's established that machines—including toy machines—have a soul, it's only natural to accept that they go through existential issues and may suffer jealousy or delusions of grandeur. In *Toy Story*, Buzz Lightyear (Tim Allen's character) a battery-operated, talking action figure, at first thinks that he really is a space ranger, and so Woody (Tom Hanks's character) angrily warns him that he's just a toy. This self-awareness at times hilariously embraces spirituality; when asked who's in charge, the plush prices in the arcade game machine point their fingers to the Claw and solemnly state: "HE chooses who will go and who will stay." The film *Cars* (Pixar, 2006) like *Wall-E*, also directed by John Lasseter, depicts another diverse community of machines who think and feel: each one of them has a particular age, gender, education, distinct socio-cultural background, and ethnicity, complete with grudges against each other or against life in general. By the way, *Cars* also speaks of a universe where life, either vegetal or animal, simply does not exist. Unlike in *Wall-E*, there is no environmental remorse here: echoing the ideology of the Futurama exhibit at the General Motors pavilion on the 1939's New York World Fair, the argument of this movie is that cars should get what they want, namely tires, pavement, and gas.

Whether we like it or not, intelligent machines will live among us, and we'll live among them. Already, a quick glance at our kitchen at night resembles the view of an airport: blinking lights coming from the residual energy of the entertainment system, thermostat, air conditioner, electronic clock, radio, computer, monitor, printer, stove, microwave oven, coffee maker, cable modem, wireless router, charger for the cell phone, and many more microchip devices silently serving us while also keeping track of our habits and needs. It's inevitable that their descendants will be ever smarter, to the point that they may actually enjoy listening to Broadway songs. But then, in our darkest hour, will machines come to our rescue, like Wall-E? Or will they take over and annihilate us, like Terminator and his friends? This is an open question. What's for sure, though, if we are to believe Hollywood and their accomplices in the computer industry, our metal-and-silicon roommates are here to stay.

INTERPRETATIONS

1. In his essay, Kutnowski uses allusions—references to a person, place, or thing generally possessing mythological, cultural, or historical significance. How do these references affect your understanding of the work? (You might review such allusions as "Robinson Crusoe," "Friday," "Giza," "Teotihuacan," "Louis Armstrong," "Terminator," and *Toy Story*.)

2. What do you think is the main point of Kutnowski's essay? Where does this idea appear? Provide sufficient explanations and evidence for your answers.

CORRESPONDENCES

1. Jack Solomon (p. 374) writes: "The success of modern advertising, its penetration into every corner of American life, reflects a culture that has itself chosen illusion over reality." How do you think this perspective relates to both the movie *Wall-E* and Kutnowski's essay?

2. How do Kutnowski's ideas about robots compare to those presented by Turkle?

3. In "Why We Crave Horror Movies" (p. 418), Stephen King refers to the "hungry alligators" that represent our basest instincts. In his essay about *Wall-E*, Kutnowski maintains that the robot protagonist has a soul. From King's essay, what do you think those characteristics are that lay at the bottom of human consciousness and represent our worst selves? From Kutnowski's, what are those characteristics that elevate human consciousness and present us at our best? After rereading both essays, create a chart that represents King and Kutnowski's respective answers to the above questions.

APPLICATIONS

1. In his essay's final paragraph, Kutnowski asks: "But then, in our darkest hour, will machines come to our rescue . . . Or will they take over and annihilate us . . . ?" What do you think will be the future of technology? Design with words or through images two robots—one a friend and the other a foe. Your descriptions or drawings should demonstrate clearly those features that would be beneficial or detrimental to human kind. Then, in an essay, provide your answer to Kutnowski's question. Refer to your drawings in your written response.

2. These days in theaters, there always seems to be a movie made for children. Go see one, and then write a review of it. (Check the form of a movie review in your local newspaper.) In your review, stress how you think parents will respond to this movie and what they may learn from it.

The Knowing Eye

READING IMAGES

1. What is your response to the photograph with the bicycles? Would
    you classify the objects in the photograph as popular culture or as
    art? If there is a difference between these terms, what is it and how
    might it influence your interpretation of the objects in the photo-
    graph and the photograph itself?

2. What kind of music is being played by the person in the second
    photograph? What kind of music do you think would be played
    by the trio? What details in the image help you to form your
    opinion?

MAKING CONNECTIONS

1. What specific aspects of popular culture do you find in these pho-
    tographs? What additional kinds are identified in the essays pre-
    sented in this chapter?

Arnold Asrelsky

2. Review the photographs that have appeared in earlier chapters. Which ones show evidence of popular culture? What specific details can you locate to support your claims?

WORDS AND IMAGES

1. What music do you think would be listened to by the musician in the second photograph? Create a tune in this style and write a brief explanation of the music you have composed and how you came to create it.

2. Popular culture or classic? Consider the analyses contained in the essays by Tom Lee, James Geasor, and Todd Craig. For each of the photographs, consider whether the artifact depicted or implied

Elissa R. Schlau

(the installation of objects, the music produced by the guitar player, the music sung by the three women) is more likely to be classified as "popular culture" or "classic." As you set up your analysis essay, first establish clear and complete definitions of these terms before applying them to your exploration of the photographs.

Additional Writing Topics

1. Both Tom Lee and James Geasor hold the Beatles up as a paragon of popular culture. Is such attention and tribute deserved? Do some research about John, Paul, George, and Ringo. Listen to their records, watch their films, read some articles, and ask your parents (or someone of their generation) about them.

    Next, write an article for your college newspaper about rock and roll's first supergroup from the vantage point of history. Consider creating a headline such as "The Beatles: Yay or Nay," "She Loves You, Yeah, Yeah . . . So?," "The Beatles: Hype or Hip?," or anything that reflects your undertaking to separate truth from fiction. Here are two Web sites to get you started:

    http://en.wikipedia.org/wiki/The_Beatles

    http://www.beatles.com

2. Now that you have read Martín Kutnowski's essay, view *Wall-E*. In addition to interpreting the film's story, pay careful attention to the score. How do you think the music relates to what is happening on screen? What specific examples can you provide to support your observations? Cite two other films in which the music plays a role in theme, characterization, or setting.

3. Custom ("vanity") license plates for automobiles also make use of shorthand text. Using the concepts presented by Charles McGrath (see paragraphs 2–5 on pp. 377–8), design a license plate that describes you. Then use your license plate as the title for a descriptive essay about yourself.

4. Write a comparison and contrast essay about the films *8 Mile* and *Hustle & Flow*. What is the main idea that you will present to your reader? What specific similarities or differences will you choose as the basis for your arguments? Reading Todd Craig's analysis of hip-hop should help to provide you with points to focus upon.

5. Choose an influential rock, hip-hop, or movie star popular with your generation. Review tapes and interviews with him or her, and write an essay analyzing the causes and effects of his or her influence on your age group. Support your analysis with creative, specific examples.

6. Write a persuasive essay comparing and contrasting your responses to seeing a movie in a theater as opposed to viewing it at home on a DVD. Provide as many specific examples as you can to convince

your target audience. Remember to take into consideration the genre of your film: comedy, thriller, romance, action, or horror.

7. Todd Craig writes "Now in 2006, we have reached the era where hip-hop is no longer the subculture, but is indeed popular culture. We see it on a daily basis in the fashion choices of youth, the words they choose to speak in everyday language, and the shift in lifestyle." In their respective essays, James Geasor and Tom Lee also note the power of popular culture to minister to prevailing ideas and trends.

Explore the music, dress, and lifestyles of a bygone era or another culture. Examine photographs, movies, paintings, recordings, and newspaper and magazine articles. Write a consolidated report of what you have discovered, defining "popular culture" for that time or place.

You will find the Internet to be an invaluable tool for locating source material. Keying search terms such as "the 1880s" or "the 1920s" or "Mexico 'popular culture'" or "modern Japan" into a Web search engine will present you with many options for finding information. Be creative with the search terms you use. You can even limit your search to images or sound clips, and access to full-text original documents might be available in the licensed resources subscribed to by your college library.

8. Some teachers and administrators argue that cell phone usage by students is getting in the way of their educational mission and have called for legislation that would ban the phones from schools. As the leader of a student governance group, prepare a speech that you will deliver to either support or refute such an iniative. Included in the group you will address are students, teachers, and parents.

9. Check out the following Web sites:

Movies:

http://www.ericenders.com/100films.htm

http://www.bfi.org.uk/sightandsound/topten/poll/critics.html

Music:

http://www.xpn.org/885ATGA.php

http://www.listsofbests.com/list/38

Television:

http://43best.weblogswork.com/
    pmwiki.php?n=Main.43BestTVShows

http://www.the-top-tens.com/lists/top-ten-tv-shows.asp

Each list reflects the opinion of the webmaster who maintains it. Select only one "best of" list to work with. Do you agree or disagree with the choices? When you explain your answer to this question, identify those qualities that the webmaster seems to value in choosing his or her favorites. Also in your essay, present the criteria *you* would use for including an item in *your* "best of" list. Fully explain why you favor your criteria as opposed to those of the webmaster. Conclude your essay with your list!

Rhetorical and Cultural Glossary

Abstract   Without physical, tangible existence in itself; a concept as opposed to an object. A "child" is a concrete object that our senses can perceive, but "childishness" is an abstract quality. *See* Concrete.

Addition   A revising technique that enables you to add information to your draft. Words, phrases, or paragraphs may be inserted to clarify or enhance what you have written.

Analogy   A comparison that points out a resemblance between two essentially different things. Sleep and death are analogous, although certainly not identical. Often an analogy is drawn to explain simply and briefly something that is complex or abstract by pointing out one way in which it resembles something that is simpler or more concrete. To explain how the mind processes and stores information in its memory, an analogy might be drawn to the way in which a bank processes and stores deposits.

Antonym   A word of opposite meaning from another word; "good" is an antonym of "bad." *See* Synonym.

Argumentation   In persuasive essays, a unit of discourse meant to prove a point or to convince; the process of proving or persuading.

Audience   A work's intended readership, the author's perception of which directly affects style and tone. As a rule, the more limited or detailed the subject matter, the more specific the audience. An author may write more technically if the intended audience is composed of specialists in the field and may write less technically if the writing is for the general public.

Brainstorming   A prewriting technique in which you rapidly write down ideas in list form. Each idea is usually represented by only one or two words.

Cause and Effect   A type of exposition used primarily to answer the questions "Why did this occur?" and "What will happen next?" The structure of a cause-and-effect essay is a series of events or conditions, the last of which (the effect) cannot occur without the preceding ones (causes). When you write a cause-and-effect essay, it is helpful to keep chronology clearly in mind: remember, causes always create effects and effects are derived from causes.

Class   A group of related objects or people. Those who share the same economic status in a society are said to be of the same social class, such as working class, middle class, or upper class.

Cliché   An expression so overused that it has lost its ability to convey a sharp image or fresh idea. Clichés, such as "busy as a bee," diminish clarity and precision. Familiarity reduces them to little more than vague generalizations.

Coherence   The sense of connection and interrelationship present among the parts of a work. In a coherent piece of writing each sentence leads reasonably to the next sentence, and each paragraph follows reasonably from the preceding paragraph. A lack of coherence is evident when gaps are left between parts. The reader of a poorly written essay might begin to ask, "Why does the writer say this here?" or "How did the writer get to this idea from the preceding idea?" *See* Transition and Unity.

Colloquialism   A conversational or folksy word or phrase deemed inappropriate in formal writing. Using colloquialisms ("booze" for "whiskey" or "loosen up" for "relax") imparts a less dignified, less studied quality to one's writing. *See* Slang.

Combining   A rearrangement strategy that helps you to concentrate information in a draft by taking ideas expressed in two or more locations and placing them together. Such a change can improve essay organization and the logical presentation of main ideas.

Comparison and Contrast   A type of exposition that states or suggests similarities and differences between two or more things. Two types of organization for comparison and contrast essays are point by point and subject by subject.

Conclusion   A summing up or restatement of the writer's thesis. A strong conclusion imparts a sense of completion and finality to a piece of writing. The conclusion may be no more than a sentence in a short essay; it may be many paragraphs in a long report. A short conclusion may restate the writer's thesis in a memorable way, place the specific topic being discussed within or against a broader framework, or suggest answers to questions raised in the essay. A summary of the writer's main points may be effective as the conclusion to a long paper, but in a short essay it will seem unnecessarily repetitious.

Concrete   Specific and tangible as opposed to general and abstract. "Wealth" is an abstract concept of which "gold" is a concrete form. The use of concrete details, examples, and illustrations is a key to clear and effective writing. *See* Abstract.

Connotation   The implication(s) and overtones, qualities, feelings, and ideas a word suggests. Connotation goes beyond literal meaning or dictionary definition. "Sunshine" denotes the light rays of the sun, but connotes warmth, cheer, happiness, and even prosperity. *See* Denotation.

Culture   The total pattern of human (learned) behavior embodied in thought, speech, action, and artifacts. It is dependent on the human capacity for learning and transmitting knowledge to succeeding generations through the use of tools, language, and systems of abstract thought.

Deduction   A logical or argumentative appeal in persuasive essays; deductive reasoning elicits a specific conclusion from a generalization. Deduction as a logical approach proceeds from the general to the particular. For example, if we assume that cigarette smoking causes cancer, we may deduce that a person who smokes is liable to contract the disease. *See* Induction.

Definition   A type of exposition that explains the meaning of a word or concept by bringing its characteristics into sharp focus. An **extended definition** explores the feelings and ideas you attach to a word. Extended definitions are suited to words with complex meanings, words that are subject to interpretation, or words that evoke strong reactions. Such definitions are an appropriate basis for organizing exposition. A **dictionary definition** places a word in a class with similar items but also differentiates it from members of the same class.

Deletion   The revising strategy that enables you to remove unnecessary information from your draft. Words, phrases, or paragraphs may have to be dropped if you find they clutter or digress.

Denotation   The literal meaning of a word as defined in a dictionary. *See* Connotation.

Description   A method of paragraph development that conveys sensory experience through one or more of the five senses: sight, hearing, touch, taste, and smell. Description is generally either objective or subjective and can be organized in three broad categories: spatial, chronological, or dramatic. *See* Mode.

Diction   The writer's choice of words. Writers are said to employ proper diction when the words they choose to express their ideas are accurate and appropriate; that is, when what they write says exactly what they mean. Poor diction stems from choosing words whose denotation does not accurately convey the author's intended meaning or from choosing words regarded as inappropriate because they are nonstandard ("ain't"), colloquial, or obsolete.

Editing   The final stage of revising, not to be substituted for careful revision. Changes in punctuation, spelling, and word choice are all editing changes.

Epiphany   A moment of insight for a character, often resulting in a turning point.

Exposition   A mode or form of discourse that conveys information, gives directions, or explains an idea that is difficult to understand.

Fetishism   The worship of inanimate objects believed to have magical or transcendent powers. Some people obtain sexual arousal and satisfaction from an object, for example gloves or shoes.

Figure of Speech   An imaginative phrase and comparison that is not meant to be taken literally. "He ran as fast as the wind" is a figure of speech known as a simile. *See* Analogy, Hyperbole, Metaphor, Personification, Simile, and Understatement.

Frame of Reference   Broadly defined as those ideas or assumptions that affect how one perceives and approaches the world. Such factors as age, gender, ethnicity, nationality, and life experiences help to determine how an individual processes new information.

Freewriting   A prewriting activity that requires you to write down thoughts about a subject as they occur to you. Essentially, you are taking dictation from your brain.

Function   The utility of an object, as opposed to its cultural meaning.

Generalization   A broad statement, idea, or principle that holds a common truth. Despite many possible exceptions, it is generally true that a soldier's job is to go to war. Writing that relies too much on generalization is likely to be vague and overly abstract. *See* Specificity.

High Culture   Classical music, serious novels, poetry, dance, high art, and other cultural products that are usually appreciated by a small number of educated people.

Hyperbole   Obvious exaggeration, an extravagant statement, intentionally designed to give the reader a memorable image. A fisherman who brags that the one that got away was "big as a whale" almost certainly is speaking hyperbolically. *See* Understatement.

Image   In writing, an image is a picture drawn with words, a reproduction of persons, objects, or sensations that are perceived through sight, sound, touch, taste, or smell. Often an image is evoked to visually represent an idea. *See* Symbol.

Impressionistic   Depicting a scene, emotion, or character so that it evokes subjective or sensory impressions. An impression is an effect produced upon the mind or emotions. The more writing emphasizes the effects on the writer of scenes, persons, and ideas, the more impressionistic, and hence the less objective, it will be. *See* Objectivity and Subjectivity.

Induction   The process by which one draws a generalized conclusion from specifics. If it is a fact that a high percentage of people who die from lung cancer each year also smoke cigarettes, one might safely induce that cigarette smoking is a contributing factor in the disease. *See* Deduction.

Introduction   An introduction sets forth the writer's thesis or major themes and establishes tone (attitude toward one's subject), and—particularly in a long paper—suggests an organizational plan. The introduction, or opening, of an essay should capture the reader's attention and interest. Like the conclusion, it may be no more than a sentence or it may be many paragraphs.

Irony   The undermining or contradicting of someone's expectations. Irony may be either verbal or dramatic. **Verbal irony** arises from a discrepancy, sometimes intentional and sometimes not, between what is said and what is meant, as when a dog jumps forward to bite you, and you say, "What a friendly dog!" **Dramatic irony** arises from a discrepancy between what someone expects to happen and what does happen; for example, if the dog that seemed so unfriendly to you saves your life. *See* Sarcasm and Satire.

Jargon   The specialized language of a trade, profession, or other socioeconomic group. Truck drivers employ a jargon on their citizen's band radios that sounds like gibberish to most people. Writing that employs contextless jargon is inappropriate.

Journal   A daily written record of ideas, memories, experiences, or dreams. A journal can be used for prewriting and as a source for formal writing.

Journalism   The profession of writing for newspapers, magazines, the Web wire services, and radio and television. Journalistic writing emphasizes objectivity and factual reportage; the work of editorial writers, columnists, and feature writers often is a more subjective form of reportage.

Literal   The ordinary or primary meaning of a word or expression. Dwelling on literal meaning can promote erroneous thinking. The sentence "Childhood is a time of sunshine" should be read figuratively, not literally. (The sun does not always shine during childhood; rather, childhood is a happy time.)

Metaphor   A figure of speech in which, through an implied comparison, one object is identified with another and some qualities of the first object are ascribed to the second. *See* Simile.

Mode   A conventional form or usage. Writing includes four customary modes of discourse: description, narration, exposition, and persuasion (argumentation).

Multiculturalism   Assimilation of several cultures while allowing each culture to retain its separate identity.

Myth   A traditional or legendary story with roots in folk beliefs.

Narration   A narrative essay is a story with a point; narration is the technique used to tell the story. When writing a narrative essay, pay close attention to point of view, pacing, chronology, and transitions.

Objectivity   Freedom from personal bias. A report about a scientific experiment is objective insofar as facts in it are explained without reference to the writer's feelings about the experiment. But not even the most factual piece of writing is completely uncolored by the writer's attitudes and impressions. Objectivity is best thought of as a matter of degree, increasing in direct proportion with the writer's distance from the work. *See* Subjectivity.

Paradox   A statement that sounds self-contradictory, even absurd, and yet expresses a truth. It is paradoxical, though nonetheless true, to say that one person can simultaneously feel both love and hatred for another person.

Parallel Structure   The association of ideas phrased in parallel ways, thus giving a piece of writing balance and proportion. "He loves wine, women, and singing" lacks parallelism. "He loves wine, women, and song" is parallel; the verbal noun "singing" interrupts the series of nouns.

Personification   A figure of speech in which abstract concepts or inanimate objects are represented as having human qualities or characteristics. To write that "death rides a pale horse," for example, is to personify death.

Persuasion   The art of moving someone else to act in a desired way or to believe in a chosen idea. Logic and reason are important tools of persuasion. Equally effective may be an appeal either to the emotions or to the ethical sensibilities.

Point of View   The vantage point from which an author writes. In expository prose, an author may adopt a first-person or a third-person point of view. *See* Style and Tone.

Politics   The practice of promoting one's interests in a competitive social environment. It does not only have to do with running for government office; there are office politics, academic politics, classroom politics, and sexual politics.

Popular Culture   Sometimes called mass culture. It is accessible to everyone and is dominated by sports, television, films, and popular music.

Purpose   A writer's reason for writing. A writer's purpose is clarified by his or her answer to the question "*Why* am I writing?"

Rearrangement   The revising process that enables you to reorganize your draft by changing the placement of information. Three subsidiary rearrangement techniques are moving, combining, and redistributing.

Redistributing   A rearrangement strategy that helps you to reorganize your essay by taking a block of information and breaking it up into smaller units. Such a revision might help you to explain ideas more carefully or divide main ideas into more understandable units.

Revising   The writing process that enables you to change what you have written. Revising implies rethinking, rereading, and rewriting and does not necessarily come after a whole essay is created. Revising helps you bring what you have written into line with what you want to write.

Sarcasm   An expression of ridicule, contempt, or derision. Sarcastic remarks are nasty or bitter in tone and often characterized by irony that is meant to hurt. You might express your displeasure with those who have given you a hard time by sarcastically thanking them for their help. *See* Irony.

Satire   A genre of writing that makes various use of irony, sarcasm, ridicule, and broad humor in order to expose, denounce, or reform. Satires dwell on the follies and evils of human beings and institutions. The satirist's tone may range from amusement and gentle mockery to harsh contempt and moral indignation.

Simile   A figure of speech including *like* or *as* and stating a direct, explicit comparison between two things: he ate *like* a pig; her heart felt light *as* a feather. *See* Metaphor.

Slang   Colloquialisms and jargon are deemed inappropriate in formal writing. Whether a word or phrase is considered colloquial or slang is often a matter of personal taste. Also, slang often gains acceptance in time. A word such as *uptight*, once considered slang by cultivated people, is now an acceptable colloquialism. *See* Colloquialism and Jargon.

Specificity   Precision, particularity, concreteness. Specificity, like generalization, is a matter of degree; the word *horse* is more specific than *animal* but more general than *stallion*. *See* Generalization.

Style   The "fingerprint," the identifying mark, of a writer—both as an individual and as a representative of his or her age and culture. An author's style is the product of the diction employed, sentence structure and organization, and the overall form and tone in which thoughts are expressed. Style is variously described, depending on the analyzer's purpose. It may be simple or complex, forthright or subtle, colloquial or formal, modern or classical, romantic or realistic, "logical" or poetic. It may be anything, in short, that reflects the writer's personality, background, and talent. *See* Point of View and Tone.

Subjectivity   The personal element in writing. The more subjective a piece of writing, the more it is likely to be focused on the writer's opinions and feelings. *See* Objectivity.

Substitution   A revising strategy that allows you to replace unsatisfactory words, phrases, or paragraphs with ones that are more desirable. Substitution uses both addition and deletion in the same place in the draft.

Syllogism   A high formal three-part form of deductive logic. The syllogist argues that if a generalization (major premise) is true and a specific case of the generalization (minor premise) is also true, then any conclusion reached is necessarily true. If the major premise is "smoking causes cancer" and the minor premise is "John Doe smokes," then the conclusion is "John Doe will contract lung cancer." Syllogisms often sound logical, but are not true because one or both premises are faulty. *See* Deduction.

Symbol   Something that stands for something else. An eagle is a conventional symbol of the United States. Any word, image, or description, any name, character, or action that has a range of meanings and associations beyond its literal denotation may be symbolic, depending on who is interpreting it and the context in which it appears. The word *eagle*, therefore, may bring to mind different images or ideas; it may connote freedom or power or solitude.

Synonym   One of two or more words having approximately the same meaning. "Happiness" and "joy" are synonyms. *See* Antonym.

Tautology   Inherent or pointless repetition. To write that a person was treated with "cruel inhumanity" is tautological: inhumanity is always cruel.

Thesis   The main idea or theme of an essay. In expository prose, the writer usually states the thesis clearly in the introduction. The thesis statement should establish point of view, the primary point(s) intended for discussion, and the writer's attitude toward it.

Tone   Tone of voice; an author's attitude toward his or her subject, and, at times, audience. Tone is caught in the "sound" of a piece of writing. The tone of an essay may be angry, resigned, humorous, serious, sentimental, mocking, ironic, sarcastic, satirical, reasoning, emotional, philosophic—anything, in short, that echoes the voice of the author. One tone may predominate or many tones ("overtones") may be heard in any work. *See* Style.

Topic Sentence   The sentence in a paragraph that states clearly the main theme or point of the paragraph.

Transition   A bridge between one point or topic or idea and another. The logical movement from sentence to sentence and paragraph should be easy to follow if a piece of writing is coherent. This logic is often emphasized by means of transitional expressions such as *therefore, hence, similarly, however, but, furthermore, also,* and *for example. See* Coherence.

Understatement   An obvious downplaying or underrating of something. It is the opposite of hyperbole, although use of either may create a memorable image or an ironic effect. To say that "after they ate the apple, Adam and Eve found life a bit tougher" is to understate their condition. *See* Hyperbole.

Unity   The basic focus or theme that permeates a piece of writing, thus lending the piece a sense of wholeness and completeness. The words and sentences and paragraphs, the images and ideas, the explanations and examples, the characters and actions, the descriptions and arguments—all should be relevant to the overriding purpose or point of a work. *See* Coherence.

Geographic Index

Africa

Swahili Folktale   The Wise Daughter (East Africa)
Senegalese Myth   The Falsehood of Truth
African Legend   In the Beginning: Bantu Creation Story
(Southern Africa)

Asia

China
John King Fairbank   Footbinding
Shirley Geok-lin Lim   Two Lives

Indonesia
Trikartikaningsih Byas   Where the Land Is Stepped on, the Sky Above
It Must Be Upheld

Japan
Garrett Hongo   Fraternity

Korea
Chang-Rae Lee   Mute in an English-Only World
Kenneth Woo   Konglish

India
Gautum Bhatia   New (and Improved) Delhi
Mark Fineman   Stone-Throwing in India: An Annual Bash
Lalita Gandbhir   Free and Equal
A Folktale from India   How the Wicked Sons Were Duped
R. K. Narayan   Forty-Five a Month

Pakistan
Mahwash Shoaib   Treasures

Central America and the Caribbean

Guatemala
Quiché-Mayan Legend   Quiché-Mayan Creation Story

Mexico
Ramón "Tianguis" Pérez   The Fender-Bender

South America

Chile
Marjorie Agosín   Always Living in Spanish

Europe

Middle East

North America

United States: Ethnic Groups

Credits

445